THE CITY IN CULTURAL CONTEXT

TITLES OF RELATED INTEREST

★ Published in North America by the University of Minnesota Press and in South Africa by Human & Rousseau.
† Published in North America by the University of Alabama Press.

THE CITY IN CULTURAL CONTEXT

Edited by

John A. Agnew, John Mercer and David E. Sopher

Syracuse University, New York

Boston
ALLEN & UNWIN
London   Sydney

Allen & Unwin Inc.,
9 Winchester Terrace, Winchester, Mass. 01890, USA

George Allen & Unwin (Publishers) Ltd,
40 Museum Street, London WC1A 1LU, UK

George Allen & Unwin (Publishers) Ltd,
Park Lane, Hemel Hempstead, Herts HP2 4TE, UK

George Allen & Unwin Australia Pty Ltd,
8 Napier Street, North Sydney, NSW 2060, Australia

First published in 1984

Library of Congress Cataloging in Publication Data

Main entry under title:
   The City in cultural context.
Includes bibliographies.
1. Cities and towns—Cross-cultural studies.
2. Urbanization—Cross-cultural studies. 3. Social
change—Cross-cultural studies. I. Agnew, John A.
II. Mercer, John, 1934– . III. Sopher, David Edward.
HT119.C59 1984   307.7′6   84-2851
ISBN 0-04-301176-4
ISBN 0-04-301177-2 (pbk.)

British Library Cataloguing in Publication Data

   The City in cultural context.
1. Urbanization
I. Agnew, John A.   II. Mercer, John, 19— –
III. Sopher, David
307.7′6   HT255
ISBN 0-04-301176-4
ISBN 0-04-301177-2 Pbk

Set in 10 on 12 point Bembo by Computape Limited, Great Britain
and printed in the United States of America

Preface

Although there has been an explosion of information and research in urban geography and in urban studies generally since 1960, the study of cities and of urbanization has remained unbalanced. We have often forgotten that it is people – through institutions – who have the central rôle in building and developing cities, and in bringing about the various transformations embodied in the urbanization process.

A major problem has been caused by assigning too much explanatory power to such concepts as 'the market,' and 'the mode of production,' while not paying enough attention to human actions and to the attitudes, values, and beliefs that relate to those actions. We have not attended to Park's dictum (Park 1936, p. 133): 'Cities ... are, with all their complexities and artificialities, man's most imposing creation, the most prodigious of human artifacts.' By saying so, however, we are not imputing unlimited authority or even equal authority to all individuals to make decisions regarding city building or urbanization. Nor do we endorse the beguiling but dangerous notion of consumer sovereignty. The self-confidence of behavioral studies and analyses of decision making has been shaken by work that has laid bare the constraints under which human intentions are realized. These constraints, which are real enough and have had varying influence on different people in different contexts, are themselves socially constructed. They are the result of human agency, past and present.

This book, then, has a central purpose: to begin to restore balance to our perspective on cities and urbanization by emphasizing their cultural context. A full treatment of what we mean by this is given in the Introduction, and in varying ways the individual authors also articulate their understanding of the notion. We ourselves understand culture to embody not only elements that reflect continuity, but those that arise from change as well, and we have therefore wanted to emphasize the continuous interaction that goes on between the making of cities and the making of culture.

The Introduction has other purposes. One is to review the literature of urban studies critically. Our survey of the literature is organized around the principal objects of analysis in urban studies, disciplinary orientations to them, and collective and particular failures to recognize the relevance of cultural context. Another goal is to elaborate the problems that face any study using cultural context in an explanatory fashion. The last section of the Introduction tells how and why the papers have been organized as they have been in this book. The contents of the papers are summarized to provide an overview of the collection at a glance.

The book is intended for two audiences. One comprises students of human geography, simply because, as geographers, we editors are convinced that our discipline suffers as much as any from the lack of balance we have spoken of. The lack of intellectual exchange and collaboration between urban geographers and cultural geographers is especially disturbing. The second audience consists of students of cities and urbanization no matter what their discipline. The field of urban studies has been notably multidisciplinary, rather than interdisciplinary, although signs of mutual recognition are appearing now. By bringing together contributions from a number of disciplines, including anthropology, sociology, history, and planning, in addition to geography, we have tried to make a collection of work that will be of interest and value far beyond our discipline.

Because the contributions suppose the reader to have a certain familiarity with basic concepts, the text is not intended for beginning undergraduates. On the other hand, because most of the papers were first presented as public lectures to a general university audience, they are not so specialized as to be understood only by *cognoscenti*. The book might therefore be used by senior undergraduates and graduate students, for whom the collection as a whole and the particular thrust of individual essays can serve as a springboard for an exciting leap in their urban studies. In short, we believe that the book points in a new and necessary direction in urban geography and, in varying degree, in other urban fields.

Except the two editorial chapters and the contributions of Allinson, Claval, the Duncans, and Western, the papers were first delivered in the spring of 1981 in a series of public lectures sponsored by the Department of Geography in the Maxwell School of Citizenship and Public Affairs, Syracuse University. The editors, who organized the series, then requested revisions in the written versions of the lectures, and solicited other essays to broaden the geographic range of the whole set.

Some of the authors from whom papers were solicited in the later stage did receive provisional drafts of the essays that had first been written for the lecture series. In addition, the authors of some of the essays were able to see drafts of certain papers by other authors in the series. We hope that these exchanges have gone some way to achieve a degree of integration that is often missing in collections of this sort.

Few papers are themselves explicitly comparative (Hall's is an obvious exception). It was, however, our intention to allow the reader to draw conclusions by comparing the statements of experts in various culture regions on particular aspects of urbanization and urban development in those regions. We try to help the reader to do so in the concluding chapter. Among our objectives in that chapter is to point out connections, some involving similarities, some contrasts, among the papers. Style and approach of individual essays are of course varied. We can even expect that the work of some authors will elicit strong criticism from other authors.

There is, however, a common theme, and we have tried editorially to resolve some of the discordance, in addition to effecting a large integration in our chapters at the beginning and end.

Clearly, the individual essays raise a number of theoretical questions that are not immediately resolved. Placed in the context of this thematic collection, they present a challenge to conventional and current practice in urban studies. Ignore the rôle of culture and its manifestations, they tell us, and theories of city structure, city building, and urbanization will continue to suffer from premature closure and incompleteness, and the dangers they entail of misunderstanding and policy error.

We do not regard this characterization of urban studies as too severe. But neither do we see the increased understanding of cultural context and its incorporation in urban studies as providing a simple nostrum. A quick cultural 'fix' would be no better than behavioral or structural ones. Rather, we see that the work presaged by this book will require urban scholars to have command of a broader literature and a wider range of research methodologies than they now have as a rule. It will require an end to the Western ethnocentric parochialism (Masotti & Walton 1976) that has marred urban studies. This is too much to expect from one individual, but with collective attempts to achieve this goal we may yet see urban studies transformed from a multidisciplinary enterprise into a truly interdisciplinary one. We hope that this book will be a step in that direction.

A number of debts are incurred in preparing a book such as this for publication. We wish to thank Pam Walker for her editorial assistance. D. Michael Kirchoff made a number of the maps. Harriet Hanlon and Pam Walker shared the typing. Finally, we would like to thank Bob Jensen, chairman of the Department of Geography at Syracuse University, for his encouragement and support.

JOHN A. AGNEW, JOHN MERCER AND DAVID E. SOPHER
October 1983

References

Masotti, L. H. and J. Walton 1976. Comparative urban research: the logic of comparisons and the nature of urbanism. In *The city in comparative perspective*, J. Walton and L. H. Masotti (eds.), 1–15. New York: Sage, and Halsted Press for Wiley.

Park R. E. 1936. The city and civilization. Reprinted in *The collected papers of Robert Ezra Park9. Vol. II: Human communities: the city and human ecology*, E. C. Hughes, C. S. Johnson, J. Masuoka, R. Redfield & L. Wirth (eds.), 128–41. Glencoe, Ill.: Free Press.

Contents

JOHN A. AGNEW, JOHN MERCER
AND DAVID E. SOPHER

PAUL CLAVAL

AMOS RAPOPORT

List of tables

List of plates

1 Introduction

JOHN A. AGNEW, JOHN MERCER
and DAVID E. SOPHER

The study of the city in cultural context implies two things. First, networks of practices and ideas exist that are drawn from the shared experiences and histories of social groups. Secondly, these practices and ideas can be invoked to account for specific patterns of urban growth and urban form. Such a study does not imply acceptance of a questionable and now largely discredited concept of 'urban culture' (Benet 1963). That concept would have a universal rural–urban continuum (defined by population density) provide the essential kernal of explanation for all urban phenomena. Instead, consideration of the city in cultural context implies an emphasis on the practices and ideas that arise from collective and individual experiences, and that are constitutive of urban life and form. The practices and ideas are not themselves uniquely urban but derive from the social, economic, and political situations that have shaped group and individual existence. In turn, the practices and ideas – in short, 'culture,' – have shaped urban worlds.

An enduring Western conceit in urban studies has been that all contemporary cities can be explained by reference to a 'rational' economic calculus of profit and loss for the individual or group. This explanation itself comes out of a contemporary Western cultural context (Poggi 1972, p. 116). Applied to other places and times, it improperly projects recent Western experiences on to other contexts, accounting in an invalid, a priori fashion for urbanization and urban life.

The basic premise of this book is that culture counts. The concept of culture is, however, notoriously difficult to grasp (Bauman 1973, Williams 1977, 1982). There is some agreement that culture refers to the 'ways of life' and the 'systems of meaning' established by groups of people who form communicating networks, or did so at one time. How culture comes to be constituted and how stable it is are more controversial matters (Duncan 1980). For many (like Sahlins 1976), culture is largely equated with 'tradition,' and contemporary populations are seen only as its carriers. For others, including most of the contributors to this volume, culture is created by thought and actions of both historical and living populations. Culture can change because it refers to material and symbolic contexts or limiting conditions for individual behavior; it does not comprise an *entity* that governs what every human being thinks and does

(Williams 1958, 1977, Geertz 1973, Beeman 1977). Nor is the idea of continuity in culture without problems. The assumption of inertia that underlies much culture theory plays down the need for culture to be created anew in each generation. As Moore (1966, p. 486) puts it:

> To speak of cultural inertia is to overlook the concrete interests and privileges that are served by indoctrination, education, and the entire complicated process of transmitting culture from one generation to another.

Culture is the 'glue' of society, but it cannot exist independent of human action.

To study the city in cultural context therefore requires us to use a concept of culture that is sensitive to the *causes* of both cultural continuity and change. It also requires us to insist on the importance of the collective experience of national, ethnic, and social groups. It is thus set apart from other contemporary approaches to the study of cities and urbanization, such as those outlined by Saunders (1981). The emphasis on culture helps to resolve four fundamental problems that occur in other approaches: (a) the structure–action problem; (b) the problem of 'Eurocentric evolutionism;' (c) the 'base–superstructure' problem; and (d) the problem of student 'self–consciousness.'

First, much conventional reasoning in urban studies deduces the causes and features of urbanization and urbanism in specific contexts from 'structures,' either empirical or abstract, that are held to operate in or through human agents. The early urban sociology of Manuel Castells (1977) and the environmental psychology based on behavioristic postulates are examples. For other writers, 'action' is primary: for them, 'individuals' are 'free' to behave 'as they please,' or according to rules 'freely' negotiated with others. Much work in urban economics and in the sociology that focuses on 'urban life' is of this kind. We discuss this literature in more detail later.

The structure–action problem refers to the difficulty of finding a way to avoid these extremes while recognizing the significance of both human agency and structural constraint (Abrams 1980, Manicas 1980). One solution is to focus on 'cultural contexts' as we have defined them, to recognize human action as both motivated and intended, and at the same time both mediated by social structure and generative of it. This is not an easy task. There is a strong tendency to slip toward an emphasis on either structure or action. The cultural–context approach holds out at least the possibility of resolving this venerable and stubbornly persisting dilemma.

Secondly, a conspicuous feature of Western social science that deals with cities and other phenomena has been a 'Eurocentric evolutionism.' In much modernization theory and in Leninist interpretations of Marx, the world is divided into regions at different 'stages of development' (Gusfield 1967, Tipps 1973, Pletsch 1981). Although 'the West' (or by some 'the East') is defined as the most 'advanced' or 'modern,' the populations of other world regions need not despair. They will advance inevitably as they follow the Western experience. Cities will follow suit, moving from the traditional end of the continuum to the modern one and losing their individual characters along the way. Apart from its Eurocentric view of world history, this line of thinking involves a denial of human agency. However, when urban growth and urban form in a particular region are seen in cultural context, the basis for understanding their patterns is provided by the region's historical experience, including the changing character of the region's ties to an increasingly integrated world political economy. Calcutta, then, need not 'evolve' in the same way as Chicago, nor need Tokyo come to be like Los Angeles.

A third advantage of the cultural–context approach to urbanization and urbanism lies in its potential for resolving the 'base–superstructure problem' that has bedeviled most of the other approaches. The problem has been articulated most clearly in discussions among Marxists on certain questions: 'economic determinism,' the 'relative autonomy of the state,' and the rôle of thought in social change (Brenner 1977, Williams 1980, Wood 1981). The problem is not merely one of Marxist exegesis ('what Marx really meant'). Many Marxists as well as others used to see cultural phenomena – ways of life and systems of meaning – as mere 'reflections' of the economic base, serving the function of 'reproduction' for its survival. The resolution that seems to be emerging would collapse the base–superstructure metaphor into a concept of productive activity, or 'praxis.'

The concept of cultural context that we have outlined then becomes crucial. Williams (1980, p. 38) writes:

> . . . In any society, in any particular period, there is a central system of practices, meanings, and values, which we can properly call domi-nant and effective . . . which are organized and lived . . . It is a set of meanings and values which as they are experienced as practices appear as reciprocally confirming. It thus constitutes a sense of reality for most people in the society.

Thus, the *practical* nature of everyday life, rather than the abstracted nature of economic organization or superorganic culture, becomes an alternate focus for social explanation. Not only does this point to resolution of the base–superstructure problem, but it directs attention to what we are calling cultural context.

Finally, openness to the possibility of a world marked by cultural variety has an important methodological implication for the student of cities. It helps to unveil the attitudes and assumptions brought by the student to the research. This need not lead to cultural relativism, although there is always that danger. What it will do is to encourage development of a critical self-consciousness in selecting and applying concepts, and watching for those that may be bound to a particular context of time and place. Encounters with unfamiliar cultural contexts can also deepen understanding of what we think we know. In a challenge to 'common-sense' views of knowledge, the familiar may prove to be less familiar than was previously thought (Grew 1980). The cultural-context approach thus opens up the possibility of exploring the 'taken-for-granted' in cultural contexts that we all think we know 'from the inside.' We may find that truth in Fuentes' words (1982, p. 69): 'To discover the other is to discover our forgotten self.'

While an examination of the city in cultural context moves toward resolutions of the problems in contemporary urban studies that we have outlined, the approach is certainly in need of additional elaboration and criticism. We try to provide these in the next part of this chapter (and again in the concluding chapter). Next, we identify some of the chief themes and objects of analysis in the urban literature and, at the same time, outline the particular concerns of different disciplines involved in the study of urban questions.

The city in cultural context

We have made some bold claims for studying the city in cultural context, and their validity will have to be measured by the individual contributions to this book. Here we want to lay out some of the problematic issues that face a study of this kind. In the closing Commentary we deal with some of the problems as they have arisen in individual chapters. Taken together, then, Introduction and Commentary are our attempt to provide a critical perspective on the theme of the book and on the chapters themselves.

First of all, the concept of the city itself is problematic. In recent years, the separation of 'the urban' as an object of study has often been questioned. The city, it is said, cannot be a significant unit of study in its own right. It should be seen as an 'ideal type' that cannot have much use in the development of sociological theory (Saunders 1981). But this criticism confuses two different questions. One is whether cities in their various aspects can be the objects of analysis. The other is whether explanations of 'urban phenomena' can themselves be restricted to the level of the urban.

A negative answer to the second question does not, as some critics seem to think, require a negative answer to the first. For the geographer, the historian, and the political economist, (if not for the sociologist as well – Saunders 1981), the city is not merely a research milieu or a population concentration – it is also a place. Its study has usually involved concepts that presuppose the insufficiency of explanation at the level of the urban itself. One can therefore reject the idea of 'urban explanation' while accepting the urban object of analysis.

For the sociologist, however, the *significance* of distinguishing the urban is clearly problematic. Although the city can be a significant condition for the development of social forces, as it was for the division of labor in medieval Europe, the concept of the urban is typically not equatable with the physical object of the city. In societies dominated by urbanization and urban ways, the division between city and country is not of much significance. Saunders (1981, p. 13) concludes that in 'advanced capitalist countries,' and perhaps in others:

> the city . . . is no longer the basis for human association (Weber), the locus for the division of labor (Durkheim), or the expression of a specific mode of production (Marx), in which case it is neither fruitful nor appropriate (for the sociologist) to study it in its own right.

But even such critics acknowledge that this is a recent condition in a few parts of the world. It is dangerous to project it to other times and places.

The second problem in our approach is with the basis for the concept of culture. Our analysis here owes a special debt to the writing of Raymond Williams. Cultural anthropologists and cultural geographers in the United States have tended to view culture in transcendental–idealist terms. It is a superorganic entity, the 'informing spirit' through which a social order was reproduced (Duncan 1980). Some anthropologists and sociologists now prefer to see culture as a 'realized signifying system' (Williams 1982, pp. 207–9), embedded in everyday life through 'activities, relations, and institutions.' For some, such as Geertz (1973), this system seems to be largely symbolic in nature and mental in origin. For others (such as Williams 1980, 1982), culture is practical in origin if also symbolic in nature. For Williams (1982, pp. 207–8):

> a signifying system is intrinsic to any economic system, any political system, any generational (kinship and family) system, and, most generally, to any social system.

Emphasis on the practical, the grounding of culture in everyday life, is a position that has been criticized (Sahlins 1976, Cosgrove 1982). However, much of Sahlins' argument rests on a conflation of the terms 'practical' and 'utilitarian.' The practical is reduced to 'the economic,' as reference to everyday life is taken to represent the workings of an 'economy' in which people persistently take a cost–benefit approach to individual and collective decisions. The argument is an example of a naïve dualism in which 'ideas' are separated from 'material reality.' This is an important failing of most modern social theories. Rather, as Williams (1977, pp. 59–60) argues, 'consciousness is seen from the beginning as part of the human material social process and its products in "ideas" are then as much part of this process as material products themselves.' Culture, then, need not be thought of as superorganic or mental in origin and continuation, but as practically rooted in material social life.

A related issue is the extent to which culture is equated with tradition and continuity. Anthropology and geography, and to some degree all the social sciences, have emphasized cultural inertia and continuity (Duncan 1980), reflecting the perception of culture as a superorganic entity or a social fact. An alternative view is that it cannot be reduced to 'fixed forms.' As collective social experience changes, so must the signifying system that defines a culture. The dominant set of meanings and symbols held by a social group in any period represents both continuity and change. How much of each is represented is an empirical rather than a conceptual question.

Such a wide range of ideas and activities has been taken in the anthropological literature to form the bundle called 'culture,' so as to give the term the sense of 'a whole way of life.' This has the merit of avoiding the strong social-science tendency to engage in the 'separated analysis' of 'economic,' 'political,' 'social,' and other aspects of life (Williams 1982, p. 209). But the view of culture as a whole way of life suffers from insufficient attention to the relational aspect of culture as a mechanism for weaving ideas and practices together into a framework that has meaning for people. To regard culture as a signifying system produced and reproduced by collective experience emphasizes the centrality of symbolism, and avoids the generality and lack of analytic clarity in the definition as a way of life. There is another advantage. It draws attention to the political and social orders with which culture as a signifying system is interwoven, and which together form the context for the genesis of symbols and meanings.

The concept of 'hegemony' is sometimes used now to extend this concept of culture. It contributes a sense of what is found in most societies, the dominance and direction of one part vis-à-vis another. Williams (1977, p. 108) explicates:

'Hegemony' goes beyond 'culture,' as previously defined, in its insistence on relating the 'whole social process' to specific distributions of power and influence. To say that 'men' define and shape their lives is true only in abstraction. In any actual society there are specific inequalities in means and therefore in capacity to realize this process.

One can therefore conceive of hegemonic or dominant cultures which give meaning to the 'whole social process,' including the character of domination and subordination, in all societies (Anderson 1976, Cheal 1979, Della Fave 1980). In addition, the concept of hegemony opens up the possibility of viewing cultures as contestable. Contrary to the usual sense of the term 'ideology,' according to Williams (1977 p. 112), a hegemony:

> does not passively exist as a form of dominance. It has continually to be renewed, recreated, defended, and modified. It is also continually resisted, limited, altered, challenged by pressures not at all its own.

While a hegemonic culture is always dominant by definition, it is rarely totally dominant or exclusive (Wrong 1969, Williams 1977). There can be alternative or directly opposing cultures within a society at any time. In one terminology, these would be labeled 'autonomous' in contrast to the 'directed' nature of a hegemonic culture. Alternatively, they can be seen as either 'residual' or 'emergent' cultures, depending on their historical origins (Williams 1980, p. 204).

Not only culture, but the concept of culture itself, is then clearly contestable. Whether one chooses to identify culture with continuity, with the superorganic or with practical reason, as a whole way of life or as a signifying system, as directed or autonomous, one's definition is open to challenge and discussion. In one respect, however, most recent usage has tended toward a consensus in taking national societies as the units to which the concept of culture is most appropriately applied. In cultural anthropology, of course, tribes or ethnic groups have always been the typical units of analysis, although a problem has been recognized in the range in size of such units (from a few people to several hundred million). Cultural geography has faced the same difficulty in its search for cultural expression in lands ranging in size from county to continent. In other social sciences, too, there are references to 'ethnic cultures,' 'subcultures,' and 'class cultures,' including those that are 'feudal' and 'bourgeois.' (In social history and historical sociology, concepts of 'class-consciousness' and 'minority-group consciousness' are more common.) But the sense of culture as a national entity, developing as the global system of states develops, seems prevalent now.

We have decided to use the term 'cultural context' rather than 'culture' because we do not want to be tied to the concept of culture as national or hegemonic. The term we prefer should suggest a nesting of contexts, from class and ethnic to national and global, by which specific cultures are defined and relate to one another. The term also strengthens the sense of culture as a contextual matrix of symbols and activities which give meaning and direction to people's lives.

To put the city in cultural context is to view it as the product of both hegemonic and subordinate cultures and, at the same time, as the site for their production. Placing cities in the context of their societies, we are able to see how the cultural motifs of a society are embedded in the form of its cities and in the lives of its urban population. We can also see the city as a socioeconomic and political factor in the organization of the society as a whole.

The idea of the city in cultural context has sometimes been realized by treating the city as solely a product of culture rather than as both producer and product. The Turkish cities of Anatolia have been viewed as the products of a cultural context in which the patrimonial claims of the Ottoman state left little scope for local control, and 'the culture of the Palace' dominated the urban scene (Mardin 1969). In Brazilian cities, the clientelist culture of the countryside has been transferred through migration to the class-based context of the cities, and provides the dominant frame of reference that is still evolving for the mass of the urban population (Oliven 1979). Finally, in 19th-century French cities, local loyalties were replaced by national ones, and the solidarities and antagonisms of social class replaced the ties of trade and patronage as French society experienced intensive industrialization and the growth of a national education system (Aminzade 1979).

Until this century, city life was the experience of a minority. Only in England in the middle of the 19th century did the urban population of a region exceed the rural population for the first time anywhere. Massive urbanization in the 19th century involved concomitant changes in the social organization of culture. The cities created by the new urbanization in turn represented and communicated the new culture as well as significant aspects of both older and emergent cultures.

However, the 'dialectic' between city and cultural context is not entirely a modern phenomenon, as cultural anthropologists and other students of urbanism remind us (Thrupp 1961, Fox 1977, Lefebvre 1978, 1980). What is different now is that urban living and the influence of the urban have become pervasive. In a discussion of urbanization and culture in 19th-century France, Merriman (1979, p. 131) captures both the transformational and the reflective aspects of their relationship:

> The city itself – its configuration, neighborhoods, and relationship to its region – is often the neglected historical personage in the drama of social and political change when in fact it came to define and shape those changes. The impact of large-scale industrialization, the creation of a working class, and the development of the labor movement cannot be divorced from its physical setting.

In their form and in the lives of their inhabitants, cities have reflected the working of dominant, residual, and emergent cultures. To study the city in cultural context therefore requires us to acknowledge that cities are cultural creations and that they are best understood as such.

Urban studies: themes and perspectives

In the past two decades, the literature of urban studies has grown exponentially. In the established social-science disciplines, new or expanded urban subfields are now thriving. In the United States, some came early (urban sociology), some much later (urban history), and some were, so to speak, force-fed by money from foundations (urban economics). Reflecting a basic uncertainty about the theoretical significance of the city as object of analysis, the literature of these subfields ranges across a surprisingly wide variety of themes. The city may appear as agent, as cause, or as backdrop, a stage for large social events and trends.

Like their parent disciplines, these proliferating subfields have undergone marked changes of direction. Even in specialties of short pedigree, redefinitions of the field have been striking enough to warrant the label 'new' for the later work (e.g. Masotti & Lineberry 1976, Richardson 1977). Nevertheless, we have tried, at the risk of being somewhat reductive, to identify persistent, dominant themes in the literature and to discern the different perspectives on the city that each discipline has.

Here we must enter a disclaimer regarding what follows. However much we may hope for the emergence of a more balanced understanding of the city in cultural context, we must face the fact that what we present here has a decidedly ethnocentric cast. Irrespective of discipline, most of the literature of urban studies has been written by Europeans and Americans about European and American cities. In geography we can of course point to the existence of some regional surveys of cities in the 'Second World' (e.g. Bater 1980) and the 'Third World' (e.g. McGee 1967), but the overwhelming mass of urban geographical study and writing has been about North America and Western Europe. Here, to our regret, we can only handle the core of the mass, to the neglect of some fine, important work.

The literature we have surveyed has several principal themes: urban origins, urbanization, urban form, urbanism, urban systems, city government, and the distribution of community power. Some of these present problems of definition: 'urbanism' is sometimes used as an umbrella category, subsuming the others, as in the title of an eclectic reader edited by Fava (1968). Urbanism and urbanization have been treated both as processes (Harvey 1973) and as products. The other categories are generally treated as products.

These themes have received different degrees of attention from the disciplines whose work on cities we are reviewing – anthropology, economics, geography, history, political science, and sociology. To guide the reader as our survey proceeds, we have indicated the different disciplinary emphases in the form of a necessarily crude scheme (Table 1.1).

Table 1.1 Disciplinary emphases in urban studies.

| | Emphasis | | | | | | |
Discipline	Urban origins	Urbanization	Urban form	Urbanism	Urban systems	City government	Community power structures
anthropology	×	×		×			
economics		×	×		×	×	
geography	×	×	×		×	×	
history	×	×		×	×	×	
political science				×		×	×
sociology		×	×	×			×

Urban origins How and where cities came into being, and what consequences urban settlement had for the conduct of daily life are questions that have been important to some disciplines although not to others, such as urban economics. In line with their primary concern with the city, political scientists find early cities of interest chiefly in relation to their forms of governance.

For the most part, questions about urban origins have not been explicitly considered as related to the 'base–superstructure' problem although it is certainly an appropriate frame of reference. The contention surrounding urban origins hinges on what is truly the basis of city formation and growth. For some (Childe 1950), the economic base in the form of the emergence of a sufficient surplus is the fundamental prerequisite. Political and religious organization then develops as superstructure on the material base. The argument advanced by some Marxists (among others) that city growth is a function of intercity trade in the regional surpluses appropriated by the cities also ascribes significance to the incipient urban economy; other forms of organization are secondary, derived from conditions pertaining to the base.

Alternative positions regard spheres of activity other than the economic as basic. For Boulding (1963), cities arise when political means are employed to convey food surpluses into authoritarian hands, and other urban activities follow. But this begs the question of how authority can emerge with sufficient capacity to employ 'political means.'

Except recently, and then perhaps only in Western society, religious institutions have played an important rôle in urban life, and their buildings have been focal points in many cities. In the early cities, the ruler could be an authoritarian figure in a political sense *and* a religious leader, even a deity. For Wheatley (1971), the symbolic integrative functions of the early cities were of the first importance. Wheatley (1971, p. 282) cannot accept the economic base as an explanation of urban origins:

Despite the emphasis which has been placed on trade as a primary motivating force in the generation of urban forms, it has not yet been demonstrated clearly and unequivocally first, that a generalized desire for exchange is capable of concentrating political and social power to the extent attested by the archaeological record, or second, that it can bring about the institutionalization of such power.

Somewhat surprisingly, the potential significance of ancient city formation is ignored by theorists of urban society, notably Marx and Weber (Saunders 1981). Urban economists, moreover, have not seen the question as providing matter for their classification of functions as 'basic' and 'nonbasic' (Thompson 1965).

As we pointed out earlier, the base–superstructure question is a dilemma which we should want to avoid, in connection with urban origins as much as with any other urban question. Wheatley (1971, pp. 318–19) hints at recognition of this:

> It is doubtful if a single autonomous, causative factor will ever be identified in the nexus of social, economic, and political transformations which resulted in the emergence of urban forms, but one activity does seem in a sense to command a sort of priority . . . This does not mean that religion . . . was a primary causative factor, but rather that it permeated all activities, all institutional change; and afforded a consensual focus for social life.

Whenever possible, we need to turn to studies by the historian of the practical nature of everyday life in the ancient city (e.g. Carcopino 1940). These studies throw light on the relationships between such activities as the production and appropriation of the surplus, trade, the exercise of authority, religion, and ceremony, and the origin and initial growth of cities.

Within the category of urban origins, other questions have been debated. One has to do with the rate of change in urban development, that is, evolutionary change (Mumford 1961, Adams 1966) versus urban revolution (Childe 1950). Another is the question of the geographic diffusion of cities (as a settlement form and as an idea) from one source, most likely the Near East or a number of independent cultural hearths (Hammond 1972, Carter 1977), with the latter argument now replacing the conventional wisdom of the former. These issues are ably reviewed by Carter (1977).

Urban form   Urban form can be narrowly conceived as the physical arrangement of structures and open spaces, including streets and other pathways, within some defined area, such as the space enclosed within a wall that is called a town or city. Urban form then becomes synonymous with urban morphology.

Urban morphology has a distinguished tradition in geography (e.g. Conzen 1960, Whitehand 1981), and also in other fields (e.g. Gutkind 1964–72, Reps 1965). However, much of the work has been confined to a particular national context, and only a few studies (e.g. Dickinson 1961) have explicitly attempted to make comparisons among different countries. Apart from an effort to find the morphological features common to certain conventional regions ('the Islamic city,' for instance), there has been a notable lack of attention to theory.

Vance (1977) and Michael Conzen (1978) have gone some way to extend this literature. For Conzen (1978, p. 134), 'cultural differences of all kinds within and between cities play significant rôles' in the full geographic reality of cities, and cultural context demands a sensitivity not shown by an urban geography concerned with 'general forces' as explanations. He suggests, however, that American cities are less in need of a cultural–geographic analysis than Old World cities because American urban history has been short, and American urban life is dominated by the values of economic Darwinism. This implies a notion of culture that diverges from ours. We understand both duration of urban experience and a particular set of economic mores to be fundamental elements of cultural context that *must* be a part of any morphological analysis. As the urban sociologist Scott Greer (1972, p. 2) says: 'To understand our cities . . . one must know something about the culture and organization of the United States as a whole.'

Vance (1977) is no nearer to sharing our interpretation of culture. His study of urban form and morphogenetic processes does cross national boundaries freely within the somewhat arbitrary framework of 'Western civilization.' However, the emphasis is on technology as a variable and on the city as both place of production and market. Scale and physical process take precedence in explanation, notably in his discussion of suburban morphology (Vance 1977, p. 405), over such matters as social values, attitudes toward land as private property, and homeownership.

Urban form has a broader meaning as 'internal structure' of a city. As such it includes the geographic patterning of activities and social groups within a city or metropolitan area (Palm 1981). Whether studying the unique form of individual cities or generalizing about urban patterns, geographers have been chiefly associated with the description and analysis of urban form. What theory there is of urban form in geography, however, is largely derived from other fields. One is urban sociology, especially the human ecology school of Chicago (Park, Burgess, and others). Another is land economics, which has a longer intellectual lineage than urban economics proper; it runs from Hurd (1903) and Haig (1926) to Alonso (1965) and Muth (1969).

The distribution of activities within a city has almost always been explained by competition for a scarce resource (i.e. urban location with good access) and the importance of the market as almost the only mechanism of allocation. This set of ideas could accommodate the models of the human ecologists, which rested on Darwinian principles. Park and his associates did recognize the importance of cultural factors, in the adjustment to urban life for example, but these factors were placed on a separate analytical level and given less attention than the 'biotic' context (Saunders 1981).

The market perspective has now been challenged because of a growing conviction that the processes of land allocation are increasingly mediated by political institutions and processes. Whether these institutions are subservient to the interests of private capital in capitalist societies or truly reflect autonomous state interests remains a troublesome question. Ley and Mercer (1980) argued for the importance of political mediation in their study of locational conflict in Vancouver (more generally, see Kirby 1982). They found that the social values held by the city government and beliefs in what constituted a 'livable city' influenced and in some cases directed land-use patterns and changes in urban form. Although the stability of these values remains in question, they may be a portent of new value structures (Inglehart 1977, Kirby 1982).

Some of the debates on urban form in urban economics have been technical ones, referring to a received methodology such as regression analysis (Ball 1979). Others have been concerned with the need to relax the basic assumptions used in reducing the city to one-dimensional space and with the consequences of doing so, as in the debate over monocentricity versus polycentricity (Richardson 1976). Ball (1979), in an assessment of urban economics, criticizes the economic theorist for looking for general urban characteristics and for asking questions that imply the existence of a universal city structure. More reductionism is applied both to social relations, converting them into 'technical' or 'policy' problems by limiting them to the city itself (Ball 1979, p. 325), and to the varied social nature of people by inventing a universal economic man (Alonso 1965, p. 1).

The result is that cultural context is ignored by most urban economists. The primacy of the market's rôle in allocating private goods and services is assured. Some commentators (e.g. Lineberry 1980) now discern a 'political economy of the right' that looks to market primacy in the provision of *public* services and the making of social choices, processes which inevitably affect urban form.

In urban sociology, human ecology has foundered and some new modes deny the importance of the urban place (Saunders 1981). It is reduced to a container (like a beaker in a science laboratory) with little impact on the catalysis within. The implications for what Berry and

Kasarda (1977) call contemporary urban ecology are serious. Its shaky theoretical base is made up of social area analysis and human ecology, including spatial models of city structure derived from the Chicago work. Social area analysis never made the internal structure of the city or the urbanization process a central object of enquiry. Neither it nor the human ecology school, with its ecological framework of competition, gave much attention to cultural context.

As urban–ecological analyses were extended to non-American settings, questions of cultural context might well have arisen in connection with factorial structures and urban patterns that differed from those found in the United States. Had their practitioners developed the critical self-consciousness we have urged, these issues would surely have surfaced. But the questions posed were derived from Western, chiefly American, experience in urban research. Not being grounded in indigenous experience, they exemplify for Masotti and Walton (1976, p. 2) the 'parochialism' that appears:

> when researchers venture into 'foreign' settings with a prefabricated set of theoretical and methodological tools which presuppose the order and meaning of events.

While there is good reason to question basic economic assumptions regarding dominance and competition in the context of the United States they are less believable when applied to 'Third World' cities. Human ecology remains, as Hunter (1980) describes it, 'a macrostructural perspective,' although he claims that it can incorporate the case study of everyday urban life at the local scale. The macrostructural perspective is illustrated by the work of Kasarda (1978), but he provides no local case study and says nothing about values, beliefs, or the ordering of social relations. Other than in the mass, people are not his chief concern.

An alternative path in urban ecological analysis was pointed out by Firey (1947), Form (1954), and Willhelm (1962). But neither in human ecology nor in the urban geography that drew upon the work of the Chicago school did the intention of emphasizing symbolism, social structure, and values redirect the basic approach. These were minor modifications, still accepting the structural imperatives of 'competition' and turning to culture only for supplementary explanation.

Other limitations are clear. In urban economics, as in land economics, the rationally calculated self-interest of the individual economic man has never lost importance, and there has been little or no concern with the origins of individual preferences or wants. Even in urban sociology, despite Greer's remark about the need to look at American culture and organization to understand American cities, values and beliefs are usually subsumed under macrosocial processes that are not closely tied to urban ones. He is correct in charging that human consciousness has been suppressed as an important aspect of human behavior (Greer 1972, p. 3).

The literature on urban form has not resolved the structure–action problem referred to earlier, and in most cases has failed to address it. Spatial models of city form – more broadly, factorial ecology and urban sociology – embody a structural view of human behavior. An action-oriented view of the city, on the other hand, is present in studies that look at the choice of residential sites, residential mobility, and the locational strategies of development and construction firms. These studies characteristically overemphasize individual decision making and do not specify context adequately. We believe that a successful integration of both human agency and structural constraint can be realized, although it is hardly to be found at present.

This alternative perspective has been employed with a measure of success by some American urban historians (Thernstrom 1964, Warner 1968, 1972, Hershberg 1981). To take but one example of this genre, Warner, in *The urban wilderness*, provides:

a sweeping narrative of urbanization in American history . . . which . . . demonstrated how insights about the structure of cities and the dynamics of urbanization could inform, and yet be informed by, a general cultural analysis of American society (Frisch 1979, p. 375).

The potentials and pitfalls of this and related historical work are reviewed forcefully by Frisch (1979).

Urban systems   Traditional urban geography concerned itself with the 'situation' of the city, chiefly in relation to its region, that is, to the terrain and to the location of other settlements. This interest is transformed in the contemporary theme of urban systems: the city is now a node linked to and interacting with other large nodes, and also acts as the center of a 'functional' or 'nodal' region (Bourne & Simmons 1978). The idea of a hinterland, involving relationships between town and country, persists. Urban and regional economists try to explain the structure of the urban system and the changes in it and its associated set of regions as a response to a pattern of investment decisions, the comparative advantages of places, and exogenous influences, exerted most importantly by commodity and final demand markets (Hansen 1972, 1975a, 1978). Urban historians have focused on the changing relationship between the city and the surrounding region or countryside (Pirenne 1925, Weber 1958), while historical and urban geographers have sought to describe and explain the evolution of urban systems (Pred 1966, Ward 1971, Conzen 1977, 1981).

Urban geographers in particular have wanted to learn the structure of the system and how it operates. System organization, involving the

notion of hierarchy or core–periphery relationships, which imply dominance and exploitation by the core, and the direction and magnitude of
flows have engaged most attention. Regional development is understood
to be intimately linked with the performance of the urban system, and
geographers, economists, and regional planners have joined in studying it
for this reason. Their aim has been to discover ways of reducing regional
inequalities, in particular to stimulate economic growth in lagging
regions; the city is conceived as 'growth pole' (Berry 1973b, Friedmann &
Alonso 1975, Hansen 1975b). City–countryside relationships have been
viewed in two ways. In Christallerian terms, the city is a 'central place'
serving the smaller settlements and dispersed population of the countryside. Through Marxist lenses, it is dominant and powerful, exerting force
when necessary to appropriate the surplus value generated by the
countryside.

While notions of culture are largely absent from these analyses,
awareness of the need for a culturally informed approach seems to be
growing. Berry (1973b, p. 36) now thinks that the essential motor for
growth in the American urban system is to be found in social rather than
economic dynamics. Basic to these dynamics is a significant element of
American culture, the personal drive for success and achievement that
fosters social and spatial mobility. There is here some intimation of people
sharing in a collective self-portrait and acting upon the values and beliefs it
embodies. Lacking theoretical development, this view is still a minority
one in the study of urban systems (Gilbert 1978).

However, values and beliefs do appear explicitly in the study of
city–country relations. Perhaps the most loudly expressed modern
Anglo-Saxon attitude to the city is that it is loathsome and corrupting,
degrading to the human spirit as an embodiment of the headlong pursuit
of profit. The countryside is morally superior, a place where people are
ennobled through close contact with natural rhythms. Others see this
view of the countryside as highly romantic and quite inaccurate and feel
that the positive virtues of the city have been ignored. Conceding that
'chaos and misery' are a part of life in the new metropolis, they suggest
that out of the struggle of the city there arises 'a new vision of society'
(Williams 1973, p. 231). The experience of urban life is first needed to
demystify social processes before new value systems can emerge. One
illustration of this is the rise of the cooperative movement from its
founding in industrial Rochdale in 19th-century northern England.

Community Power and Urban Government   The closely linked themes of
community power structure and city government seek answers to a
central question: who 'really rules' this place? Sociologists, working in the
community-studies tradition established by the Lynds in the United
States, and political scientists have long argued the question, although

without giving the place itself particular significance. The question of whether the distribution of power is 'élitist' or 'pluralist' has been debated in a large body of work (Lineberry 1980).

The debate led social scientists to look closely into the meaning of power and the way decisions regarding the city are made (Bachrach & Baratz 1970, Lukes 1974, Wrong 1979), but the problems encountered had the effect of reducing interest in this research. There were endless conceptual difficulties and operational dilemmas. How, for example, should one measure 'nondecisions?' There was also a failure to show that differences in the character of community power can explain why the material results of policy making are distributed unevenly. Attention turned to the bureaucracy as studies showed that elected politicians in city hall seem less important than professional administrators who implement policy and often set it (Burnett 1981, p. 203, Crenson 1982). The classic Weberian theme of the rôle and power of bureaucracies has been given a specific new focus, the geographic and distributional consequences of administrative decision making (see the extensive bibliography in Burnett 1981).

Little in this recent work is concerned with cultural context, but such a point of view might raise intriguing questions. As a professional field of public administration grows in the United States in urban planning for example, does an administrative or bureaucratic subculture appear into which the practitioners are socialized (cf. Nachmias & Rosenbloom 1978, 1980)? What value system and set of meanings does such a subculture share? How does an administrative élite relate to community groups that have different subcultures?

Urbanism   Conceptual confusion over 'the urban' as an object of study goes back to different interpretations of 'urbanism.' Wirth's seminal paper (1938) has been a mixed blessing. Wirth conceived urbanism as 'a distinctive mode of human group life' by distinguishing between the ideal types of urban–industrial society and the rural–folk one. But urbanism was then restated as 'that complex of traits which makes up the characteristic mode of life in cities.' Wirth could even claim that it was not the result of 'specific locally or historically conditioned cultural influences.' However important, these were not the 'essential determinants' of the character of a city – clearly, we disagree.

The sociological definition of a city rested on size, population density, permanency of settlement, and social heterogeneity, and a number of propositions were formulated relating these variables to urbanism as manifested in the daily lives of people. The propositions remain unverified, chiefly because a wide range of settlements was found to be arrayed on each variable.

Nevertheless, these relationships remain the central concern in the study of urbanism, although the focus has shifted. Many writers now simply equate urbanism with urban ways of life. They do not question its theoretical status, especially the claim that it is *the* urban way of life. What matters for them are the consequences for individuals of leading urban lives. Are the behavior and attitudes associated with urban living caused by urban living? Reviewing both theoretical and empirical work, Fischer (1976) identified three sociological theories of urbanism.

(a) Determinist theory follows Wirth in making urbanism foster social and individual personality disorders in contrast to the rural mode of life.
(b) Compositional theory (expounded by such as Herbert Gans and Oscar Lewis) denies urbanism any direct effect. Urban–rural differences arise from the different composition of the populations involved, and the urban experience operates indirectly at most.
(c) Subcultural theory, of which Fischer himself is the leading advocate, adopts the compositional perspective but holds that urbanism does have direct measurable effects on urban folk.

Cultural characteristics acquire importance in compositional and subcultural theories. For Gans (1962), there can be more than one way of life in the city, but each is little affected by the surrounding urban environment. Fischer argues that the urban environment promotes the heterogeneity of residents, as groups, fostering subcultures or 'social worlds.' Structural differentiation arising from the division of labor in large settlements also fosters subcultures. In contrast to compositional theory, subcultures are both created and strengthened by urbanism, which is thus assigned a causal rôle, as it is in determinist theory.

The perhaps simplified conclusion is that people living in cities, especially large ones, differ in behavior both qualitatively and quantitatively from rural and small-town populations, even allowing for the spread of urbanism beyond the metropolis (Sedalla 1978). Just as the city is seen negatively, so are the personal consequences of urbanism, which is held responsible for the individual's detachment, insulation, and excessive concern with self. Alienation is only a step away. But to what extent are individualism and privatism features of American society rather than urbanism per se?

Moving from the question of whether urban life is disintegrative, Fischer (1982) now wants to understand the different *integrations* of urban and rural life. But the particularities of historical period continue to constrain generalizations about the consequences of urbanism for human behavior, as, even more, does cultural context, ignored by Fischer except for the notion of American subcultures.

Fischer's framework can accommodate political studies of 'public-regarding' and 'private-regarding' ethos (Banfield & Wilson 1963). Those adhering to a particular ethos might represent a subculture, although perhaps one with less intense interaction than a 'social world' (Fischer 1982, pp. 233–49, on alienation in public life). But the question remains: does the social and political behavior that constitutes a distinct ethos arise from the experience of urban life, particularly the personal adjustment of the migrant, or from political and social value systems that are more or less independent of the urban experience? The question bears on (among other things) the understanding of the rôle of the political machine in American city politics. The machine has been considered, on the one hand, as a response to urban immigrant experience with remote, incomprehensible institutions, and, on the other, as a means of immigrant adaptation to the new urban experience (Crenson 1982).

In seeking answers to such questions, it is difficult to isolate the effect of urbanism as 'a distinctive mode of life' and all the more difficult to attribute causality to it, either in the modern period or in earlier ones that historians have studied. What the sociologist has done is to define urbanism operationally as 'the number of people living in and near a community' (Fischer 1982, p. 23). Certain associations between a scale of urbanism and measures of psychological strain, social involvement, and traditional values are then demonstrated. While circumventing some problems of definition, this procedure sharply diminishes the social and cultural content of urbanism as a way of life.

Urbanization Of all the urban themes we have identified, the most widely studied has been urbanization, the process whereby the settlement system, the regional organization of the economy, and the mode of life for millions of people have been fundamentally transformed.

There are two conventional ways of studying urbanization, which is defined demographically as the proportion of a regional or national population living in urban places. One is to treat it as a dependent variable and to hypothesize a range of social, demographic, and economic variables which, working in conjunction, give rise to it. The other way is to make urbanization the independent variable that is shown to be related to certain consequences, or, in some theories, to cause them. Regions or countries with different levels of urbanization might be expected to have urban systems with different kinds of spatial articulation: the more urbanized the country, the more fully developed the urban system is expected to be. According to Goldstein and Sly (1978), other expected consequences of urbanization include:

(a) the development, maintenance, and expansion of urban infrastructures;
(b) social control, and the breakdown of traditional institutions;
(c) transformation of a largely subsistence agrarian economy into one with an industrial orientation;

(d)   environmental degradation, and ecological pressures.

The implicit claim to universal validity in these propositions illustrates the potential for error in using European historical experience as the paradigm of world development.

There are substantial differences in the way each of the urban-oriented disciplines looks at urbanization, which is an important theme in all but political science. There it is usually treated as a component of modernization, which is of interest primarily as it relates to political development (Friedmann & Wulff 1975, pp. 30–33, Olsen 1981).

To generalize broadly, anthropology and sociology are most concerned with urbanization as a social process – changes in behavior and mores, emergence of new roles, and altered relationships among groups (Meadows & Mizruchi 1969, Schaedel et al. 1978). Although viewed as a cultural phenomenon, urbanization is seen to depend upon the conjuncture of technological and social processes. Urbanization somehow consists of several distinct processes: the diffusion of urban values, migration from country to city, and adjustment to urban ways. This confuses what is arguably a symptom of urbanization, namely migration, with urbanization itself.

Urban and regional economists and planners study urbanization mainly in connection with models of regional growth, emphasizing development on a broad scale. (For a comparative introductory treatment of urbanization in certain developing nations see Friedmann & Wulff 1975, pp. 10–37, 56–63.) Degrees of urbanization are seen as determining types of urban systems and changes in them. Current debate, in which urban geographers are also involved, centers on the nature of the population changes, the direction of migration flows, and their impact on both origin and destination that are accompanying what appears to be a new developmental phase in economically advanced countries, Berry's 'counterurbanization' (Berry 1976).

Dissatisfaction with the conventional wisdom of the early 1970s has grown. One no longer thinks that urbanization is a universal process that follows from modernization, and that all nations move inevitably through a series of stages to a final convergence of form in urban systems and structures (Hawley 1971, pp. 313–15). Reality has compelled a different view. Berry himself (1973a, p. xii) came to see that:

> we are dealing with several fundamentally different processes that have arisen out of differences in culture and time . . . these processes are producing different results in different world regions, transcending any superficial similarities.

There is at last a prospect, if not indeed a demand, for the culturally informed study of urbanization.

Berry's response to the imperatives of his own position can be contrasted to that of the sociologist Roberts (1978). The latter agrees that urbanization produces divergent processes within and between nations, in addition to convergent ones. The diversity does not arise from the regional uniqueness of culture, however, but from increasing economic interdependence in the world (Roberts 1978, p. 593). Berry is more explicit regarding the place of culture in American urbanization. In the decreasing rate of population growth in many metropolitan centers and the increasing rate in other than metropolitan counties, often distant from them, we are witnessing, he says, 'the reassertion of fundamental predispositions of the American culture' (Berry 1976, p. 24).

However Berry's discussion of American culture harks back to the basic traits discerned by Crevecoeur (1782), Berry conceives of culture as received and handed down almost without change over a long period of time. It diverges from our view that culture is actively constructed and renewed by people as they confront situations that are patently not the same as those that obtained 200 years earlier.

Urbanization has also been analyzed by various scholars from the viewpoint of what they call 'political economy' or 'critical science' (Dear & Scott 1981, Procter 1982). For them, the theory of urbanization 'generally insists upon the explicit derivation of contemporary urbanization processes out of the structure of the capitalist mode of production' (Dear & Scott 1981, p. xiii). Roberts (1978, p. 596) says much the same:

> Urbanization processes in different parts of the world are indeed related; they are interdependent processes. Urbanization is the product of capitalist development and expansion.

We agree that 'urbanization (and planning) can never be effectively treated as objects of theoretical study divorced from some wider theory of society' (Dear & Scott 1981, p. 4). We are, however, separated from these writers by our belief in the need for an understanding of cultural context.

Organization of the book

Apart from the Introduction and Commentary, the chapters have been organized in three groups. The first comprises the essays by Claval, Rapoport, Walton, Abu-Lughod, and Hall. These are at a continental or global scale, or have developed a general framework that is examined in a preliminary way with selected data.

The second set consists of the papers by Bater, Allinson, and Murphey, which rest on a base of solid empirical work and first-hand experience with the phenomena discussed. Each happens to deal with a region where there has been a history of centralized state direction of the economy, of political life, and, to some extent, of cultural change. The long duration of some form of control, however different, of the cities in the Soviet Union, Japan, and China has made for the maintenance of continuity there despite important social change in all three countries.

The last group is made up of the papers by Western, Lewandowski, and the Duncans, which blend a concern for conceptualization with original substantive research. Each addresses two important questions in a distinctive way. To what extent is cultural change autonomous or directed? And what are the implications of either type of change for urbanization, as in the case of largely directed change in South Africa, for urban morphology, as in directed change in the symbolic landscape of southern India, or for both autonomous and locally directed change in the form of élite residential districts in American and Canadian cities?

In the first paper, Claval shows the limitations, for the understanding of urban reality, of conceiving culture as an ensemble of techniques and artifacts. Culture for Claval encompasses ways of thinking and behaving, custom and habit, preferences and styles of life, in addition to norms, rules, and values. The expression of culture in urban morphology is documented for several urban regions that have existed in Europe since the Middle Ages and transcend the modern nation–state. Claval also notes regional differences among European cities that are based on culturally conditioned forms of social interaction.

Rapoport's conception of culture is of a set of values and beliefs from which develops a characteristic way of viewing the world. The relationship between culture and different 'urban orders' is manifested in the landscape (particularly in the shape of settlements), for it is the view of the world that shapes the urban scene. Illustrating his thesis from a range of urban orders, Rapoport argues that urban morphology can only be interpreted and made sensible if one knows the cultural context.

Walton thinks that most conventional notions of culture are not adequate for theories about its relation to urbanization and urban form. He looks at these from a political–economy perspective, but recognizes that such a view cannot deal with culture effectively or systematically. Culture is something that is made, a set of beliefs that is held by a group about itself and that arises from political and economic struggle and that in turn influences the struggle. Tending to view culture as akin to ideology, he identifies the different cultures that are associated with the groups whose collective action shapes the city in important ways. He does so by looking at the links between economic organization, urban life, and spatial structure in Guadalajara, the second largest Mexican metropolis. There he finds four cultures: civic culture, modernity culture, working-class culture, and the political culture of developmentalism.

A framework that is also based on political economy is used by

Abu-Lughod, an authority on cities in the Arab World whose early work attached considerable importance to the commonalities among Arab cities arising from culture history. Here, she proposes a taxonomy for the Arab countries of the Middle East, including North Africa, that is based on their different national roles within the world economy and the international division of labor. She insists on the need for such a framework to understand current trends in the urbanization of the Arab World, especially the startling morphological changes that are taking place in such cities as Amman and Riyadh. Her rejection of culture as solely equatable with tradition suggests that she has in mind cultures of modernity and developmentalism such as those discerned by Walton.

The last paper of the first set takes us to the industrially advanced countries and the idea of competing cultures. These are cultures defined in geographic terms that compete in the sense that Hall sees his fellow planners as preferring 'urban culture' and disdaining 'suburban culture.' Suburban culture is most developed in the United States, typified in such cities as Los Angeles and San Jose. Nevertheless, a comparative analysis leads Hall to detect a strong trend toward suburban and even non–metropolitan styles of living (cultures, in his sense) in Europe as well as the United States. He concludes that planners who hold to an urban culture and admire it are in danger of committing a serious mistake. They may be imposing their own values and beliefs about the proper form of cities on people who have already expressed their preference for certain locations and associated styles of life, and thus, presumably, their own values. These people have done so through residential location – voting against the city with their feet, as Hall bluntly puts it.

Bater's synthesis of the form of Soviet cities and the life of their inhabitants is constructed around the notions of continuity and change. He accepts that cultural traditions continue to be of importance in Soviet society. Spanning a period from the pre-Revolutionary era to that of the contemporary socialist city, cultural values are shown to affect urban form, mediated as they are through the residential segregation of specific social strata. The geography of status groups (and associated privilege) persists in Soviet cities, despite official statements to the contrary. A second theme of this essay hinges on the city–state relationship. On the one hand, both in the pre-Revolutionary era and more recently, the state has proven to be ineffective in controlling urbanization, though its desire to do so rested upon quite different motivations. On the other hand, cities have increasingly become both instruments and examples of change directed from the center, in what has always been a highly bureaucratized society. The state has consciously constructed city form, seeking an accord with the ideals of a socialist society. As Bater indicates, urban experience often does not correspond with the state ideology.

Tradition and continuity are also emphasized in the essays on Japan by

Allinson and on China by Murphey, but the authors are also quite aware of the impact of change. Allinson properly focuses on the capitalist managerial center of Tokyo and the peculiarly Japanese nature of Japanese cities. Nevertheless, his history of central direction of economic organization and the emphasis on tradition give the paper a conceptual commonality with Murphey's paper on China, regardless of the differences in the central structure in each case and in the outcome of its direction. In China, traditional ways led to a distinct hierarchy of urban settlements and to definite geographic patterns in urban form. Modern transformations changed urban ways of life perhaps more than the urban system or urban form, although the significance of the treaty ports remains somewhat problematic. Both system and form retain the stamp of preceding eras, and urban–rural tensions (a central theme of Murphey's paper) have not disappeared.

In the last set of essays, culture is conceived in a way that lends itself to operational treatment, and the ideas about culture are then given detailed substantive application to a particular case. To study the interactive relationship between cities and culture in South Africa, Western finds it necessary to distinguish between autonomous and directed cultural change, while recognizing that they are not independent. Autonomous change arose with the onset of capitalism in the region, and the attendant rise of industrialization and urbanization. To achieve political ends, Afrikaners and their Nationalist Party have sought to modify culture. In trying to do so, they have had great effect on the process of urbanization, most notably for Black Africans, but also for Coloureds and Afrikaners themselves. The impact of directed cultural change and of the laws that express it is also evident in social patterning in the cities, overwhelming the allocation processes of the market.

In some societies, the values, beliefs, and customs that constitute culture are suffused with what is understood by the West as religion. Nowhere is this truer than in India, where people customarily interpret their culture in a religious context. Lewandowski shows that the expression of religious culture, as in the building of temples, has a significant effect on key landscape complexes in certain Indian cities. One aim of her paper is to show how the state consciously manipulates urban features to convey symbolic meaning, to foster identity, and to enhance the political legitimation of the incumbent administration. This is a form of directed cultural change that is, in Lewandowski's phrase, 'the institutionalization of cultural aspirations.'

The Duncans' paper extends the theme by relating the conscious manipulation of suburban landscape symbols to the wish of particular social groups to preserve their distinct identity. They suggest that what seem to be autonomous or 'vernacular' landscapes of a particular cultural coloration are in fact in some sense 'directed' by the use of such political tools as zoning regulations and legislation regarding environmental quality. These tools, they argue, are used to plant and maintain the cultural signature of a particular group in the landscape, a group that has the power to do so. While the signature they are concerned with, in two North American locales, happens to be a translation of the idealized country homes of English gentry, their study invites analogous interpretation of other landscape forms in other times and other places.

This overview of the chapters of this volume shows that urban form has been most emphasized and the process of urbanization almost as much, mostly as the increasing metropolitanization of people and the ascendancy of urban life. On the other hand, there is little comment on city–country relationships apart from in Murphey's paper and to a lesser extent in those by Bater and Hall. Even less attention is paid to the concept of urban systems. These particular emphases reflect the predilections of our contributors, our charge to them, and the difficulties of placing urban systems in cultural context, although some attempts to do so have recently been made elsewhere (Conzen 1981).

It may be analytically desirable to separate such objects of analysis as urban form, urbanization, or urban systems, but their fundamental relatedness must always be kept in mind. It is necessary to eliminate such artificial distinctions. Work on the city in cultural context promises to do so. It is an approach that can lead us to a synthesis of our knowledge about the city and to an appreciation of it in different cultural contexts. Thus we may come to understand what causes cities, why they take particular forms, and how the urban experience is involved in the production of culture. It is our hope that this book will stimulate interest in a variety of work along a wide front that will have the effect of ending the sway of the culturally uninformed in urban studies.

References

Abrams, P. 1980. History, sociology, historical sociology. *Past and Present* **87**, 3–16.

Adams, R. McC. 1966. *The evolution of urban society*. Chicago: University of Chicago Press.

Alonso, W. 1965. *Location and land use*. Cambridge, Mass.: Harvard University Press.

Aminzade, R. 1979. The transformation of social solidarities in nineteenth-century Toulouse. In *Consciousness and Class experience in nineteenth-century Europe*, J. M. Merriman (ed.), 85–105. New York: Holmes and Meier.

Anderson, P. 1976. The antinomies of Antonio Gramsei. *New Left Review* **100**, 5–78.

Bachrach, P. and M. S. Baratz 1970. *Power and poverty: theory and practice*. New York: Oxford University Press.

Ball, M. 1979. A critique of urban economics. *Int. J. Urban Reg. Res.* **3**, 309–33.

Banfield, E. C. and J. Q. Wilson 1963. *City politics*. Cambridge, Mass.: Harvard University Press.

Bater, J. H. 1980. *The Soviet city: ideal and reality*. London: Edward Arnold.

Bauman, Z. 1973. *Culture as praxis*. London: Routledge & Kegan Paul.

Beeman, R. R. 1977. The new social history and the search for 'community' in colonial America. *Am. Q.* **29**, 433.

Benet, F. 1963. Sociology uncertain: the ideology of the rural–urban continuum. *Comp. Stud. Soc. Hist.* **6**, 1–17.

Berry, B. J. L. 1973a. *The human consequences of urbanization*. New York: St Martin's Press.

Berry, B. J. L. 1973b. *Growth centers in the American urban system*, Vols. 1 and 2. Cambridge, Mass.: Ballinger.

Berry, B. J. L. (ed.) 1976, *Urbanization and counter-urbanization*. Beverly Hills, Calif.: Sage.

Berry, B. J. L. and J. D. Kasarda 1977. *Contemporary urban ecology*. New York: Macmillan.

Boulding, K. 1963. The death of the city. In *The historian and the city*, O. Handlin and J. Burchard (eds.), 133–45. Cambridge, Mass.: Harvard University Press.

Bourne, L. S. and J. W. Simmons (eds.) 1978. *Systems of cities*. New York: Oxford University Press.

Brenner, R. 1977. The origins of capitalist development: a critique of neo-Smithian marxism. *New Left Review* **104**, 25–92.

Burnett, A. D. 1981. The distribution of local political outputs and outcomes in British and North American cities. In *Political studies from spatial perspectives: Anglo-American essays in political geography*, A. D. Burnett and P. J. Taylor (eds.), 201–35. Chichester: Wiley.

Carcopino, J. 1940. *Daily life in ancient Rome*. New Haven: Yale University Press.

Carter, H. 1977. Urban origins: a review. *Prog. Hum. Geog.* **1**, 12–32.

Castells, M. 1977. *The urban question*. London: Edward Arnold.

Cheal, D. J. 1979. Hegemony, ideology and contradictory consciousness. *Sociol. Q.* **20**, 109–17.

Childe, V. G. 1950. The urban revolution. *Town Plann. Rev.* **21**, 3–17.

Conzen, M. P. 1977. The maturing urban system in the United States, 1840–1910. *Ann. Assoc. Am. Geog.* **67**, 88–108.

Conzen, M. P. 1978. Analytical approaches to the urban landscape. In *Dimensions of human geography*, Research Paper No. 186, K. W. Butzer (ed.), 128–65. Chicago: Department of Geography, University of Chicago.

Conzen, M. P. 1981. The American urban system in the nineteenth century. In *Geography and the urban environment: progress in research and applications*, Vol. IV, D. T. Herbert and R. J. Johnston (eds.). 295–347. Chichester: Wiley.

Conzen, M. R. G. 1960. *Alnwick, Northumberland: a study in town-plan analysis*, Publication No. 27. London: Institute of British Geographers.

Cosgrove, D. E. 1982. Problems of interpreting the symbolism of past landscapes. In *Period and place: research methods in historical geography*, A. R. Baker and M. Billinge (eds.), 220–30. Cambridge: Cambridge University Press.

Crenson, M. A. 1982, Urban bureaucracy in urban politics: notes toward a developmental theory. In *Public values and private power in American politics*, J. D. Greenstone (ed.), 209–45. Chicago: University of Chicago Press.

Crevecoeur, J. H. St John de 1782. *Letters from an American farmer*. London: Thomas Davies.

Dear, M. and A. J. Scott (eds.) 1981, *Urbanization and urban planning in capitalist society*. New York: Methuen.

Della Fave, L. R. 1980. The meek shall not inherit the earth: self-evaluation and the legitimacy of stratification. *Am. Sociol. Rev.* **45**, 955–71.

Dickinson, R. E. 1961. *The West European city: a geographical interpretation.* London: Routledge & Kegan Paul.

Duncan, J. S. 1980. The superorganic in American cultural geography. *Ann. Assoc. Am. Geogs.* **70**, 181–98.

Fava, S. F. (ed.) 1968. *Urbanism in world perspective.* New York: T. Crowell.

Firey, W. 1947. *Land use in central Boston.* Cambridge, Mass: Harvard University Press.

Fischer, C. S. 1976. *The urban experience.* New York: Harcourt Brace Jovanovich.

Fischer, C. S. 1982. *To dwell among friends: personal networks in town and city.* Chicago: University of Chicago Press.

Form, W. 1954. The place of social structure: the determination of land use. *Social Forces* **32**, 317–23.

Fox, R. G. 1977. *Urban anthropology: cities in their cultural settings.* Englewood Cliffs, NJ: Prentice-Hall.

Friedmann, J. and W. Alonso (eds.) 1975. *Regional policy: readings in theory and application.* Cambridge, Mass.: MIT Press.

Friedmann, J. and R. Wulff 1975. *The urban transition: comparative studies of newly industrializing societies.* London: Edward Arnold.

Frisch, M. 1979. American urban history as an example of recent historiography. *History and Theory* **28**, 350–77.

Fuentes, C. 1982. Writing in time. *Democracy* **2**, 1, 61–74.

Gans, H. J. 1962. Urbanism and suburbanism as ways of life. In *Human behavior and social processes*, A. M. Rose (ed.), 625–48. Boston: Houghton Mifflin.

Geertz, C. 1973. *The interpretation of cultures.* New York: Harper and Row.

Gilbert, A. G. 1978. The dynamics of human settlement systems in less developed countries: the priorities for urban policy formulation. In *Human settlement systems*, N. M. Hansen (ed.), 177–94. Cambridge, Mass.: Ballinger.

Goldstein, S. and D. F. Sly (eds.) 1978. *Patterns of urbanization: comparative country studies*, Vols. 1 and 2, International Union for the Scientific Study of Population: Commission of Urban and Population Redistribution, Working Paper No. 3. Dolhain, Belgium: Ordina Edition.

Greer, S. 1972. *The urban view: life and politics in metropolitan America.* New York: Oxford University Press.

Grew, R. 1980. The case for comparing histories. *Am. Hist. Rev.* **85**, 763–78.

Gusfield, J. R. 1967. Tradition and modernity: misplaced polarities in the study of social change. *Am. J. Sociol.* **72**, 351–62.

Gutkind, E. A. 1964–72. *International history of city development.* New York: Free Press.

Haig, R. M. 1926. Toward an understanding of the metropolis: the assignment of activities to areas in urban regions. *Q. J. Econ.* **40**, 402–34.

Hammond, M. 1972. *The city in the ancient world.* Cambridge, Mass.: Harvard University Press.

Hansen, N. M. (ed.) 1972. *Growth centers in regional economic development.* New York: Free Press.

Hansen, N. M. 1975a. *The challenge of urban growth.* Lexington, Mass.: D.C. Heath Lexington Books.

Hansen, N. M. 1975b. An evaluation of growth center theory and practice. *Environ. Plann.* **7**, 821–32.

Hansen, N. M. (ed.), 1978. *Human settlement systems: international perspectives on structure, change and public policy.* Cambridge, Mass.: Ballinger.

Harvey, D. 1973. *Social justice and the city*. London: Edward Arnold.

Hawley, A. H. 1971. *Urban society: an ecological approach*. New York: Ronald Press.

Hershberg, T. (ed.) 1981. *Work, space, family, and group experience in the nineteenth century*. New York: Oxford University Press.

Hunter, A. 1980. Why Chicago: the rise of the Chicago School of Urban Social Science. *Am. Behav. Sci.* **24**, 215–27.

Hurd, R. M. 1903. *Principles of city land values*. New York: The Record and Guide.

Inglehart, R. 1977. *The silent revolution: changing values and political styles among Western publics*. Princeton, NJ: Princeton University Press.

Kasarda, J. D. 1978. Urbanization, community, and the metropolitan problem. In *Handbook of contemporary urban life*, D. Street (ed.), 27–57. San Francisco: Jossey-Bass.

Kirby, A. 1982. *The politics of location*. New York: Methuen.

Lefebvre, H. 1978. *De l'etat*. Vol. 4: *Les contradictions de l'état modern*. Paris: Union Generale des Editions.

Lefebvre, H. 1980. *Une pensee devenue monde – faut-il abandonner Marx?* Paris: Fayard.

Ley, D. F. and J. Mercer 1980. Locational conflict and the politics of consumption. *Econ. Geog.* **56**, 89–109.

Lineberry, R. L. 1980. From political sociology to political economy: the state of theory in urban research. *Am. Behav. Sci.* **24**, 299–317.

Lukes, S. 1974. *Power: a radical view*. New York: Macmillan.

McGee, T. G. 1967. *The Southeast Asia city*. London: Bell.

Manicas, P. 1980. The concept of social structure. *J. Theory Soc. Behav.* **10**, 65–82.

Mardin, S. 1969. Power, civil society and culture in the Ottoman Empire. *Comp. Stud. Soc. Hist.* **11**, 258–81.

Masotti, L. H. and R. L. Lineberry 1976. *The new urban politics*. Cambridge, Mass.: Ballinger.

Masotti, L. H. and J. Walton 1976. Comparative urban research: the logic of comparisons and the nature of urbanism. In *The city in comparative perspective*, J. Walton and L. H. Masotti (eds.), 1–15. New York: Halsted Press/Wiley.

Meadows, P. and E. H. Mizruchi (eds.) 1969. *Urbanism, urbanization and change: comparative perspectives*. Reading, Mass.: Addison-Wesley.

Merriman, J. M. 1979. Incident at the statue of the Virgin Mary: the conflict of old and new in nineteenth-century Limoges. In *Consciousness and class experience in nineteenth-century Europe*, J. M. Merriman (ed.), 129–48. New York: Holmes and Meier.

Moore, B. Jr. 1966. *Social origins of dictatorship and democracy: lord and peasant in the making of the modern world*. Boston: Beacon Press.

Mumford, L. 1961. *The city in history*. New York: Harcourt, Brace and World.

Muth, R. C. 1969. *Cities and housing: the spatial pattern of urban residential land use*. Chicago: University of Chicago Press.

Nachmias, D. and D. H. Rosenbloom 1978. *Bureaucratic culture: citizens and administration in Israel*. New York: St Martin's Press.

Nachmias, D. and D. H. Rosenbloom 1980. *Bureaucratic government, USA*. New York: St. Martin's Press.

Oliven, R. G. 1979. Culture rules O.K: class and culture in Brazilian cities. *Int. J. Urban Reg. Res.* **3**, 29–48.

Olsen, M. E. 1981. Comparative political sociology. *Int. J. Comp. Sociol.* **22**, 40–61.

Palm, R. 1981. *The geography of American cities*. New York: Oxford University Press.

Pirenne, H. 1925. *Medieval cities*. Princeton, NJ: Princeton University Press.

Pletsch, C. 1981. The three worlds, or the division of social scientific labor, circa 1950–1975. *Comp. Stud. Soc. Hist.* **23**, 565–90.

Poggi, G. 1972. *Images of society: essays on the sociological theories of Tocqueville, Marx, and Durkheim*. Stanford, Calif.: Stanford University Press.

Pred, A. R. 1966. *The spatial dynamics of U.S. urban–industrial growth, 1800–1914: interpretive and theoretical essays*. Cambridge, Mass.: MIT Press.

Procter, I. 1982. Some political economies of urbanization and suggestions for a research framework. *Int. J. Urban Reg. Res.* **6**. 83–97.

Reps, J. W. 1965. *The making of urban America: a history of city planning in the United States*. Princeton, NJ: Princeton University Press.

Richardson, H. W. 1976. The new urban economics: an appraisal. *Socio-Econ. Plann. Sci.* **10**, 137–49.

Richardson, H. W. 1977. *The new urban economics and alternatives*. London: Pion.

Roberts, B. R. 1978. Comparative perspectives on urbanization. In *Handbook of Contemporary Urban Life*, D. Street (ed.), 592–627. San Francisco: Jossey-Bass.

Sahlins, M. W. 1976. *Culture and practical reason*. Chicago: University of Chicago Press.

Saunders, P. 1981. *Social theory and the urban question*. New York: Holmes and Meier.

Schaedel, R. P., J. E. Hardoy and N. S. Kinzer (eds.) 1978. *Urbanization in the Americas from its beginnings to the present*. The Hague: Mouton.

Sedalla, E. K. 1978. Population size, structural differentiation and human behavior. *Environ. Behav.* **10**, 271–91.

Thernstrom, S. 1964. *Poverty and progress: social mobility in a nineteenth century city*. Cambridge, Mass.: Joint Center for Urban Studies of MIT and Harvard University.

Thompson, W. R. 1965. *A preface to urban economics*. Baltimore: Published for Resources for the Future by Johns Hopkins.

Thrupp, S. 1961. The creativity of cities: a review article. *Comp. Stud. Soc. Hist.* **4**, 63–4.

Tipps, D. 1973. Modernization theory and the comparative study of societies: a critical perspective. *Comp. Stud. Soc. Hist.* **15**, 199–226.

Vance, J. E. 1977. *This scene of man*. New York: Harper's College Press.

Ward, D. 1971. *Cities and immigrants: a geography of change in nineteenth century America*. New York: Oxford University Press.

Warner, S. B. Jr. 1968. *The private city: Philadelphia in three periods of its growth*. Philadelphia: University of Pennsylvania Press.

Warner, S. B. Jr. 1972. *The urban wilderness: a history of the American city*. New York: Harper & Row.

Weber, M. 1958. *The city*. New York: Free Press.

Wheatley, P. 1971. *The pivot of the four quarters*. Chicago: Aldine.

Whitehand, J. W. R. (ed.) 1981. *The urban landscape: historical development and management papers by M. R. G. Conzen*. London: Academic Press.

Willhelm, S. 1962. *Urban zoning and land use theory*. New York: Free Press.

Williams, R. 1958. *Culture and society: 1780–1950*. New York: Columbia University Press.

Williams, R. 1973. *The country and the city*. London: Chatto & Windus.

Williams, R. 1977. *Marxism and literature*. London: Oxford University Press.

Williams, R. 1980. *Problems in materialism and culture*. London: New Left Books.

Williams, R. 1982. *The sociology of culture*. New York: Schocken Books.

Wirth, L. 1938. Urbanism as a way of life. *Am. Journ. of Soc.* **44**, 3–24; *Louis Wirth: on cities and social life*, Reprinted in Reiss, A. J. (ed.). Chicago: University of Chicago Press.

Wood, E. M. 1981. The separation of the economic and the political in capitalism. *New Left Review* **127**, 66–95.

Wrong, D. 1969. The oversocialized conception of man in modern sociology. In *Sociological Theory*, L. A. Coser and B. Rosenberg (eds.), 122–32. London: Collier-Macmillan.

Wrong, D. 1979. *Power: its forms, bases and uses*. Oxford: Basil Blackwell.

2 Reflections on the cultural geography of the European city*

PAUL CLAVAL

Introduction

Cultural geography has long been concerned with small, archaic societies or societies in which the population remained largely rural. It tended to neglect the facts of urban existence.

What, then, was understood by culture? An ensemble of techniques and artifacts that were transmitted from one generation to another. A village cell is easy to define to the extent that the mode of life of its members is based on a few patterns following universal rhythms. The skills and knowledge needed to mold the enviroment would be possessed by all the members of the community. Even where there were specialists whose particular skills would be recognized by all, the principles of their crafts would be understood by most of their fellows.

It is possible to explore urban realities by means of this concept of culture, but not without considerable difficulty.[1] In the city, the division of labor is taken much further than in the country: thus, the part of the whole culture known by everyone is much more modest. Each occupational milieu tends to assert its own distinctiveness and to ignore the others. If there remains one domain in which everyone can communicate, one would have to look for it in the forms of consumption, in modes of dress and habitation, rather than in the area of production techniques.

To the extent that writing comes to play an important role in the diffusion of knowledge, one finds in general two sectors within the domain of culture whose connection is somewhat limited: that of folk or popular lore, vernacular architecture, for example; and that of élite knowledge, exemplified by what is known as *architecture savante* in France, 'professional architecture.' The two sectors have neither the same significance nor the same distributional dynamic. Forms tied to oral traditions can be diffused, but much more imperfectly and slowly than those that are easily transmitted over great distances by writing. How then is it possible to speak of urban culture? How could areas of culture analogous to those

* Original French manuscript translated by David E. Sopher

that are so clear in the countryside be outlined if their most distinguishing traits obey a different logic?

Even if researchers take these difficulties into account, and work out ways of resolving them, their task remains extremely arduous because of the great variety of artifacts that confronts them. What should one select in a city? Monuments, churches, temples, seats of civil government? Of course. But one will grasp thereby only a part of the whole, only one kind of activity – that which is out of the ordinary. Should one not be concerned with the plans of towns, with the configuration of streets, with the space occupied by the plazas and other areas of public encounter? These are elements that are important for understanding how a city functions and the social relations that characterize it, for marking out the places where all sorts of people mingle, and where the differences among them are certainly less evident.

But once laid out, plans are only altered with difficulty. That is, of course, what makes for their archeological interest – in Western Europe, for example, there are hundreds of towns in which one can recognize the traces of the Roman grid layout.[2] Groups learn to adapt to forms which they did not create, so much so that the evidence of the ancient traces is difficult to interpret: it can instruct us about the realities of different periods, both about the forces at work in the society which founded the town and sketched out its system of roads, and about the capacity for reinterpretation displayed by succeeding generations.

Finally, the residential habitat deserves our attention, even when it involves only modest homes. But here again, the result of a real choice on the part of those using them is restricted: many live in apartments or single houses which they were not instrumental in building and which they have to accept simply because these were what they could afford. The individuals who build the rental properties or the public agencies which occupy more and more space in this sector are motivated by economic reasons; they are looking for the most appropriate way of satisfying potential clients without regard to long established traditions

Despite these very real difficulties, it would be possible to have a cultural geography of cities, understood as an inventory of the techniques and artifacts displayed there, but its interest would diminish as technology progressed. As the conditions for the exchange of scientific information improve, the material facet of culture – that which is the result of special skills and methods of production – has a tendency to become universal and to lose its geographic interest. Structures which rely on concrete, steel, and the lighter alloys are everywhere and nowhere.

Does this mean that the modern city evades the aims of cultural geography? Not at all, and for two sets of reasons. First, every landscape contains inherited elements which include some from a period when communications were more difficult, and the art of building more diverse. Second, culture (what is learned) cannot be reduced to the sum of techniques and skills. It consists of habits, of behavioral schemes, of customs, fashions, and norms. Here, too, the development of means of circulation allows convergence, but the choices made do not arise from utilitarian considerations. They respond to a much more complex logic, such that the tendency to homogenization is much less marked. From city to city and from class to class, cultural differences appear which have a pronounced effect on the rhythms of daily life, on the bustle or quiet of the streets, and on the security or violence in public places. In the long run, they are expressed in morphological arrangements

Modern cultural geography is thus learning to read the mark of values in traditional cities, after having long neglected to do so, and is thereby finding a way to contribute an original approach to contemporary urban reality (Claval 1981). Thus, to speak of a cultural geography of European cities is to confront a many faceted question. One must take into account differences that are related to the folk traditions of an ethnically and religiously diverse space, the super-positions which have resulted from the evolution of forms that were more widely diffused by an élite culture, and styles of living that express the wish to affirm original values.

Despite its fundamental importance, the domain of relations between the social architecture that dominates during a particular period and the social order, behavior, and culture which characterize it remains regrettably little studied. A cultural geography that investigated actual, living differences in regard to urban organization would certainly be heading in the right direction. It is this, rather than economic or philosophical principles, that defines the opposition between the Eastern European city and the city in the liberal or social democratic countries.

Is there a European city?

To begin with, is there any sort of unity in the cities of Western Europe, something that would allow us to group together these very heterogeneous cities? At first glance, the answer is not at all clear, so different are the urban forms of the Mediterranean shores, the Central European lands, and the Atlantic margins of the continent. Everything west of the Rhine and south of the Danube has inherited something of Roman traditions and urban spatial order, but this is not a truly distinctive feature: it appears also in the cities of the Middle East and North Africa which were part of the Roman Empire. Central, Northern, and Eastern Europe cannot claim this legacy, at least not directly.

Nevertheless, it is the transformation of the urban forms of antiquity which allows us to reply in the affirmative to the question of the identity of European cities. The ancient city, whether Hellenistic or Roman, was built around a square; it had an agora or a forum. These squares have always constituted one of the common traits of European cities, both those that date from antiquity and those that developed in areas in which urbanization occcurred late. In the Islamic world, as de Planhol has correctly shown, the evolution of the city was very different. In the decades that followed the Muslim conquest, a progressive closing of the forum took place (de Planhol 1983). It represented a danger for the Muslim community, which still constituted a minority in the newly conquered lands: why allow the unbelievers the opportunity of uniting and perhaps revolting? The only space for meeting which survived then was the courtyard of the mosque; in a society which did not distinguish between clergy and laity, it was unnecessary to provide public spaces for secular relationships. Commercial forms evolved accordingly: the suqs, which came into being toward the end of the medieval period and which gave to the urban cores the structure of long corridors of intense circulation, were adapted to this civilization.

In underscoring the distinctiveness of the ensemble of European cities, it is the town square that must be emphasized. But the existence of this common trait does not imply uniformity: the morphological differences bespeak a complex history of contrasting ethnic and cultural influences.

Urban regions of medieval Europe

The general morphological characteristics and the layout of the great axes and public spaces allow us to distinguish certain regions whose origin is ancient and often unrelated to the present boundaries of linguistic regions and administrative units.

In most English towns, the emphasis was placed on the convergence of the axes, rather than on large spaces open to the public at the heart of the urban agglomeration.[3] The ancient cathedrals often occupied sites that were toward the side of the old town. Today they appear striking in the extent of the open space on which they are set – we are all familiar with the Salisbury meadows immortalized by Constable. However, the origin of these spaces was complex – ancient graveyards, cloisters or houses of the clergy destroyed during the Reformation – and their present appearance may date only from the last century. The town itself was based on a quarter that grouped municipal administration, trades, and crafts (today it is business) around a crossing. Here, some widening might take place, one of the streets might open up enough to allow a market to be held, but the crossroads was the most striking feature. It was as if the presence of a highcross sanctified the place.

In cities developed on Roman sites, this feature hardly appears remarkable, since it appears to be derived directly from the ancient *cardo* and *decumanus* (the intersecting perpendicular axes of the planned Roman town). What is more noteworthy, however, is the appearance of the same forms in later cities (such as Oxford or Bristol), in which the axes are roughly perpendicular and oriented toward the cardinal directions. Similar arrangements exist in many cities of Saxon origin. Perhaps this is not surprising among people with a preference for astronomical orientation and axes laid out north–south or east–west.

Another equally ancient feature, fortifications, might well have been obliterated by later development, but a combination of circumstances in England has always favored the prominence of routes radiating out rather than ring roadways. The fortifications, which elsewhere gave rise subsequently to encircling boulevards, were there so degraded that their moats were filled in and their sites occupied without provision for circulation (Johns 1965). In the modern period, municipal authorities have lacked the power of expropriation which is generally indispensable for opening up transportation lines along the course of the ancient walls. The emphasis on the central crossing is thereby heightened.

From the Vistula to northern France, there exists a broad region whose urban features recall certain traits of the English city, but without the emphasis on cardinal axes and converging routes (Flatrès 1983). What is most striking throughout this zone is that the city was not centered on its great religious edifices, on its cathedral, but on a large square that was basically a market place. Merchants put up their stalls there on certain fixed days and enclosed market-halls often allowed transactions to be carried on in a climate that could be changeable and harsh. The community's civic life was also anchored on the place, as indicated by the presence there of the town hall and its various equivalents in different regions. The high clocktower signaled from a distance the civic center and counterbalanced the spires of the churches.

We cannot be certain about the origin of this type of spatial organization. It is certainly old, going well back in the Middle Ages, and is found on both sides of the Rhine, which suggests a Germanic influence rather than a legacy from antiquity. Of more interest than its age are its social and political meanings: the duality of its religious center on one side and its political and commercial one on the other discloses a type of social order in which the secular played a chief role.

Toward the west, the organization of medieval towns and the urban centers which are their heirs today has been more strongly marked by the dominance of the church (Flatrès 1983). Throughout the Paris Basin, it was the cathedral which was at the heart of city life; commercial life was intimately tied to it and the market took place in the open space in front of it or immediately next to it. The same type of organization and the same type of ordering of social life were found in a good part of the South of France.

Italian cities were diverse. Among them, the cathedral sometimes occupied a situation somewhat to the side of commercial and business life, as in Rome (but there the religious constraints were quite special), or as in Pisa, or Siena. Elsewhere, the civic center and the religious center overlapped (in Milan, for example, or, an even better example, in Venice). What was perhaps more characteristic of the Italian city than these broad morphological features was the multiplicity of small piazzas (Guidoni 1978, Muret & Courtois 1980), indicating a community based on living neighborhoods, with multiple foci for meeting and animated activity; Provence also had this type of organization.

It was mostly in the Middle Ages that the cultural typology of European cities was established as a function of the layout of squares, open spaces, and religious foci, and in certain regions the pattern still remains fundamental. The *plaza mayor* has been a notable feature of the morphology of Spanish towns since the 12th and 13th centuries, but it was during the Renaissance that the model achieved perfection and became very widely diffused throughout the Peninsula and beyond in the colonial empire that was coming into existence – in the USA and even in the Philippines. The grouping around the same square of the municipal offices, the cathedral, and the governor's mansion indicates a density of central functions and a symbolic hierarchicalization of the sacred and the secular, which were nowhere as marked in any other part of Europe.

These morphological contrasts were, in part, the result of conscious policies of management of space on behalf of royal or municipal authorities. They are thus evidence of the action of ruling élites whose ideology we do not know and whose reasoning we can barely follow, but who must have had some comprehensive vision of urban life. The marked divergence that arose subsequently between vernacular and cultivated aspects of urban form and design was then not very evident. The forms established then do not have the appearance of having been conceived from above to fit the aims of solitary thinkers, but rather of having represented the needs of the whole community.

The art of building urban houses only began to be perfected around the 12th and 13th centuries, when people learned how to build chimneys and to heat their places of residence properly (Braudel 1967, Platt 1976). The rules of house construction then became fixed and, according to the region, diversified. There is thus an element of differentiation in this area which goes back in part to the Middle Ages, and in part dates from the modern period, and which combines with the morphological differentiation discussed above. In Mediterranean Europe, urban structures are tall and built close together. In Central Europe, in the Alpine world, or at least on its borders, the city house resembles in its size the great farmhouse with enclosed barn, characteristic of the region, that is intended to accommodate animals and people under one roof. Since the Middle Ages, such urban dwellings have sheltered several families. Elsewhere, in most of western and northern France, in Great Britain, and across the great North European Plain, dwellings are more modest, scaled for single families, so much so that the urban landscape sometimes seems to lack grandeur. Rather, it appeals by the intimacy of its little squares and its winding and often narrow streets.[4]

Because of their functions, certain cities had more complex activities and greater interaction. Ports, in particular, were often built differently from inland towns. The crowding together of buildings is often more marked in such port towns, and tall houses are more common. All along the Atlantic littoral, there is a thin facing of such cities which bespeaks a history of trade between the Low Countries, England, the Hansa ports and the Baltic Sea.

Impact of the Renaissance

From the Renaissance, the separation between vernacular and cultivated forms of architecture and town layout grew wider. The groups of people able to direct large works of construction changed; they were no longer made up solely of artisans trained directly by experience on the work site, but included true intellectuals, people who had come out of the colleges and the universities. Their work involved a mastery of design and calculation and a knowledge of classical antiquity as the universe of reference. At the same time, the areas characterized by common forms tended to become broader. Even toward the end of the 18th century, architects and town planners were still working with local traditions, adapting their academic models to the roof types and residential patterns that people were used to; but this flexibility was gradually lost, and in the end formalism took over.

The distribution of these new creations was sometimes unrelated to already well defined culture areas or to the boundaries of the nation–states that were then coming into being. This accounts for the type of construction that gives towns in the Piedmont, the French Alps, the Franche-Comté, Burgundy, and a part of Switzerland and Austria a sort of family resemblance: the main streets there are bordered by vaulted arcades (like the squares), which give the impression of a particularly urbane, elegant landscape. Similar arrangements are sometimes found in other places (at La Rochelle, for example), but they are always creations of the same period, the 17th century.

In most cases, the models devised had a wider diffusion. The origin of these new experiments was to be found in Italy, but there were a number of transfer points that came to have a decisive rôle (Lavedan 1926–50, Giedion 1941, Argan 1968, Tafuri 1981). A new esthetic of geometrical plans, perspective composition, and grand places designed to show off a monument or statue was worked out successively in Rome, Florence, Genoa, and Venice, and in the surrounding regions during the 16th century. The exporting of these forms was in part accomplished by the church, which thus brought about the glory of the Baroque in Spain, Bohemia, and Poland, after it had passed across Italy, Bavaria, and Austria. In the Protestant lands, design and composition always remained less exuberant, although one may speak of 17th-century Holland as a secondary hearth of the Baroque. The imitation of Italian models was also the work of enlightened élites, of merchants, bankers, men of the law, and governments. The former were inspired by the models of palaces, mansions in the city, and great country villas, and drew from sources that owed much to Brunelleschi, Michelozzo, and Sangallo in 15th-century Florence and to Bramante, Giulio Romana, Sanmicheli, and Palladio in Rome and northern Italy in the 16th century. These models were adapted to the taste of middle and northern Europe in the first decades of the 17th century, with the first Paris mansions in the style (Lavedan 1975), and with the work of Inigo Jones in Great Britain (Summerson 1966). The long isolation of the countries of the Reformation, cut off from the Mediterranean hearth of the new esthetics, explains the mutations which the borrowings underwent, such as the early success of the Palladian style in Great Britain. The princes and the municipalities drew more from the example of Michelangelo in the Capitoline Square and from the plans and their implementation that Pope Sixtus V entrusted to Fontana, but it was Paris that soon became the essential source of transmission; it was toward the *places royales* of that city (the royal squares) that people of means turned for structures of both stateliness and symmetry (Francastel 1969).

The Europe of the town mansions, the palaces, and the grand vistas was perhaps more homogeneous than that of the churches, Catholic and Protestant, and their religious architecture. One can discern a province of the Baroque and one of Neoclassicism, more faithful to the Classical model – this was the area of the Anglican Reformation and of Gallican Catholicism, somewhat hostile to certain excesses of Roman art and architecture – but these are nuances rather than well marked differences. By placing beside the still contrasted monuments of the 16th and 17th centuries the structures of the 18th century, history has blunted such distinctions. It is in little towns long cut off from the mainstream that pure forms, urban landscapes all of a piece, can still be found; one must go to certain Spanish towns to see the Baroque in all its splendor, and, even better, to the small cities on the Bohemian border to find a picture that has not been altered for three centuries, as at Ceske Budejovice, at Tabor, and at Telc (Gutkind 1972, Morris 1979).

Toward the end of the 18th century, from one stage to another, through one influence or another, the Europeanization of the urban scene was completed. Structures built as late as the 16th century in Eastern Europe, particularly in Russia, seem strange to people in the West in their underlying concepts, their colors, and their forms, even when they were the work of artists from the West, especially Italy, as one sees in the Kremlin. On the other hand, the use of perspective and symmetry and the taste for grand ensembles made the core of St Petersburg the most European of cities at the end of the Neoclassical period. It hints of a mix of Italian models, of Dutch and Baltic contributions, of French regularity, and of Neoclassicism in the Prussian manner, with the accent everywhere on a monumental scale and the choice of white and ocher as dominant hues.

This combining of architectural ideas does not imply the suppression of every sort of difference. National cultures were asserting themselves and the cities were not slow in giving evidence of this. It was in England that such unity was most swiftly asserted (Summerson 1953, 1962, Johns 1965, Claval 1970). In the Middle Ages, the national tradition was already one of unity, in contrast to what was found in France or Germany. For lack of direct and continuous communication with Italy, the Renaissance in England was more involved than was the case elsewhere, with an extension of the designs and construction of the Late Gothic period. There is no abrupt break between the Tudor and the Elizabethan in architectural decor. Everything changed with the Stuarts. The English then discovered the models provided by antiquity and Italy, and their building methods underwent a radical transformation. With its wars and other troubles, the 17th century was not a major period of urban growth in Britain; construction was tied to exceptional events – the most noteworthy was the Great Fire of London – and to the resumption of church and university building. Conditions changed in the 18th century; peace reigned and prosperity grew. The competition that had developed in the 17th century between the Dutch Baroque and the Neoclassical models disappeared; the former had been better suited to bourgeois and popular building, the latter, to construction on a more splendid scale. In the 18th century the grammar of architectural forms became simpler: Palladianism became dominant; but, at the same time, the English broke with some of the rules that in other places characterized the esthetic of Italian derivation. They readily discarded the rigid ensemble and the straight line in favor of a more flexible architecture involving freer use of curved lines. This gave rise in the same period to the English garden and to the first residential terraces and crescents (Summerson 1953). Even when the forms most resembled those of Italy, the residential pattern remained British: the ground floor remained the prestigious level and the single house was the rule. This is what impelled the two Woods to find a solution in the terrace when they were trying to create a gracious decor in a beautiful arrangement at Bath, where everyone wanted to be as independent as possible from their neighbors.

British urban design subsequently became a series of transformations of this pattern as it was successively imposed on the less privileged and less educated classes. The forms became simpler and the Neoclassical details were confined to particular points, such as the entry porch. In the 19th century, when tastes were modified under the influence of the Gothic revival, the formula for building large ensembles, with uniform façades reproduced by the score and by the hundred along parallel streets, was retained. Even in our time, when the attempt has been made to break with the oppressive uniformity of the Victorian scene, the most frequently used solutions remain tied to the single house, to the use of the curved line, and to the play of volumes which are created by the repetition of a small number of forms; instead of a single model, we find the combination of two or three elementary ones.

In other Western European countries, the development of urban models reflecting the emergence of a national culture appears to have occurred somewhat later, except in Spain (as was noted earlier with reference to the *plaza mayor*). France continued to display great diversity – in the canon of its urban residential building, in its vernacular architecture, and in its large ensembles.[5] Even in the Neoclassical period, architects continued to respect some of this diversity: the fortifications built by Vauban all along the kingdom's frontiers present many different details in their form. What gave an increasingly expressed unity to these heterogeneous elements was the adoption of several elements inspired by the urban forms of the capital – the grand monumental square, the vista of symmetrical or almost symmetrical form, and those monuments of Neoclassical inspiration, the churches and especially the palaces intended for the civil administration. Individuals sought to outdo each other in following the model of the town mansion.

Until the middle of the 17th century, unity remained barely recognizable. The north looked to the Low Countries while the south maintained its direct ties with Italy, which had provided many of its architectural formulas. The Neoclassical models only supplanted houses in the Gothic tradition quite late, often no earlier than the end of the 16th century. In the east, which was not yet incorporated into the kingdom of France, there were discernible Parisian influences, but relations with Central Europe remained vigorous; they remained so in Lorraine until the middle of the 18th century, as witness the arrangement of the great squares of the time of Stanislas Leczinski. The forms which won out had already found expression in Britain, at Rennes, and at Montpellier in Languedoc before the end of the reign of Louis XIV, but it was the 18th century which saw the triumph of a national urban architecture; the cities under the administration of the intendants during that century display its mark and owe to it some of their magnificence.

Despite its aspirations, the period of the Revolution was hardly favorable to the creation of a common style. There was little construction; the most that could be done was to make use of the property of the church and the former aristocracy in accommodating the most varied needs. Napoleon had more resources for government, but even in his case, time was too short for him to make his mark on the provincial towns, with but few exceptions. Building began to be active again under the July Monarchy, but it was only Haussmann's model for Paris (Saalman 1971, Sutcliffe 1981) that succeeded in giving unity to the French cities: large perspectives, regular rather than uniform facades, standardized forms, and building facade heights limited to three, four, or five levels according to the scale of the aggregation. All this disclosed a taste for urbanity that had not been weakened since the Renaissance.

In Germany, the emergence of a national urban style came even later (Claval 1972). Political unification was achieved late and the pre-existing urban forms were almost as varied as in France. The new Reich was not a unitary state, so that a certain diversity of architectural ideas could be retained, but the forms inspired by the Prussian experience rapidly tended to become dominant everywhere (Sutcliffe 1981). Designs owed much to the example of Paris, as shown by the formal aspect of the finished work and the monumental character of the new residential quarters. The splendor that the new state sought to create everywhere is to be seen in the width of the main arteries and the breadth of the squares and their side streets.

In France, as in Germany, the portion of the city that exhibits the national characteristics occupied only a part of urban space – the rebuilt or renovated city centers or the expansion on the periphery, while the earlier diversity is still very much evident to the alert observer.

In Eastern Europe, history has often been too short for unitary national experiences to be similarly expressed in the landscape; Polish towns, for example, retain in large measure a Prussian, Austrian, or Russian urban character. The interwar years were marked by studies and experiments intended to create a national style, but eclecticism was too deeply rooted to disappear quickly. Since 1945, in Poland, as in other countries of Eastern Europe, the norms sought are socialist rather than nationalist. The medieval or classical sections of the cities, which have been part of the history of the country, have been rebuilt at great cost, but in the new extensions there has been no attempt to express in any way what might correspond to a tradition anchored in the national soil. In the German Democratic Republic, the town planners are now proud of having brought into being something less bleak than the products of the Stalinist period, and the Hungarians and Rumanians have also displayed taste in making use of some ideas from contemporary architecture, but homogenization is far more marked than in the countries of the West. There has been very little concern with the private residence, closer to the dimensions of the traditional dwelling and therefore easier to fit out according to traditional rules. As far as multiple-family accommodations are concerned, the prescriptions of the Charter of Athens (modern architecture as viewed by Le Corbusier and his supporters) have done even greater damage than in the West, although everywhere in Europe there is a tendency for the same structures to be imposed on the landscape.

We thus find both unity and diversity in Europe's urban culture, here understood as the assemblage of artifacts, of concrete structures conditioned by technics and know-how and adapted to the prevailing forms of group life. What is common to the whole continent is a certain dualistic conception of social life that makes a distinction between private and public, religious and secular, and that therefore requires spaces open to everyone for varied transactions and for bringing many people together.

The diversity of urban forms no doubt derives in part from very ancient ethnic traditions, evident in medieval organization, as is suggested by the Saxon characteristics or those of the great plain of Northern Europe, as well as by early Slavic settlement forms, although the latter were generally displaced during the Middle Ages by urban centers that had borrowed extensively from the more advanced, nearby German achievements. The conditions for the transmission of technology in the traditional world thus made for a permanent element of diversification, such as one discerns in the types of domestic architecture.

The unity, which was made possible by a common basis of social relations accepted by everyone, was to a considerable extent the work of élites, whose rôle became more pronounced during the Renaissance. The convergence in urban form was achieved by imitation of models inspired by antiquity and the Italian Renaissance, but the diffusion of these ideas, and the mutations that they underwent as a result, have outlined much larger regions than had existed earlier, which provide an essential element to the urban personality of the countries of Europe. Nationalist ideas were expressed in part subconsciously and in part deliberately in the emergence of forms specific to this or that political entity; the borrowings, that different countries have not ceased to make from each other, have not prevented them from keeping alive some of their own distinctiveness.

Forms of social interaction and the regionalization of European cities

However, as noted already, culture, does not consist simply of techniques and artifacts. It consists of ways of thinking, habits, styles of life, preferences, as well as norms, rules, and values. The cultural geography of European cities requires in addition, then, a different approach, one that emphasizes fashions in living and the way these spread, the ideologies that mold them, and the processes by which they have come to pervade whole societies or to characterize certain social groups (Claval 1981).

There were many groups which set the style in medieval Europe (le Goff 1980): men of the church who were learning new forms of religiosity, so important to our understanding of the multiplication of shrines and organized social services, and the mushrooming of monastic orders that channeled collective effort; next, nobles set up in the towns during the winter season in order to spend their income in a more rewarding milieu than the countryside; finally, well-to-do artisans and traders, who provided a model of independence and freedom gained through labor and skill. These different elements were present in every feudal town, but the mix varied from place to place. Stein Rokkan (1980) has demonstrated a contrast between the medieval band, which runs from northern and central Italy to the Low Countries, and the peripheral territories. At the core of the European economic space, the interactions were sufficiently intense to assure prosperity to those centers that lived by production and exchange. The merchant élite thus played a major role, while the church was open to social experiments, and tried by every means to foster Christian thought and practice in the world of the petty bourgeoisie. In the peripheral lands, the possibilities open to men of business were far more restricted, so much so that the cities were landowning rather than hearths of production. The social hierarchy was modified accordingly, with the aristocracy endowed with land in the central zone. The city did not live from its work, it was a setting of transactions, of communication, and sometimes of corruption. It was readily damned, and urban society often seemed to be living in a state of fundamental repentance.

The separation between the two models of social and cultural organization was not rigid. When business decreased in an area, the merchant bourgeoisie might convert to landownership, buying lands and learning to improve them. In the 16th century, Italy provided many examples of this sort of shift, while France was most commonly the scene of evolution of this kind between the 15th and the 18th centuries.

The city was an environment that offered much the same opportunities to women as to men. In the cultural tradition common to Europe, women were not shut away, and even where they were strictly supervised, as they were in parts of the Mediterranean Basin, they were able to practice some professions, to work at crafts, to engage in trade, and to assure themselves thereby some degree of economic independence. They thus found themselves closely involved in public life, with no possibility of being shut out. The houses of merchants and artisans were purely urban in character; they rarely contained gardens, and thus limited the possibility of distancing from the larger community. This prevented the families of public persons from avoiding neighborhood interaction: a situation conducive to social homogenization, or to social strife. To avoid this interaction if all the townspeople did not share the same ideas, sometimes even the same religion, the only alternative would have been to have one homogeneous quarter next to another. While the medieval city often consisted of a mosaic of independent nuclei, the urban crucible brought that diversity to an end (le Goff 1980). Almost throughout its history, the European city has been strongly assimilative, and remains so today. Identifying elements are basically not ethnic but territorial in most of Europe. It was by being based in the milieu where one lived that recognition and approval were earned, much more than by reference to a community related by blood. There were, of course, variations in this condition. Central Europe, where the ghetto had long been present, was less homogenizing than Western Europe. Many of the towns built in Eastern Europe had institutions whose purpose was the preservation of diversity among the populations living side by side.

Where an aristocracy that was rich enough to control sizeable lots existed in the city, the situation was quite different. The urban mansion of the French type indicates clearly the desire of newly rich people to isolate themselves from communal life. The street frontage would be occupied by ordinary people and sometimes by rented shops. The family lived sheltered from observation in a building between the front court and the garden. This permitted the occupants to hold their children back from public activity and, at least in part, to segregate the women. What developed was an organization of space that led to the self-containment of different ways of life according to income. Urban society was structured in classes that did not experience the city in the same way (Claval 1981). Nevertheless, until the beginning of the Industrial Revolution, and the emergence of economic liberalism, this did not lead to neighborhoods segregated by income. Wealthy people were quite happy to have nearby the service people they had need of and the artisans who would work for them; they felt themselves powerful enough to put down any disturbance that might break out among them. In countries where economic modernization occurred without a concomitant political evolution (in Poland under the Czar, for example), this condition continued until the beginning of the present century; the rich industrialists of Lodz lived in mansions at the front of the parcels of land on which they built their factories and placed part of their workforce.

From the beginning of the Industrial Revolution, the rise in levels of living allowed a growing section of the population to have the means to isolate themselves and to create voluntary relations away from the pressures of the immediate neighborhood. The response to these new possibilities was quite diverse, following ideologies whose importance in this regard has not yet been adequately analyzed. In Great Britain and part of Northern Europe, the élite took advantage of these new opportunities to isolate themselves further, to escape from the crowded living in the center of the city, and to lead a way of life, half urban and half rural, that was in part a copy of the old aristocratic life, but under quite different geographic conditions. The middle class followed their example precisely. Elsewhere, in most of continental Europe, this movement came much later and has remained more restrained. The automobile finally overturned the balance established a century ago, but the contrast between the two Europes remains clear – the north-west, where the wealthiest city folk want to deny their urban identity, and the center and south, where they prefer to remain close to the foci of collective existence. Basically, the dividing line between the two Europes was based on more fundamental cultural differences: the idea of nature as the place of health and of moral virtues was more popular among Protestants than among Catholics.

The new ways of dwelling in the city and of experiencing the city were brought into existence by a series of social revolutions and technical mutations. To be a city person today involves patterns of existence very different from those that once prevailed. The urban social order first developed through a diversification of the opportunity for interaction, through an increasing possibility of social encounter. The Neoclassical city was the city-as-theater,[6] and was so at several levels. It multiplied shows, theaters, operas, places where the comedy and drama of power, splendor, and even faith could play themselves out. But it was also designed so that everyone could make a show of themselves for others; it was the city-as-mirror.

The models were Italian. Rome, with its papal court, and Venice had great influence on the transformation of Europe, but Paris, Madrid, London, and the great cities of Central Europe were quickly won over. The adoption of the continental model is illustrated in England by the rapid rise in the fortunes of Bath (Johns 1965).

The style of life presented for imitation by the many was quickly modified in several ways. Tourism called forth the creation of urban settlements, which, even more than others, were made for presentations of self and the game of society. That was the case in Bath, and was soon to become the case in all the spas (bathing places where the idle nobility began to gather at the beginning of the 19th century). The morphology of these places exhibits some distinctive traits. Within a rather modest area, they provided at their core a particularly high density of shops, cafes, tearooms, pastry shops, theaters, and night-time places of entertainment. They were, in particular, organized around promenades where people were eager to display themselves and observe the idiosyncrasies of others. This was the development of the city at its most urbane, and one still can sense today its double origin, English and continental.

But the life of leisure is not made up only of spectacles. The English taught the rest of Europe, which had been on the way to forgetting it, the need to keep fit through sports. Just when French cities were losing their courts laid out for the *jeu de paume* (an early form of tennis), England was popularizing its descendant, the modern form of the game. Little by little, the space devoted to these activities grew, and ended by forming, around the urban core, more or less continuous girdles containing parks, public gardens, playing grounds, fields for sports, stadiums, and race-tracks. Everywhere in Europe, the vocabulary of these activities discloses their British origin. But despite their fashionable success among some of the continental nobility, it took a long time for these sports to become truly popular. The Latin countries remained more faithful than the rest to the conduct of individual sports – walking, cycling, swimming – which required much less in the way of plant, and modified the urban fabric far less profoundly. This is one of the reasons that movement toward the periphery on the part of those aspiring toward a new style of life was much less marked there than elsewhere in Europe. In Eastern and Central Europe, on the other hand, the collective aspect of the athletic activity was emphasized, with the result that the city was shot through with the sorts of installations that were elsewhere placed on the periphery.

Conclusion

These, then, are some of the directions in which it would be desirable to look for the origin of the behavioral differences which today distinguish the cities of Western Europe so profoundly, which make them so different from what they were a century ago, and which have generated differences between their populations that are not only those of income and status.

The organizational revolution was born in Europe at the time of the Renaissance, but it matured over such a long period, in forms often so subtle that its influence is much less clearly perceived in the development of social relations there than in North America or the Eastern countries. Apart from public administration, the church, the army, and industry, bureaucratic structures such as those of corporations remained of minor significance, so much so that business life in the city at the beginning of this century still involved the contact of individual persons rather than of anonymous employees of large firms. This situation has been changing rapidly, especially since the end of World War II.

In Great Britain, the bureaucratization of urban life had progressed much further than in the rest of Europe from the 1930s onward; it was in the city center itself that the change took place, and the core of the urban agglomeration came to resemble the trans-Atlantic one. In continental Europe, acceleration of this movement has been more recent, coinciding with the development of the automobile, and the growth of construction on the periphery.

In the last generation, the countries of Western Europe have seen a great increase in the flow of immigrants. In the large cities, laborers no longer come from the nearby countryside; rural exodus has emptied it of its surplus population. Now it is workers from sharply different culture areas who have been pouring into the low-rent zones – at first the Mediterranean peoples, Italians, Spanish, and Portuguese, then Greeks, Cypriots, and Moroccans, West Indians, Pakistanis, Indians, and sometimes Filipinos and Malays. Almost the whole world contributes to the flow that governments are now, since the end of the period of rapid growth, trying to stem.

How do these newcomers react to the unknown conditions in which they are plunged? The situation differs very much according to national traditions and the political orientations of the governments involved, but certain dominant trends have emerged. The ease of communications and the often higher cultural level of today's immigrants compared to earlier ones make them much more conscious of their national identity and more concerned to preserve it. As a result, the traditional assimilative rôle of the West European city no longer seems effective. As in North America, ethnic tracts begin to form. Will they last? We cannot tell, but this development reminds us how fluid is the cultural reality of the European city and how much it is liable to change in the space of a generation.

Notes

1   In this introduction, I summarize ideas about the relations linking social order, models of behavior, social architecture, and culture that I have developed (Claval 1981).
2   The importance of this heritage has long been underestimated, especially in France under the influence of the pro-Gaulish sentiment of historians like Camille Jullian. Recent research has brought much that is new to the question, as is indicated in two reviews presented at a colloquium on the historical geography of the cities of Western Europe held at the University of Paris-IV in January 1981 (Chevalier 1983, Pinon 1983).
3   On the origins, partly Anglo-Saxon, of the English town, see Biddle (1974), Guidoni (1978), Platt (1976) and Hill (1971). David Sopher stresses the preference of peoples around the North Sea, particularly the Anglo-Saxons, for the cardinal directions as reference points (Sopher 1978).
4   For some idea of the great variety in this vernacular architecture, one should leaf through the eight volumes of E. A. Gutkind (1964–72).
5   Perhaps this has discouraged attempts at synthesis, since there are few studies on the French city (Lavedan 1960).
6   The rôle of the theater in the development of urban design in the Renaissance was first emphasized by Francastel. Sociologists such as Sansot and Remy have been concerned with something of the sort in emphasizing the importance of primary places and secondary places, that is, the organization of life like a stage set. This allows us to have a better grasp of the meanings of the city for those who dwell there and to see more clearly its place in the culture of those who inhabit it (Francastel 1977, Sansot et al. 1978, Remy & Voye 1981).

References

Argan, G. 1968. *The Renaissance city*. New York: Braziller.

Biddle, M. 1974. The development of the Anglo-Saxon town. In *Settimane di Studio del Centro Italiano di Studi sull'Alto Medioevo, XXI, Spoleto, 1973*, 203–30. Spoleto: Centro Italiano di Studi sull'Alto Medioevo.

Braudel, F. 1967. *Civilisation matérielle et capitalisme*. Paris: Armand Colin.

Chevalier, R. 1983. Présence de l'architecture et de l'urbanisme romains. In *La géographie historique de la ville en Europe occidentale*, P. Claval (ed.). Paris: CREDIF.

Claval, P. 1970. Les villes britanniques. *Norois* 17, 327–50.

Claval, P. 1972. La grande ville allemande. *Ann. Géog.* 81, 538–54.

Claval, P. 1981. *La logique des villes*. Paris: Librairies Techniques.

Flatrès, P. 1983. Essai de typologie morphologique des villes traditionnelles en France. In *La géographie historique de la ville en Europe occidentale*, P. Claval (ed.). Paris: CREDIF.

Francastel, P. (ed.) 1969. *L'urbanisme de Paris et l'Europe 1600–1680*. Paris: Klincksieck.

Francastel, P. 1977. *Peinture et société*. Paris: Denoël Gonthier.

Giedion, S. 1941. *Space, time, and architecture*. Cambridge, Mass.: Harvard University Press.

le Goff, J. (ed.) 1980. *Histoire de la France urbaine*, G. Duby (ed.) Vol. 2: *La ville médiévale*. Paris: Le Seuil.

Guidoni, E. 1978. *La città europea*. Milan: Electra Editrice.

Gutkind, E. A. 1964–72. *International history of city development*, 8 vols. New York: Free Press.

Gutkind, E. A. 1972. *International history of city development*. Vol. 7: *Urban development in East-Central Europe*. New York: Free Press.

Hill, D. 1971. Late Saxon planned cities. *Antiq. J.* 51, 70–85.

Johns, E. 1965. *British townscapes*. London: Edward Arnold.

Lavedan, P. 1926–50. *Histoire de l'urbanisme*, 3 vols. Paris: Laurens.

Lavedan, P. 1960. *Les villes françaises*. Paris: Vincent Fréal.

Lavedan, P. 1975. *Histoire de l'urbanisme à Paris*. Paris: Hachette.

Morris, A. J. 1979. *History of urban form before the Industrial Revolution*. London: George Godwin.

Muret, J.-P. and M. Courtois 1980. *La ville comme paysage*. I. *De l'antiquité au moyen age*. Paris: CRU.

Pinon, P. 1983. La persistance des trames urbaines d'origine romaine. In *La géographie historique de la ville en Europe occidentale*, P. Claval (ed.). Paris: CREDIF.

de Planhol, X. 1983. La cour, la place et le parvis: éléments pour une morphologie sociale comparée des villes islamiques et européennes. In *La géographie historique de la ville en Europe occidentale*, P. Claval (ed.). Paris: CREDIF.

Platt, C. 1976. *The English medieval cities*. London: Secker & Warburg.

Remy, J. and L. Voye 1981. *Ville, ordre, violence*. Paris: PUF.

Rokkan, S. 1980. Territories, centers, and periphery: toward a geoethnic, geo-economic, geopolitical model of differentiation within Western Europe. In *Center and periphery*, Jean Gottmann (ed.), 163–204. Beverly Hills, Calif.: Sage.

Saalman, H. 1971. *Haussmann: Paris transformed*. New York: Braziller.

Sansot, P. (ed.) 1978. *L'espace et son double. De la résidence secondaire aux autres formes de secondarité de la vie sociale*. Paris: Editions du Champ Urbain.

Sopher, D. 1978. The structuring of space in place-names and words for place. In *Humanistic geography*, D. Ley and M. Samuels (eds.), 251–68. Chicago: Maaroufa Press.

Summerson, J. 1953. *Architecture in Britain 1530–1830*. Harmondsworth: Penguin.

Summerson, J. 1962. *Georgian London*. Harmondsworth: Penguin.

Summerson, J. 1966. *Inigo Jones*. Harmondsworth: Penguin.

Sutcliffe, A. 1981. *Towards the planned city: Germany, Britain, the United States, and France, 1780–1914*. Oxford: Basil Blackwell.

Tafuri, M. 1981. *Architecture et humanisme: de la Renaissance aux Réformes*. Paris: Dunod.

3 Culture and the urban order

AMOS RAPOPORT

Introduction

This essay makes two principal, related points. The first is that rather than to speak of urban order as opposed to disorder or chaos, it is more appropriate to speak of different urban orders. The second is that these various orders are related to culture, and can only be studied and understood in that context.

These themes are developed first by discussing the concept of culture; then, the rather elusive notion of order is discussed briefly. The difficulty of interpreting various orders is addressed. It is suggested that those urban environments considered to be disordered or chaotic are better understood as unacceptable or inappropriate for given observers or users. A number of urban examples are considered, and it is argued that meaning plays an important role in the understanding of urban order within cultural context.

The argument is 'nonlinear:' certain points are made, themes are discussed in different ways, and a complex set of relationships is developed. The principal objective is to suggest a particular way of looking at cities in relation to their cultural context.

Culture

The concept of 'culture' is rather complex, and there is a large body of literature dealing with it from many points of view. Consequently, I have argued elsewhere that, for some aspects of environmental analysis and design, it may frequently be more useful to break this rather global concept down, and to begin with 'lower order' concepts such as activity systems and life-style (e.g. Rapoport 1976, 1977, 1980a). For the present purposes, however, it is more useful to consider the broad concept of culture.

While anthropologists agree about the centrality of culture in humans, they disagree about its definition. As a result, many different definitions are found. However, the apparent confusion may be simplified by suggesting that all the definitions fall into one of three general classes. One defines culture as a way of life typical of a group, a particular way of doing things; the second as a system of symbols, meanings, and cognitive schemata transmitted through symbolic codes; the third as a set of adaptive strategies for survival related to the ecological setting and its resources.

These three views are not in conflict, but are complementary. Thus, built environments of particular groups are settings for the kind of people which that culture sees as normative, and the particular life-style which is significant and typical, distinguishing the group from others. In creating such settings and life-styles, a set of cognitive schemata symbols is used; some visions of an ideal are given form, however imperfectly (i.e. an order is expressed); finally, both the life-styles and symbolic system form part of the group's adaptive strategies within the ecological setting – or at least did at one time.

For our purposes, then, culture may be said to be about a group of people who have a set of values and beliefs which embody ideals and are transmitted to members of the group through enculturation. These lead to a world view – the characteristic way of looking at, and, in the case of design, of *shaping* the world. The world is shaped by applying rules which lead to systematic and consistent choices, whether in creating a life-style (i.e. the specific way of allocating temporal, material, and symbolic resources), a building style, or a landscape of a settlement. In all these cases, choices are made from among the possible alternatives.

It is of particular interest to consider landscapes and settlements. These are the result of the individual decisions and acts of very many individuals and groups, which yet add up to a recognizable whole. If one knows the ordering system (i.e. understands the code), it is possible to identify landscapes and cities. Habits, manners, food, rôles, and behaviors, i.e. life-styles, also result from choices. All the elements mentioned show, or should show, regularities due to the common underlying schemata.

This suggests that the link between order and culture is that order (and ordering) – the product and process respectively – is in the mind; environments are thought out before they are built or given physical expression. The link is in the *cognitive schemata* of a group which is minimally defined in cognitive anthropology as mental constructs which allow groups to select those material phenomena which are significant to them and to organize them in some way (Tyler 1969). These schemata can be understood as resulting from processes which make the world meaningful by classifying, naming and ordering through some conceptual system (for a more extensive discussion of how this relates to the built environment, see Rapoport 1975, 1976, 1977, Ch. 3).

Order

Our discussion of cognitive schemata has involved the notion of order – which is, of course, the topic under discussion. This is rather an elusive concept. One interpretation is that it is anti-entropic, i.e. involves organization, but that idea is equally difficult to define; replacing one concept by the other is not useful. Assuming, then, that order involves organization, we return to that elusive concept of order.

A rather thorough multidisciplinary exploration of this concept (Kuntz 1968) well illustrates its difficulty and complexity. Moreover, it is used differently in philosophy, art, science, everyday speech, and so on.

It would be inappropriate to become too involved in reviewing the many interpretations of this concept. It seems more appropriate, for the present essay, to develop a minimal definition useful for the task.

A useful starting point is the comparison of different types of order with their opposites. Clearly, order involves a relation, or a set of relationships, of a definite sort. As such, the concept has no opposite. It involves elements or parts which relate to each other, these relationships being of different kinds (Kuntz 1968, p. xxxiii). In this sense, we speak of different orders, rather than order as opposed to its lack. The relationships involved can be understood and described in terms of some specified formal type (Kuntz 1968, p. xxxiv). The opposite of any given order is then an order of a different type, for example axial orders versus radial orders, grids versus nesting areas, symmetry versus asymmetry, and so on. Such orders then differ in the nature of the formal rules involved. Note that this relates to our discussion of cognitive schemata involving how phenomena are organized. The other aspect of schemata – the selection of phenomena – also links to the notion of order, since orders may also vary in the nature of the material being ordered, i.e. the elements important to the group and hence selected by them. In terms of our topic, the relationships may be among spatial elements, temporal elements, social elements, sensory ones, and so on.

Note that in all these notions of order there are different orders, rather than order opposed to disorder. That definition of order to which the opposite notion of chaos or disorder can be applied is the order of the world, a 'categorical order' the opposite of which is an undifferentiated state of things. Chaos is thus a negation of such an order and is only a hypothetical state (Kuntz 1968, p. xxxv).

In terms of all urban environments, categories of some sort clearly do apply; 'city' itself is such a category. Thus it seems more valid to speak of different orders rather than order versus disorder. This is a major argument of this chapter, to be developed later.

When one examines the various possible meanings of 'order' having to do with relationships, arrangement, rules, patterns, organization and the like, then two major notions seem common to all. One is *recognizability*, one knows that a thing is A or B, A not B. The other, related to the first, is *predictability* (which also implies stability). Once A is recognized, one can predict occurrence, use, behavior, sequence, or whatever. These also imply identity – since a thing is recognizable as itself, and, by contrast to others not itself, has identity – and can be used to communicate identity (Rapoport 1981b).

Given that different orders do exist, part of the problem one has with the concept is one of understanding, which will also preoccupy us. The discussion above has already intimated why misunderstanding can occur. The elements being ordered may not be 'appropriate,' for example social relations may be organized but not expressed spatially, whereas the observer expects space to be organized. This is precisely the problem with the understanding of the order of precontact African cities (Hull 1976). Alternatively, the type of relationships may be 'inappropriate,' religious or sacred rather than geometric (Lannoy 1971, Wheatley 1971, Rykwert 1980). Or again, the formal rules may be 'wrong:' instead of a system of linear roads and sequentially numbered points (as, for example, in American cities), a system of nesting areas (as in Japan) may be used (Rapoport 1977, Fig. 3.15), or the experiential order may be wrong.

The implication is clearly that different cognitive schemata are being used to organize these different urban environments. The problem with understanding such differing schemata is partly one of what are called emics and etics. These terms, developed by cognitive anthropologists and commonly used on cross-cultural analysis, are not widely known and may require some explanation.

Cross-cultural approaches are used to establish generalizations which are valid in all cultures. This is considered to be an *etic* goal, categories which an analyst may use to compare widely differing cases and situations. But these theoretical frameworks, the categories used in comparisons, cannot be *imposed* a priori, since that may eliminate precisely these elements which are important (for urban examples, see Wheatley 1971). Thus the frameworks and categories need to be *derived*, and this can only be done by understanding the units valid within a given culture, how members of that culture define and understand things. These are the *emics* of the given problem.

It follows that our task now is to understand the various urban orders in terms of emics, the cognitive schemata of the various groups which have created them. Only then can one hope to begin to derive some etic categories which will make sense of these orders cross-culturally.[1]

The urban order

I have already pointed out that the elements being ordered can be of different types – spatial, temporal, or social. The misunderstanding (or inappropriateness) of such orders (as in the case of the African city for example) is clearly due to the use of an imposed etic, in that case spatial organization. That list can be expanded: the elements being ordered may be domains or sensory, perceptual qualities.

In dealing with the urban order, it may be useful to begin with the sensory, experiential qualities of cities which are also organized or ordered. Cities, among other things, are physical artifacts, experienced through all the senses by people who are in them. They are also experienced sequentially as people follow different paths and use different movement modes through them. Cities look, smell, sound and *feel* different; they have different character or *ambience*. This is easily felt, but is very difficult to describe.

These sensory qualities are ordered – they can be understood as an experiential order. This experiential order can be, and needs to be, studied by abstracting it in various ways. But even then, it is still rather less abstract than the approach commonly employed by geographers. The latter tend to study urban environments mainly through plans and maps, and rarely discuss the experience of that environment by the people in it. The experience is partly visual, but also involved are kinesthetics, textures, colors, sounds, sequences, smells, breezes, thermal qualities, etc. (Rapoport 1969a, 1977). In fact, one of the characteristics of my approach based on man-environment studies, which should be emphasized in this geographical context, is its stress on experiential, sensory qualities and relationships.

Each setting can be seen as a place having an order which becomes recognizable, because it can be described by a set of characteristics:

(a)   its location,
(b)   its relation to landscape,
(c)   having certain elements,
(d)   having certain settings,
(e)   having spaces of a certain type,
(f)   being named in particular ways,
(g)   using certain orientational systems,
(h)   having certain colors, textures, etc.,
(i)   having certain sounds, smells, temperatures, air movements,
(j)   having certain people engaging in certain activities, and so on.

There are two important points (among many) to be made about any such set of examples.

(a)   It is possible to identify, from a single photograph (if one knows the 'code'), the general location (e.g. Middle East, Northern Europe, etc.), sometimes the specific country (Norway, Mexico, Peru, USA, Australia), and occasionally even the city (Guanujuato, Trondheim, Sydney, Milwaukee). In other words, urban landscapes (like other

cultural landscapes) can be identified: they are distinct and recognizable entities – the minimal definition of order.

(b)   At the same time, as already pointed out, urban landscapes (again like
other cultural landscapes) are typically the result of many independent decisions and actions by very many people. In fact, one of the
interesting things about cities and landscapes is that they are very
rarely designed, in the commonly accepted sense (like a building), by
a single person (a 'designer') at a single moment in time.

In fact, 'design,' as a process, needs to be seen much more broadly than
is common: *design is any purposeful change to the physical environment.*
Designed environments thus include places where forests have been
planted or cleared, or fields fenced in certain patterns. The placements of
roads or dams, of pubs and cities are all design. Roadside stands and
second-hand car lots are designed environments. The work of a tribesman
burning off, laying out a camp or village, and building his dwelling is an
act of design. These apparently mundane activities are more significant in
their impact on the earth, and on people, than the work of professional
designers. Cities, like all cultural landscapes, are generally not designed
(or even planned) by a central authority, let alone a single individual. Even
when there is planning or design, it generally only applies to small
portions of cities. Even those few cities which begin as designed entities
tend to be open ended; they develop and change greatly over time.
Eventually, only a few major 'designed' elements remain, although these
may be very important since they provide the guiding and organizing
framework (Bacon 1967). For example, major elements like the axis from
the Louvre to the Arc de Triomphe and beyond (in Paris), and other axes
around which exists the urban fabric which results from the many
decisions of individuals; in London, the equivalent is the axis linking
Regents Park and St James's Park; in Rome, the axes and nodes laid out by
Pope Sixtus V; in Isfahan, the Maidan-i-Shah; in Peking, the north–south
route from the Southern Gate to, and through, the Forbidden City. Many
other such examples can be given: the axial sequence of open spaces,
avenues and boulevards of Mexico City stretching from the Zocalo, via
the Alameda, the Paseo de La Reforma to Chepultapec Park (Violich 1981)
around which is the incredible variety of very different urban fabrics of the
over 800 km^2 of the urban agglomeration.

Note that while these tend to remain, or change slowly, the urban fabric
around changes much more, as a result of the more typical processes
already described. In such cases, then, cities have *two* orders, i.e. two
recognizable cultural landscapes: a *high-style order* based on the schemata of
small groups, including professional designers, and a *vernacular order*
expressing more widely shared (and sometimes very different) schemata.
These two orders, of course, not only coexist, they also interact and

mutually reinforce one another. The experience of each is strengthened and heightened by the contrasting presence of the other. In fact, to understand either fully, the other must be considered (Rapoport 1969b, 1977).

Given the fact that urban landscapes are typically the product of design as described above, i.e. the result of many decisions by many people over long periods of time, it is very striking indeed that they 'add up.' They develop coherence, they are instantaneously recognizable; if one knows the cues, a single slide can be enough to identify a place.

If the independent decisions by many individuals and groups, over long periods of time, produce recognizable landscapes, that suggests that these decisions must have things in common. It would seem to follow that the people whose decisions create these landscapes share certain ideals or images, certain *schemata* which provide rules for making choices, for deciding what to include and which things to eliminate. Those cognitive schemata, which guide the decisions made in a given cultural context, can be conceived as models, or mental templates, or schemata, which makes possible the statement that all cities, like all built environments, have some order in the sense that none of them is a random assemblage of elements but a systematic arrangement of elements. In this they are like culture, since they are based on *shared schemata*; these, in fact, characterize cultures, as we have seen.

This is the key argument of this chapter: all cities have an order, and that order is intimately (and ultimately) related to culture via schemata.

The schemata lead to certain choices being made from among the alternatives which are possible. It is the fact that the nature of these specific choices made tends to be lawful, which makes places recognizably different one from the other (Rapoport 1972). One can, in fact, think of design as a *choice process* which produces environments (or other artifacts) by eliminating some alternatives and retaining others, thus approaching as closely as possible those ideal environments embodied in schemata. Similarly, life-styles are the result of sets of such consistent choices, which is another way of linking environments and culture. This is the process which I have called the 'choice model of design' (Rapoport 1973, 1976, 1977).

One can also use this model to examine the choices people make in moving, i.e. at various forms of migration from intra-urban to international. In that connection, it becomes particularly interesting to look at immigrant landscapes. In many cases, the types of landscapes chosen for settlement tend to resemble some ideal recalling home, although recently this notion that immigrants (at least in the USA) selected landscapes like those 'back home' has been questioned (McQuillan 1978). Whatever the truth of that, the *transformation* of landscapes to create cultural landscapes approximating as closely as possible an ideal resembling home seems quite clear. For example, New Zealand was transformed into an English landscape (Shepard 1969), as were parts of Australia. The colonial cities of Africa created by the English, French, Portuguese or Germans differed from each other but resembled the cultural landscapes of the home cultures (Rapoport 1977, pp. 351–4). In the Middle East, one finds that the monastic landscapes in the desert or in the city tend to be Greek, Italian or Ethiopian, depending on the place of origin of the founders. Even neighborhoods of cities in countries of recent migration show attempts at this down to the level of individual houses, as in Australia (Stanley 1972). Moreover, the ability to recreate such landscapes can play a significant rôle in the success or failure of immigration (Eidt 1971).

As already suggested, this consistent system of choices applies not only to the built environment; it also determines how people dress and behave, what they eat, and their table manners while they eat. It leads to the ways in which they interact and structure space and time, and so on. In fact urban, architectural and art styles, and life-styles have at least one thing in common – they represent systematic choices among alternatives. All of these can also be used to establish various forms of identity, although they need not play that rôle (Rapoport 1981b). Not only are those choices related to culture, but they reflect the culture of the group in question (via schemata). In fact, *one way of looking at culture is in terms of the most common choices made.*

Even if we disregard life-style, activities and behavior, and only consider the built environment (at least for now), one can see different orders which are related to culture. To be able to understand these orders, whether at the experiential level or at a more abstract level, *one needs to understand the cultural context of that particular urban order.* In other words, one needs to look at them in emic terms before one derives (rather than imposes) etic categories.

Various urban orders
MEXICAN SETTLEMENTS A settlement such as San Cristobal de Las Casas shows more clearly than others, perhaps, a number of features typical of a common type of traditional settlement in Mexico. The first is the consistent use of a single scheme to organize the dwelling, the neighborhood and the whole town (Wood 1969, Rapoport 1977, p. 11, Fig. 1.4). Within that order a variety of sensory modalities (colors, smells and sounds) is used to create distinct experiential qualities, characters and ambiences in the various neighborhoods. At the same time, one can better understand the organization of the neighborhoods, their salience and social meaning, and the social relations within them, if it is realized that different groups live in them and how far back this ordering schema goes, i.e. its extraordinary persistence over time. The pattern of neighborhoods still found in Mexican settlements goes back at least to Aztec cities

organized into areas called 'Calputlin,' which were physical expressions of symbolic, social and kinship relations (e.g. Ingham 1971); these were combined with the layout based on the Laws of the Indies.

THE TRADITIONAL CHINESE CITY   The overall layout, organization, and significance of the traditional Chinese city expresses a cosmic or sacred order. It can hardly be understood without a knowledge of its rôle as a 'cosmic machine' (Wheatley 1971). At the same time, its internal organization of enclosed wards for various groups (stronger at some periods than others) and the relation of high status to central location is an expression of culture and needs cultural understanding (e.g. Tuan 1968).

THE ROMAN CITY   In ways analogous to the Chinese city, the ancient Roman city can only be fully understood if one appreciates its cultural context and significance; once again, its order is a *sacred* order (Rykwert 1980). More generally, the examples of the Chinese and Roman cities suggest that even the purely *spatial* order depends on the *kind* of space involved, and even that is a function of culture. Thus, one can distinguish between human and nonhuman space, abstract geometric space contrasting with sacred, or religious space; space can be symbolic, it can be behavioral, it can be subjective, experiential or sensory, and so on (Rapoport 1970a, pp. 81–6). Clearly, in the examples above of the Chinese and Roman cities, we are dealing with an order based on sacred space which is, of course, the basis of many (if not most) traditional cities (e.g. Indian, Yoruba, Maya, and so forth). This sacred space is then organized differently by different cultures to produce different sacred orders, but all can only be understood in these terms (Rapoport 1979a). This situation can be contrasted with cities which can only be understood in terms of orders related to efficiency, comfort or health – or an abstract geometric or esthetic order. Similarly, the USA city can be understood as expressing an order based partly on an important value of maximum mobility for most people, whereas some traditional Chinese and Indian, and most traditional Moslem cities exhibit an order based on severe limitations on mobility (Rapoport 1977, p. 21, Fig. 1.10). These are different orderings of behavioral space.

THE MOSLEM CITY   If one looks at the control of mobility in the Moslem city, and the use of this control for social control, one finds that the behavior space for any given individual is restricted to a small area around the dwelling, and that this area is smaller still for women (Wheatley 1976). The town tends to be divided into areas (usually called 'Mahallas') which 'belong' to particular groups, and distant quarters are not used and not even visited (see the examples in Rapoport 1977). In the Moslem city, whether in North Africa, the Middle East or North India, one also finds the bazaar as a linear element (as opposed to the node markets – market squares – of Europe). Behind and between these linear bazaars, one finds the residential communities described above. These named quarters, and very small, tightly knit subareas of clans, large families, occupational or common origin groups, may only be accessible through culs-de-sac off the bazaar, and sometimes even through single gates which can be closed, which are found in Antioch, Damascus, Isfahan, Ahmedhabad, Lahore, and so on. This order, which is so 'strange' to Western observers that they have sometimes denied the *existence* of an order in the Moslem city, can only be understood if the cultural schemata are understood. It is also critical to realize that the spatial order described is only significant if related to the social order – in the above example the control of mobility, the definition of semi-private areas, the reduction of public space in the city, and so forth.

It is, of course, possible (in fact *necessary*) to go beyond the mere spatial organization of the built environment and to realize that the order can be social. In some cases, this social order may not be manifested spatially, i.e. in terms of spaces, buildings or other features; it may not be *visible*. What is being organized are social relationships, networks and group member-ship. Experientially there is no order, but once the social order of the culture is understood, what appeared chaotic becomes comprehensible and hence orderly. Examples of this are provided not only by African cities already mentioned, but also by the settlements of the Pomo Indians of California (Rapoport 1969b, p. 64, Fig. 3.8), or contemporary Aus-tralian Aboriginal, or Quebec Indian settlements (Rapoport 1977). In these cases, the apparently disordered physical environment is highly organized in terms of social groups and relationships. Other examples of this type of order will be discussed later, as will examples of other kinds of orders (e.g. eikonic orders superimposed over the spatial order of the city). Orders can also be geometric rather than sacred, as in the USA West (Rapoport 1970a), allowing for easy subdivision and 'endless' expansion, stressing process (Rapoport 1969b, cf. Kouwenhoeven 1961). The order can also be highly experiential, as in the different sensory ambiences of Middle Eastern or Indian bazaar and the North American supermarket.

The relation of the urban order to culture, and the difficulty of understanding these, suggests that urban orders are related to *meaning*. This is, in fact, the case.

Meaning in the urban order   For example, location in space expressed by the spatial order is intimately related to meaning. In most traditional cities, central location indicates higher status than does peripheral location; this is still the case in certain European cities such as, for example, Paris (Lamy 1967), and Bologna (Schnapper 1971). In a given country (e.g. Mexico), different meanings (or *lack* of meaning) can be attributed to such central location: in Spanish-origin settlements there is a connection between centrality and status; in those of Indian origin there is none (Stanislawski 1950, cf. Rapoport 1977, p. 49, Fig. 2.2). Finally, one finds that in the contemporary USA and, increasingly, other modern cities, there is an inverse relationship: status goes up as one moves from the center towards the periphery, although distance from the center and specific location play important rôles.

The space organization related to the two orders of high style and vernacular is also related to meanings and to the groups using them. Thus, it seems apparent that the plan of the ancient Peruvian city of Chan Chan (Moseley & Mackey 1974) shows that size and scale of spaces, and their regularity, are clearly related to the degree of 'high-style' and, through this, to status. This is also clear in ancient Nubia and Egypt, where the high-style centers of the élite retain the grid, whereas the more vernacular, lower status parts of settlements tend to change to a more 'organic' layout (Kemp 1972a, b). These two orders, rather than ordered and disordered parts of the city, are thus related to meaning and, once understood, can be read in this way. This change in the grid is related to the general tendency for the grid to 'disintegrate' (Stanislawski 1961, Eliseeff 1970, Kemp 1972a, b); its survival in those cases indicates high-style, higher status areas contrasting with areas where it is absent, which are lower status, 'vernacular.' Note that this is also culture specific; in some cases, for example the USA, there has been no tendency for the grid to disintegrate, although, as can be seen in any suburb, new orders have sometimes replaced it in later periods (Rapoport 1977, p. 348, Fig. 6.3).

Such meanings become even clearer when a variety of means is used to reinforce the message, i.e. when spatial organization and many other elements together create two distinct experiential orders, characters, or ambiences. For example, in Latin America generally, these two orders are both common and very clear. A regular, grid street layout, a continuous building fabric (what one could call an urban wall), man-made materials, a general absence of visible vegetation with what little there is confined to plazas and highly controlled, all indicate high-status, and hence Mestizo, areas. The opposite set of characteristics, irregular, twisting streets, free-standing buildings made of natural materials, high levels of natural vegetation, all indicate low status, and hence Indian areas (Redfield 1950 (cf. Rapoport 1977, p. 348, Fig. 6.3), Hill 1964, Richardson 1974). These ambiences are, of course, further reinforced by the type of people present, their dress, their behavior, the various activities, where and when they occur, the types of goods (and hence smells), the sounds, the types of shops and what they sell, and so on.

The fact that urban orders have meaning implies that any given order is interpreted (or read) as a nonrandom and hence systematic set of relationships between things and things, things and people, and people and people. These relationships are based on schemata which lead to rules, including those used in making choices (as discussed above). Frequently, these relationships may be more important in terms of the urban order than the elements involved. Thus, for example, many outdoor markets and bazaars, which provide most exciting experiences in all sensory modalities, are composed of rather 'scruffy' elements, for example awnings made of sacking, galvanized iron roofs, orange-box display stands and the like. This is in terms of their *esthetic* order (given a particular value orientation). Given different values, they may be seen as 'disorderly' or 'chaotic' esthetically. The meanings they communicate will then make them inappropriate for particular groups of people; the presence of other groups will then reinforce these meanings, as in the case of Latin American urban areas discussed above.

Similarly, urban designs may consist of rather 'scruffy' elements – ramshackle, rusty, even semiruined. The relationships may, however, be such that they become highly significant and highly appealing to some groups of users or observers (Rapoport 1969a, 1977). As in the case of markets, other people may find these totally repugnant, and hence unacceptable. Moreover, the nature of the elements cannot be totally ignored. First, as in the case of markets, they communicate meanings about the urban order influencing behavior (for example, understood as 'slums,' they will be avoided). Secondly, through increasing redundancy, they make clearer other meanings inherent in the urban order. Finally, they do play a rôle in establishing ambience, i.e. in the experiential order.

The nature of elements is also important at a larger scale, because the definition of 'city' in different cultures may depend on the presence or absence of specific elements, for example mosques, cathedrals, baths, markets, city walls, or whatever (Krapf-Askari 1969, Wheatley 1971, Rapoport 1977, 1979a).

Even the deliberate 'denial' of order may be a form of order, i.e. the use of a specific set of elements and of specific relationships among them. An example is a 'counterculture' community on the outskirts of a Californian town which has been called a 'libertarian suburb' (Barnett 1977). In my view, there would be two interpretations of this particular urban organization, i.e. two meanings in the eyes of 'insiders' and 'outsiders.' The insiders would read the arrangement positively, as an order indicating a rejection of establishment values, an assertion, expressed in physical form, of freedom, ideological purity and the like; outsiders, in the adjoining town, would see it as a slum, a scruffy and undesirable setting for equally scruffy and undesirable people. Their negative evaluation would be interpreted by them as a lack of order – as disorder or chaos.

These interpretations are also clearly related to the ways in which spontaneous settlements are interpreted and to the changes in the ways in which they have been perceived – as areas to be pulled down or as highly positive areas. They are also clearly related to the ways in which 'slums' are defined, which depend on the meaning attached to particular orders (Rapoport 1977, especially Ch. 2). In those cases also, where some observers see chaos, a lack of both social and physical order, others see order reflecting culture, social relations, the use of space and time according to definite, but different, rules, the action of various constraints, and so on.

It again follows that in this sense it may be incorrect to contrast urban *order* with *chaos* or *disorder*; it is more valid to speak of *different orders*, some of which (called 'chaotic' or 'disordered') may be imperceptible, incomprehensible or unacceptable because incongruent with a particular set of norms, preferences, cultural rules or schemata of given individuals or groups (cf. Rapoport 1977). In other words, *all* cities, indeed *all environments*, have an order almost by definition, since they are nonrandom, the result of sets of consistently made choices.

The incomprehensibility of particular orders is frequently due to a lack of knowledge of the culture, and hence of the cues which communicate meaning. It is useful to think of settings as providing cues which, when noticed and understood, define the social situation. The knowledge of that situation then elicits appropriate behavior, enabling people to co-act (cf. Rapoport 1977, 1979b). Not knowing the culture may mean that the cues are not noticed; if noticed, not understood, or they may be wrongly understood, i.e. they define an inappropriate situation. Finally, the situation, even if understood, may demand different behaviors or use different rules. In such cases it is then unclear how these cues define settings and situations, and through them the rules for expected and appropriate behaviors. Since the urban order (like other environmental orders) consists of settings which define situations, rules and behavior, it again follows that, instead of the dichotomy or opposites of urban order and disorder, we are dealing with *different orders related to culture*.

Consider an Indian city. On first sight it is chaos: dust, noise, smells, a great variety of people in a variety of costumes, widely different building styles. There is apparently random and continuous movement, a bewildering mixture of animals, people, bicycles, rickshaws, trucks, and buses. Activities seem equally bewildering: all kinds of activities and users are found intermingled at an extraordinarily fine grain and close juxtaposition; all is 'jumbled up.' The streets and other spaces are full of people not only walking and riding, but sleeping, cooking, eating, getting their hair cut or shaved, working, and playing. One's senses reel.

Yet, if one has studied the Indian city, or if one is already familiar with it, or if one gets a chance to explore and is sensitive to urban cues, one quickly realizes that there is a strong order. It is based on two morphological units already briefly mentioned: the linear bazaar and a sociospatial residential unit – known variously as the Mahalla, in North India (see above), the Pol in Gujarat (cf. Desai 1980, Appleyard 1981, p. 245), the Pada in West Bengal, the Busti in Bihar, etc.

These morphological units can be understood in terms of access and control, penetration gradients, publicness versus privacy. Each of these residential units is socially homogeneous, i.e. there is a *social order*. The whole city is made up of agglomerations of these smaller units creating separate, larger sections which further define the social order through group membership, location, name, and visible characteristics and cues. Activity systems also begin to reveal a clear order and meaning: activities are organized in space and in time, have clear linkages and separations. Thus activities of the bazaar and public realm are accessible, access to the semi-private units strictly controlled and separated; penetration is difficult and discouraged. The activities in the public domain are different from those in the semi-private; different people are there at different times. Within these units are further orders at even finer scales.

There is thus a strong and complex order: spatial, social, in terms of land uses, in terms of activity systems, in terms of domains (e.g. private/public, men/women, group A/group B, etc.), of territories and of degrees of penetration, of status. These result in a sensory order: noise in the bazaar, the quiet of the residential unit, different temporal rhythms and tempos, different smells, thermal qualities, light levels, colors, textures, enclosure, and many others. Once grasped, it is difficult to believe that one ever thought it to be chaotic.

Of course, this order (as all the others described) may still be unacceptable, undesirable, offensive or inappropriate for particular individuals or groups. It may even be more generally less or more acceptable or appropriate using criteria such as health, sensory needs or limitations, or other pancultural psychological or biosocial human characteristics. One might find that a given order is, in fact, generally undesirable. However, the fact remains that *there is still an order*.

Urban order and environmental order Cities constitute a specific type of environment. Thus urban orders or organizations are a special case of environmental orders or organizations. It has been suggested above that orders can differ in the nature of the elements being organized or ordered. But for cross-cultural comparison, we need some generalization. The example of the Indian city, and others given, suggests such a generalization (which also helps cope with the problem that 'environment,' like culture, is an excessively broad term). The environmental order goes beyond the order expressed merely in the built form, the 'hardware.' One can say that four variables are being ordered: space, time, meaning, and communication. Moreover, they fall into three major classes: fixed-feature elements (those which change little or slowly: buildings, highways, roads, bridges etc.); semifixed-feature elements (the 'furnish-ings' of the city: plants, signs, neons etc.); and nonfixed-feature elements (people and animals, their behaviors, etc.) (cf. Rapoport 1977, 1980a, b).

It follows that the order of the environment (in this case urban environments) is to be understood as particular forms of organization of space, time, meaning and communication, through fixed-feature, semifixed-feature and nonfixed-feature elements, as a function of a par-ticular way of life of groups, their cognitive schemata, rules and sym-bolic codes, i.e. their culture.

In terms of this redefinition, one can begin to understand and analyze apparently 'disordered,' 'chaotic,' or 'irrational' urban forms. This applies not only to 'slums' or spontaneous settlements, but can also begin to clarify other kinds of urban order. For example, the arguments about whether Maya settlements were cities are resolved both by using a derived etic definition of what is a city – that which organizes a region (Wheatley 1971) – and then through an understanding of the organizing role of ritual movement over time (Vogt 1968, 1976), i.e. organizations of communication, meanings, and time. Similarly, one can then under-stand the order underlying Australian Aborigines' environments (Rapoport 1975), and nomads generally (Rapoport 1978). Immigrant cities and landscapes can be understood in terms of certain organizations of meaning which symbolize *home* as well as of space-facilitating critical forms of social support, i.e. organization of communication. Traditional African cities which seem to have no spatial order become comprehen-sible, and hence orderly, in terms of social relationships, i.e. the organization of communication (Hull 1976).

Furthermore, apparently different urban forms – a city of courtyards, a low-density area of widely spaced elements and a city of 'ethnic villages' – can be shown to be different versions of a single principle, the control of unwanted interaction, i.e. organization of communication (Rapoport 1977, pp. 337–9, Figs. 6.1 & 2). In the case of a city of courtyards, physical elements, such as walls, doors and gates, are used; in a low-density area it is distance; in a city of 'ethnic villages' or other homogeneous areas, communication is controlled among groups more than among individuals. This then allows the interpretation of two adjacent, but very different, urban orders such as the indigenous and British colonial cities in India (King 1976). In that case, as in many others, more than one element may be used, for example in the indigenous North Indian city, courtyards and homogeneous areas; in the colonial portion of the city, distance and homogeneity. Apparently similar spatial organizations, such as Chinese and Baroque urban axes, can be shown to be different (Rapoport 1977, p. 350, Fig. 6.4) in terms of the organization of meaning: the former indicating control of access and hence limited movement, the latter freedom of access and hence free movement; this also results in different organizations of communication.

Note two things. The first, already mentioned, is the importance of meaning and its relation to communication as they influence the organization of space and time. In this context, latent functions and aspects of activities play a more important rôle than do manifest ones. The distinction between the two is, in fact, partly related to meaning, and can more usefully be made by noting that any activity can be understood as consisting of the activity itself, the specific way of doing it, additional, adjacent or associated activities, and the meaning of the activity. The first and partly the second are the manifest aspects of the activity; the second and mainly the third and fourth are the latent aspects which vary more with culture as one moves towards the latent end of the scale (Rapoport 1977). Consider one urban activity, shopping. It is basically the exchange of goods, either directly or through the medium of money. The specific way of doing it may vary – shopping in a bazaar or supermarket, relying on hawkers or mobile shops. Associated activities may include exchanging gossip while shopping, or information exchange while shopping. The meaning of shopping may be recreation or conspicuous consumption related to status. One also finds, of course, that there are different cultural rules that go with each. The sensory, experiential orders are also very different: compare an Indian outdoor market or bazaar with an American department store or supermarket.

The second point to be noted, which has already been made, and which also follows, is that one needs to begin with *emics* and, for comparative purposes, use *derived* etics. Imposed etics should never be used since it is precisely their use which leads to accusations of chaos or disorder, i.e. to a perceived lack of comprehensible order.

This becomes clear from a consideration of the mutual incomprehension and denial of order to the Chinese, African, Maya, Moslem, North American or other city by observers from other cultures – the rules of organization are misunderstood (Rapoport 1977, especially Ch. 1). This applies not only to the physical order, but to the social orders of various cities or parts of cities. Much of the discussion about whether neighborhoods or clustering of groups in modern cities are still significant or have been replaced by network relationships, has to do with an imposition of criteria; so does the use of a priori categories for homogeneity in neighborhoods rather than the use of the concept of *perceived* homogeneity, which is a derived etic category. The fact is that neighborhoods are still salient for many, if not most, groups if one studies their subjective cognitions, and that they tend to be homogeneous, if one uses perceived homogeneity as the criterion; perceived homogeneity can be based on many different variables (the specific choice depending on the culture – Rapoport 1977).

The result of this continued salience of neighborhoods is, of course, the importance of the social geography of the city, the social organization of people in urban space; it, in itself, constitutes a most significant urban order related to culture. This also has experiential implications, since areas 'belonging' to particular groups take on clearly different characters. Even when the fixed-feature elements are similar, variations in the semifixed- and nonfixed-feature elements generate noticeable difference, making the city both more legible and more complex, and perceptually richer. In homogeneous areas, all the cues 'add up' and reinforce each other, whereas in heterogeneous areas they are highly varied; they therefore 'point' in different directions and tend to cancel out.

Note that both complexity and legibility depend on noticeable differences. Regarding legibility, some level of redundancy is necessary, so that different cues, in different sensory modalities, need to be communicating the same meanings. This implies some measure of congruence between form and activities, among organization of space, time, meaning, and communication; congruence among fixed-feature, semifixed-feature and nonfixed-feature elements.

The legibility depends not only on redundancy, which has to do mainly with making cues noticeable. Noticing cues is a necessary but not sufficient condition for comprehending the urban order. Cues must also be understood. To understand these cues (which communicate the various urban orders) one needs to know the codes, i.e. cues are culture specific. It is culture-specific cues which define the settings within the environment, the situations and the rules which go with them and hence indicate appropriate behavior, making co-action possible (cf. Rapoport 1979b).

One of the reasons modern cities are frequently accused of being chaotic, in contradistinction to traditional cities which are seen as having an order, is that in modern cities the cues may be neither noticed nor understood. Meanings in modern cities are much more numerous, as are settings; at the same time, modern cities are pluralistic, having a number of different cultures. The result is that meanings are also much less lexical, more idiosyncratic than in traditional situations (Rapoport 1970b, 1980b). Thus, the relatively subtle cues which frequently worked in traditional environments do not work in modern cities; higher redundancy is needed.

Redundancy in modern cities, and the need to make cues much more explicit to diverse groups with varied and mutually incomprehensible codes, is frequently achieved by superimposing new kinds of systems over the spatial order (or at least more elaborated versions of them) – eikonic, verbal, or symbolic. Distinct, explicit, and complex information and meaning systems are added to the spatial, locational and other systems. This insight enables one to link apparently diverse studies stemming from very different traditions and with very different points of departure (cf. Choay 1970-71, Venturi et al. 1972, part I, Carr 1973). All of them comment on the proliferation of new, nonspatial systems such as signs, neons, billboards and the like – a whole new urban order. Since that order is incongruent with the values and schemata of many academics, planners, designers etc., it has been seen as chaotic and disordered, in fact as the most chaotic aspect of modern cities (Nairn 1955, 1956, 1965, Blake 1964, among many others). One may personally intensely dislike this particular order, while being able to understand the cultural reasons for its development and the need for higher redundancy and more explicit cues when idiosyncratic, noncommunicative cues replace lexical, communicative ones. Also, that particular order may not only be disliked; analysis may show that it may not even work in perceptual terms (Carr 1973, Rapoport 1977). The essential point, however, is that the more complex and varied a cultural system, the more different schemata and meanings are employed. A pluralistic cultural system, and large-scale social and physical systems, consist of a number (sometimes a large number) of subcultures and settings. If the same urban settings are to be used successfully by diverse groups, the more redundant, multichannel and complex must be the communication systems in order to become legible and successfully coordinate activities, i.e. help people co-act (Rapoport 1977, especially pp. 325–33). This seems to be a general finding: among animals also, as more activities need to be coordinated, i.e. as social systems become more complex, so do communication systems become more complex and multichannel (cf. Brereton 1972).

This type of analysis also partly explains the development and success of chain food, lodging and other operations which consistently use certain sets of cues to communicate highly predictable outcomes (Rapoport 1973, 1977). These cues become highly recognizable; they predict with great certainty and clarity expected behaviors, acceptable dress and manners, prices, quality, and so forth. Their order is very clear and legible. In this case, also, the reasons for their development, and their rôle in the urban (and regional) order are lost in critical reactions of observers who dislike them, and validly see other faults in them, for example the anti-entropic process of increasing sameness in food, accommodation, and so on, with consequent loss of complexity and choice.

In all these last examples we find that the urban built order (i.e. the fixed-feature elements) is an expression of and a setting for activity systems (i.e. nonfixed-feature elements); the semifixed-feature elements (signs, billboards, neons, etc., as well as decorations, landscaping, street furniture and the like) make manifest, communicate, and reinforce the order. Note also that these semifixed elements are those which can change fairly easily; they change more rapidly and responsively than fixed-feature elements. In most cases, we 'inherit' fixed-feature elements, physical urban orders. As activity systems change, the semifixed-feature elements respond fairly easily, both reflecting these changes and helping to guide them, i.e. helping to guide behavior. This, of course, also applies at smaller scales: planting, gardens, birdbaths, gnomes, house decorations and 'whatnots' generally personalize, express, reinforce, and clarify urban and architectural orders and help guide behavior and activity systems in the various settings.[2]

It is clear that culture plays a most important rôle in people's activity systems. Recall that I suggested before that a most useful way of making operational the excessively broad term 'culture' is precisely by starting with activity systems (including their latent aspects) and life-style. The various urban (and other environmental) orders act as facilitators for some sets of activities and, at the same time, as constraints on other sets of activities (Hägerstrand 1970, Palm & Pred 1974). This is because in order to facilitate some activities, others need to be constrained; both these aspects express a cultural consensus embodied in the urban order. This consensus may, of course, not fit or suit particular groups (particularly in increasingly pluralistic cities); neither may it fit changed patterns at different times.

We are thus still dealing with congruence and incongruence but, in this case, between, on the one hand, activity systems as expressions of life-styles leading to particular behaviors, social networks, home ranges and so on, and, on the other hand, systems of settings, of which an important exemplar is the house-settlement system (Rapoport 1969b, 1977). Note that this notion of interpreting built environments, whether at the urban or smaller scales, and their orders in terms of the congruence between certain specified activity systems and systems of settings, provides a most useful way of looking at environments cross-culturally while avoiding the use of an imposed etic (Rapoport 1980a).

At this point in the argument, the definitions of culture based on cognitive schemata and on the way of life of a group are again related through the idea of choice, specifically as expressed in activity systems and also in terms of domain definition, the separation or nonseparation of domains (such as private/public, men/women, adults/children and many others), and also of more specific settings (e.g. related to dwelling, work, recreation, education, etc.). The organization of such domains and settings in terms of their linkages, separations, barriers, proximities etc. is an important aspect of the urban order. If one asks the question, *who does what, where, when and including or excluding whom (and why)*, then the rules applying to these relate the environment, as a specific organization of space, time, meaning and communication, to the environment seen as a system of settings. The cues and meanings in the environment define settings with their rules, define situations, and, in that way, guide behavior both positively and through constraints (Rapoport 1977, 1979b, 1980a, b). Using a different terminology and point of departure, they define culture spaces through an overlap of space, time, activity, ownership and rules of admission (Yamamoto 1979).

In all these cases the urban environment (physical, social and other) is then an expression of (and modulator of) activity systems in terms of who does what, when and with whom. At the same time, in a more fundamental sense, the urban order expressed physically in the urban environment is an expression of cognitive schemata. In other words, the urban environment, the recognizable and consistent urban landscape with which we began, is such not only because schemata are shared among members of given groups guiding their design decisions, but because these shared schemata also lead to rules and choices regarding life-style and hence those activity systems which are acceptable in given settings, at given times, and those which are not. The decisions about who does what, where, when and including or excluding whom are habitual, consistent, shared and regular. They, therefore, receive physical expression in the urban landscape, which is a different (but useful) way of saying that there is a relation between social and physical space, between culture and the urban order.

It is useful to have a number of different ways of looking at urban order because the more different ways one has of interpreting a particular complex phenomenon, the better it can be understood without too much loss of complexity. Thus, other ways of interpreting the above material may also be useful: for example, in terms of home ranges, core areas and territories of different groups in urban space; or in terms of different kinds of networks of groups, e.g. intensive and localized, as opposed to extensive. Such networks are related to the extent and locales of activity systems and also to the extent to which groups cluster. All of these approaches can also be interpreted in terms of systems of settings, the distribution of settings in space, and for what activities particular settings may, or may not, be used, e.g. are streets merely transitional space or also meant for various activities (Rapoport 1969b, 1977). To reiterate, these are all different ways of approaching, studying, interpreting and understanding the urban order, and more generally, the environmental order in relation to culture.

There is another link between the urban order and culture. Whereas the activities themselves, i.e. at the manifest level, in any given environment (including cities) have a limited range of possibilities for humans, they tend to be much more variable at the latent level (Rapoport 1970b, 1980a). More specifically, the activities themselves, how they are carried out, the associated activities (which turn them into systems), and the meaning of these activities tend to be increasingly more variable culturally in that sequence.

Even more variable are the sequences and other temporal organizations of activities and, of course, the systems of settings in which they occur. Also extremely variable are the cues which identify settings, and hence situations, and the rules about what is public or private, to whom it belongs, who is admitted, how it is used to place people in social space, etc., i.e. the rules about what is permissible behavior – which allows co-action to occur. (Note that culture can also be defined in terms of the knowledge needed by people in order to co-act effectively (Goodenough 1957), another link between culture and meaning in the urban order.)

Let us return to the point made at the beginning, that few cities are designed, or built *de novo*. Those few which are include colonial cities, new capitals and some new towns. When they are built thus, they reflect the schemata and hence the culture of the designers and the client groups, rarely of the users. For example, in the case of Brasilia, the culture of many users is expressed much more effectively in the urban order of the spontaneous settlements than of the planned center (Smith *et al.* 1971).

Most cities grow by expansion, new areas being added to what already exists. These additions may continue the original form, expressing the same cultural schemata. Examples of this can be found in cases where war-damaged cities had to be reconstructed. In West Germany, in contradistinction to other Western European cities, the traditional urban order was consciously preserved and recreated (Holzner 1970). In Warsaw, the old city was reconstructed to express the original schemata, as a symbol of continuity, while new areas used different schemata: a new urban order was used to express a new social order.

Frequently, forms change, expressing changes in the culture, i.e. changes in schemata, life-style and activity systems; the order changes. One example would be provided by an East Coast American city where an irregular, 'organic' street layout was first replaced by a grid street pattern, and then by curvilinear street layouts with culs-de-sac (Rapoport 1977, p. 348, Fig. 6.3).

Within cities, one finds different, and changing, preferences for environmental qualities, and hence changes in design, character and location – changes both over time and among groups. If one looks at wealthy groups, where constraints are weak, one finds major differences in the urban orders and ambiences selected even within a single city (Rapoport 1977, Ch. 2, 1980c). Immigrants, as already discussed, seem to select certain types of environments and then tend to modify them even further to express their particular notions of urban and other environmental order (Stanley 1972, Rapoport 1977). The success of such groups may depend on their ability to recreate their traditional environmental order, physical and social (Eidt 1971). In any case, within various constraints which distort this process, different groups settle differentially within cities, seeking out different ambiences, characteristics and environmental quality profiles. In doing so, they both choose different urban orders and also *create* an urban order – the social geography of the city.

Conclusion

Thus, all different urban orders are related to, and are a function of, culture. However, while this has major implications for design and planning through the notion of culture-specific design (Rapoport 1980a), it is not directly relevant to our discussion here.

What seems more relevant, in conclusion, are the reasons why we might be interested in the variety of urban orders and their relation to culture. A prerequisite for valid generalization is the ability to trace patterns and regularities. Thus, one is concerned with the underlying similarities behind apparently different urban forms, such as the city of courtyards, the low density area, and the city of homogeneous areas to which I have already referred. Another example of pattern and regularity, linking apparently diverse urban orders, is neighborhood homogeneity. Most (although not all) neighborhoods through history can be shown to have had a tendency to homogeneity if one uses emic criteria, and the derived etic characteristic of perceived homogeneity rather than an imposed etic of certain a priori characteristics (Rapoport 1977, Ch. 5). This, then, helps explain the fact that a deliberately homogeneous neighborhood, such as La Clede, in St Louis, Missouri, is in fact extremely homogeneous on the basis of a shared ideology of liberalism and of heterogeneity!

In order to trace regularities and patterns in the urban order, it is also important to consider the effect of scale on constancy and change. While the megalopolis and metropolis are greatly changed, even new, urban forms, at the neighborhood level, there are many fewer changes – traditional aspects and schemata, in any given cultural milieu, are much less changed, with implications for what we can learn from traditional settlements (Rapoport 1981a). Also, different orders can have different rates of change. The experiential order, based on perception, tends to be less changed than the cognitive; even more changeable are orders based on preference (Rapoport 1977, 1981b). This again, has implications for what, and how, one can learn from traditional settlements.

Why, finally, should we be interested in patterns and regularities? One important reason is that this search underlies all research and scholarly activity. It is related to the need for generalizations to be valid, and their validity depends on the use of the broadest possible sample; this need has been neglected in the case of built environments, including cities (Rapoport 1977, 1979a, 1980a). Thus the study of all built environments, and of environment–behavior relationships (in this case cities and their order), must include all environments built, including vernacular; must be historical, comprising the full span of history and including archeological data; and must be cross-cultural, including all cultural traditions.

Only then will we be at all likely to understand these most complex human creations – cities. This, in fact, is the reason why this chapter has looked at the urban order in the way it has.

Notes

1 Note that the notions of emic, derived etic and imposed etic are used here only to help clarify the problem. There will be no technical use of these concepts.
2 I have recently dealt with this topic in more detail in a new book *The meaning of the built environment: a non-verbal communication approach* (Beverly Hills and London: Sage Publications, 1982). This synthesizes my work on this topic and relates it to work in several other disciplines.

References

Appleyard, D. 1981. *Livable streets*, Berkeley, Calif.: University of California Press.

Bacon, E. N. 1967. *The design of cities*. New York: Viking Press.

Barnet, R. 1977. The libertarian suburb: deliberate disorder. *Landscape* **22**, no. 3, 44–8.

Blake, P. 1964. *God's own junkyard*, New York: Holt, Rinehart & Winston.

Brereton, J. L. 1972. Inter-animal control of space. In *Behavior and environment*, A. H. Esser (ed.), 69–91. New York: Plenum Press.

Carr, S. 1973. *City signs and lights: a policy study*. Cambridge, Mass.: MIT Press.

Choay, F. 1970–71. Remarques a propos de semiologie urbaine. *Architecture d'Aujourd' hui* **42**, no. 153, 9–10.

Desai, A. 1980. The environmental perception of an urban landscape: the case of Ahmedhabad. *Ekistics* **47**, no. 283, 279–85.

Eidt, R. C. 1971. *Pioneer settlement in Northeast Argentina*. Madison: University of Wisconsin Press.

Eliseeff, N. 1970. Damas à la lumiere des theories de Jean Sauvaget. In *The Islamic city*, A. H. Hourani and S. M. Stern (eds.), 157–77. Oxford: Cassirer.

Goodenough, W. G. 1957. Cultural anthropology and linguistics. In *Monograph series on language and linguistics*. Vol. 9: *Report of the seventh annual round table meeting on linguistics and language study*, P. L. Garvin (ed.), 167–73. Washington, DC: Georgetown University.

Hägerstrand, T. 1970. What about people in regional science? *Paps Reg. Sci. Assoc.* **24**, 7–21.

Hill, A. D. 1964. *The changing landscape of a Mexican municipio (Villa Las Rosas, Chiapas)*, Research Paper No. 91. Chicago: University of Chicago, Dept. of Geography.

Holzner, L. 1970. The role of history and tradition in the urban geography of West Germany. *Ann. Assoc. Am. Geog.* **60**, no. 2, 315–39.

Hull, R. W. 1976. *African cities and towns before the European conquest*. New York: Norton.

Ingham, J. M. 1971. Time and space in ancient Mexico: the symbolic dimensions of clanship. *Man* **6**(4), 615–29.

Kemp, B. J. 1972a. Fortified towns in Nubia. In *Man, settlement and urbanism*, P. J. Ucko, R. Tringham and G. W. Dimbleby (eds.), 651–6. London: Duckworth.

Kemp, B. J. 1972b. Temple and town in Ancient Egypt. In *Man, settlement and urbanism*, P. J. Ucko, R. Tringham and G. W. Dimbleby (eds.), 657–80. London: Duckworth.

King, A. D. 1976. *Colonial urban development (culture, social power and environment)*. London: Routledge & Kegan Paul.

Kouwenhoeven, J. A. 1961. *The beercan by the highway*. Garden City, NJ: Doubleday.

Krapf-Askari, E. 1969. *Yoruba towns and cities*. Oxford: Clarendon Press.

Kuntz, P. G. (ed.) 1968. *The concept of order*, Seattle: University of Washington Press.

Lamy, B. 1967. The use of the inner city of Paris and social stratification. In *Urban core and inner city*, 356–67. Leiden: Brill.

Lannoy, R. 1971. *The speaking tree (a study of Indian culture and society)*. Oxford: Oxford University Press.

McQuillan, D. A. 1978. Territoriality and ethnic identity: some new measures of an old theme in the cultural geography of the United States. In *European settlement and development in North America*, J. R. Gibson (ed.) 136–9. Toronto: University of Toronto Press.

Moseley, M. E. and C. J. Mackey 1974. *Twenty-four architectural plans of Chan Chan, Peru (structure and form at the capital of Chimor)*. Cambridge, Mass.: Peabody Museum Press.

Nairn, I. 1955. *Outrage*, London: London Architectural Press.

Nairn, I. 1956. *Counterattack*. London: London Architectural Press.

Nairn, I. 1965. *The American landscape (a critical view)*. New York: Random House.

Palm, R. and A. Pred 1974. *A time-geographic perspective on problems of inequality for women*, Working Paper, No. 236 (Sept.). Berkeley: University of California, Center for Planning and Development Research, Institute of Urban and Regional Development.

Rapoport, A. 1969a. The notion of urban relationships. *Area (J. Inst. Br. Geogs)* **3**, 17–26.

Rapoport, A. 1969b. *House form and culture*. Englewood Cliffs, NJ: Prentice-Hall.

Rapoport, A. 1970a. The study of spatial quality. *J. Aesth. Ed.* **4**, 81–96.

Rapoport, A. 1970b. Symbolism and environmental design. *Int. J. Symbol.* **1**(3), 1–10.

Rapoport, A. (ed.) 1972. Environment and people., In *Australia as human setting*, 3–21. Sydney: Angus and Robertson.

Rapoport, A. 1973. Images, symbols and popular design. *Int. J. Symbol.* **4**(3), 1–12.

Rapoport, A. 1975. Australian aborigines and definition of place. In *Shelter, sign and symbol*, P. Oliver (ed.), 38–51. London: Barrie and Jenkins.

Rapoport, A. (ed.) 1976. Socio-cultural aspects of man–environment studies. In *The mutual interaction of people and their built environment*, 7–35. The Hague: Mouton.

Rapoport, A. 1977. *Human aspects of urban form*. Oxford: Pergamon Press.

Rapoport, A. 1978. Nomadism as a man–environment system. *Environ. Behav.* **10**(2), 215–46.

Rapoport, A. 1979a. On the cultural origins of settlements. In *Introduction to architecture*, A. J. Catanese and J. C. Snyder (eds.), New York: McGraw-Hill.

Rapoport, A. 1979b. On the environment and the definition and the situation. *Int.* *Archit.* **1**(1), 26–8.

Rapoport, A. 1980a. Cross-cultural aspects of environmental design. In *Human behavior and environment: advances in theory and research*. Vol. 4: *Environment and culture*, I. Altman, A. Rapoport and J. F. Wohlwill (eds.), 7–46. New York: Plenum Press.

Rapoport, A. 1980b. Vernacular architecture and the cultural determinants of form. In *Buildings and society: essays on the social development of the built environment*, A. D. King (ed.), 283–305. London: Routledge & Kegan Paul.

Rapoport, A. 1980c. Environmental preference, habitat selection and urban housing. *J. Soc. Iss.* **36**(3), 118–34.

Rapoport, A. 1981a. *Environmental quality, metropolitan areas and traditional settlements*, Invited paper given at the 1st International Congress on Planning of Large Cities: Mexico City, June 1981 (mimeo).

Rapoport, A. 1981b. Identity and environment: a cross-cultural perspective. In *Housing and identity: cross-cultural perspectives*, J. S. Duncan (ed.), 6–35. London: Croom-Helm.

Redfield, R. 1950. *The village that chose progress (Chan Kom revisited)*. Chicago: University of Chicago Press.

Richardson, M. 1974. The Spanish American (Colombian) settlement pattern as societal expression and as behavioral cause. In *Geoscience and man*, Vol. 5: *Man and cultural heritage* (papers in honor of Fred B. Kniffen), H. J. Walker and W. G. Haag (eds.), 35–51. Baton Rouge, Louisiana: School of Geoscience, Louisiana State University.

Rykwert, J. 1980. *The idea of a town*, Princeton, NJ: Princeton University Press.

Schnapper, D. 1971. *L'Italie rouge et noire (les modeles culturels de la vie quotidienne à Bologne)*. Paris: Gillimard.

Shepard, P. 1969. Pacific viewpoint monograph No. 4. *English reactions to the New Zealand landscape before 1850*, Wellington: Victoria University of Wellington, Department of Geography.

Smith, S., E. A. Wilkening and J. Pastore 1971. Interaction of sociological and ecological variables affecting women's satisfaction in Brasilia. *Int. J. Comp. Sociol.* **12**, 114–27.

Stanislawski, D. 1950. Institute of Latin American Studies, No. X. *The anatomy of eleven towns in Michoacan*, Austin: University of Texas.

Stanislawski, D. 1961. *The origin and spread of the grid pattern town*. In *Studies in human ecology*, G. A. Theodorson (ed.), 294–303. Evanston, Ill.: Row-Peterson.

Stanley, J. 1972. *Migrant housing*. unpublished MSc(Arch.) thesis. Sydney: School of Architecture, University of Sydney.

Tuan, Y. F. 1968. A preface to Chinese cities. In *Urbanization and its problems*, R. P. Beckinsale and I. M. Houston (eds.), 218–53. Oxford: Blackwell.

Tyler, S. 1969. *Cognitive anthropology*. New York: Holt, Rinehart & Winston.

Venturi, R., D. S. Brown and S. Izenour 1972. *Learning from Las Vegas*. Cambridge, Mass.: MIT Press.

Violich, F. 1981. Mexico City and Mexico: two cultural worlds in perspective. *Third World Plann. Rev.* **3**(4), 361–86.

Vogt, E. Z. 1968. Some aspects of Zanacantan settlement patterns and ceremonial organization. In *Settlement archaeology*, K. C. Chang (ed.), 154–73. Palo Alto, Calif.: National Press.

Vogt, E. Z. 1976. *Tortillas for the gods: a symbolic analysis of Zinacantecan rituals*. Cambridge, Mass.: Harvard University Press.

Wheatley, P. 1971. *The pivot of the four quarters*. Chicago: Aldine.
Wheatley, P. 1976. Levels of space awareness in the traditional Islamic City. *Ekistics* **42**, no. 253, 354–66.
Wood, D. 1969. The image of San Cristobal. *Monadnock* **43**, 24–5.
Yamamoto, A. Y. 1979. *University of Kansas publications in anthropology*. No. 11: *Culture spaces in everyday life: an anthropology of common sense knowledge*. Lawrence, Kansas: University of Kansas.

4 Culture and economy in the shaping of urban life: general issues and Latin American examples

JOHN WALTON

Introduction

Beguiling phrases are rare in social science, and the few we have give us special comfort. Assertions about the social construction of reality, captains of consciousness, blaming the victim, or the presentation of self in everyday life (all popular book titles) seem to set the world on its proper ontological axis, just as they place the social scientist at its interpretive epicenter. Prominent in this lexicon is the idea of the culture of cities. How naturally the phrase rolls off the tongue and resonates in the ear. Culture and city come hand–in–glove. Seldom are we treated to expositions on the culture of the countryside, perhaps because the phrase itself is gratingly incongruous. Dropped into a conversation or passage, 'the culture of the farm' alerts us to the joke that must follow, but how evocative it seems to speak of 'the culture of slums'.

Of course, these curiosities of language reflect something important about the way we think and, in this case, something quite fundamental about our theories of urban society. To put it simply, cities are the home and workshop of culture: culture is produced (more or less exclusively) in cities, and cities themselves are among the archetypes of any society's cultural products. Moreover, the very life of the city, the custom and commotion of the street, is an enactment of culture.

Yet, as we reflect on the virtual identity of city and culture in this usage and theory, analytic clouds begin to gather. How are we to disentangle these soulmates in a manner that would allow analyses of the way culture affects (even produces) different forms of urban social organization, or of the way urbanization is conducive to new cultural forms? More reflection suggests that we are already in serious trouble. In these uncharted wastes lie the remains of Louis Wirth and other pioneers felled in the tautological drought that equated the culture of urbanism with a psychologized version of the characteristics of the city (e.g. density and competition). Indeed, with the exception of a few intrepid followers who share Wirth's fate (e.g. Fischer 1976), modern students of urbanism skirt this problem, going on to conceive of the city in ways that open up tractable questions and leave the matter of culture orphaned by the wayside. And so much the better in the positivistic mood that brought us social area analysis, central-place theory, factorial ecology and other less-than-alluring phrases.

Of course, the idea of culture was never banished from contemporary urban social science, but has been left to lurk in the corridors, awaiting the opportune moment of testimony when all else fails to clinch the case. More exactly, nontautological theories of urban social organization employ the concept of culture in three more and less opportunistic (atheoretical) modes of explanation. Firstly, culture is used as a *residual* explanation of phenomena that are not fully or satisfactorily accounted for in the terms of the analysis. For example, a family of theories (both *laissez-faire* and radical) explains the spatial organization of cities according to economic function.[1] Social institutions that play key economic roles with respect to, say, marketing and distribution occupy physically central places positioned along transportation routes in a cost-efficient relationship with activities such as supply of housing, describing a pattern of concentric circles, multiple nuclei, etc. Anomalies arise when we discover that next to the nucleus, where the protoplasm ought to be, lies New York's Central Park or Boston's Common and Beacon Hill. But the theory is quickly salvaged with the observation that these are cultural vestiges laden with sentiment and symbolism which, after all, should in some unspecified way be included in the explanation.

Secondly, culture is often seen as an *ensemble* of other things, each with its own explanation. Illustratively, European cities are older, more stable, and historically wiser – in short, they 'have a culture' of the city distinct from agglomerations that pretend to the same name in the United States. Similarly, the entrepreneurial rough-and-readiness of the American South-west (or lately the sunbelt) reflects a 'new urban culture' that makes up in crisis avoidance what it lacks in urbane manner.

Thirdly, culture is sometimes understood as an *emergent* phenomenon – a real and palpable fact, yet one that combines elements of geography, economy, politics, and life-style in some new chemistry whose periodic table has yet to be revealed (e.g. Meehl & Sellars 1956, Edel 1959). To avoid embarrassment or charges of mysticism, we call this a hypothetical construct (but only when 'an emergent' is not language strong enough to stop the skeptic). Examples are commonplace: San Francisco has a 'culture of civility' (or used to), affluent Eastern cities have their own 'public-regarding ethos,' and seemingly bizarre places like Los Angeles make sense from the vantage point of the 'political culture of Southern California' (Wilson & Banfield 1964, Wilson 1967, Becker & Horowitz 1970).

The point stressed in these types and examples, of course, is that none provides an adequate way of thinking about the reciprocal influence of culture and urban social organization. But they cannot be so easily dismissed. In one form or another, they are common to writing about the city, and that is because they are pragmatic 'solutions' to the dilemma of Louis Wirth and others, who err on the other side of residual treatments with overly inclusive notions. The question, then, is how can culture be fitted into a coherent theory of urbanism?

In an effort to fathom the social organization of cities (and other sociospatial forms), all of us begin with certain assumptions. My own lean toward what is today loosely termed the political economy perspective, or, with imperious simplicity, the new urban social science. Rather than being side-tracked into paradigm discussions, of which there are many on this topic,[2] I prefer to describe the approach very briefly, point to some examples, and move on to how it works, with specific reference to the question of culture.

As it has developed over the last decade, the new urban social science embraces several characteristic premises. First, from a theoretical and historical standpoint, it holds that urbanism itself requires definition and explanation rather than being taken for granted or treated simply as a phenomenon of aggregation. Urbanism and urbanization must assume the status of 'theoretical objects' in the sense of phenomena that arise (or do not) and take different forms under various modes of socioeconomic organization and political control (Harvey 1973, Castells 1978). Secondly, the approach is concerned with the interplay of relations of production, consumption, exchange, and the structure of power manifest in the state. None of these can be understood separately or as part of a causal sequence except in an intellectual exercise (i.e. *ceteris paribus*). Thirdly, as in the case of urbanism generally, concrete urban processes (e.g. ecological patterns, community organization, economic activities, class and ethnic politics, local government) must be understood in terms of their structural bases or how they are conditioned by their connection with economic exigencies, political arrangements, and the sociocultural milieu. Fourth, the approach is fundamentally concerned with social change, and conceives of this as growing out of conflicts (or contradictions) among classes and status groups. These conflicts are the basis of the political process which, increasingly, is coincident with the arena of the state. Changes in the economy are socially and politically generated as well as mediated. Political and social changes are in no sense independent of the economy. Finally, the perspective is inextricably tied to the concerns of normative theory. It is concerned not only with drawing out the ideological and distributive implications of alternative positions, but also with being critically aware of its own premises and the dilemmas they pose.

Urban research based on these premises is in flower, bringing us the first real revolution in theory since the Chicago school of urban ecology was founded in the 1920s. In the United States, it has illuminated the historical development of cities and suburbs,[3] the urban fiscal crisis (Alcaly & Mermelstein 1977), and regional shifts such as the rise of the sunbelt cities (Perry & Watkins 1977). Comparatively, it has dovetailed nicely with work on urbanization and underdevelopment in Latin America (Portes & Walton 1977, Roberts 1978), Asia (McGee 1971), and Africa (Gugler & Flanagan 1978). It is to the comparative focus that I want to direct my remarks, since that not only befits the occasion, but allows the fullest expression of cultural influences on urban life.

Despite its progress, the new urban research has not dealt effectively or systematically with culture. In comparative work, however, political economy does provide the holism and relational sophistication that join history, ecology, politics, and class struggle in the determination of urban social organization. Does it allow a useful, nonresidual conception of culture? I believe it does, and will stake my thesis on a conception of culture as ideology. Apart from all pejorative intent, and some textbook anthropology (that reifies culture as artifact), I want to suggest that culture is best understood as the beliefs social groups have about themselves: how they interpret their past, comport their present, and construct their future physical and moral accommodations. Culture is a collective self-portrait, albeit one that hangs alongside others and is frequently defaced. That is, cultures are produced by social groups in conflict. They are the ideologies of groups struggling with one another and with their own ambitions. Only in the most abstract sense is it informative to talk of *the* culture of a society. Such conventional usage hypostatizes the concept and leads us into museums rather than streets, homes, parliaments, factories, and markets. The search for a dusty object called culture obscures what is most interesting about it, namely the claims people make on its behalf and, therefore, on their own. In this sense, it is neither epiphenomenal nor merely the contextual terrain of action. On the contrary, it is the set of beliefs that are acted out in the political and economic struggle in a process of reciprocal influence. That, returning to the question, is how culture complements political economy. Devotees of political economy may be led to equate this notion of culture with class (and status) consciousness, which, indeed, is close to the spirit of my meaning, provided that consciousness is understood in an autonomous sense. But I would urge a broader meaning for culture as ideology, one that includes those less articulate beliefs that guide the uncertain course toward a consciousness of class and status, as well as those with a more cosmic aspect.[4]

The city in Latin America

Does this perspective improve our understanding of the Latin American city in cultural context? The argument that follows is illustrative and sensitizing. Regrettably, in the short space available, it cannot go much further. I believe the approach can be employed in a more exacting fashion, and that unique inferences may be drawn from it and evaluated empirically against parallel propositions derived from other theories. But that is another topic for another day, one that is not likely to be pursued unless we catch the imagination at this point of entry. Accordingly, let me provide the rudiments of a political-economy analysis of Latin American urbanism and, subsequently, develop the contribution culture makes.

We begin with the obvious, if sometimes neglected, fact that most of the major cities in Latin America were founded in the 16th century for the specific purpose of extending, consolidating, and enriching the Spanish Empire (Portes & Walton 1977, pp. 7–25). Initially, Spain wanted dominions, converts to the church, and, above all, bullion. Once these were acquired or exhausted, Spanish colonial society settled down to commercial trade, primitive production (e.g. of dyes), and agriculture. The native labor force was captured in the institutions of *encomienda* (crown grants of Indian laborer subjects), and *repartimiento* (crown-regulated participation of labor in public works). Both institutions were abused from the standpoint of crown law (e.g. grants to individuals were appropriated as family inheritance, and public labor obligations were used for private and coercive ends), as Spain found it increasingly difficult to govern the colonies, and a New World evolved according to its own exigencies.

The strategy of Spanish colonization was centered on the city, from which civil, military, and ecclesiastic authority maintained a tenuous purchase on the hinterland. In consequence, no frontier emerged in the North American sense, nor was the countryside left to the governance of rural proprietors in the European tradition of the time. 'The city did not arise to serve, but to subdue' (Portes & Walton 1977, p. 9). The ecology of the colonial city reflected this centralization. Ringed around the central plaza were the headquarters of the church and state and the residences of the social élite, passing through a second ring of public functionaries, merchants, and artisans to the peripheral ranchos or workers and *peones*. The major urban landholders were the church and the municipal (though territorially sovereign) government which reserved one-third of the land for public purposes.

Colonial cities and towns were organized as nested boxes. Authority and imported goods ran from the center outwards, and loyalty, raw materials, and artisan manufactures ran inward from the periphery. Interregional trade was discouraged or, to the extent possible, prevented, despite opportunity and natural complementarity among regional products. Benefits, and therefore development 'policy', were determined at the centers in Mexico City, or Lima, or Buenos Aires, and ultimately in Spain. Urban and regional development were predicated on the needs of the center somewhat apart from the potential of the periphery. A zone that could produce silver and timber (or indigo and cacao) specialized in the former and traded disadvantageously in the latter as long as the latter was commercially available somewhere else. From a regional standpoint, the arrangement produced monoculture and underdevelopment orchestrated by a system of blunt inequality. In brief, this was the Latin American city *circa* 1581.

Taking a historical deep breath, we can say that urban society did not change a great deal until the 1820s, when a series of independent republics was created in rapid succession in Latin America. The ideals of Simón Bolivar notwithstanding, independence failed to bring liberation, except from the long-flagging control of Spain, substituting an indigenous élite at the top of the same social order. But independence did temper the pattern of regional specialization, exploitation, and subservience. The opening of interregional trade and its stimulus to local commerce were decisive changes when coupled with a gradual increase of political autonomy. Slowly, this led to the commercialization of agriculture, the encouragement of urban artisans and merchants, and, demographically, an increase in both the size and primacy of the city.[5] The city and its economy expanded, albeit on the basis of commerce, rude industry, and the export of primary products. This pattern continued into the present century, when Latin American markets and nascent industries were invaded and in some part displaced or pre-empted by foreign investment.

The consequences of all this for urban society are found in three characteristic phenomena. Geographically, the cities grew and became 'overcrowded', as judged from the standpoint of available jobs, housing, and other amenities – hence the infamous (much maligned *and* romanticized) slums and barrios. Economically, the expanding urban population competed for the relatively few industrial jobs, or found niches of underemployment in construction and the prototypically booming, yet disparate, tertiary sector of commerce and services (hence the awkward, if informative, label of 'tertiarization' for the process). Politically, the state was hoisted on the dilemmas of how to provide jobs and industry within a system of international constraints, which also favored important local classes, and how to meet the accelerating, perhaps insatiable, need for urban development with a weak political system poor in public resources.

At this juncture, I shift from the general aspect to the development of a particular Latin American city which is typical enough for the present purpose of analyzing the contemporary urban condition. Guadalajara is Mexico's second city, a position it has occupied since the late 19th century, when it grew as the commercial center of an agricultural region and trading network extending through the northwestern reaches of the country to the United States border. That is, its rise to prominence as a provincial city corresponded to the post-independence period just described. This growth was predicated on a distinctive colonial past. Founded on its present site in 1542 as Nueva Galicia, it was the administrative and ecclesiastical focus of a vast area that now includes seven western and northern states. Given the importance of the territory it governed, including one of the major sites of silver mining, Guadalajara acquired its own legal court of the crown (*audiencia*) in 1548, and therefore political status equal to that of Mexico City. Economically, the city fitted the entrepôt rôle, exchanging silver and agricultural products for imports from Mexico City and Spain, with a minimum of interregional transactions. Next to the territorial government, the church and hacienda were the major social institutions, sharing in the political autonomy of the region, giving it a sense of independence reflected in impressive church buildings, public-spirited projects, and an air of refinement retained to this day.

The city's first major growth spurt, coming after independence from Spain in 1824, was built on these foundations. Commerce flourished in old and new ways with the advent of interregional trade and development of the western port of San Blás. Artisan manufactures, the processing of food, and construction became important industries, organized as family enterprises. Prosperity was reflected spatially as commercial profits were invested in land, and élite residences moved westward from the central zone which was given over increasingly to small business and public responsibility. Indeed, as the city grew in numbers of people and area, public works led the way with elegant avenues, parks, arches, and a profuse display of fountains, all adorning the corridors of commerce and upper-class commuters.

Prior to the Mexican Revolution (1910–17), Guadalajara was home to 120 000 people devoted to the church, civic progress, and the tenets of 19th-century political reform and economic liberalism. It was not a seed-bed of revolution – and that fact has prompted some local defensiveness ever since. The revolutionary fever was less contagious in Guadalajara for a number of reasons: the church dominated local affairs and, perhaps through its civic works, maintained legitimacy; rural society was governed by haciendas that fostered debt peonage, but were less commercialized and concentrated in the hands of absentee landlords than in more volatile regions; local business and industry were centered on small-scale family enterprises relatively unaffected by the encroachments of foreign capital in the nation's railroads, export agriculture, and large industry. Less touched by these incendiary issues, the business of Guadalajara was Catholicism, commerce, and comfort for a rural aristocracy and urban bourgeoisie. Artistic achievements that graced the cityspace were complemented in the commonweal by a passion for political theory.

The revolutionary victory, won on other terrain, brought high irony to Guadalajara. Revolutionary policy that did not reflect local ambitions was nevertheless applied more systematically. The principal goals of the new regimes of the 1920s and 1930s were the elimination of church influence, land reform, and the creation of a modern one-party state. In short, and with the exception of the local economy, Guadalajara's institutional foundations came in for a major overhaul. Although landownership was somewhat less concentrated in the region than in the nation as a whole, land reform was pursued more aggressively. The result was to break up the old and unproductive hacienda system as its former proprietors found refuge for their families and their capital in the city. The church was deprived of its land holdings, its rôle in public education, and at least its surface appearance in clerical dress. These depredations on the church were violently resisted in the Cristero rebellion (which bears many similarities to the Vendée in post-revolutionary France). Politically, the one-party state slowly took root, arrogating to itself much of the power once held by the landowners and the church in an economy that had never produced the large industrial capitalists who might have challenged the interlopers. In short, the transformation was institutional and thorough.

A new social order was created in the years between 1920 and 1950; one that combined colonial, independence-and-reform, and revolutionary influences in a special blend. The post-revolutionary politicians were now in command, but their modernizing ambitions depended upon the cooperation of merchant and family capitalists, as well as the veiled but forceful presence of the church. Moreover, if the one-party state was institutionally revolutionary, it was still staffed by locally prominent figures who understood that their own success depended on them working with what was available. The city had a 'tradition' in the sense of what had already been accomplished in response to political and economic circumstance, and it had potential. In alternating moods of suasion and coercion, the modernizing politicians saw opportunities for parlaying these resources to their own political advantage, which rested on the pleasure of an increasingly centralized and patrimonial federal state. All of the foregoing considerations come together in the contemporary city that blossomed after World War II, as signaled dramatically by a decennial rate of population increase that averaged 20 percent between 1900 and 1940, jumped to 65 percent in the 1940–50 period (and a population of 377 000 at the end of the period), 95 percent in 1950–60 (736 800), and another 62 percent from 1960 to 1970 (1 200 000). Migration and natural increase contribute in roughly equal measure to the current population that is nearing 2.5 million.

Economic change, while substantial, has been less dramatic, leading to the contemporary developmental problem. The early success of commerce and services continues as these constitute the major sector, employing about half the labor force. Commerce includes an impressive variety of retail sales made in the public markets and house-front stores, and the increasing number of chain stores, supermarkets, and international firms such as Sears. A large fraction of the service sector is made up of city and state government workers and of people engaged in a bewildering array of personal and repair services. Guadalajara's overcrowded 'tertiary sector' is typical for Latin America. A walk on the streets is a study of under-employment and labor-force characteristics: the seller of lottery tickets stopped for a shoe shine, or the automobile mechanic draped over the hood of an ancient truck opposite the open front of a beautician's salon are scenes from the economy as much as the street.

Industry of a distinctive sort also thrives. Many local firms are still relatively small, family owned, and devoted to the elaboration of agricul-tural products (e.g. food processing, beverages, shoes, soap, textiles and clothing). Equally important is the construction and construction-materials industry, which has boomed in the same metric as population. The diagnostic feature of all this industry is that two-thirds of its products are for final consumption. Stated differently, industry and product link-ages, particularly the 'forward' variety, are minimal. But locally based industry is cleanly split (or almost so) between indigenous firms with the foregoing characteristics and nonlocal firms, with headquarters in Mon-terrey, Mexico City, or abroad, that have a somewhat different profile. Nonlocal firms are larger corporate structures (i.e. of stock-holders rather than family owners), engaged more often in the production of capital goods with 'dynamic' markets (e.g. electronics, chemicals). However, the contrast should not be overdrawn. To put the matter more precisely, nonlocal firms cover a broader spectrum of industrial activities, ranging from food products and construction materials to business machines and metal products. Moreover, nonlocal firms engaged in these activities are frequently involved in joint investments and product lines with local manufacturers. The range is suggested by such familiar American multi-national names as Corn Products, Ralston Purina, Nabisco, Kodak, Burroughs, Motorola, IBM, Celanese, and Union Carbide. But other large Mexican companies are also present in fields as diverse as food, beer, textiles, and steel. Finally, if local firms are concentrated in less dynamic and low-linkage activities, nonlocal enterprises are more capital intensive and impermeable to local investment.

Gaining some perspective, we can see that the economy is rent with sectoral and social-class fissures. Population and underemployment grow in train with an economic structure low in absorbency. Commerce and services are not only 'overcrowded,' the real meaning of underemploy-ment, but also show signs of monopolization. Industry is split between an indigenous low-growth sector and a nonlocal leading sector that is less open to local labor and investment participation. Moreover, some non-local industry competes directly with home-grown manufacture and small business. At the same time, commercial wealth is generated which may be 'conservative,' reinvesting in safe, inflation-proof, and less productive areas (especially land and rentals), but is also presented with few opportunities in the high-return, dynamic fields that attract foreign investment. Some of this wealth is devoted to luxury consumption, but, as Samir Amin (1974, p. 177) observes:

> In the main, however, this enrichment attracts new capital formed in the urban sector toward the purchase of land. Merchants made wealthy by *comprador* trade in manufactured goods from the center, and in exotic products destined for the center, invest their profits not in industry, which would be unprofitable, given the foreign competition, but in the purchase of land, which constitutes a lucrative use of savings.

A sociological interpretation of the broad picture would suggest that there are two major 'fractions of capital,' the commercial and the industrial bourgeoisies, each with its own internal divisions (petty versus monopolistic commerce, and native versus nonlocal industry). A critical assessment of these social-class divisions suggests that they are at the root of the developmental problem. For example, underemployment is increasingly the rule as commerce becomes more monopolized and growth industries are more capital intensive. Locally generated surplus is either partially blocked and diverted into unproductive channels, or realized by national and multinational corporations for reinvestment in broader circuits – and so on through the familiar vicious circles of underdevelopment. What I would stress here is that the pattern of social inequality rests on the logic of classes in conflict, rather than on any immutable laws of the economy.

Yet this is only one side of a political economy interpretation that must also reckon the rôle of the state in the development process. Much of the pattern described is the direct result of actions by the government to promote a particular kind of development. And, conversely, it is a result of other official decisions not to intervene in promoting alternatives. To illustrate, public works projects have traditionally responded to the needs of commerce. Broad avenues support the traffic of goods in and out of the city. The railroad and bus terminals were impressive structures in their day, if more recently overshadowed by an airport boasting (at one time) the longest runway in Latin America. Justifiable on their individual merits, in broader context these projects often destroy small business in their path, centralize commercial activity around high-rent downtown or suburban shopping centers, and absorb public funds that might go to more egalitarian investments (such as the large public market which, to be fair, the state also built). Public works produce a redistribution of real income at the same time as they reorganize spatial arrangements (Harvey 1973). In Guadalajara, the resolution of forces generated by a wide variety of projects is in the direction of a more regressive income distribution.

The same result obtains more clearly in the case of state policies on industrial development. Local government has pursued an open-arms policy of attracting new industry, including promotional campaigns, assistance in plant location, tax incentives, and provision for infra-structural needs (e.g. transportation, and natural gas). Firms that compete with local industry or bring monopolized and capital-intensive features are, nevertheless, sought after with a flourish. To the extent that this is justified, public officials claim that the effect will be beneficial competition or benign complementarity – claims that are easily refuted, as may be inferred from other portions of this analysis. Assuming that local officials and economic planners are intelligent, public-spirited people (a valid assumption, I would add), what explains this? The answer lies in the nature of Mexican regional politics, particularly the great importance of showing evidence to the dominant federal government and one-party state that regional leaders are making significant developmental progress in the short space (four to six years) of any one administration's tenure. Individual advancement in the political system as well as the state's share of federal largesse depend on a track record of big steps towards conven-tionally defined developmental goals (e.g. the number of new industries or the aggregate value of production) in a short time. Each new adminis-tration wants to build its own monuments in the vista of the city and the record books. The successful federal careers of many one-time local officials were built on such achievements – the urban landscape is political morphology.

State policies of industrial promotion materialize in many forms. I have just indicated some of the actions that contribute to a growing number of national and multinational firms. This growth interacts with the char-acteristic features of the local economy, generating new and pressing needs. Urban transportation, housing, infrastructure, and amenities (e.g. paved streets, lighting, drainage) are all serious problems in a city whose growth outruns the public treasury. The state is presented with hard choices about what action to take, often what to build, and for whose benefit. Although seldom cast in this light, the choices must rely on a theory of development which is invariably a theory of equity: what kind of works will accomplish a desired developmental end for certain classes without harm (or, ideally, with indirect support) to others. In short, policies and works have inherent conflicts that are best illustrated in the spatial dimension.

Guadalajara has grown outwards from its traditional, commercial and administrative center to all points of the compass. To the south and south-west are zones of industry, rail transport, and many of the proto-typical repair services (Fig. 4.1). To the west and north-west, middle- to upper-class residential areas move along a suburbanization gradient. Closer to the city center is a progressive planner's dream of mixed, small

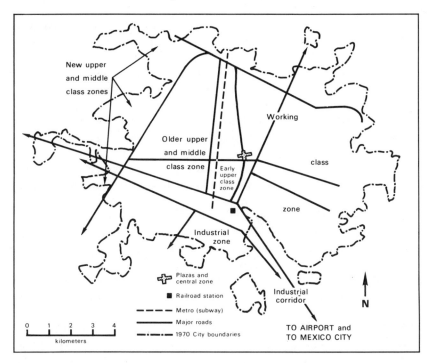

New upper
and middle
class zones

Working

Older upper
and middle
class zone

Early
upper
class
zone

class

zone

Industrial
zone

✠ Plazas and
central zone

■ Railroad station

- - - - Metro (subway)

——— Major roads

—··—··— 1970 City boundaries

Industrial
corridor

N

0 1 2 3 4
kilometers

TO AIRPORT and
TO MEXICO CITY

Figure 4.1 Guadalajara.

industry, petty commerce, and varied residential usage; further out, the complaisant 'order' of suburbs and shopping centers in the North American mold. To the north-east and east is a zone of predominantly working-class housing and the most modest brand of tertiary economy. Official estimates are that 70 percent of the population lives in these eastern quadrants in densities twice the city average. Predictably, most of the city's new infrastructure has gone westward.

This has been the setting for conflict among the costs and benefits of developmental policy and between social classes. Examples are abundant, and include the dramatic physical separation of new industrial sites (south-west) and working-class residential areas (north-east). Workers, who can scarcely afford the time and cost of public transportation, have to negotiate two to four trips daily across a diagonal of the city's expanse. A tattered fleet of city-contracted buses bravely serves the purpose, along intricately winding routes with origin and destination at the central zone. Enormous problems of congestion, smog, traffic accidents, and commuter inconvenience result. Downtown business welcomes the delivery of patrons, but resents the rest. Of course, in earlier projects of urban design and beautification, the state had helped to generate the problem, just as it recently tried to solve it anew with a subterranean electrical bus system.

The project brings class conflict into sharper focus. To connect workers directly with the industrial zone, the Metro excavation had to cut through one of the older neighborhoods of stately upper-middle-class homes. The interests in conflict here were, on one side, the large industrialists in need of a convenient labor force, and the workers desirous of efficient, low-cost transportation, and, on the other, property capital, much of it generated in downtown commerce. The state sided with the former constellation of interests, in something of a break with tradition that may continue as industrial capital gains the upper hand. This, obviously, is not to say that the working class was awarded a major, indirect benefit or that the propertied rentier class suffered a broad defeat. The latter group, with its income derived from commerce, continues inveterate speculation, driving land costs throughout the city to high and, amazingly, roughly equal levels irrespective of location. Frenzied speculation means that land anywhere in the city can command top dollar, or nearly so, because of the certainty that all of it is rising in price – nevertheless, 'overpriced' parcels sell and soon come to be seen as bargains. Choice housing sites are rented or sold and less convenient ones are overcrowded with renters, or simply held vacant for speculation. Among other things, this exacerbates the housing problem. Yet the state has not moved toward significant public-housing developments, nor has it exercized its legal right to expropriate urban lots for private or public housing. On the contrary, the few commendable public-housing projects that do exist are on land publicly purchased at full (inflated) value, a fact that both encourages further speculation and puts the public-housing market out of reach for most workers. Folding all this into a summary generalization, state policy has catered to the interests of the commercial-propertied and industrialist classes, although shifting priorities seem favorable to the latter. The working class in industry and the underemployed in commerce and services benefit only remotely, when they benefit at all. Development theory says you feed the sparrows by feeding the horses.

The cultural influence on urban life

Which brings us unceremoniously to culture. So far, I have described the political economy of unequal urban development and interpreted this as largely a consequence of class conflict. How does culture make a non-residual contribution to the analysis? Recall that we explored the idea of culture as collective self-portraits, the beliefs and ambitions that conflict-ing social (class and status) groups develop for themselves in joint action. Culture is not unitary, artifactual, or auxiliary. It follows that there are cultures associated with the major contending social groups whose collec-tive action shapes the urban environment.

The central analytic question here is how urban culture evolves in a form that is relatively independent of class interest. Let me provide as precise an answer as possible, since the theoretical status of the argument hinges on this connection. I conceive of the process as involving two steps. First, insofar as separate classes have articulate interests, those of each class are at variance with the interests of other classes. Two or more classes that act in concert by dint of affecting and sharing the same urban environment must reach some accord or compromise that is necessarily distinct from the individual viewpoint of any one. Secondly, these negotiations emerge in the political process (itself shaped by history, an inherited structure of power, and accidents of circumstance) that transforms the interests the groups bring to the process, just as it provides the experience in which urban culture and some of its products are forged. The resulting physical and social organization of the city may be viewed as a collective portrait of urban culture.

In this sense, Guadalajara embodies at least four important cultures. First is the *civic culture*, so visually evident in the architecture, urban design, art, and the places of worship and learning as to form the major and stereotypical impression of the city's high-brow 'culture.' At a deeper level, the civic culture is an amalgam of beliefs derived from the church and the aristocratic landowners and merchants, together with commercial oligopoly and property capital. It is founded on classically conservative ideas about paternalistic good government, reformism, and church and state participation in good works that serve and educate the masses. It is a belief in general prosperity as the enlightened result of entrepreneurial initiative – a portrait of the benevolent state as purveyor of bourgeois order.

Second is the *modernity culture*, reflected in new industries, the multinational presence, technocratic and planning institutions, elaborate infrastructure works such as the Metro and industrial park, and the suburbs. Materially these reflect beliefs about science and economic development as technical objectives realizable by state provision of the necessary tools for the use of planners and worldly industrialists. The modernity culture is a belief in the good life of consumer durables, 'know-how,' a golden mean calculated as a favorable balance of exports and imports or profits and wages. Fittingly, it is an imported belief whose devotees have been progressively weaned from the indigenous moral economy to join their international peers of industrial capital.

Third is the *working-class culture*, whose monuments are as modest as they are pervasive. Physically, they are found in the rustic and over-crowded housing, the occasional dirt soccer field, the street vendor's push-cart, and the sidewalk café where a hasty repast is cooked and consumed, literally on the sidewalk. But these appearances belie more noble beliefs of working-class culture rooted in the Mexican Revolution.

The idea of personal dignity is pre-eminent. Socially, this is expressed in the legitimacy of expectations for a job, public guarantees of worker rights, and responsibility for health care and education. The family is the locus of these beliefs, investing a special salience or urgency in medical care for the infirmed or schooling for the child. The post-revolutionary, one-party state is viewed as the legitimate source, if a frequently errant one, of these social guarantees. And the working class understands its obligation of party loyalty as the currency of public services. The bargain is clear, if seldom adequately struck.

Finally, we come to the *political culture* of developmentalism which is embodied in the state with its multitude of agencies and functionaries. At a rhetorical level, the state is committed to the continuation of the Mexican Revolution through social justice and economic growth. Programmatically, these beliefs translate into the provision of welfare services and enforcement of strong labor laws, on one side, and alacritous support for modern industry and related growth sectors of the economy on the other. In Guadalajara, planning is the chief vice of officialdom: agricultural plans, urban plans, guides to foreign investors, regionalization plans, and analyses of new industrial opportunities, all operationalize the understood rôle of the state in directing growth and the desired ends of the process. The physical symbols of this political culture are abundant, from the ubiquitous slogans painted on walls and buildings to the public works discussed previously, and the prepossessing state administrative headquarters.

Although the state is the dominant local institution, and in many ways autonomous (e.g. with distinct career lines for political aspirants and as the agent of policies determined at the federal level), it also endeavors to represent faithfully the interests of all classes and cultures, thus repeatedly bringing itself into potential conflict with any one. In these conflicts, the distinct cultures and their symbolic expressions are seen in greatest relief. For present purposes, the examples cited must suffice. New developments in the city's economy and social organization, particularly as they are reflected in public policy, favor 'modernization' as a specific constellation of cultural themes (e.g. planning, technocracy, industrialism). The political and modernity cultures are forging ever-closer links, based on developmental ambitions, that ultimately prove disadvantageous to working-class culture and increasingly threaten the civic culture that has long been the basis of local repute and pride.

These are the urban cultures that grow out of class interests and, in the political process, grow into relatively autonomous normative systems and collective actions. This treatment helps to demystify culture as a free-floating influence that does its work in ubiquitous but unspecified ways. Since the content and organization of these cultures are judged by the stamp they put on the urban sociospatial form, it remains to indicate

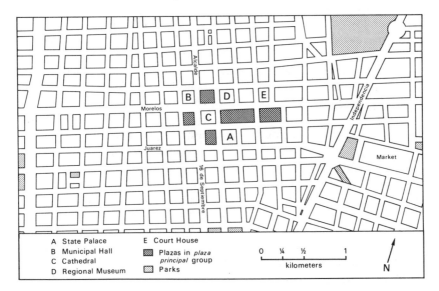

A State Palace   E Court House
B Municipal Hall ▨ Plazas in *plaza*
C Cathedral   *principal* group
D Regional Museum ▨ Parks

0 ¼ ½ 1
kilometers

N

Figure 4.2 Central Guadalajara.

briefly how culture acts as a mediating and relatively autonomous force shaping urban life. Let me conclude with two suggestive examples, one historical and connected with urban design, the other contemporary and related to function. In both cases, the point is to show how the cultures interact in the determination and use of urban structure.

In the 1920s, the city's central plaza was still of colonial proportions, a modest square bordered by the main cathedral, state palace, government buildings, and small shops. The city fathers decided to modernize the area with a huge urban renewal project. Large squares were installed around three sides of the cathedral, replete with fountains, rose gardens, and a band stand, with the fourth side given over to an even larger rectangular plaza, extending some 180 metres (200 yards) toward a new performing arts theater at the base of what now formed a cross of several acres, with the cathedral at its center (Fig. 4.2). The symbolism was appreciated by everyone, especially the church, whose post-revolutionary low profile did not restrain this expression of civic culture.

A second example concerns some of the uses the working class finds for modern urban works. The cross-shaped plaza is also a place of business for shoe-shiners, street vendors, photographers, and small dealers without their own office space. But less likely public works satisfy multiple uses. The transportation system provides a rolling stage for underemployed musicians, whose voices or guitars rise above the din of traffic, winning patronage in loose change. Public buildings are a focal point of vending and petty brokerage, including the sidelines that minor functionaries carry on from their official desks or doorsteps. As a regulator of this traffic, the doorman of the average government office building is a person of influence. In some ways, working-class culture controls, thrives in, and gets more use from official quarters than the intended beneficiaries. Put another way, cultural products have many more uses, and beliefs about legitimate use, for the working class than intended.

Culture is both a product and a determinant of class and collective action. In the awkwardly concise language of social theory, culture evolves according to its own logic in ways that are functionally autonomous: exigency leads to circumstantial accommodation out of which evolve variation, tolerable satisfaction, and new motives. Culture is what we feel about our circumstance, and what we do about it – change it, make it livable, or struggle with something between. In Third World cities, culture characteristically becomes the integrating basis for resistance to modern forms of multinational imperialism, unifying class, status, and nationalistic considerations in popular movements. Revolutions require additional precipitants, but, when they come, their greatest force derives from cultural expression.

The rôle I have assigned to culture in this discussion will doubtless offend some who savor a more idealistic taste for art and philosophical verity. Esthetically, I am on their side, but explanatory social theory only rarely achieves esthetic merit. Conversely, a less ethereal understanding of culture may lend some grace to the dour theory we have been using, mostly in the breach, to explain the warmth of social life.

Notes

1   This approach characterizes both the *laissez-faire* analyses of location and equilibrium (such as Alonso 1964), and radical political economy (as in Gordon 1971).
2   Elsewhere (Walton 1979), I have tried to review uses of 'political economy,' and to provide an effective one.
3   See especially Gordon (1978) and other articles in Tabb and Sawers (1978).
4   My approach is informed by Thompson (1966), though it does not begin to suggest the richness of his treatment.
5   McGreevey (1971). More detail on the urban development of Guadalajara is contained in Walton (1977) and Walton (1978).

References

Alcaly, R. E. and D. Mermelstein (eds.) 1977. *The fiscal crisis of American cities: essays on the political economy of urban America with special reference to New York.* New York: Vintage.

Alonso, W. 1964. *Location and land use.* Cambridge, Mass.: Harvard University Press.

Amin, S. 1974. *Accumulation on a world scale: a critique of the theory of underdevelopment 1*. New York: Monthly Review Press.

Becker, H. S. and I. L. Horowitz 1970. The culture of civility: San Francisco. *Trans-Action* **7**(6), 12–20.

Castells, M. 1978. *The urban question: a marxist approach*. Cambridge, Mass.: MIT Press.

Edel, A. 1959. The concept of levels in social theory. In *Symposium on sociological theory*, L. Gross (ed.), 167–95. New York: Harper & Row.

Fischer, C. S. 1976. *The urban experience*. New York: Harcourt, Brace, Jovanovich.

Gordon, D. M. (ed.) 1971. *Problems in political economy: an urban approach*. Lexington, Mass.: D. C. Heath.

Gordon, D. M. 1978. Capitalist development and the history of American cities. In *Marxism and the metropolis: new perspectives in urban political economy*, W. K. Tabb and L. Sawers (eds.), 25–63. New York: Oxford University Press.

Gugler, J. and W. G. Flanagan 1978. *Urbanization and social change in West Africa*. Cambridge: Cambridge University Press.

Harvey, D. 1973. *Social justice and the city*. Baltimore: Johns Hopkins University Press.

McGee, T. J. 1971. *The urbanization process in the Third World*. London: Bell.

McGreevey, W. P. 1971. A statistical analysis of primacy and lognormality in the size distribution of Latin American cities, 1750–1960. In *The urban development of Latin America, 1750–1920*, R. M. Morse (ed.). 116–29. Stanford, Calif.: Stanford University, Center for Latin American Studies.

Meehl, P. E. and W. Sellars 1956. The concept of emergence. In *Minnesota studies in the philosophy of science. The foundations of science and the concepts of psychology and psychoanalysis*, H. Feigl and M. Scriven (eds.), 239–52. Minneapolis: University of Minnesota Press.

Perry, D. C. and A. J. Watkins (eds.) 1977 *Urban Affairs Annual Reviews*. 14: *The rise of the sunbelt cities*. Beverly Hills, Calif.: Sage.

Portes, A. and J. Walton 1977. *Urban Latin America: the political condition from above and below*. Austin: University of Texas Press.

Roberts, B. 1978. *Cities of peasants: the political economy of urbanization in the Third World*. London: Edward Arnold.

Tabb, W. K. and L. Sawers (eds.) 1978. *Marxism and the metropolis: new perspectives in urban political economy*. New York: Oxford University Press.

Thompson, E. P. 1966. *The making of the English working class*. New York: Vintage Books.

Walton, J. 1977. *Élites and economic development: comparative studies on the political economy of Latin American cities*. Austin: Institute of Latin American Studies, University of Texas Press.

Walton, J. 1978. Guadalajara: creating the divided city. In *Latin American urban research. 6: Metropolitan Latin America: the challenge and the response*, W. A. Cornelius and R. V. Kemper (eds.), 25–50. Beverly Hills, Calif.: Sage.

Walton, J. 1979. Urban political economy. *Comp. Urban Res.* **7**(1), 5–17.

Wilson, J. Q. 1967. A guide to Reagan country: the political culture of Southern California. *Commentary* **43**, 37–45.

Wilson, J. Q. and E. C. Banfield 1964. Public-regardingness as a value premise in voting behavior. *Am. Polit. Sci. Rev.* **58**, 876–87.

5 Culture, 'modes of production,' and the changing nature of cities in the Arab World

JANET ABU-LUGHOD

Studies of Third World urbanization have been handicapped by the absence of theoretical frameworks that permit *analysis* rather than pure description.[1] This is particularly true with respect to cities in the Arab World, which I have been studying for over two decades. In the course of time, I have come to know a great many of the area's cities and to love not a few of them. In their historic form, I think I understand them as well as anyone. But when I examine the most recent developments of the urbanizing Arab World, I find that most of the generalizations based upon the past simply will not hold.

Urbanization in the Arab World today neither fits the dependency model so robust for other parts of the Third World, nor does it any longer fit the decolonizing model I found so useful in studying Cairo in the 1960s, or Rabat-Salé in the 1970s (Abu-Lughod 1971, 1980b). Not only do current patterns of urbanization deviate drastically from their historic antecedents, but, as subtypes proliferate and diverge, it becomes increasingly difficult to generalize about the processes of urbanization as they are occurring in different Arab countries, much less to subsume these developments neatly into some 'species' of 'genus' Third World urban.

This chapter represents an attempt to reconceptualize the problem.[2] Instead of beginning with what Arab cities have in common, culturally and historically, I want to begin with how their current economic conditions diverge; to explore the implications for urbanization of the increasingly peculiar rôle Middle Eastern states are playing in the global economy; and to propose a taxonomy, based upon modes of production, that can perhaps predict the particular kinds of urban developments now occurring in different subregions of the Arab World.

When one examines Arab countries, with a view to seeing how they fit into the regional and international divisions of labor, it becomes possible, for analytical purposes, to divide them into four 'mode of production' types. Of these, two are familiar, and existing theory can, with modifi-

Table 5.1 Countries in the Arab region classified by mode of production, with selected socioeconomic indicators of urbanization and income.

Type and countries	Total population ('000s), 1976	Per-capita income ($), 1976	Percent urban, 1975	Percent urban population in largest city	Average rate of urban growth, 1970–75
I Neo colonial					
Tunisia	5 700	840	47	35	4.2
Morocco	17 200	540	38	26	5.1
II State socialist					
Algeria	16 200	990	50	32.5	3.2
Iraq	11 500	1 390	62	49.0†	5.0
Syria	7 700	780	46	31.6	4.2
III Charity cases					
Jordan	2 200★	610★	56	46.7	4.9
Occupied Palestine	1 200‡	?	low‡	?	low‡
Egypt	38 100	280	48	38.0	3.9
Israel	3 500‡	3 920	84	?	3.4
Lebanon	3 200	1 070?	60	50.7	5.4
IV Oil and sand					
Libya	2 500	6 310	31	45.4	5.0
Saudi Arabia	8 600	4 480	21	26.0	6.3
Bahrain	300	2 140	80	100.0	6.0 (1970)
Qatar	200	11 400	88	100.0	18.0 (1970)
Kuwait	1 100	15 480	89	95.0	8.2
United Arab Emirates	700	13 990	84	—	—
Oman	800	2 680	?	—	—
V Fourth World					
PDR Yemen	1 700	280	29	83.6	5.4
Yemen AR	6 000	250	9	50.3	8.0
Sudan	15 900	290	13	24.9	5.5

★ The total population of Jordan is for the East Bank, since the 1979 census of Jordan covered only this area. According to preliminary returns, some 2 150 000 persons lived on the East Bank, of whom 1 million were in the Amman–Zarqa metropolitan area. I am not certain about the per-capita GNP figures in this table, but believe they refer to the East and West Banks combined. The East Bank alone might be somewhat higher, although I really believe none of these figures is very reliable.

† Iraqi data generally exaggerate the size of cities because provincial figures substitute for municipal. This percentage is therefore suspect.

‡ In its recent census reports, Israel has been including the approximately 100 000 Arab residents of the East Jerusalem area, a district unilaterally and illegally annexed after 1967. If this population is transferred to the West Bank, as in my computations, the Israeli total drops from 3.6 to 3.5 million, and the West Bank–Gaza total increases from 1.2 to 1.3 million. I have not adjusted the percent urban accordingly, but, clearly, the percentage in Israel would be somewhat lower while the percentage in the Occupied Areas would rise. However, the figures on per-capita GNP could not be adjusted.

Source: the figures in this table, with the changes noted above, have been taken from Clarke (1980, Table 2.3, p. 39), which in turn was based on World Bank and ECWA figures.

cations, apply to them. However, the remaining two types are relatively unprecedented. Existing theories are of little value for understanding or predicting urban developments in countries of these types. Table 5.1 shows a grouping of the major countries in the region into the four types (plus a fifth type that will not be discussed), together with some associated socioeconomic measurements.

Neocolonial countries

The first group (a familiar type) consists of imperfectly decolonized dependencies, of which only Tunisia and Morocco remain as examples. Both countries received their nominal independence from France in 1956 in relatively bloodless transitions of power. Both had inherited, from the precolonial era, numerous cities of 'pure' Arabo-Andalusian character which, until quite far into the modern era, had retained their surrounding walls, their cellular organization into quarters, their narrow and convoluted streets, their linear bazaar arteries, and their Islamic laws and precedents governing urban development and property relations. On top of this urban system, the French occupiers had superimposed an urban hierarchy based on a colonial extractive economy whose major link was to the Metropole, and, on to the major pre-existing cities of importance to the colonizers, the French had grafted new towns (villes nouvelles) for their own use, adjacent to the 'native' cities. In both cases, Metropole-directed economies stimulated the rise to primacy of very large ports. When, as in the case of Tunisia, the chief port was also the political capital, primacy was unbridled. Tunis is still five times larger than the second-ranking city of Sfax, also a port. In Morocco, in contrast, the chief port of Casablanca was virtually a new city and was consciously rejected as the political capital. The population having grown in two generations to over 1.5 million, it is only three times larger than the next-ranking urban area, Rabat-Salé, which is the political capital, and there are several other secondary cities of large size and economic importance located in the interior.

Although ostensibly the 'dual' spatial structure (in terms of both urban hierarchy and individual cities) paralleled a 'dual' economic structure (so-called modern and so-called traditional), neither was actually what it purported to be. Rather than establishing 'separate but equal facilities,' the dual system was a most efficient 'machine' for siphoning surplus value from 'natives' to foreigners. Wealth was transferred from the traditional to the modern (or foreign) economy through state (that is, French) monopolies over phosphates and other mineral resources, and through monetization and land expropriation, which threw dispossessed natives into the cities where their cheap labor subsidized development. In the cities, native land and taxes were siphoned to subsidize French urban elegance (see Abu-Lughod 1980b, *passim*).

Decolonization had remarkably little impact on this system, although the native élites began to take a larger share of the drained surplus value once independence was achieved and many of the foreigners left. Indigenous élites inherited the newly vacated administrative posts in government and modern commerce, and also inherited the commodious urban quarters formerly the exclusive preserve of Europeans. But *bidonvilles* (tin-can makeshift quarters) continued to grow for the same reason as before. Urban population was growing through natural increase and migration well in excess of the economic and spatial capacities of cities to absorb it. After independence, French researchers and planning experts continued to be retained, now to work with French-trained 'native' experts, to 'solve' urban problems, but the radical changes in the mode of production that would be required to restructure urban economies have not been attempted.

Soon after independence, leftist ministers of economy in both Tunisia and Morocco tried to socialize development plans and to focus on more diversified mineral extraction and the growth of related heavy industries. But in both countries these ministers lost out to heads of state who preferred joint ventures with foreign capitalists, creation of infrastructure, social services, and state jobs, and support to industrialists engaged in import-substitution light production. Thanks to French and World Bank advisors, tourism was accorded a central role in the development plans, and hotels and other facilities were the recipients of heightened investment.

Therefore, after brief periods of 'nationalistic independence,' both countries settled down into their current rôles as economic satellites dependent on Europe. Both countries export laborers to France; both receive their heaviest capital investments from France; both depend increasingly upon the 'invisible' export of tourism; both, but particularly Tunisia, are cooperating in the new international 'putting-out system,' whereby cheap Third World labor remains *in situ*, while parts to be assembled or goods to be hand finished are imported, finished locally, and then re-exported – still with the French or Italian labels on them.

Therefore, despite important natural resources, good man : land ratios, and talented and energetic populations, both Tunisia and Morocco seem to be operating below their potentials. This is reflected in their modest GNP/capita rates. Both countries have moderate levels of urbanization (below 50 percent), but these are symptomatic more of economic stagnation in the countryside than of economic vitality in the cities. Urban unemployment rates are high, and would probably be even higher if it were not for the safety valve offered by external employment. Marked contrasts of economic status are evident in the cities, which have retained their 'dual' character, now made 'triple' by the peripheral *bidonvilles* and public-housing projects that have been the most rapidly growing urban zones. Reformist measures to improve these districts are the primary focus of urban planning, but these activities have done little to ameliorate the lack of jobs and development underlying their existence. Up to 70 percent of the labor force in these economically and spatially marginal districts is 'employed' in the tertiary sector. Unless Tunisia and Morocco are able to break from their pasts, this situation is not likely to improve.

State socialist countries

In contrast, the 'state socialist' countries of Algeria, Iraq and, to a lesser extent, Syria show far greater discontinuities with their pasts. Coming from quite different backgrounds, these countries I have classified as Type II now have much in common, at least in terms of avowed goals. For example, Algeria was a French colony for 130 years, until it gained its independence in a bloody and long struggle, whereas Iraq was only briefly and lightly ruled by Britain. And yet their present policies are remarkably similar, suggesting that history can be less determinant than contemporary political ideologies, especially when countries have ample funds to implement them. Current policies are beginning to 'wash out' prior differences in urban historical development, yielding quite similar patterns of urban change.

The long history of urbanization in Syria and Iraq had bequeathed full urban hierarchies to both countries. Iraq's cities were regularly spaced along the north–south axis of the country, as it had been shaped from time immemorial by the Tigris–Euphrates valley. The more diffuse and regular distribution of cities in Greater Syria (which, before the dismemberment of the Ottoman Empire, also included Palestine, Jordan and Lebanon) focused on a north–south axis in the western portion of the country, but also spread east and west, connecting the interior with the Mediterranean. Precolonial Algeria was less well endowed with cities, in part because, throughout the changing dynasties of Islam, eastern Algeria was usually controlled from Tunis, while western Algeria was dominated by Morocco. Nevertheless, by the time the French colonists departed in 1963, they left behind not only the inflated port/capital of Algiers, but a string of other minor ports along the Mediterranean littoral, as well as at least a few towns, such as Bougie and Tlemcen, of historic significance.

Iraq, Syria and Algeria have each built on their urban inheritances, but have also been transforming and decentralizing them. Some 50 to 60 percent of the population in each country lives in urban areas,[3] even though each country has traditionally been, and continues to be, richly agricultural. The capital of each is a sizeable metropolis: Baghdad's population may now have reached 3.5 million, Algiers has at least 1.5 million inhabitants, and Damascus has almost a million. But it is interesting to note that, because of government development planning, aided in all three cases by oil deposits located far from the capital city, secondary cities have been growing – not in a vacuum, but in the context of major agricultural schemes, oil fields, and pipeline terminals and/or heavy industrial developments.

Thus, while the Syrian 'second city' of Aleppo has not quite held its own in the north-west region of the country, the western port cities of Lataqiyah and, especially, Tartus (the terminus of the oil pipeline and the site of oil refineries) have been growing rapidly. Even more dramatic developments are taking place in the north-east extremity of the country where the large dam on the Euphrates, built with Russian aid, has led to the booming urban development of such towns as Raqqah (with a population of over 80 000 now, in comparison to 16 000 in 1960), Hassaqah, and Taqba al-Thawrah (a new town planned and built by the Soviets with some 75 000 residents today).[4]

In Iraq, where urban developments had always been more heavily concentrated in the southern region between Baghdad and the Gulf port-city of Basra, the highest rates of urban growth are now being experienced in the northern part of the country – a development not unrelated to the location of the oil fields, but also stimulated by massive agricultural schemes. Towns of northern Iraq, such as Mosul and especially Kirkuk, are among the fastest growing in the country, and they are being supplemented by new centers as well.

In Algeria, which prior to independence was totally dominated by Algiers, there has been a highly self-conscious planning effort to create counter-poles of attraction by connecting the oil fields of the interior to ports both east and west of Algiers. The mushrooming city of Azrew at the western end of the coast, with its oil terminal, refinery, and iron and steel plants, is not the only, simply the most obvious, fruit of a national policy to spread urbanization more widely.[5]

I would suggest that the similarity in current national planning for urbanization in these three countries is not an accident: it flows quite naturally from a national ideology which has stressed more egalitarian and balanced development, and it has been made possible by state 'socialism' (funded in part through oil and, in the case of Syria, foreign loans) that has favored large development schemes both in land reclamation/irrigation and in heavy industry. Not all of these schemes have been successful, and many are too recent to show dramatic results, but centralized power has made it possible for them to be attempted.

This 'mode of production,' combined with adequately diversified natural resources and a population neither too large nor too small for its economic base, has led to increased utilization of local labor forces. All three countries formerly 'exported' labor. These exports have been reduced, as the surplus has increasingly been absorbed at home. Syria formerly provided seasonal agricultural laborers to Lebanon; not only the political/economic disturbances in Lebanon in recent years, but the agricultural improvement projects connected with the new dam in Syria seem now to have reduced this flow. Algeria, like Tunisia and Morocco today, had formerly disposed of its surplus labor by exporting it to Europe; not only a decline in the demand for such labor in France and Switzerland, but also developments at home have caused a decline in emigration. Iraq, formerly a major exporter of unskilled labor to the countries of the Arabian Gulf, has gradually ceased to play this rôle; cheaper Asian immigrants have taken the Iraqis' place in Gulf economies, and schemes in Iraq have started to absorb more of the surplus.

Under these circumstances, urbanization has been relatively healthy, and linked to economic developments. In all three countries, the location of new cities has been planned in conjunction with development and jobs, and advanced planning has allowed these new cities to follow an orderly process of growth, despite the incompatibility between the needs of construction crews and those of the established cities. Older parts of historic cities are being renovated, or have been displaced by newer constructions, although much remains to be done. The outskirts of existing cities are increasingly ringed with new residential zones which, while perhaps of undistinguished architectural quality, are nevertheless providing mass housing for the growing urban population. Sarifas (provisional reed dwellings formerly used by squatters) are virtually gone from the vicinity of Baghdad, and a curb has finally been placed on the squatter bidonvilles outside Algiers. Syria has been somewhat less successful in 'cleaning up' Damascus, both because it lacks the resources of the other states and because it must cope with a problem that the others do not face, namely, the existence of residual refugee camps of Palestinians. On the other hand, Damascus always grew more slowly than the other capitals, and squatter settlements per se never constituted as great a problem there as they did in either Baghdad or Algiers.

What variations exist among the three 'state socialist' countries are due more to the relative availability of resources than to historic antecedents or future goals. Algeria and Iraq are well endowed with petroleum deposits, and have had sufficient time to begin to reap and reinvest profits from them. (Although development in Iraq has recently been interrupted by the Iraq–Iran War.) Syria is only now beginning to exploit its oil. Estimates of her reserves have recently been revised upwards several times, indicating potential prosperity, but thus far oil has not had a substantial impact upon income. Expenditures for nondevelopmental purposes have also been higher for Syria than for Iraq or Algeria. Syria provided shelter and economic absorption to Palestinian refugees, who now number over 200 000 in the country. Syria experienced the loss of agricultural land on the Golan Heights in the 1967 war with Israel, as well as the devastation of Quneitra, a city that formerly housed about 80 000 persons. Since 1975, Syrian peace-keeping forces have been stationed in Lebanon. But the main handicap Syria has faced is the climate of insecurity which, given the country's greater dependence upon private capitalism, has made development plans particularly vulnerable to the suspended animation and increased uncertainty that has characterized the region since 1967. That physical conditions in Damascus have deteriorated in recent years cannot be denied. That they would have slipped much farther, *ceteris paribus*, without the subsidies Syria has been receiving from wealthier Arab states and from low-interest loans from the Soviet Union and even China, also cannot be denied. Syria is a borderline case. It could easily slip into the third category.

'Charity case' countries

The third type of economy found in the Arab World has no name. I have termed it the 'charity case,' since the countries that fall in this category all depend essentially on 'welfare.' Not one of the remaining countries of the Fertile Crescent – Lebanon, Palestine (both Israel and the Occupied Areas) and Jordan – lives within its means; each is subsidized from outside, and for noneconomic reasons. To these countries, one must now add Egypt, despite its greater size and its more ample resources. Granted, each country lives at a different level of penury or luxury, and each receives its subsidies from different benefactors and through different forms of transfer payments. But in terms of 'mode of production,' one must categorize them together.

The key characteristic of the welfare mode of production is that decision making is disengaged from economic rationality. The key consequence for urbanization of the welfare mode of production is that settlement patterns *need not* have any relationship to internal economic developments. This mode of production operates in the same way that any 'third party payment' does in an economy. It raises prices and allows administrative (or political) discretion to outweigh economically measurable costs and benefits. While, for convenience, I have placed these countries in the same mode of production category, to explain *how* this mode of production affects urbanization it is necessary to treat each country or region separately.

Egypt is a unique case. The giant of the Arab World, with over 40 million inhabitants, Egypt formerly depended almost exclusively on agriculture and the processing of agricultural raw materials (foods and textiles). Although it suffered from a labor shortage at the beginning of the 19th century, by the 20th century that shortage changed to a glut, despite the quadrupling of agricultural production through improvements in irrigation and the introduction of new crops, such as cotton. Population increased even faster than the expansion in the country's economic base, and even though agricultural production has remained labor intensive, surplus population has been thrown into the cities, especially into Cairo since the 1920s. That city now houses some 10 million residents in its metropolitan region, almost one-fourth of the total population.

In the 1950s and 1960s, a corporatist 'socialist' government, under Nasser, attempted what Syria, Iraq and Algeria are now doing, namely, to invest heavily in agricultural expansion (the High Dam at Aswan represents the same strategy as the Euphrates Dam), and to use energy (in this case hydro-electricity) to power heavy industry. This program essentially failed. It failed in part because Egypt lost her sources of foreign exchange in the war of 1967, when Israel conquered the oil fields along the Red Sea and when the Suez Canal, whose user fees had been Egypt's major source of foreign exchange, was closed to traffic. But it also failed more directly through military defeat and through a change in ideology.

Since 1967, Egypt has been heavily subsidized from outside, first through small grants from wealthier Arab states (which, until 1973, were not very wealthy), then, after 1973, through more liberal government-to-government grants as well as personal investments from nationals of *nouveau riche* oil states, especially Saudi Arabia. Much of the rebuilding of the war-damaged cities along the Suez Canal was financed through foreign government subsidies,[6] and much of the incredible real-estate speculation in Cairo must be attributed to the inflow of private capital from the Gulf during the early 1970s. Since the Camp David agreements, the source of Egypt's subsidies has changed. A billion dollars a year has been ear-marked from the USA to 'sweeten the pot' of Egyptian concessions. The economy has had difficulty in absorbing these massive government-to-government payments, since they must pass through the narrow eye of the needle of the Egyptian state, notoriously lugubrious. One of the results is that Cairo is now a vast sea of unfinished construction projects: flyovers that end abruptly, bridges and cloverleafs that do not connect with highways. Clearly, the manner in which city improvements are determined is the key to understanding what is happening in Cairo, and this manner is obviously the result of the 'charity' mode of production. Projects are not subject to cost–benefit considerations. Bribes are paid at the initiation of projects, and there is, therefore, a recurring incentive to begin new ones rather than complete those in progress. Under these circumstances, responsible planning is impossible.

Deficit financing, as a way of life, is inevitably inflationary, whether the deficit is covered by local printing of money or by external infusions. Indeed, Egypt is suffering badly from inflation, which has pushed the cost of living beyond the means of most. Food prices are rigidly controlled to prevent the full impact from being felt by consumers. (When, at the insistence of the World Bank and the AID advisors, Sadat tried to remove part of the subsidies, food riots were the result.) Rents are similarly controlled, which leads to an inevitable deterioration of urban plant, as owners cannot afford to maintain buildings, and the proliferation of hidden bribes (called 'key money') that are necessary to obtain an apartment. No wonder there is a severe housing shortage in Cairo, and heightened occupancy densities.

Although Egyptians were previously reluctant to leave their country, since the mid-1950s Egypt has become a country of labor emigration. While the first emigrants were well educated, mostly Christian and primarily headed for the West, since 1973 particularly, migration has swelled to a massive stream, consisting largely of unskilled and even agricultural laborers, who have gone mainly to adjacent Arab countries. At the minimum, 2 million Egyptians now work outside Egypt, increasingly in the oil countries, but even, ironically enough, in countries such as Jordan, where wages have risen to the point where cheap Egyptian agricultural workers are in demand in that falsely flushed economy.

I say falsely flushed, because Jordan is another economy without 'visible' means of support. It too exists on the largesse of subsidy. Subsidies are of three kinds. First, there is the continuing American subsidy of the military and security forces of the states. While America long ago took over that function from Great Britain, in recent years its price tag has increased enormously; these costs are supplemented by American AID funds directed towards infrastructure and agriculture. Secondly, there is the increasing subsidy from Saudi Arabia and, to a lesser extent, the other Gulf countries; these funds pay for the operation of the civil service and other governmental ventures. And thirdly, there is the more indirect subsidy from the oil states of the Gulf that comes in the form of remittances from Jordanians (mostly of Palestinian origin) who occupy the middle cadres in Kuwait, and increasingly in other places as well. While it is impossible to determine exactly how much money comes to Jordan from these three sources, it is clear that such funds constitute an extremely high proportion of the 'gross domestic product.' (Ameri 1981). Otherwise, it would be impossible to account for the fact that Jordan, and particularly its capital of Amman, has an increasingly higher standard of living, despite the absence of all but the most tenuous local economic base.

Jordan is the chief exporter of labor in the region. It has been estimated that up to half of its labor force may actually be working abroad, primarily in the Gulf.[7] Paradoxically, the situation has become so extreme that there is now a 'labor shortage' in Jordan. The gap between need and availability of labor is being filled by the temporary import of cheaper labor, from Egypt for agricultural and unskilled jobs, from the Far East for construction labor and semi-skilled technicians, etc.

Because of the disengagement between the mode of production and the manner of consumption, Jordan's pattern of urbanization cannot be predicted from internal resource analysis. The remarkable growth of the Amman metropolitan area – which now contains over a million persons (or half of the entire population of the country), and which, in a mindless burst of speculative wheeling and dealing, has now subdivided land for expansion which, by rough calculations, would be sufficient to house the other 50 percent of the country's population – is inexplicable according to the ordinary laws governing urbanization. But then, Amman has been a peculiar case from the very beginning. A small town of 40 000 inhabitants prior to the 1948 expulsion of Palestinians from what then became the territory of Israel, Amman grew within a brief period of time to a quarter and then a half million in size, without essentially altering its economic rationale for existence. Now reputed to contain a population which is 70 percent or more Palestinian in origin, the city has grown by leaps and bounds, despite a terrain and an organization of space which are completely unsuited for such developments. Constructed on seven hills, all of which debouch into the narrow defile of a valley 'downtown,' in good weather the city is snarled by the traffic which congests the center, and in rainy weather is immobilized by the flood waters that collect in the same valley. (The floods are intensified by the hard surfacing of the former wadi and the runoff is increased by erosion, caused by the heavy building that has removed all absorptive ground on the mountains.) Elaborate plans for rectifying the situation have been made by Japanese consultants, who suggest bridges to connect peripheral mountain districts by passing *over* rather than through the downtown – an expensive but probably inevitable expedient (International Engineering Consultants Association (Japan) 1978).

However, the country in the region which has, by far, been on the most liberal 'dole' is Israel which, since its inception, has existed on subsidies, both internal and external. At the time the state came into existence, it was not only funded heavily from outside contributions, but was also the beneficiary of the property, land and infrastructure belonging to the 700 000 Arabs whom it had driven from the country. These subsidies were gradually supplemented by USA government subventions and German reparations, as well as extensive loans. None of these has been able to make the country self-supporting.

According to the International Monetary Fund (reported in *The New York Times* of January 5, 1981), in 1980 Israel had the distinction of topping all other countries in the world in its rate of inflation, while still suffering from unemployment and emigration. (The Jewish Agency recently estimated the number of emigrants during the past five years at about half a million, on a population base of 3.5 million.) In 1980, prices rose by over 130 percent, and the outstanding foreign debt, as of June 1980, stood at over 20 billion dollars. Despite infusions of uncounted billions of dollars in military aid, plus some 3 billion dollars a year, presumably for nonmilitary purposes, from the USA government, in addition to private donations and the now ending reparations from the German government, the economy has not only failed to expand, but investments have been dropping. It is no wonder that Israel is experiencing heightened emigration; Israelis are seeking their livelihoods in New York in the same way that Egyptians and Jordanians are seeking theirs in the Gulf.

In Israel, even more than in Jordan, there is virtually no congruence between 'development' and the evolving pattern of urbanization. But, whereas in Jordan the lack of congruity is due to an artificially stimulated market demand, in Israel it is due to state policy. Within Israel, urbanization is seen as a tool for military and political purposes, rather than as a concomitant of changes in the mode of production. Plans for settlements are devised not as a means of economic development but as a method of territorial delimitation and consolidation of control, as demonstrated by the almost exclusive preoccupation with Jerusalem ever since the 1967 war. Thus, the old walled city of Jerusalem (Arab) is now ringed with skyscrapers whose fortress-like architecture reveals their true purpose. The satellite towns now under construction deep in the West Bank are similarly designed to solidify territorial expansion. Built at a scale far exceeding demand, population has had to be encouraged to move there, in part through rent subsidies, in part by the lack of housing units elsewhere. The settlements in the West Bank territories conquered in 1967 are even more blatantly designed for military and political purposes.[8]

The other side of this distorted process of urbanization has been the systematic destruction of urban and village settlements occupied by Israel's Arab minority. Regulations that prevent the buying and selling of properties, and that make it impossible for non-Jewish citizens to obtain clear title, have resulted in rapid deterioration in the Arab quarters of existing cities in Israel, and their rebuilding for Jewish occupants. The use of eminent domain powers to take land and buildings (from Arabs) to support 'public' purposes (for Jews) is another mechanism that has transformed existing towns (Mushkatel & Nakhleh 1978). More forthright is the bulldozing of sections of, or whole, Arab villages; the subtler version is to deny these settlements water rights, electricity and other infrastructural necessities. All of these techniques are now being extended, with even fewer inhibitions, to the territory of the West Bank.

Given the politicization of urbanization in Israel, it is difficult to evaluate the fact that at present some 84 percent of the country's population lives in urban areas – a level of urbanization unmatched by any other country in the region, except for the pure city-states along the Arabian Gulf. In fact, this degree of urbanization would be even higher if it were not for the peculiar system of ethnic segregation that confines the Arab minority to their villages of origin, despite their increased integration into the urban economy as daily commuters. If this anomaly were taken into account, one would find that well over 90 percent of the Israeli population is urban or is 'supported' by nonrural modes of production, making it comparable to such city-states as Singapore and Hong Kong.

The West Bank and Gaza, under Israeli occupation since 1967, are similarly living 'on the dole,' although at considerably lower levels of affluence, as might be expected given their more restricted sources of support and the fact that their labor power and other resources are drained into the Israeli economy by familiar colonial methods. Civil servants on the West Bank are still paid by the Jordanian government, which (as pointed out above) gets its funds from outside. Almost every family remaining has at least one member, and often more than one, working outside the country and sending remittances home, although after the 1973 war a large number of families gave up the struggle and joined the expatriot abroad. The 80 000 West Bank refugees still in camps, and the more than 200 000 Gaza refugees living in camps, receive direct 'doles' from the United Nations, although the three cents a day per refugee of UNRWA assistance could hardly support a cat or small dog, and must be supplemented in order to survive.[9]

In the Gaza Strip, the distinction between urban and rural has not made sense since 1948, when that formerly rural area became crowded with refugees; there are now some 400 000 persons living in that tiny district. As a consequence, settlements are closely grouped, even though the main form of economic production was, until the 1967 conquest, agricultural. Since the incorporation of the Gaza Strip into the 'Administered Territories' of Israel, the district has served as a vast reserve labor pool of workers who can be trucked in and out daily to provide Israel with cheap agricultural, service and construction laborers when they are needed, but can be left marginalized when the Israeli economy contracts, as it has recently.

On the West Bank, the population is still largely rural in residence, while increasingly less agrarian in occupation. There are, of course, substantial urban concentrations in Jerusalem and its environs, and in major regional centers such as Nablus, Hebron, and Jenin. But most West Bankers live in smaller places, even though they no longer make their livings in agriculture. (By 1977, only 28 percent of the male labor force living in villages of the West Bank were farmers, which was less than the close to 30 percent who were construction workers, largely working for the Israelis.[10]) This peculiar situation requires explanation. The confiscation of farmlands, the deflection of irrigation water away from Arab settlements, the laws preventing the drilling of new wells by Arabs, etc. have virtually destroyed Arab farming, but the system of military passes and enforced residence in their own communities has prevented them from moving to cities. Instead, they, like the Israeli Arabs and the Palestinians in Gaza, have increasingly become daily commuters, working either in Israel or on projects run by Israelis. Given this disjuncture between their places of residence (rural) and their places of employment (largely urban), none of the usual theories linking forms of settlements to modes of production has much relevance.

Such things have even less relevance in Lebanon, the final country to be discussed as an example of the dole or charity mode of production. Prior to the Israeli invasions of southern Lebanon (beginning in the early 1970s), and the not unconnected civil war that erupted in earnest in 1975 onward, Lebanon would have been in a class by itself: it was a country living by the compradore mode of production. Center of banking and finance for the Arab World, port of entry for goods from all directions, chief nexus for a communication network that made it possible to 'do business' in the Arab World, vacation magnet for wealthy Saudis and Kuwaitis – Beirut had no lack of means or livelihood. By the early 1970s, about 1 million, out of a total population of 3 million, were concentrated in and around that major city (half within the city limits, half within commuting distance in the suburbs). The standard of living was one of the highest in the region, and the literacy rates and the amount and diversity of economic activities were far and away the highest in the Arab World.

The devastations of the 1970s have disturbed the pre-civil war system so drastically that all one can do is to list the symptoms of the disaster; data are obviously lacking to evaluate their magnitude. First, the constant warfare in the south, the Israeli bombardments and strafings, the persistent and occasionally massive incursions, etc. have virtually emptied the southern region of the country. While this region was primarily rural, it did contain the important port-towns of Tyre and Sidon. The former, in particular, was the object of heavy bombardment and an aborted invasion. As early as 1970, the population from the south began to flee to squatter camps on the outskirts of Beirut. That thin trickle grew in intensity in the years that followed, as refugees were forced from the battle zones. Their growing presence in Beirut was highly visible evidence of the government's total impotence to protect its borders, and their needs and pressures helped to light the spark that ignited into the civil war.

Since then, the population has been sorting itself out regionally, until West Beirut has come to be the domain primarily of Muslims, Lebanese and Palestinian alike, while East Beirut and northward has become the province of Christians. Beirut is now a dual city with its former downtown (devastated and destroyed by the fighting) serving as a no-man's land between two hostile camps. Within each subcity there is much more vitality than one would expect, given the newspaper accounts of disorder. New commercial quarters have evolved, squatters have pre-empted abandoned buildings and sea resort cottages, utilities have been reconstructed, and people have adjusted their lives to the volcano by picking their paths carefully, by staying inside at night, and by literally becoming immune to the sounds of explosions and gunshots.

The civil war not only disrupted settlement patterns, but, far more important, it disrupted the entire economic base upon which Beirut life had been built. No longer could the port function as entrepot for the region. New routes had to be found, accounting in part for the impressive growth of Syrian ports to the north and Gulf and Red Sea ports to the south and east. The banks were pillaged, and some foreign banks have never re-opened. Communication is often interrupted, and Bahrain has taken advantage of this to offer itself as a substitute gateway to the great markets of the oil rich. No single country has attracted all the foreign corporations that were formerly based in Beirut: some withdrew to Athens, others attempted (with great frustration) to set themselves up in Egypt, Amman wooed some, and still others have never found a convenient substitute.

How, then, does Lebanon make its living, now that its old bases are destroyed? While the statistical evidence is missing that would permit an estimate of the magnitude and sources of its receipts from abroad, the only logical answer to that question is that Lebanon subsists upon foreign subsidies. The sources are multiple, reflecting a variety of political interests, and being funneled through very different channels. The secessionist forces of Haddad in the south are subsidized by Israel; the Palestinian forces of West Beirut are supported in part by Syria, in part by the oil states; the Christian forces of the north are presumably being aided by the USA, possibly indirectly through the Israelis. With multiple sources and multiple sets of recipients, and a country in the midst of war, it is clear that, especially in Lebanon, there can be no connection between patterns of investment and patterns of urbanization. The situation demonstrates, to a degree bordering on parody, the pitfalls of the 'dole' mode of production and the urbanization associated with it.

Oil and sand countries

An even stranger mode of production is beginning to characterize the Arab countries blessed with petroleum and little else – our fourth type of economy, based on oil and sand. I have been hard pressed to find an adequate term to denote the mode of production in these countries. To some extent, the old 'Asiatic mode' might be made to apply, although that application is close only for the mode of appropriation; it does not fit the form of labor being utilized, for which I have had to invent a new term, 'rent-a-slave.' Let me try to explain what appears to be going on, and give my tentative analysis of it.

The exploitation of the oil resources concentrated near and in the Arabian Gulf goes back in time to the third and fourth decades of this century, but it was neither on the scale of the present nor were operations in the hands of the occupants of the countries from which oil was being extracted. The mode of production was that of an enclave; it was an extraterritorial mining operation. Concessions were held by foreigners who controlled the rate of removal, who supervised the transfer to and the exchange on the world market, and who handled all technical and business operations. A subset of 'natives' provided cheap, unskilled labor as needed. In an enclave economy, it is assumed that profits will be repatriated, that the concession area will be 'a world unto itself,' and that there will be little local spillover to affect the indigenous economy. That, indeed, was the early situation in Saudi Arabia and Kuwait, some of the first Arab countries to produce oil.

After the middle of this century, this situation began to change, although more slowly than one might have expected. First, there was a growing sentiment that the rulers of the producing countries should be given a higher share of the profits; later, that demand was expanded to include a larger share of the decision making as well. In the meantime, other places were entering the picture. Oil was discovered in Libya by the late 1950s, and in the 1960s it was being extracted in quantity all along the Arabian Gulf to meet growing world demand. But, as yet, there were only a few governments autonomous enough to negotiate with the foreign companies for greater returns and control. Not until independence was achieved could the mode of production change from an enclave to a national economy. Table 5.2 shows the approximate dates of discovery and large-scale extraction of oil in selected Arab states, together with the date of the establishment of independence, current government, or newly constituted state.

From the table, it is evident that, prior to 1971, the idea of an official Arab oil embargo was inconceivable. Since the early 1960s, the states of the Organization of Petroleum Exporting Countries (OPEC) had been trying to create a producers' cartel to counteract the foreign cartels that had previously colluded to set prices and control supply. In the late 1960s, the Organization of Arab Petroleum Exporting Countries (OAPEC) was established, but full membership had to await the early 1970s. By 1973, Saudi Arabia was in a position to lead the latter in an oil embargo. While the embargo failed to achieve its avowed political ends, it did strengthen the producers' cartel, or at least demonstrate that it could cut off supplies and thus force prices to rise to world demand.

Table 5.2   Arab states totally dependent on oil exports, by dates of oil discovery, large-scale extraction, and political constitution.

Name of country	Year oil first discovered	Year oil first extracted in quantity	Year of establishment of current government
Bahrain	1932	1940s*	1971
Kuwait	1938	1946	1961
Libya	1958	1961	1969†
Oman	1964	1967	1970
Qatar	1939	1971	1971
Saudi Arabia	1933	1958	1932
United Arab Emirates‡	1960s		1971
(largest components)			
Abu-Dhabi		1962	
Dubai		1969	
others		1970s	

* These reserves are now close to depletion.
† Libya independent of Italy in 1951; monarchy overthrown 1969.
‡ Seven 'city states' united.
Source: data compiled from separate entries in Haddad and Nijim (1978).

The trebling of oil prices between 1973 and 1975, coupled with the new *modus vivendi* with the oil companies, unleashed a dramatic process in which the walls surrounding the enclave economy broke down, flooding the surrounding societies with wealth. This process (which had earlier begun in Kuwait) spread to Saudi Arabia, to Libya, and to the several small principalities of the Gulf. In each country, elaborate plans were devised to utilize the glut of foreign exchange which was suddenly available, in part because of greater autonomy, in part because of the higher per-barrel prices. Local economies were infused with wealth, and the commensurate expansions in local facilities (for both production and consumption) generated an enormous demand for labor.

However, the physical characteristics of these beneficiaries of the oil boom made it difficult to absorb either the wealth or the ambitious plans. All were sparsely populated zones, as was appropriate to their terrain (largely desert), and their prior mode of production. Modest agrarian settlements were found in small and especially favored spots along the coast in Libya, in the extreme south-west of Saudi Arabia, and on the coast of Oman. Fishing, pearling, and some sea trade were also to be found in scattered enclaves along the coast of the Gulf. Mostly, however, there was nomadic herding throughout the desert areas. This was hardly an economic base capable of supporting a large population, or of providing the kind of labor force that instant industrialization/modernity demanded.

The fact that so many of the nearby Arab states were in severe economic difficulties, and that many had been victimized by the festering hostilities in the region, meant that they could easily provide the needed labor force. The first place that began to absorb labor in large quantities was, of course, Kuwait, to which displaced Palestinians flocked from the late 1950s onward. Their numbers increased in the 1960s and early 1970s, and were supplemented by immigrants from other Arab countries as well. By 1965, there were a quarter of a million migrants living as 'foreigners' in Kuwait, of whom close to 190 000 were from Arab countries. The remainder hailed primarily from Iran, India and Pakistan. By 1975, the number of noncitizen residents had more than doubled. Almost 420 000 Arabs had migrated to Kuwait (or had actually been born there, since a second generation was appearing), their numbers augmented by another 100 000 migrants from Asian non-Arab countries. Given the fact that, in 1975, Kuwaiti nationals numbered only 472 100, and that, of these, fewer than 20 percent were economically active, one can readily see the extent to which the economy had become overwhelmingly dependent upon migrant labor.[11] By that year, some 70 percent of the economically active members of the labor force in Kuwait were foreigners (Birks & Sinclair 1980, Table 8, p. 132).

Over time, other oil countries began to emulate Kuwait, becoming increasingly dependent upon immigration for their labor supplies. Table 5.3 summarizes, as accurately as possible given the poor quality of the data, the extent to which non-nationals had become an important component of total population in various oil states by 1975. The table also shows the number of 'guest' workers in each country by that year, and the ratio of workers to dependants.

As can readily be seen, by 1975 citizens of Kuwait, the United Arab Emirates, and Qatar had already become minorities in their own countries, while foreign nationals constituted between a fifth to a fourth of all residents in the other countries. This posed an important political and moral dilemma. To what extent should the migrant population share in the wealth that came from the mineral resources of the land – wealth that, given a political system that approximated the Asiatic mode, was gathered into the patrimonially organized state, and then redistributed largely in the form of welfare payments ('free' educational, health and utility services, heavily subsidized housing, pensions, etc.)? To what extent should the migrant population share in the privileges of citizenship and potential political power?

The answer to both questions was essentially negative. Foreign migrants have largely been denied citizenship through naturalization (the number of foreigners nationalized annually is minimal in all states), and the distribution of welfare services has been distinctly two tiered. Nationals receive preferential treatment in the distribution of public

Table 5.3 Importance of migration and immigrant labor in the oil-producing Arab states, 1975.

Country	Citizen population (1)	Non-national population (2)	Total resident population (1) + (2)	Percentage of total population who are non-nationals	Number of 'guest workers'	Percentage of non-nationals who are workers
Kuwait	472 100	502 485	974 585	52	208 000	41
United Arab Emirates	200 000	456 000	656 000	70	251 000	55
Qatar	70 000	97 000	167 000	58	53 700	55
Libya	2 223 000	531 475	2 754 475	19	332 400	63
Saudi Arabia	4 592 500	1 565 000	6 157 500	25	773 400	49
Oman	550 000	132 250	682 250	19	70 700	53
Bahrain	214 000	56 000	270 000	21	30 000	54

Source: data have been assembled from entries in Tables 1, 3, 6, 9, 13 and 14 of the statistical appendix to Birks and Sinclair (1980). Computations mine.

goods, and dual salary scales are used to widen the income gap between national and foreign workers further. (In Kuwait, salaries of nationals are twice those of foreigners in the same occupations.) The 'drain' on the economy from foreign workers has been further minimized through rigid restriction of work permits, and through control over the admission of dependants. As can be seen from the final column in Table 5.3, the ratio of dependants to workers among foreign nationals averages less than 1 (Birks & Sinclair 1980, Tables 13 & 14, pp. 137–9). Obviously even before 1975, attempts were being made to keep the potential contradictions within each society to a minimum, by excluding foreigners from the political system, by regulating their numbers through immigration restrictions, and by requiring annual work permits, which made the right to renew residence contingent upon labor needs in the national economy, and upon cooperative behavior on the part of migrants. But the fact that in Kuwait, Saudi Arabia, and Libya, the overwhelming percentage of the migrants shared Arab identity, culture and language with their hosts meant that discriminatory treatment was mitigated to some extent by other considerations. On the other hand, such places as the United Arab Emirates, Qatar, Oman, and Bahrain had already devised an alternative arrangement. They were already importing their labor from the non-Arab countries of Asia, according to a system which contained the nucleus of what elsewhere I have called the 'rent-a-slave' mode of labor relations (Abu-Lughod 1981a). Whereas only 11 percent, 3 percent and 6 percent of the immigrant populations in Kuwait, Libya and Saudi

Arabia respectively were of non-Arab origin in 1975, the proportions in UAE, Qatar, Oman, and Bahrain were, respectively, 68 percent, 60 percent, 78 percent and 65 percent. And these proportions had shown an increase during the preceding five-year period (Birks & Sinclair 1980, Table 12, p. 136).

Since 1975, the number of migrant workers in the economies of the oil-producing states is estimated to have doubled, although exact figures are impossible to obtain. With the exception of Libya, which has drawn its guest workers increasingly from adjacent Tunisia, the rest have taken advantage of their proximity to the vast labor reserve armies of Asia to supplement or replace their Arab guest workers by importing their workforces not only from India and Pakistan (the traditional Asian sources), but, increasingly, from Korea, Thailand, the Philippines, and Sri Lanka.

The advantages are enormous. First, migrants lay no moral claims to nationality. Secondly, migrants are recruited for specific tasks, with the understanding that their sojourn will be temporary; they are therefore not accompanied by dependants. Thirdly (and increasingly), such recruitment is carried out through a 'turn-key' contract, in which an Asian government or entrepreneur agrees to provide the labor required for a specific construction project, to discipline the workforce it recruits, to house it in barracks located on site (and therefore insulated from native residential zones), to provide food and maintenance as well as housing for its workers, and to repatriate them when the project is completed.

This system keeps labor costs to an absolute minimum, while also eliminating any prospect of welfare and political demands – the two dilemmas that Arab labor migrations had posed. In its purest form, the new system is equivalent to 'renting' a labor force, rather than either 'owning' it, as in slavery, or buying it, as in a free-wage labor economy. In both of the latter cases, wages must be partially determined by the costs of reproducing the labor. In the former case, such costs are borne by the sending country which has raised the workers to adulthood, which will support them in old age, and which provides shelter and food to wives and children. And yet, given the differential wages, Asian countries are eager to provide unlimited quantities of cheap labor on this basis. The host country gains not only an inexpensive labor force, but one which makes no political or social demands.

The result of this process is turning the oil-producing countries of the Gulf (with the possible exception of Kuwait) into the obverse of the old foreign enclave economy – the system with which they began. Initially, it was the foreign enclave that controlled production and siphoned off profits made from the mineral wealth and the labor power of the host society; little of that wealth seeped through to the larger society. Today, increasingly, wealth is being generated by a combination of local mineral resources and a foreign enclave of labor power, with little of that wealth filtering through to the foreign enclave of workers.

What are the implications of the system for urbanization? First, cities serve mainly as sites for consumption, rather than production. They are the arenas in which patrimonial largesse is chiefly distributed, in the form of housing, utilities, schools, health services, and the like. Cities, therefore, exert an irresistible attraction for citizens. Nomads are sedentarized there. Agriculturalists abandon their poor-yielding occupations to resettle there. The élite must be in the major city in order to participate in the political division of spoils, and royalty, merchants and traders benefit enormously from their new rôles as legally required 'national' partners for international firms, as agents for importers, and as influence peddlers for lucrative spot oil contracts.[12] As centers of consumption, the cities also attract the lion's share of migrants who perform many of the governmental and service functions oriented toward public and private consumption. As much as 75 percent of the labor force in each country is engaged in services; only a small percentage is involved in manufacturing or other industry-related production; and only 5 percent is involved in agriculture, or other primary production.

Secondly, given the inhospitable terrain, cities are the only way in which the greatly increased population can be absorbed and handled. In the case of such city–states as Bahrain, Kuwait, Qatar, and the seven principalities that make up the United Arab Emirates, this is literally correct, with the additional proviso that only one urban center per mini-state is sufficient, in most instances, to absorb virtually all of the population. As can be seen from Table 5.1, the result is that from 80 to 90 percent of the population in each state lives in the city. While the overall percentages are lower in the geographically more extensive states, i.e. Libya, Saudi Arabia, and Oman, this situation appears to be only temporary, unless agriculture can be rescued from its declining spiral.

Thirdly, because of the extremely rapid rates at which the major cities have been growing during this recent period of dramatic shift from nomadism to urbanism, an extraordinarily high percentage of current urban residents are 'migrants,' in the sense of having moved to the city from elsewhere. Findlay (1980) has attempted to rank order a selected number of Arab cities by proportion of migrant–residents. It is significant that nine of the top ten cities on his list were located either in Saudi Arabia, Kuwait, Qatar, or the United Arab Emirates. Some of these percentages were as high as 85 or 90 percent.

This prevalence of migrants in the cities gives rise to the fourth characteristic of the cities – their ethnic segregation. As has been noted earlier, migrants are of three basic types. First, there are local citizens who have gathered increasingly in the cities. These tend to reside in their own quarters, their segregation ensured by preferential land distribution and the loan and rental subsidies earmarked by the government for nationals. Secondly, there are the migrant workers, mostly from Arab countries, who are accompanied by their families and view their sojourn as long term, if not permanent. They occupy multi-family housing within the city, for which they compete on the open market. Unable to qualify for housing in the subsidized quarters occupied by nationals, they are *de facto* segregated – by nationality at the minimum, but often according to even finer breakdowns of life-style, income, and class as well. In places which, even before oil, were hospitable to Asian residents (such as Dubai, for example), there may also be ethnic-specific quarters for Pakistani and Indian families. The third type of migrant, newly imported as part of the evolving 'rent-a-slave' system, is even more isolated, physically and socially, from the urban population. If employed in the city, this exclusively male labor force will be housed in isolated 'camps' at the outskirts. If employed in construction projects in developing areas, these workers will be accommodated in temporary structures distant from established urban areas. Only the minority who work as domestic servants are not residentially segregated, but that is only because they often live on the premises in which they work.

These four characteristics of the process of urbanization yield the new type of city that is appearing in the countries of oil and sand. The fact that these countries are primarily centers of consumption (and conspicuous consumption at that), rather than of production, gives them the appearance of gigantic 'display cases' for goods. Not only are vast areas given over to shops where imported goods are redundantly displayed, but even the new buildings themselves look as if they are on display. Set next to straight, wide boulevards (the urban design least adapted to the climate), the new buildings, shiny and often decorated, almost bejeweled on their surfaces, symbolize the ability to buy. Many of the residences are palatial in size, with interiors copied from glossy 'House Beautiful' advertisements. While obviously most residents do not occupy palaces, class gradations are mainly apparent through a diminution of scale and opulence, rather than through any difference in taste or aspiration.

Because the cities have been growing so quickly and have been drawing in, like some powerful vacuum cleaner, populations from decidedly different backgrounds, they have a distinctly uneven and unfinished quality. Construction cranes hover over the skyline like a herd of giraffes. Construction materials clog the ports, or lie, in untidy piles, on almost every vacant lot. Isolated structures arise without warning in the midst of sandy wastes. Into this unfinished urbanscape are going unfinished urbanites. Neatly arranged bungalow housing projects contain families whose teenage children were born in tents. The dwarfed remnants of the Gulf's traditional cities (graceful constructions of warm-toned pressed brick and mud-wash) end, without grace, at arbitrary points where a new highway interrupts their former flow. Often, the indigenous population has abandoned these areas for new quarters built in the Western style; their places have been taken by Pakistani or other Asian families. At the outskirts of these cities are other unfinished zones, temporary shack-towns, some containing newly sedentarized bedouins, others containing Filipino laborers, or only partially demobilized soldiers from Korea.

And, finally, because of the system of multiple-status labor migration, and the increasingly uneasy relation between foreigners and citizens, caste-like residential segregation is coming to characterize the evolving spatial pattern. Ethnicity, not unrelated to class, is the dominant different-iating element in the various urban quarters. One is told, 'this is where the . . . live, and this is where the . . . live,' as if this were the natural order of things. In fact, however, such segregation is the conscious product of government policy. While, presumably, the temporary quarters for tem-porary laborers will eventually disappear, the more permanent ethnic ghettos will be harder to eliminate. Indeed, with time, they grow increas-ingly, institutionalized into some present-day version of the millet system, as they develop their own social and commercial services, and as they are held accountable, by the government, for their own good conduct.

Summary

It has not been possible to do more in this chapter than sketch the main outlines of the diverse forms of urbanization that now co-exist in the Arab World. If, at some previous point in time, it was possible to generalize about cities in the wide region encompassed by Arabo-Islamic culture, it is clear that such generalizations are no longer realistic. I have tried to show how the wide variations that exist are directly related to the rôle each country and/or region has come to play in the global division of labor. Thus, within such residual neocolonies as Morocco and Tunisia, slower growth, plus a weak economy that cannot do without the input from self-help, have led to the perpetuation of many of the older traditional architectural urban forms. In the national socialist states, some reno-vations of older cities have been possible, and new mass housing has been added which, while scarcely 'traditional' in style, is at least designed and constructed locally, with an eye to cultural preferences. In countries I have classified as living 'on the dole', no single pattern of urbanization prevails, but in all cases one notes a progressive disengagement between urban expansion and the economic development that fails to keep pace with it. And, finally, in the hastily expanding cities of the oil-producing states, the evolving urban design and architecture are as unindigenous as the labor that constructs and runs them.

Although we are therefore unable to generalize about urbanization in the region, we can place the entire region within a common framework, albeit one that has a different impact on the individual parts. The Arab World, unlike China, or even India, continues to be deeply enmeshed in the political and economic system of the world. Because of its geopolitical position and its vital resources, it has not been permitted the luxury of temporary 'withdrawal' which might give it the chance to determine the modalities of its connection to the world system, or to experiment with indigenously generated forms of development or urbanization. It is unlikely that this situation will change drastically in the near future. Thus far, however, because the region is fragmented into so many separate political units, inequities have been growing, and overall strength has been handicapped. The effects of the inequities actually give rise, in large measure, to the four contrasting types that are causally linked to one another. The problems in each cannot be solved without reference to the others, and the overall problem of impotence in the international arena cannot be overcome without greater unity and the equity such unity could engender. Only in such a case might it be possible once again for urbanization in the Arab World to take on a common character.

At the moment, then, it appears that the cultural context of urban development is taking second place to the political and economic context. And yet this would not be totally accurate, nor need it be true in the future. Arab cities, regardless of which mode of production dominates their national economies, retain social and familial patterns, unique to their culture and incorporate urban and architectural features, that recall an earlier era of cultural unity. If economic and political stability can be achieved through unity and more equal sharing of resources, it is possible that cultural and architectural authenticity and commonality may once again fill the Arab World with great cities to rival those created in the historic past.

Notes

1 See, for example, the attempt in Abu-Lughod and Hay (1979).
2 The beginning of the classification system used in this chapter was attempted (although not without confusion) in Abu-Lughod (1980a, pp. 39–44).
3 The congruence in their levels of urbanization is partially masked by the different definitions used. The most 'precise' definition is that used in the Syrian census, which makes a distinction between the urbanized population *within* administrative units which are primarily 'urban,' and the rural population of the same zones. Only the urbanized population is included in computing the overall urbanization rate. Algeria includes the total population of all legally constituted 'communes,' whether these populations live under urban or rural conditions. And, in the case of Iraq, no real attempt is made to distinguish between the urbanized portion of provinces and the rural, which makes all calculations of the Iraq urbanization rate somewhat tentative.

4 Among the sources that can be consulted on recent developments in Syria (based primarily upon findings released in the *Statistical yearbook* since a new census was conducted only in 1980) are: United Nations Economic Commission for Western Asia (1980), David (1978), and Mahayni (1980). Two volumes of the proceedings are forthcoming.

5 I depend in part upon Sari (1980).

6 The various quarters are actually named after the donors, e.g. Shaykh Zayd City, etc.

7 The standard source is fast becoming Birks and Sinclair (1980), authors of the general book that evolved as a culmination of their various country-specific studies. In these earlier (mostly unpublished) papers, there was already recognition of Jordan's rôle as a supplier of manpower in the Gulf, and the hint that the local economy was already suffering from 'excessive' labor export. I have my own reservations about the accuracy of some of their figures, and, in any case, caution must be exercised when dealing with Jordan per se, since West and East Banks must be analyzed separately.

8 There has been a whole series of plans in Israel which have made no secret of these connections. Some, like the Allon plan, have been made public; most exist in typescript and are intended only for limited circulation. A fuller survey of these plans (including those for Galilee, the main concentration within pre-1967 Israeli borders of its Arab population) can be found in Abu-Lughod (1981b). In this, I depend heavily on the scholarly dissertation of Harris (1980).

9 The population living in camps is smaller than the population classified as refugees and therefore receiving UNRWA assistance. Detailed figures are issued annually through the United Nations. See the *Annual reports* of the Director-General of UNRWA and the series entitled *Registration statistical bulletin*.

10 *The statistical abstract of Israel, 1978*, Table XX. This volume contains a length appendix presenting data from a 1977 survey of the 'administrative territories', i.e. the West Bank and Gaza. It should be noted that these figures constitute a minimum, rather than a maximum, since they include only *legally* employed workers. According to Farajun (1978), illegal employment is extensive on the West Bank.

11 Excellent census publications are available for 1957, 1965, 1970, 1975, and should soon be available for 1980. However, many of these figures have been incorporated into the tables presented in the appendix to Birks and Sinclair (1980). For the 1975 labor force participation rate of Kuwaiti nationals (19.4 percent), see Table 6, p. 131.

12 Ibrahim (1982) gives an excellent account of the laws and new 'rôles.'

References

Abu-Lughod, J. 1971. *Cairo: 1001 years of the city victorious*. Princeton, NJ: Princeton University Press.

Abu-Lughod, J. 1980a. The growth of Arab cities. *Middle East yearbook 1980*. London: IC Magazine.

Abu-Lughod, J. 1980b. *Rabat: urban apartheid in Morocco*. Princeton, NJ: Princeton University Press.

Abu-Lughod, J. 1981a. *Labor migrations in the Arab region*. Unpublished paper.

Abu-Lughod, J. 1981b. *Israeli settlements in occupied Arab lands*. Presentation to United Nations Seminar on the Question of Palestine. Unpublished paper.

Abu-Lughod, J. and R. Hay Jr (eds.) 1979. *Third World urbanization*. New York: Methuen.

Ameri, A. 1981. *Socioeconomic development in Jordon 1950–80: an application of dependency theory*. Doctoral dissertation, Detroit: Wayne State University.

Birks, J. S. and C. A. Sinclair 1980. *International migration and development in the*

Arab region. Geneva: International Labour Office.

Clarke, J. I. 1980. Contemporary urban growth. In *The changing Middle Eastern city*, G. H. Blake and R. I. Lawless (eds.), 34–53. London: Croom Helm.

David, Jean-Claude 1978. L'urbanisation en Syrie. *Maghreb-Machrek* **81**, 40–9.

Farajun, E. 1978. Palestinian workers in Israel: a reserve army of labour. *Matzpan Red Pages* **5**.

Findlay, A. M. 1980. Migration in space: immobility in society, In *The changing Middle Eastern city*, G. H. Blake and R. I. Lawless (eds.), 54–76. London: Croom Helm.

Haddad, H. and B. Nijim (eds.) 1978. *The Arab World: a handbook*. Wilmette: Medina Press.

Harris, W. W. 1980. *Taking root: Israeli settlement in the West Bank, the Golan and the Gaza–Sinai, 1967–1980*. New York: Wiley.

Ibrahim, S. E. 1982. *The new Arab social order: a study of the social impact of oil wealth*. Boulder, Colorado: Westview Press.

International Engineering Consultants Association (Japan) 1978. *Preliminary study on the city center development for municipality of Amman, the Hashemite kingdom of Jordan*. Mimeo report.

Mahayni, R. 1980. *Impacts of urbanization on Syria*. Unpublished paper presented to the International Symposium on Islamic Architecture and Urbanism, Dammam.

Mushkatel, A. and K. Nakhleh 1978. Eminent domain: land use planning and the powerless in the United States and Israel. *Social Problems* **26**, 147–59.

Sari, J. 1980. Le cas de l'Algérie. In *Systeme urbain et développement au Maghreb*, A. Mouschi, F. Stambouli, K. Chateur *et al*. (eds.), 105–116. Tunis: Cérés Productions.

United Nations Economic Commission for Western Asia (ECWA) 1980. *The population situation in the ECWA region*. Series of pamphlets dealing with individual countries.

6 The urban culture and the suburban culture: a new look at an old paper

PETER HALL

Aging academic authors are occasionally permitted the indulgence of re-reading favorite old papers, and considering how well they have stood the test of time. This contribution represents one such rare luxury. In 1967, I delivered a paper (published in 1968) that incorporated some views on the evolution of cities in North America and in Europe (Hall 1968). Its title, *The urban culture and the suburban culture*, encapsulated its major theme: that a new kind of suburban form and suburban culture was evolving in the United States, different in kind from (but in no sense necessarily inferior to) the traditional urban form and urban culture that had characterized Europe since the time of the Ancient Greeks. Here, I want to re-examine these views of the 1960s to see how well, or badly, they stand up in the very different world of the 1980s. I will first try to summarize the argument of the paper. Then, I will try to give a personal view of the main changes that have occurred to the world – and to ask, in that light, how valid the paper still seems to be. Lastly, I will try to speculate on changes still to come, and on their implications for the thesis.

The argument

American cities, the paper suggested, had begun to develop in ways quite unlike the traditional city that had characterized the Western urban world for at least 2000 years. This traditional city was compact and centered. There was a defined central business district, which was also the center of administration and of culture. Around it were dense residential areas, the inhabitants of which enjoyed a high density of face-to-face contacts with each other. The two together gave the city a sense of form, of coherence, of organic life. In contrast, the new city – which reached its classic form west of the Mississippi, in the cities that had developed in the 20th century under the influence of the automobile – had no dominant central business district, or any other center; it consisted of low-density suburbs, loosely strung together; it lacked face-to-face contact. In consequence, it was attacked by traditional urbanists, who saw in it the disintegration of the values they associated with urban culture: propinquity, interaction, diversity, and richness were replaced by separation, segregation, remoteness, privacy, and heterogeneity.

It followed, logically, that these traditional urban planners should deliberately aim to frustrate what they saw as the 'disintegration' of the city and of the urbanity that it represented. They could do this by maintaining existing centers, and developing new ones; by restricting suburban sprawl, through policies of urban containment; by promoting neighborhood ties, through the planning of neighborhood units and the maintenance of social mix within them; and by giving ready access to the open countryside, again through policies of urban containment. European planners had been fairly successful in achieving these ends; American planners, sharing the same values in a different culture that was less hospitable to the planning idea, had been more frustrated because their rôle was less generally accepted.

Looking in depth at the planners' case for intervention, we find that it was a mixture of the esthetic, the social, the economic, and even the organic. Sprawl was described as 'bad esthetics' and 'bad economics' (Whyte 1958 p. 117); urban form was described as having 'disintegrated,' and a 'raw, dissolute environment' was alleged to produce 'a narrow, constricted and baffled social life' (Mumford 1938, p. 8). Basically, though, it appeared that the charge brought against the 'new city' was one of lack of form: '. . . a modern city, no less than a medieval town . . . must have a definite size, form, boundary' (Mumford 1938, p. 397). The new city lacked these qualities, and so, by definition, must stand condemned.

However, the embarrassing fact remained that people were voting for it – with their feet. The new cities were burgeoning in what has since been christened the American sunbelt, while the older cities were stagnating. Furthermore, if the new cities had any intellectual defenders at all, they were in the sunbelt itself, and especially in California. The intriguing possibility thus existed that the new urban culture was in reality not an aberrant form, but a prototype for the year 2000 and beyond. The real criterion, the paper went on to argue, was not the personal or group values of the 'expert,' but the quality of life as perceived by the ordinary person. And here the evidence failed to support the prejudices.

The first question was whether the quality of life in the new suburban areas of the 'new cities' was in any sense different from, or inferior to, the quality of life as lived in older suburbs of older cities. Suburbs after all, are not a new urban form: both in Europe and the USA, they are at least as old as the 'streetcar suburbs' of the last quarter of the 19th century (Warner 1962). There is not much evidence that life in these suburbs, or the values that underlay that life, have ever varied very much. Suburbanites are not the 'cosmopolitans' of the middle-class, gentrified inner city; nor do they represent ethnic or class enclaves ensconced in their 'urban villages;' nor yet do they demonstrate the pathological culture characteristic of the 'urban jungle.' Rather, they constitute the great mass of the population of any city in any advanced industrial society. They are the people who build nuclear families, and seek the most suitable physical environment for that purpose. The only difference, comparing streetcar suburbs in 19th-century Boston with automobile suburbs in 20th-century Los Angeles, is that the greater mobility of the latter-day suburbanites gives them command over more space per family. Yet the way of life lived in that space, in both new and old suburbs, was intensely private and familial.

This fact had to some extent been obscured, because some of the classic sociological studies of suburbs had not been of standard cases, but rather of upper-middle-class suburbs where the inhabitants had rather different values. The danger was that, by and large, sociologists were themselves upper middle class; they did not necessarily understand the values of the great bulk of suburbanites. But there were honorable exceptions: Herbert Gans, in his classic study *The Levittowners*, was one (Gans 1967).

The other question was whether, in fact, the new suburbs lacked the essential quality of centrality, which detracted from their urbanity. To this, the answer seemed to be that indeed the new suburbs had centrality – but in a different way. Because of its great size and scale, the new urban form was characterized by the development of subcenters. By the early 1960s, the work of Vance had already indicated that in North America, a diverse, high-level center could develop with a minimum supporting population of about 300 million (Vance 1962, p. 517). Thus, in a metropolitan area of several million, the original central business district progressively became merely the principal center among a number of important subcenters. It might stagnate, as the main weight of population and employment growth took place in distant suburbs, but nowhere at that time was there serious evidence that it was decaying into oblivion. Indeed, even while it might decline as a general shopping center, its status as office center and specialized boutique shopping center might be enhanced. Finally, the paper pointed out, the new city could even manage to produce its own forms of psychological excitement. The characteristic suburban roadside strip, most dramatically illustrated by Las Vegas (a landscape, not of buildings, but of signs, as Tom Wolfe put it in a celebrated essay – Wolfe 1966, pp. 7–8), offered the same kind of sensation to the spectator as Times Square or Piccadilly Circus – except that it was designed to be seen not by a pedestrian, but by a spectator in a car.

Thus, the charges against the new urban form could not be substantiated (or so I argued in 1967). However, in Europe, there was not even a chance to raise them, for, by and large, the new city did not yet exist. Urban containment policies had blocked the growth of extensive low-density suburbs and of new suburban subcenters, but, since populations had continued to grow, and their demands for shopping and other services had to be met somewhere, the result had been higher density suburbaniz-ation coupled with drastic surgical reconstruction of existing city centers.

The conclusion in 1967 was that in the United States, overall, the suburbanization trend would continue. A minority of upper-middle-class cosmopolitans (university professors, media people, other professionals, and especially the unmarried and the childless) would continue to want to live their own preferred life-style in some central cities; and, maybe, their numbers would grow. But the great majority of the population would continue to migrate to the suburbs, and even the more distant exurbs, where they could find the family-centered life-style they wanted. For them, the so-called burden of commuting (which meant perhaps a 30- or 40-minute auto ride along a fairly uncongested freeway) was in reality no burden at all. And (I might have added, though I did not) they doubtless also found in suburbia an escape from the racial tensions, then most obvious in American cities.

In Europe, probably, the planners would continue to ensure that the superficial signs were rather different. But strangely, under the surface, the essential organization would be the same. There too, the monocentric urban form would progressively give way to a polycentric one. There too the suburbs would grow to accommodate inexorable demands, and the suburban style, and the suburban values would dominate. Still, the outward manifestations would be very different.

Changes since 1967

Here, we start by looking at measurable changes that have occurred to the American city since 1967. Then, more speculatively, we discuss possible contributory causes.

Measurable changes   Clearly, the decentralization of the American city, already under way in the 1960s, proceeded apace in the 1970s. But in the latter decade, it took on a new dimension. Standard metropolitan statis-tical areas (SMSAs) continued to decentralize population and employ-ment from central cities to suburban rings; and, by the 1970s, many central cities returned absolute declines in population. However, there was a further outward shift: the growth of SMSAs as a whole began to stagnate, while nonmetropolitan areas grew vigorously. Table 6.1, drawn from preliminary returns of the 1980 census (Hauser 1981), documents these trends.

The evidence suggests that about one-half of this nonmetropolitan growth took place in counties directly adjacent to SMSAs, and thus represented a continuation of the wave-like outward motion of the earlier

Table 6.1   United States population trends, 1970–80.

Area (as of June 19, 1981)	1980 population (millions)	1970 population (millions)	Change 1970–80 (percent)	Percent of US total
USA	226.5	203.3	11.4	100.0
SMSAs (318)	169.4	153.7	10.2	74.8
central cities (429)	67.9	67.8	0.1	30.0
suburbs	101.5	85.6	18.2	44.8
nonmetropolitan areas	57.1	49.6	15.1	25.2
SMSAs and SCSAs of more than 1 million	100.2	93.8	6.7	44.2
SMSAs and SCSAs of more than 2.5 million	68.1	65.2	4.5	30.0

Source: Hauser (1981).

decade (Hall & Hay 1980, pp. 10–14). But about one-half was in non-adjacent counties, often quite remote and far from major cities. This growth, it appears, is directly related to the pressures of tourism, recreation, and retirement.

There was a clear tendency for the bigger SMSAs to show the strongest tendency to stagnation, and even to decline. Smaller SMSAs, in contrast, were often still growing quite vigorously. In the case of the so-called standard consolidated statistical areas (New York–Newark–Jersey City, Chicago–Gary, Los Angeles–Long Beach–Anaheim), there was an obvious tendency for the big, central SMSA to stagnate, while smaller, peripheral SMSAs grew. At the same time, there was also a regional effect: in the sunbelt, some large SMSAs were still growing, though even there (with rare exceptions) central cities tended to be in decline.

To summarize, then: there is a continuing core-ring movement, on to which, in the 1970s, was superimposed a further, more distant movement – from SMSAs to nonmetropolitan areas. There is also a relative shift down the urban hierarchy, as larger SMSAs stagnate, while smaller ones grow. And, finally, there is the regional shift from frostbelt to sunbelt. The clear losers in this process are the larger, older frostbelt cities. The clear gainers are the smaller SMSAs, the sunbelt SMSAs in general, and the nonmetropolitan cities almost everywhere, but especially in areas attractive for recreation and retirement.

Reference here is to population shifts, as chronicled by the first results from the 1980 census. There is still some doubt about the associated shifts in jobs, and in commuting patterns. But one inference can already be drawn: that, on the whole, the outward movement of population has the effect of further weakening the pull of central business districts, especially those in the larger cities. More and more people are almost certainly commuting from suburb to suburb within SMSAs, or within small, nonmetropolitan cities.

The obvious question is whether the United States is unique in these trends. Here, fortunately, we have good evidence from recent studies of Japan and of Europe, conducted within broadly similar spatial frameworks, similar in character to the SMSAs of the American work (Glickman 1978, Hall & Hay 1980). It appears from this evidence that advanced industrial nations are arrayed on some kind of historic continuum, in which Great Britain is the country most like the United States: it began to decentralize populations from cores to rings of metropolitan areas quite early (by the 1960s), and, by the 1970s, its bigger central cities were in a state of rapid decline. Scandinavia, the Benelux countries, and Germany (as well as Japan) are in an intermediate position: they began to exhibit some degree of decentralization in the 1960s, and on a more general scale in the 1970s. Southern Europe and, even more so, France have been at the rear end of the process: though southern Europe showed some degree of decentralization by the early 1970s, France hardly did so at all. And, most extreme, Eastern European cities seemed to have demonstrated a marked degree of *centralization* – even in the 1970s (Table 6.2).

Contributory forces First, the factors that affect the location of employment are changing. The forces behind these major shifts, both in the United States and in other industrial economies, are fairly evident. Manufacturing industry is deserting the inner, older, bigger cities because they are now almost the worst possible locations in terms of appropriate labor supply, accessibility, and land availability or cost. For tertiary industry, the factors are more complex, but even here the pull of the central business district is not as strong as it was: suburban subcenters or campus office parks represent strong rivals in terms of availability of a white collar labor force, ease of access generally, and office rentals.

The second element, highly relevant to change since 1967, is the impact of energy shortages and energy costs in the years since 1973–4. To interpret this is singularly difficult, not least because the situation is so fluid. But, at the start of 1981, the best summary seemed to be: in the United States, annual gasoline consumption was falling and was expected to continue to do so. This was partly due to a quite radical change in the mix of available vehicles under the impact both of market demand and federal regulation (Shackson 1981, p. 77). But there had also been a new feature in comparing 1980 with 1979: a 6 percent fall in miles travelled by vehicle. It seems certain that this had been concentrated on optional vacation or recreational trips, leaving work trips unaffected. And this might be expected to continue as a result of the deregulation of oil prices,

Table 6.2 Europe and regional groups: metropolitan and nonmetropolitan population change, 1950–75.

	1950–60			1960–70			1960–70			1970–75		
	Absolute change ('000s)	Percent change	Percent of total	Absolute change ('000s)	Percent change	Percent of total	Absolute change ('000s)	Percent change	Percent of total	Absolute change ('000s)	Percent change	Percent of total
Atlantic Europe												
core	511	1.87	21.92	−673	−2.42	−22.23	−673	−2.52	−24.36	−628	−2.42	−222.74
ring	1 975	8.75	84.63	3 628	14.78	119.82	3 342	14.52	120.96	951	3.61	337.20
nonmet	−153	−4.47	−6.54	73	2.25	2.41	94	5.44	3.40	−41	−2.24	−14.46
total	2 334	4.38	100.00	3 028	5.44	100.00	2 763	5.37	100.00	282	0.52	100.00
Northern Europe												
core	594	11.99	58.49	396	7.14	31.45	396	7.14	31.45	−267	−4.49	−69.17
ring	315	5.02	30.98	814	12.35	64.54	814	12.35	64.54	604	8.16	156.48
nonmet	107	31.79	31.79	51	1.45	4.01	51	1.45	4.01	49	1.39	12.69
total	1 016	6.95	100.00	1 261	8.07	100.00	1 261	8.07	100.00	386	2.29	100.00
Western Europe												
core	3 981	17.50	63.85	3 992	14.94	53.16	3 988	14.96	53.29	528	1.72	19.96
ring	2 037	7.36	32.67	3 049	10.26	40.60	3 028	10.28	40.46	1 812	5.58	68.51
nonmet	217	2.24	3.48	468	4.73	6.23	468	4.73	6.25	305	2.94	11.93
total	6 235	10.38	100.00	7 509	11.32	100.00	7 484	11.34	100.00	2 645	3.60	100.00
Southern Europe												
core	5 020	22.02	85.80	5 525	19.86	80.75	5 507	20.57	74.05	1 078	3.38	45.68
ring	949	2.51	16.22	2 729	7.05	39.89	2 833	6.58	38.09	2 358	6.35	99.92
nonmet	−118	−0.56	−2.02	−1 413	−7.25	−20.65	−903	−4.88	−12.16	−1 076	−6.11	−45.56
total	5 851	7.17	100.00	6 341	7.82	100.00	7 437	9.39	100.00	2 360	2.72	100.00

Central Europe												
core	3 463	17.98	65.11	na	na	na	914	4.02	14.39	782	4.25	15.46
ring	1 825	4.43	34.32	na	na	na	5 387	12.51	84.85	4 276	12.25	84.54
nonmet	31	9.28	0.57	na	na	na	48	13.38	0.76	0	0	0
total	5 319	8.74	100.00	na	na	na	6 349	9.60	100.00	5 058	9.49	100.00
Eastern Europe												
core	na	na	na	na	na	na	1 974	16.50	58.50	1 212	8.70	70.15
ring	na	na	na	na	na	na	1 400	5.11	41.50	516	1.79	29.84
nonmet	na	na	na	na	na	na	—	—	—	—	—	—
total	na	na	na	na	na	na	3 374	8.57	100.00	1 728	4.04	100.00
Europe												
core	13 570	13.98	65.38	10 153	9.18	40.63	11 192	11.51	50.15	na	na	na
ring	7 102	5.24	34.21	15 607	10.94	62.46	11 417	9.46	51.16	na	na	na
nonmet	85	0.22	0.41	−772	−2.32	−3.09	−290	−.00	−1.30	−763	−2.29	−10.30
total	20 757	7.68	100.00	24 988	8.58	100.00	22 318	8.87	100.00	7 401	2.70	100.00

Source: Hall & Hay (1980).

which would bring the cost of gasoline progressively closer to world market values. Overall, then, there would probably be some shift in behavior patterns. But it was far from clear that this would involve the kind of basic trips made every day in urban areas. In other words, urban travel behavior – and with it, urban form – could be expected to remain much as it has been in the recent past.

Thirdly, and more significant, have been shifts in the financial position of public transportation systems. Throughout 1980 and 1981, regular reports in the American press repeated the same story for city after city: public transportation was going through a period of crisis. British cities reported the same stories; on the European continent, only massive subsidization avoided this fate. The root of the problem is its labor-intensive and fuel-intensive character in a time of inflation, coupled with the failure to renew old and decaying infrastructure, that arose from the fiscal crisis in older American cities. In order to avoid bankruptcy and provide some reserve for the rehabilitation or renewal of equipment, cities have been forced to approve large fare rises that threaten loss of patronage. The problem, which will be only exacerbated by threatened cuts in operating subsidies from Washington, particularly affects the cores of the larger, older eastern and midwestern cities, such as New York, Boston and Chicago, where central business district commuters are reliant on public transport. Here, the risk is that continued fare rises will cause commuters either to seek suburban jobs, or to demand salary rises that in turn will lead their employers to relocate. Whatever the case, there can be no doubt that the crisis in public transportation can only further weaken the position of the central city, and of its central business district.

The fourth major change that has affected cities since 1967 (arguably), is a change in basic values. Throughout the Western world, the late 1960s and the first half of the 1970s saw a reaction against scale, against high technology, and against drastic urban surgery. In city after city, urban freeways and comprehensive redevelopment schemes were stopped in their tracks. Rehabilitation, upgrading, management, and incremental change became the approved jargon of planning. However, the effect of all this on the geography of change is hard to gauge. Some would argue that it has helped make cities more livable, and has thus slowed the rate of potential decline. Others might argue that it has aided the out-movement to small towns and villages in nonmetropolitan America (though, as already noted, no such large-scale movement seems to have occurred in Britain).

In any event, the largely negative image of the big city – as a place of high crime and of general social malaise – has not substantially improved in the United States during the past dozen years, and indeed has spread powerfully to Britain. Within the United States, even cities that until recently prided themselves on their relative freedom from crime (such as

Los Angeles and San Francisco) are now fighting a wave of burglaries and muggings. To some degree, this may have been offset by the general growth of tourism in the more attractive major cities, and by the associated development of hotel, restaurant, and convention facilities. Such a development is general in all Western cities. What is unusual in American cities is the form it takes: highly specialized and integrated interior space, hermetically sealed from the outside world through a battery of security devices, and concentrated in a relatively small part of the former central business district. The visitor to such an area leaves by the way he comes: by taxi or by airport limousine, direct via a freeway ramp from the hotel to the highway that leads to the airport, which invariably, runs for many miles through a landscape of urban decay that has no connection with the life at the center.

Summing up, then: at least in the opinion of this author, the significant developments since 1967 have further weakened the viability of the big cities rather than strengthening it. If there have been pockets of renewal and revival, they are dwarfed by the evidence of further decay. This conclusion applies unequivocally to the American and to the British city. Elsewhere in the world, the evidence is so far not as clear. But numerous pieces of evidence, some of them anecdotal, suggest that the same forces of decay are beginning to make themselves felt there also.

Factors for the future

How far are these forces likely to continue? And what new factors might emerge to change the balance between old city and new suburb? Here, we must necessarily enter into subjective territory. What follows is a strictly personal interpretation.

The first critical element is the availability and cost of energy. In the section above, we suggested that the advanced industrial nations were adapting to higher real energy costs without drastic changes in life-style – and, in particular, without abandonment of the suburban and exurban styles that had characterized the 1960s. But, of course, this comfortable conclusion could be completely upset by a permanent and drastic shortage of energy, or a very rapid increase in costs. Paradoxically, the energy glut of the early 1980s has resulted from the sharp economic recession that has everywhere reduced the demands of the Western nations for oil. An economic upsurge could again transform this equation. The best informed guess is that, though there may again be sudden interruptions in supply as a result of instability in the Middle East or other parts of the world, the overall prospect is for a degree of stability in supplies and in prices – if only because, with the entry on the market of large supplies from new producers like Great Britain (which is now self-sufficient in oil overall), and Mexico, the OPEC cartel is unlikely ever again to exert the same stranglehold as in the late 1970s.

The second element is the possibility of quite large changes in the composition of the total fleet of vehicles and the energy required to fuel it. Since 1967, one quite unforeseen change in the industrialized world has been the startling increase in the numbers of bicycles. In countries like the United States and Great Britain, more bicycles than cars have been produced in each of the recent years. Bicycles, it appears, are replacing the second car as a convenient short-distance means of urban transportation. It appears that the shift is partly a direct response to the costs of motoring, especially in a period of recession. But a general change in values and in attitudes – particularly the ecological movement, and the new emphasis on exercise – is another major factor. This is likely to intensify rather than weaken. At the same time, research is already producing a generation of very small, very economical cars. The Japanese industry, which over the past two decades has set so many market trends, is selling large numbers of these new vehicles in its home market. A breakthrough in fuel supplies, through the development of an efficient electric car, could prove an enormous fillip to this trend. All in all, one should expect a general shift towards a much higher proportion of small, limited-range vehicles, propelled either by human energy or by very small fuel-sparing motors. These will be used mainly for urban trips, and have an effective range of a few miles. They might have some impact in reducing average commuter range, though they may well be used primarily by workers who in any event do not travel far to work. Thus they will tend to reinforce the trend towards short journeys to work at decentralized, small-scale employment centers.

The third new factor, and the one with perhaps the most controversial impact, is the substitution of information for movement of people and goods through the development of the microprocessor and its derivatives. During the 1980s and beyond, virtually all experts are agreed that we shall see a several-fold increase in computing power, and a several-fold decrease in cost. Home computers with a wide range of functions, sophisticated telecommunications able to communicate a great variety of information over long distances, and a gradual linkage of what are now disparate pieces of electronic equipment (the telephone, the television, the calculator), are almost certain developments by 1990. The critical question concerns their impact, particularly upon patterns of living and working, but also on functions like education, shopping, visits to doctors and clinics, and a wide range of functions whose purpose is to gain information. There is no agreement on this point: one viewpoint sees an almost universal displacement of travel by electronic exchanges, the other – pointing to the 100-year history of the telephone – sees the new equipment as merely increasing the need and the desire for further face-to-face contact. Oddly, both effects are possible simultaneously:

there might be a reduction in some kinds of commuting to routine jobs, with a replacement by home work for all or part of the time, but, at the same time, an increase in journeys for higher level professional and managerial contacts, including journeys over long distances by specialists. Insofar as the new technologies affect the location of workplaces themselves, it seems likely that, by equalizing the costs of obtaining information almost anywhere in the globe, they will further reduce the traditional locational advantages of the central city.

All this powerfully suggests that the recent trends in the geography of employment will continue into the 1980s. Not only will manufacturing industry (itself increasingly automated) continue to decentralize to locations more suitable for large-scale integrated processing; additionally, a wide range of tertiary employment will move to locations readily accessible to a suburban or exurban workforce, especially if these have special locational advantages in the form of good environment or access to long-distance transportation facilities (such as the vicinity of major international airports). There may be some differences here between one nation and another, depending on the long-distance transportation mix: Europe and Japan, where the railroad is a much more important factor than in the United States, may find the central locations close to terminal train stations retain their attraction. But, in general, the tendency should again be outwards.

Fourthly, demographic changes may affect the relative position of central city and suburbs – and here, the consequences could just be the reverse of what has been previously outlined. Even in 1967, the original paper called attention to the 'cosmopolitans' who preferred life in the central city. Since then, a rapid (and indeed unforeseen) fall in the birth rate has been accompanied by a tendency to higher rates of household formation. More young people are living alone, while divorce also adds to the numbers of singles. This is related to a profound change in the values of many women, who have rejected familial ties in favor of their careers. Reacting against their suburban childhood backgrounds, many of this generation are seeking homes in the inner cities, thus significantly aiding the process of gentrification (itself a word imported from England but now a force in many American cities). However, for every gentrifier there is also a gentrifiee: a displaced person or persons who must find a home elsewhere. In fact, all the evidence suggests that the net effect of gentrification is further outmigration from the city, since the middle-class gentrifiers demand and obtain more space per person than the largely blue-collar (and minority) people they displace.

At the same time, as already mentioned, other middle-class Americans are rejecting the big city altogether, and seeking homes (and careers) in small towns. This is partly related to the new economic opportunities there in the burgeoning recreation and tourism industries. Whether they continue to burgeon, of course, will depend not only on the growth of discretionary income of urbanites and others, but also on the availability and cost of the fuel necessary to take those urbanites out of the cities at weekends and on vacation – and, as already noted, neither of these elements is likely to be as plentiful in the 1980s as in the 1960s or early 1970s. But, on the other hand, other factors of a social and cultural kind – the rejection of the city as a place of high crime and social malaise, the desire to escape the recession in the worst-hit northeastern and mid-western cities – may continue to aid the outmigration process. Thus, overall, the pattern may increasingly be one of voluntary segregation by life-style and, to some extent, age.

Conclusion

To sum up, then: precisely how much have developments in the last 14 years (and will the possible developments in the next 19) changed the picture given in the paper of 1967? The answer, I think, must be: not very much. Broadly, trends have continued as then predicted. It would take a revolution to affect most of them; we have not had one, and the best guess is that we shall not have one. There is no better reason now than then for planners to impose their personal value systems on the living patterns and life-styles of other people. The job of planning is to facilitate the kinds of development that most of the clients would want but could not have without planning; and to mediate in cases of conflict between the interests of different groups, according to clearly stated principles of efficiency and equity. Beyond that it should not go, and (at any rate in the United States) is unlikely to go.

There is, however, a real danger: that in the necessary job of mediation, planners may give greater weight to the interests of those whose values they share, at the expense of the rest. That is the lesson of the study of planning in Britain after World War II, as undertaken in the years immediately after the 1967 paper (Hall *et al.* 1973); it also seems to be the lesson emerging from studies of trends in the San Francisco Bay area, that may set some kind of a precedent for the rest of the American sunbelt (Dowall 1981). In both cases, the planners have backed policies of urban containment that happened literally to favor the 'haves' at the expense of the 'have-nots:' those who already live in an area versus those who would like to; homeowners at the expense of potential homeowners; older versus younger; richer versus poorer. This may represent conventional good planning on the European model, but its results are predictable: in both cases they are housing shortages, impeded mobility, and escalation of land and housing values. Good planning, in other words, can mean question-able ethics.

Finally, the distinction between the urban culture and the suburban culture remains. Despite the undisputed fact of gentrification, the suburbs continue to grow at the expense of the cities. And this is now true of an increasing number of European cities, as recent research has shown. Whatever the precise reasons – and, in Europe, these have not yet been sufficiently probed – people are voting with their feet (and with their wheels) against the city and against the countryside. Some are going the opposite way, and perhaps in time their minority movement may become the majority. But, if anything, the trend now in more and more Western countries is even further from the city and into the small rural towns. A latter-day version of the paper, written for the mid-1980s instead of the mid-1960s, might indeed have to contrapose the big-city culture and the small-town culture – to the advantage of the latter.

References

Dowall, D. 1981. *The suburban squeeze*. Berkeley & Los Angeles: University of California Press.

Gans, H. J. 1967. *The Levittowners: ways of life and politics in a new suburban community*. New York: Pantheon.

Glickman, N. J. 1978. *The growth and management of the Japanese urban system*. New York: Academic Press.

Hall, P. 1968. The urban culture and the suburban culture. In *Man in the city of the future*, R. Eells and C. Walton (eds.), 99–145. New York: Collier-Macmillan.

Hall, P. 1981. Urban change in Europe. In *Space and time in geography: essays dedicated to Torsten Hagerstrand*, A. Pred (ed.), 129–46. Lund: Gleerup.

Hall, P., and D. Hay 1980. *Growth centres in the European urban system*. Berkeley & Los Angeles: University of California Press.

Hall, P., R. Thomas, H. Gracey, R. Drewett, 1973. *The containment of urban England*, 2 vols. London: George Allen & Unwin.

Hauser, P. 1981. The census of 1980. *Sci. Am.* **245**, 53–61.

Mumford, L. 1938. *The culture of cities*. New York: Harcourt, Brace.

Shackson, R. H. 1981. Transportation and energy futures. In *Proceedings of the Aspen conference on future urban transportation (June 1979)*. Aspen: Aspen Foundation.

Vance, J. E. 1962. Emerging patterns of commercial structure in American cities. In *Proceedings of the IGU symposium on urban geography, Lund 1960*, K. Norborg (ed.), 485–518. Lund studies in geography, Series B, 24. Lund: Gleerup.

Warner, S. B. 1962. *Streetcar suburbs*. Cambridge, Mass.: Harvard University Press.

Whyte, W. H. 1958. Urban sprawl. In *The exploding metropolis*, Editors of *Fortune* (ed.), 133–56. Garden City, NJ: Doubleday.

Wolfe, T. 1966. *The kandy kolored tangerine flake streamline baby*. New York: Farrar, Straus & Giroux.

7 *The Soviet city: continuity and change in privilege and place*

JAMES H. BATER

The Russian Revolution of 1917 created a new ideological blueprint for a society molded over the centuries by the values and precepts of an absolute autocracy. Social-class relationships were transformed, perhaps nowhere else so palpably as in the city. Fundamental changes occurred. All resources, including land, were nationalized; land uses were to be planned, not market determined; most forms of privatism were to be abolished, and the ethos of collectivism cultivated instead. Equality was heralded. Socialism portended new possibilities for charting the course of urbanization, even if the precise direction and tempo of change were not always immediately clear. In Marxist–Leninist doctrine, the conscious manipulation of the urban–industrialization process assumed an important rôle in the transformation of the values of society. Thus, the Soviet city became both an instrument and example of directed social and economic change; it served to legitimate the ideology of the state itself. The extent to which the built environment of the Soviet city actually reflects the prevailing ideology is clearly a multifaceted issue. So, too, is the way in which the Soviet city has influenced human behavior, the way in which it has helped to shape urban values. Constraints of space dictate that this discussion of the Soviet city in a cultural context be selective. Moreover, the emphasis will be on synthesis and generalization, rather than on detailed documentation. Given the dearth of pertinent information on many urban topics, some of the judgments offered on the continuities and changes in privilege and place within the Soviet city are necessarily tentative.

Two broad lines of enquiry will be pursued. The first concerns the general relationship between the city and the state. The second concerns the way in which cultural values have shaped the built environment through the residential segregation of specific classes or strata of society, clearly one of the more important ways in which human actions have influenced urban form the world over. In approaching these issues, I believe there is a need for a broad historical perspective. It has been contended that Soviet society, notwithstanding the importance of the revolution of 1917, is 'embedded in a socio-historical milieu, where every generation inherits and shares with the past its cultural traditions' (Lewin 1979, p. 119). This is a contention I share. Thus, the relationship between the city and the state, between urban form and residential segregation, will be examined first of all in the context of the Russian city on the eve of World War I. The discussion will then turn to an examination of what Soviet socialism meant in terms of these two broad lines of enquiry. Finally, the extent to which the situation at present conforms to the ideals laid down more than half a century ago will be assessed.

The Russian city and the autocracy

The proportion of Russia's population living in towns was never very great; at no time was it more than one-sixth. Moreover, the urbanization which did occur differed in a number of important respects from what took place in Western Europe and North America. There, cities developed in response to a host of economic, social, and political pressures, with few institutional checks on city growth. In Russia, on the other hand, the development of cities and life within them was very much under the thumb of officialdom from at least the middle of the 17th century until well into the 19th. Of course, the institution of serfdom, formally abolished in 1861, presented numerous barriers to free migration from the countryside to the town. Under the conditions of serfdom, there seems to have been a compelling necessity for the state to regularize relationships between the various constituents of Russian society, and between them and the state itself. The process of bureaucratic pigeonholing of the various estates, or *sosloviya*, into which Russian society was divided, meant that the right to reside permanently in a town, and there to engage in some form of economic activity, was accorded only a tiny fraction of the Empire's population. In an absolute autocracy, in which the city performed an administrative service on behalf of the state, where the mercantile function was purposely restricted, and where an industrial function with the specter of a seething *lumpenproletariat* was perceived as a real threat to political and social stability, city growth was something to be closely monitored and to be limited in impact.

Thus, the state attempted to regulate the duration of residence in the city. An elaborate bureaucracy arose to monitor the comings and goings of huge numbers of temporary city dwellers. The movement of peasants especially was affected, and, as they came to comprise the largest share of the urban population by the end of the imperial era, Russian cities came to be characterized by transience (Johnson 1979, pp. 28–50, for a discussion of Moscow). The fact that peasants did become so important an element in the city is, first of all, testimony to their persistence in overcoming institutional barriers to migration, and, secondly, testimony to the poverty of life in the countryside. As more and more peasants left the villages for the city, albeit usually on a temporary basis, the state's bureaucratic machinery for superintending population movement was severely tested. When the Stolypin Reform of 1905 enabled peasants to migrate at will, an unprecedented flood-tide of rural migrants was unleashed, and in the process any remaining hope for an orderly develop- ment of the Russian city evaporated (Hamm 1976, pp. 182–200).

The uneasy relationship which existed between the state and the city in Russia was never resolved. Rapid urban-industrialization had ushered in a new reality, one which challenged the very basis of the traditional, deferentially structured, and essentially pre-urban social system on which the autocracy was founded. The town plan of the 18th century, so avidly endorsed by the autocracy, envisioned an ordered and orderly urban environment (Shkvarikov 1954, Luppov 1957). By the late 1800s, any notion that the town plan might still serve as a tool for social control was an anachronism. Architectural controls and zoning restrictions, for instance, had long since collapsed in the face of rapid in-migration. The perceived threat to the *status quo* which the state saw in uncontrolled urban-industrialization was borne out in the events of 1905. The revolu- tionary upheaval which occurred then was eventually snuffed out through some accommodation to popular demands, and through brute force. But the events of that troubled year clearly demonstrated the ability of the masses to orchestrate a real challenge to authority. Each year thereafter, maintaining public order demanded more and more of the state's resources (Thurston 1980).

Thus, the state did not view the city positively. Certainly, urban growth was deemed necessary, but, when possible, it was controlled. While the membership of the ostensibly urban *sosloviya*, that is, the honored citizenry, the merchants and that amorphous collection of what passed for the urban lower and middle bourgeoisie (the *meshchane*) is far from an entirely reliable measure of the size of the permanent city population, it is nonetheless instructive that few major Russian towns had more than 20 percent of their population in these estates in 1914.[1] The state had long attempted to monitor the social-class composition of the urban population through the discretionary allocation of permits to live in cities. It also attempted to limit the size of the urban industrial labor force. For instance, it has been argued that zoning regulations within cities were sometimes nothing more than attempts to control urban- industrialization under the guise of invoking sanitary regulations (Zelnik 1971, pp. 23–5). The promotion of industrial development in the countryside, ostensibly to ensure manufacturers an adequate and perhaps more malleable labor supply, may be viewed in the same way. In the early 1900s, more than one-half of Russia's factory labor force was in fact located in the countryside (Fedor 1975, p. 139, Blackwell 1983, pp. 415–17).

Deep-seated disquiet about the rôle of the city was by no means exclusive to the authorities, but often colored what was written by the few who were literate. Despite attempts by Westernizers to see in the Russian city, and especially the capital St. Petersburg, some prospect for the modernization of society as a whole, the literature of the 19th and early 20th centuries frequently portrays the city as a hostile, even uncivilized environment.[2] Pathological features of the urban environment figure prominently in some of Dostoevsky's and Gorky's work, for example *Crime and Punishment* (1866) and *The lower depths* (1902). For symbolists like A. Biely, *St. Petersburg*, as portrayed in the 1913 novel of the same name, did not offer hope, but was oppressive and alienating. Literary works set in the countryside frequently cast city-experienced peasants as bereft of morals, or worse (Donskov 1972, pp. 66–116). Of course, there is not necessarily a connection between what might be said about the city, or, indeed, even the actions of authorities toward the city, and the actual conditions of daily labor and life for those who lived there. Peasants, as we have noted, came and went in response to the seasons and the expiry dates on their permits. But such transient behavior was by no means restricted to the peasantry. Available data indicate that for all classes and socioeconomic groups, the ties with the city were often short term and tenuous (Bater 1980a). Amongst the social élite, for instance, residence in the city was frequently a seasonal affair, though for very different reasons than for the peasant. The winter's heavy schedule of social events and festivities in the city was a marked, and usually attractive, contrast to the somnolence of estate life in the summer. For those concerned with the rituals of society but obliged to live permanently in the city, a *dacha* in a bucolic suburban retreat was a necessary compromise. Put simply, rural values figured prominently in the culture of the Russian city. As might be expected, the form of the built environment bore mute testimony to these prevailing values and customs.

Privilege and place in the Russian city

During periods of rapid, and frequently unwelcome, change, such as that occasioned by industrialization, a commonly observed tendency is for some privileged socioeconomic groups within cities to express social distance in terms of physical separation of housing.[3] Residential segregation is perhaps the most obvious instance of the territorial manifestation of social position. By the turn of the 19th century, the form and fabric of most European and American cities already bore the indelible stamp of this process (Warner 1962). Social values, ability to pay, and technological innovations in public transport had facilitated the creation of more homogeneous than heterogeneous social-class areas within the city. Urban élites, in particular, had adopted residential segregation as one defensive strategy in response to perceived social and environmental disorders such as insurgency, disease, and blight. Few Russian cities were immune to these 'problems.' But how was the social geography of the Russian city shaped by people's responses to them? Specifically, to what extent was residential segregation adopted as a defensive strategy?

In the early 1900s, social position in Russian society was still determined to a considerable degree by the traditional system of legal estates and ranks. Titles, rank-specific uniforms, decorative paraphernalia, etc. not only added a dash of color and a sense of occasion to street life, but they were personal manifestations of one's place in the hierarchy. Whereas in European, and especially North American, urban cultural milieux, wealth, and social position were more nearly synonymous, society in Russia continued to be more strongly influenced by the nobility, often profligate and sometimes penurious, and the upper echelons of the bureaucracy and military, than it was by the merchants and industrialists who contributed to the city's economic viability. Furthermore, in Russia, élites were less attached to the city as a place; indeed, in the typically multistorey built environment of the central city of moderate-to-large size, accommodation was usually rented rather than owned. On the street, time-honored, personalized symbols of rank and class helped élites to maintain social distance, to distinguish themselves from the seeming confusion of classes and activities (see also Lofland 1973, and Sennett 1977). Thus, the voluntary isolation of social classes in homogeneous residential areas seems to have been only little developed (Bater 1976, pp. 193–201 & 369–81, Bater 1981). Ability to pay was perhaps as often reflected in the size of the apartment, and the manner in which it was fitted out, as it was through an exclusive claim to territory. Even in some of the ostensibly better parts of major Russian cities, the lower orders were found in the garrets above and the cellars below, creating a kind of three-dimensional segregation. Lavish decoration of living space on the middle floors of the multistorey built environment insulated élites from the burgeoning masses. Toward the periphery of the city, land-use intensity fell off, and the proportion of the lower orders amongst the population increased correspondingly.[4]

Of course, such countryside values and actions were increasingly at odds with the reality of urban life. By the early 1900s, reliance on personalized manifestations of privileged position in society could no longer guarantee a deferential response from the lower orders. Deficient municipal services had made the Russian city uncommonly hazardous in terms of public health (Bater 1978a). For the social and bureaucratic élites, residence in the city was becoming increasingly hazardous in other ways as well. The revolution of 1905 had shaken the foundations of Russian society to its very roots: the revolution of 1917 pulled the entire structure apart.

The new Soviet government inherited cities whose form and fabric were very much shaped by essentially pre-urban cultural values, values which reflected little commitment to the city as a place. By changing the ideological blueprint of society, the revolution of 1917 portended a new rôle, and a new form, for the city in Soviet society.

The ideal urban culture and form of the Soviet socialist city

The transformation of the values of society through the conscious manipulation of the urban–industrialization process is an integral part of Marxist–Leninist doctrine. Thus, the state's relationship to the city was altered from something colored by deep-rooted distrust, to positive endorsement. The creation of a new urban form figured prominently in the task of inculcating the values of a proletarian culture. Individualism and privatism, in all their manifestations, were to be supplanted by the proletarian principle of collectivism. In the first few years of revolutionary fervor, this led to much experimentation, especially in art and architecture (Lissitzky 1970). However, in terms of actual urban development, the chaos of civil war, and reconstruction of the national economy, meant that little was accomplished outside the municipalization of property and the reassignment of housing space. Indeed, the massive urban–rural migration, which the chaos of the times occasioned, significantly eased the long-standing housing crisis, though the benefits were both relative and temporary.

The fundamental contradiction between city and countryside, which Marxists claimed was produced under capitalism, was somehow to be resolved in a socialist society. Much was said about the rôle of communal living in the new order, some enthusiasts even arguing that it would eventually replace the nuclear family (Strumilin 1961). These were just two of the many potential social changes introduced by the revolution which had some important implications for urban design. But there were no readily available models to accommodate the profound changes set in motion by the revolution. Lenin himself noted the dilemma: 'It is imposs-ible for us,' he said in 1920, '. . . to solve the question of proletarian culture without a clear understanding and exact knowledge of that culture which was created in the course of humanity's development; it is only by remaking this [culture] that proletarian culture is possible' (quoted in Voyce 1948, p. 125). For the rest of the decade, the debate over the relationship between city form and proletarian cultural values intensified, and, despite Lenin's caution, many of the participants in this debate were still attempting to manufacture culture, to manufacture utopia. Town-planning proposals were plentiful, many inspired by the *avant-garde* movements in architecture and planning spawned in Europe and America (Starr 1978). Given the radical nature of these ideas, it is hardly surprising that most remained on the drawing board. However, one proposal did make the transition from drawing board to bricks and mortar – N. Miliutin's linear city (Miliutin 1974). This scheme merits brief description because it embodied a number of the most important principles from the leading schools of thought about the future Soviet socialist city.

Miliutin's proposal for a linear city was not original. The concept had been developed by the Spanish architect de Matya, and, by the late 1920s, had a sizeable international roster of adherents. Miliutin's adaptation of the concept was used in the planning of Stalingrad (now Volgograd), and in part for the design of Magnitogorsk. The linear city incorporated about half a dozen strictly segregated zones (Fig. 7.1). A green buffer served to separate the industrial and transport zones from the residential zone. The parallel development of industry and housing was intended to facilitate a short, pedestrian journey to work. The perceived need to create an alternative to the large city and agglomeration, both judged to be inevitable by-products of capitalism, led all planners to try to create urban environments which would generate a sense of community. Miliutin, in common with many others, reckoned that the best balance between economic provision of urban services and potential for creation of a sense of community, if not a communal ethos, was in a town of 50 000 to 60 000 inhabitants. Thus, city populations were to be strictly limited. Under ideal circumstances, the Marxist objective of breaking down the difference between town and country could be realized by accommodating both agriculturist and proletarian in the same, or similar, housing. The provision of consumer and cultural services would be in accordance with the concept of spatial equality. Decentralization, not concentration, of items of collective consumption was therefore demanded.

Whatever the merits of the architectural and town-planning schemes produced during this era of 'cultural revolution,' most were denied a place in the real world. As in literature and art, this visionary, utopian and, not uncommonly, totally impractical experimentation had little impact on the ordinary Soviet citizen. After all, only 18 percent of the population lived in cities at the time of the first Soviet census in 1926, a share scarcely changed from the late imperial era. Moreover, illiteracy was still widespread. The debate over the form of the Soviet socialist city was ended in 1931, when it was decreed that all Soviet cities must be socialist by virtue of their being part of the Union of Soviet Socialist Republics. While this pragmatic policy statement, coming as it did with the full authority of the Communist Party, served to stifle further debate, and especially the oft-cited criticism that the existing urban system, being capitalist in origin

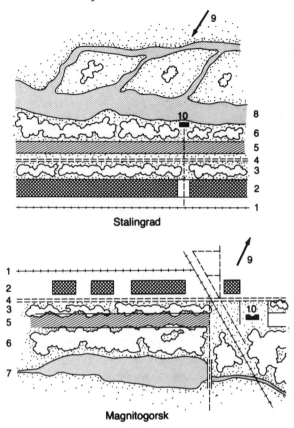

Stalingrad

Magnitogorsk

1, railway; 2, industrial zone; 3, green zone; 4, thoroughfare; 5, residential zone; 6, park; 7, Ural River; 8, Volga River; 9, prevailing wind; 10, House of Soviets.

Figure 7.1 Miliutin's linear city (after Parkins 1953, p. 22).

and in form, should be eradicated, it did not mean that all the ideas so vigorously enunciated during the 1920s were without impact. In fact, a number of them reappeared, albeit sometimes in modified form, in the Plan for the Reconstruction of Moscow, adopted in 1935. The party had effectively limited the terms of reference for the international competition to reconstruct the new Soviet capital to a moderate reworking of the existing urban form, and had ruled out the possibility of a new capital being built from scratch. Still, the principles upon which the plan was based are important, because they became the guidelines for town planning throughout the country. Among the more notable were: limited city size; an ideological rôle for the city center; state control and allocation of housing; spatial equality in the distribution of consumer and cultural services; and a limited journey to work. Planned urban development and limited city size dictated some mechanism for controlling population movement. An internal passport system and residence permit for city dwellers already existed, having been instigated in 1932. The central city had to be designed to accommodate massive, orchestrated public ceremony. The optimal city size was one of between 50 000 and 60 000 inhabitants even though Moscow already exceeded 3 million. Public space, in general, and central city space, in particular, were assigned an ideological, or symbolic, rôle. State control of housing was intended to ensure an egalitarian distribution at essentially nominal rents (Bater 1980b, pp. 27–30). However, the state evidenced little interest, and invested little of the scarce financial resources, in private space – that is, in housing. By assuming responsibility for the provision of a wide range of consumer, cultural, and perhaps ultimately household services, housing space was envisioned as having a largely dormitory function for future Soviet citizens.

The relationship between the city and state

Outwardly, the relationship between the state and the city was entirely positive. After all, urban culture was, by definition, superior to countryside customs. While the new Soviet city was scarcely what the utopian architects and planners of the 1920s had envisioned, the planning principles embodied in the Moscow Plan of 1935 nonetheless constituted a sharp break with the past. The Soviet socialist city was intended to bring into existence a new and higher form of society: one in which collectivism would supplant privatism: one in which the traditional cultural values and religions would be obliterated: and one in which the primacy of the family would eventually disappear. While there is no doubt as to the official view of the relationship between the city and state, what is of interest is the extent to which the official viewpoint is shared by those who live in the city. Of course, this line of enquiry is complicated by a real dearth of information. Still, there is scope for a few observations.

For the early Soviet period, our perception of the city tends to be clouded by official pronouncements of government and party spokesmen, and by the voluminous, and frequently effusively enthusiastic, commentary of contemporary architects, planners, and the like. What the average person in a Soviet city thought, faced as he was with a rapidly deteriorating built environment, and possibly being a part of the sizeable roster of the unemployed, is impossible to ascertain. However, Soviet literature was certainly not always at one with the official view depicting the city as a positive force in society. In L. Leonov's *The badgers* (1925), for example, the city as a corruptive environment is developed in a Soviet setting, thereby perpetuating an important theme in Russian literature. In

M. Zoshchenko's *Short stories*, materialism and privatism are the dominant traits of urban dwellers, and invariably the acquisitiveness of a would-be bourgeoisie corrupts human relationships. As late as 1930, I. K. Paustovsky's *Moscow summer* still depicted the city as an essentially negative and oppressive force in society, a stark contrast to the positive spiritual qualities engendered by the countryside. Even in literature with a futurist bent, like V. Mayakovskiy's *The bedbug* (1928), the portrayal of the city did not echo the official viewpoint. Regimentation and alienation, not selflessness and fellowship, were the principal feelings of urbanites.

While the advent of socialist realism and the censor soon strictly limited the scope of Soviet literary endeavor, the theme of middle-class, bourgeois preoccupations was not entirely erased. Nor should it have been, for contrary to original principles, beginning in the early 1930s, Stalin entrenched a system of privileges, benefits, and salary differentials to enhance participation in the industrialization drive, then the war effort, and reconstruction.[5] In the Stalin era, private values were converted into public values (Dunham 1976, pp. 15–19). The middle class – the *meshchanstvo* of the imperial era – was legitimized, and, hence, so was privatism. In censor-approved socialist realist literature, the hero contributing in his own special way to the development of Soviet socialism could be portrayed as a dedicated, career-minded manager, aspiring to own a house, and perhaps a *dacha* as well. Not for him the cramped quarters of the average citizen. He could even be depicted as driving his own car! (Dunham 1976, pp. 18–19). Meanwhile, in the real world, those who could not, or would not, participate in the now firmly ensconced system of perks and privileges, travelled to work six days a week on an overcrowded tram, returning home to scarcely less congested conditions. The long-standing housing crisis deepened with each passing year. For example, the sanitary minimum allotment of 'living space' per urban inhabitant had been set at $9 m^2$ in 1922. At that time, the per-capita average was around $6 m^2$; by 1940, it was barely $4 m^2$; by 1950, it had slipped a shade under 4, less than half the national sanitary standard established nearly three decades earlier (Jacobs 1975, p. 67). By the latter date, a family per room was the rule, not the exception, in many Soviet cities (Bater 1980b, p. 99). The portrayal of privilege in literature was not entirely divorced from reality, of course. Positions of perceived importance in Soviet society did bring a variety of special dispensations, including an above-norm allocation of housing (Morton 1980). As in the Russian city, however, it seems that privilege and territoriality were not strongly developed. Space, rather than location, was no doubt the more important consideration, given the acute nature of the housing shortage. But there were also rituals for public behavior which helped to distinguish those who had arrived from those who were still *en route*, rituals which acknowledged, in personal, rather than spatial, ways, one's place in society.

The accommodation, indeed promotion, of a Soviet middle class during the Stalin era spawned *kulturnost*. This, Dunham has defined as constituting a '. . . program for proper conduct in public,' one whose special function was 'to encode the proper relationship between people through their possessions and labels,' something which clearly facilitated the continuation of declaration of position in society through appearance and behavior, instead of territoriality (Dunham 1976, pp. 13 & 22). The Soviet system sanctioned *kulturnost* because it was a device for social control. The growing middle class in Soviet society was dependent upon the régime for its perpetuation, and the regime upon the middle class for its support. Thus, while egalitarian principles shaped the official view of the relationship between the city and society, it should not be assumed that ideal and reality in the city were at one during the Stalin era. In an urban system where scarcity and shortage were the norm, where public space and public values were accorded most attention, privatism not only had a place, it was nurtured.

In Soviet literature since the late 1950s, depiction of the reality of Soviet life, the so-called *byt* genre, has emerged as one of the more controversial themes (Shneidman 1979, p. 25). While important in its own right, it also tends to cast a rather different light on the relationship between the city and society than does state ideology. First, there is the village prose tradition in which countryside cultural values are frequently juxtaposed to urban values, to the latter's detriment. Fedor Abramov's work, especially his trilogy *The Priaslins* (1958–73), figures prominently in the village prose, but many other writers have developed this theme as well. In it, inhabitants of the contemporary Soviet village are portrayed as having retained high moral qualities, having preserved the essence of important cultural values despite the corruptive impact of widespread urbanization (Hosking 1980, pp. 50–83). The apparently wide popular appeal of this literary genre probably has more to do with the fact that a very large proportion of the urban population has itself only recently departed the village than it has to do with it being a realistic portrayal of the countryside. Thus, on the one hand, the countryside is, in some Soviet literature (as it was in some late 19th-century Russian literature), imbued with cultural values which the city has corrupted. On the other hand, the literary theme of the reality of urban life which has developed since the 1960s does little to offset the message conveyed.

Yuri Trifonov, the best known exponent of the city prose tradition, paints a somewhat dismal picture of the reality of contemporary Soviet urban life (for instance, Trifonov 1969). The central figures are frequently cast as unethical and acquisitive. Concern with self, with privatism, and with gaining a larger share of whatever is available, is linked directly to the prevailing values of the urban milieu. Those who get ahead are not the ones who are selfless and sharing, but those who know how to work the

te 7.1 Vladimir: traditional wooden housing of the inner city.

ate 7.2 Samarkand: traditional quarter of privately owned housing.

Plate 7.3 Samarkand: state-owned, Soviet-era housing on the outskirts.

Plate 7.4 Akademgorodok: semi-detached housing for the academic élite (academicians).

Plate 7.5 Akademgorodok: state-owned apartments.

Plate 7.6 Moscow: state-owned housing in a new *mikrorayon*.

Plate 7.7 Privately owned *dachi* (summer homes) near Moscow.

system best. There are few instances of endings where the spirit of collectivism prevails over privatism. As with the village prose, Soviet literary critics often label such works as unrepresentative, untypical, and too much preoccupied with the ordinariness of day-to-day existence (Shneidman 1979, p. 26). Evidence of cultural advancement, of a communal ethos, is overlooked, or downplayed, they claim, and perhaps with some truth. But available sociological studies suggest that there is more to Trifonov's interpretation of the relationship between the Soviet city and society than there is substance to the scenario conveyed by official statements and ideology. Egalitarian principles were to have guided cultural change, but, in cities, there is much to suggest that the ethos of collectivism is fast being eroded by privatism.

We can elaborate this line of argument by turning our attention to the relationship between residential segregation and the built environment itself.

Privilege and place in the contemporary Soviet city

Since 1926, the share of the urban population has increased from 18 percent to about 64 percent of the total (Fig. 7.2). Despite government policies to the contrary, the largest cities have garnered the largest share of this growth. During most of the 1970s, for example, cities with more than 500 000 inhabitants have exhibited the fastest rate of growth in both relative and absolute terms (Bater 1980b, pp. 78–9). Whereas, in 1959, three cities had 1 million inhabitants, this figure is now 21 cities. While there is nothing magic in 1 million, the point is that most Soviet citizens live in large cities, far larger than even original town-planning principles intended, and these cities are invariably part of rapidly growing agglomerations. The concept of the optimal city size is now regarded by many to be a bankrupt planning objective (Bater 1980b, p. 81). Within the Soviet city, other planning ideals have been similarly compromised by the reality of urban growth.

The late official response to the housing crisis meant that it is only in recent years that the average family has seen much improvement in its accommodation. Nonetheless, between 1960 and 1975, fully two-thirds of the population were assigned improved housing. In keeping with the egalitarian spirit of town-planning principles, Soviet cities would not exhibit residential segregation by class or stratum of society, or by ethnicity. State control over housing allocation suggests that this was a realizable objective.

The standard approach in development of state housing is to use the *mikrorayon* as the basic building block. Comprising a set of smaller housing units or living complexes (traditionally referred to as a super

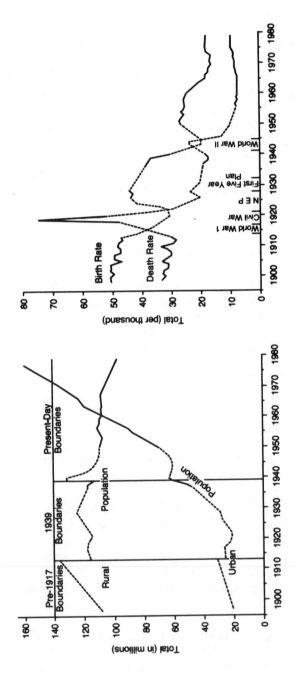

Figure 7.2 Population trends (after French 1965, *Narodnoye Khozyaystvo SSSR v 1977* 1978, p. 25, *Narodnoye Khozyaystvo SSSR 3a 60 Let.* 1978, pp. 7 & 69).

block, or a *kvartal*), the *mikrorayon* usually has somewhere between 8000 and 12000 residents. Several *mikrorayon* are then grouped into residential complexes. Something of the population and spatial dimensions of this system is indicated by the following figures: five to eight living complexes, each with a population of 1000 to 1500, and a radius of perhaps 50 to 100 meters, comprise a *mikrorayon*; four to five *mikrorayons*, each with a population of between 8000 and 12000 inhabitants, and a radius of between 300 to 400 meters, comprise a residential complex. One variant of this type of hierarchical system is portrayed in Fig. 7.3. Standardized apartment units occupied by a representative mix of the city's socioeconomic and ethnic groups, ample green space, perimeter thoroughfares with public transport facilities, day-care, educational and health services – all are common denominators of long standing in the planning of residential areas. In theory, there is a logical progression of facilities such that all the day-to-day requirements can be met with a short pedestrian journey. Higher order goods and services are located strategically within the *mikrorayon* and residential complex, with only infrequent journeys to the central city expected, and then more for the purpose of mass culture than personal consumption (Bater 1980b, pp. 102–03).

The *mikrorayon* was intended to provide the physical environment appropriate to the task of engendering a sense of neighborliness, of collective responsibility; in short, a communal ethos. Sociological evidence suggests that this has not yet occurred on a very large scale. Socializing with neighbors, for example, tends to vary inversely with position in the social hierarchy. The few at the top give little indication of even recognizing their neighbors, let along socializing with them. Amongst workers and service personnel who occupy the lower echelons of the hierarchy, where socializing with neighbors is most common, more time is still spent with relatives than with neighbors (as quoted in Frolic 1970, p. 322). Alienation, rather than a sense of collectivism, is a more commonly reported psychological trait of residents of *mikrorayons*. It is manifested in most of the usual ways – withdrawal from community endeavors, indifference to the maintenance of public space, and, of growing concern, vandalism and hooliganism amongst the young in particular. Given the massive scale of rehousing since 1960, it is hardly surprising that the disruption of social networks has generated in some a feeling of alienation. Indeed, there is a sizeable body of opinion in the Soviet Union that regards the concept of a *mikrorayon* being the focal point of human interaction as a contradiction of the urbanization process which promotes greater, not less, mobility (Bater 1980b, pp. 101–05 & 156–8).

About one-half of the Soviet population currently lives in a *mikrorayon*, in housing which is apparently more standardized than differentiated.

Figure 7.3 Residential complex (after Kravchuk 1973, p. 48).

1 - 4, 8 and 16 Storey
    Apartment Buildings

2 - Children's Day Care Centre

3 - School

4 - Home for the Aged

5 - 20, and 25 Storey Buildings
    of Hotel Type for Youths

6 - Trade and Social Centre

7 - Central Park

8 - Parking Lots

However, as we have noted already, there always has been variation in apartment design since some groups in society are entitled to above-norm allotments of space. Professionals, such as architects, for example, receive additional space. Certainly, municipal authorities can and do make adjustments in housing allocation based on social need, as opposed to occupational reward. But municipalities, in theory the principal arena for decision making in matters related to housing, in fact control only about one-half of the state housing supply. The rest is owned, operated, and maintained by ministries, departments and enterprises whose self-interest in attracting and holding a highly fluid labor supply is often best served by differential housing allocation procedures. Despite years of promoting the concept of municipal control over the state housing supply, central government has been unable to persuade its own ministries, departments, and enterprises to relinquish control to urban government. But even if this were to happen, the Stalin era entrenched system of housing perquisites as a reward for career mobility is unlikely to be dismantled. It seems to be too important an element in rewarding incentive, and is now part and parcel of the privatism of Soviet urban culture. However, this has not manifested itself to any great extent in residential segregation within the state housing sector. But, as we have already suggested, for élites living in the state housing sector, apartment size and furnishing may matter more than location. And once outside the apartment, a chauffeur waiting with the Volga (or possibly a Zil or Chaika), and the rituals of *kulturnost* may establish position in society even more demonstratively than territorial exclusivity of housing. In any event, the state only owns about 70 percent of the total urban housing stock. The remainder is made up of cooperative and privately owned housing. If residential segregation is to be found anywhere in the contemporary Soviet city, it is in these two components of the housing stock.

The construction of cooperative and private housing has had a some-what checkered history, as might be imagined. In the case of cooperatives, a substantial number were created during the early Soviet period when the state's housing construction efforts were decidedly limited. A need was met, and in an ideologically more acceptable manner than by means of construction of privately owned housing. But official sanction was withdrawn in the late 1930s, when all existing cooperatives were taken over by the state. They were, so to speak, nationalized, and the former cooperative member became a tenant, albeit one paying the characteristically nominal rent. Given the official recognition of a major housing crisis in the post-Stalin era, the attitude toward the potential rôle of cooperatives in ameliorating the housing shortage softened. By 1962, cooperative apartment ownership was made legal once more. The state now provides loans to cover 60 percent of the cost of construction. Information on the location, and intensity, of cooperative housing is extremely sparse.

However, it seems that the larger the city, the more common are the cooperatives. In Moscow, for instance, 11 percent of all housing put up in 1973 was cooperative: it is probable that the share at present is even higher. While of growing significance in many major urban centres, the overall share of cooperative housing of the total stock is not likely to be much above 5 percent at present. However, if current trends continue, this share is likely to increase. In the late 1970s, some 25 000 cooperatives accommodated 2.2 million people (Bater 1980b, pp. 99–100); who they are, how they are accommodated, and where, are important issues.

The success of a housing cooperative depends upon the occupants ability to get along with other members in order to get things done in the bewildering maze of government regulations. Thus, the membership of cooperatives tends to be drawn from particular socioeconomic groups (or strata) in Soviet society, rather than from a broad cross section, official intentions otherwise notwithstanding. The needs to have a sizeable down payment in cash and a monthly income large enough to meet the required payment are other restrictions to cooperative membership, but these are probably not as significant barriers as the need for organizational expertise amongst the collective, and a sense of group identity. Thus, the cooperative apartment block tends to house what might be broadly labelled a segment of the Soviet middle class. Outwardly, the state-owned and cooperative apartment block may not be easily distinguishable. But, according to one, no doubt not entirely apocryphal observation, there are some visible signs that the two types of housing accommodate different populations. In the state-owned apartment building, lights go on in the early morning hours, as the inhabitants prepare to leave for work. In the cooperative, lights come on later in the morning, a reflection of the different circumstances of their, presumably more professional than worker, social-class composition (Morton 1980, p. 255).

As a rule, cooperative housing, while built according to government norms and limitations, is nonetheless of higher quality than that available in the state sector. Public space, that is, halls, foyers, courtyards, and so on, tends to be better maintained as well. Since some cooperative members build apartments as large as the regulations permit, they tend to be more generously housed in a qualitatively better environment than would be their lot in the state sector. Where in the Soviet city cooperative housing is built is an intriguing question. If spatially segregated, then, in view of the social-class composition not reflecting the full spectrum of Soviet society in a representative manner, a type of residential segregation may be taking form. Available information on this issue is limited in the extreme, and may not be typical of all Soviet cities. Still, it is notable that a recent study of the social geography of Tallin did reveal a measure of spatial concentration, or segregation, of cooperative housing. In 1975, when the study was undertaken, cooperatives comprised 4.3 percent of the total housing stock; but in areas of recent housing construction, the percentage was rather higher. In two peripheral regions characterized by new housing, the share of cooperatives ranged between 15 and 16.3 percent. Many of the apartment owners were bureaucrats and professionals. Workers were not necessarily excluded, but they did not dominate the socioeconomic composition of cooperative housing membership (Rukavishnikov 1980, p. 180). Tallin, with 436 000 inhabitants, and capital of the Estonian Republic, has, like other cities in the Baltic region, a far higher standard of living than is found in the rest of the country. Overall, the share of cooperative apartments does not appear to be at all high; thus, the intraurban concentration is particularly noteworthy. Clearly to the extent that spatial differentiation of cooperative members from society at large occurs, a form of residential segregation is being created. Yet it would probably be a mistake to regard the cooperative as home to a Soviet élite. Given the nature of the rather generous housing perks for the Soviet government, military, economic and artistic élites, most observers reckon that such groups have every reason not to give up a state apartment, with its nominal rent, for a cooperative costing substantially more (Matthews 1978, p. 46).

Privately owned housing has been permitted throughout the Soviet period, though under various pressures at various times. In the countryside, such housing is by far the most common type; in the city, its share has been steadily reduced over the years, but with about 25 percent of all urban housing in private hands, it is still important (*Narodnoye Khozyaystvo SSSR v 1979* 1980, p. 419). Moreover, this share is the national average, and there are marked deviations from the mean. As a general rule, the smaller the urban centre, and the more remote its location, the higher the proportion of privately owned housing. Since the early 1960s, construction of such accommodation has been precluded in most regional capitals and major cities. In the smaller cities, construction continues; indeed, state loans of up to 1500 rubles have been authorized recently to assist with construction. Thus, the supply of such housing increases each year, even though its share of the total stock slips. In much of the Soviet Union, the privately owned house is a detached, wooden structure, not always in a good state of maintenance, the overall floor space of which must conform to the prevailing norms. But there are examples of well constructed, well maintained private homes in most Soviet cities. The continued construction of such accommodation will help to ensure the 'wooden' fabric of so many of the small- to medium-size cities of European Russia and Siberia (Plate 7.1). But whether the local building materials are wood, stone, cement, or adobe, the land on which such construction occurs, of course, remains the property of the state. The private housing sector adds much more character to the texture of the urban fabric than either of the other two, and, by dint of who tends to live in privately owned housing, it perpetuates residential segregation. Residential segregation occurs on both ethnic and socioeconomic bases.

The legacy of autocracy included territories with distinctly non–Slavic populations, some acquired only late in the imperial era, some in the Middle Ages. The Central Asian realm is an example of the former. Despite the fact that all major Central Asian cities are now dominantly Slavic, the indigenous population has not been entirely submerged, since a sizeable number still choose to live in the traditional quarters. The situation in Samarkand is typical in many ways. The built environment of this city (of about 0.5 million people) in Uzbekistan mirrors the cultural values of three epochs (Fig. 7.4). The traditional quarter is still more or less the exclusive territory of Uzbeks, and reflects the centuries old traditions of social custom and architecture (Plate 7.2). The colonial outpost of the Russian government now comprises part of the central city. With its broad thoroughfares, liberally endowed with shade trees, and laid out with some attention to the classical notions of town design of the 18th century, it stands in stark contrast still to the hotch-potch of streets and alleys in the traditional quarter from which it was once separated (much like New Delhi was separated from Delhi). Of course, not all indigenous central Asians live in the old quarter: many have voluntarily taken up residence in the standardized state housing which now surrounds most of the colonial and traditional parts of the city (Plate 7.3). Others have had to relocate because of man-made incursions into a housing stock which does not meet contemporary Soviet town-planning standards, or because of destruction wrought by the occasional earthquake. But within the sector of the traditional quarter still intact, the resistance to change is considerable. Such housing provides the physical basis for the perpetuation of cultural values which are not in any sense mainstream Soviet: birth rates are high, women have a subordinate rôle in the family, wives are rarely employed in 'socially productive' labor outside the home, and so on. Segregated housing of an ethnic minority provides a cultural staging post in the transition from village to city. But this phenomenon is not peculiar to Central Asia, nor is it restricted to specific ethnic groups.

Kazan, capital of the Tatar Autonomous Soviet Socialist Republic, and located at the confluence of the Volga and Kama rivers in European Russia, was brought under Russian hegemony in the 16th century. As in Samarkand, the indigenous population comprises about one-third of the total population, now just over the 1 million mark. While Tatars live throughout the city, a recent study reveals that some areas are still dominantly Tatar in ethnic composition. For the most part, the areas of concentration of Tatars (depicted in Fig. 7.5) reflect, in the first place, pre-revolutionary inner city patterns of residence which have to some extent persisted to present times, and reflect, in the second place, former villages which have been engulfed in the process of urban expansion.

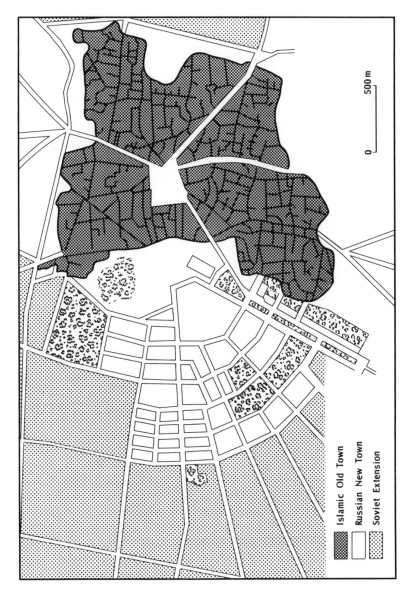

Figure 7.4 Samarkand – built environment (after Giese 1979, p. 158).

Islamic Old Town

Russian New Town

Soviet Extension

500 m

0

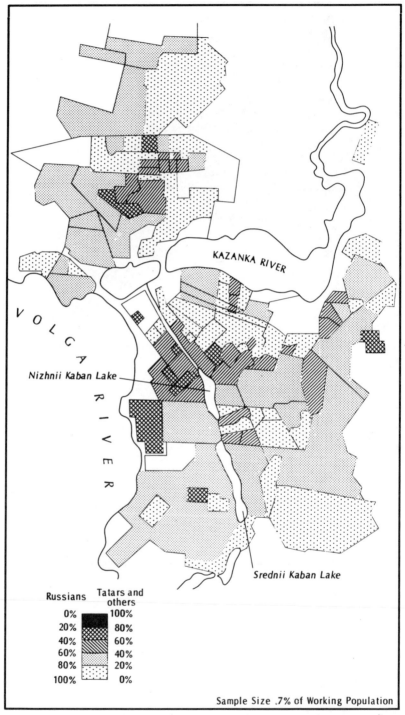

Figure 7.5 Kazan – residential segregation of tatars, 1974 (after Rukavishnikov 1978, p. 71).

Thus, while the level of concentration of Tatars in Kazan is less than that of indigenous Central Asians in Samarkand's traditional quarter, such residential segregation as does exist certainly helps to perpetuate cultural traditions of a minority group. And it is the stock of older, inner-city, privately owned housing, and the counterpart on the outskirts of the city, which are important factors in facilitating voluntary segregation. The private housing, which makes up such a large component of the peripheral areas of the Soviet city in general, and its small- to medium-size member in particular, is, as a rule, the realm of the working class. Many rural migrants apparently find that the privately owned detached house, with its customary garden, provides a more agreeable entry to urban life than an apartment or room in the state-owned housing stock (Rukavishnikov 1978). However, just how many recent migrants can afford such accommodation is a moot point. Indeed, it often takes several years before the young rural migrant secures a room or apartment for himself and his family. But for those with some capital, the possibility to buy or build still exists in many cities, especially the smaller ones. What this leads to, of course, is a type of socio-economic segregation. The peripheral dominance of workers in Kazan (depicted in Fig. 7.6) is far from uncommon. Notwithstanding the egalitarian principles endorsed by the state, the reality of the hierarchy of strata of Soviet society is that the working class, and, most notably, the recently arrived peasant and unskilled members, are nearer the bottom than they are the top. A close inspection of Fig. 7.6 reveals the central city orientation of the professional (*intelligentsia*) group. It is the central city which usually has the highest level of provision of amenities; indeed, such intracity disparities in consumer and cultural services, public-transport servicing, quality of housing, in short, in the quality of life offered by residence in particular neighborhoods, is reflected in the differential rents charged for state housing. Although the rent is nominal, and the variations to allow for preferred neighborhood residence small, the fact that such differences exist at all speaks to the reality of the urban environment (Matthews 1979, pp. 109–10). Part of this reality is a perpetuation of residential segregation on ethnic and social-strata bases.

Of course, it is in the new town, rather than in the city pre-dating the Soviet era, where reality might be expected to match most closely the town-planning ideal of social-class heterogeneity and egalitarian dispensation of state housing. Akademgorodok, the science town of about 30 000 inhabitants to the south of Novosibirsk, is indeed unique, but so too, in some way or another, are most new towns. But here there is a very sharp spatial segregation of the academic élite. Leading academicians occupy semi-detached dwellings of substance in a bucolic suburban environment (Plate 7.4). Those lower down the academic ladder are entitled to accommodation in apartment buildings commensurate with their particular status (Plate 7.5). In Bratsk, a new town of 219 000

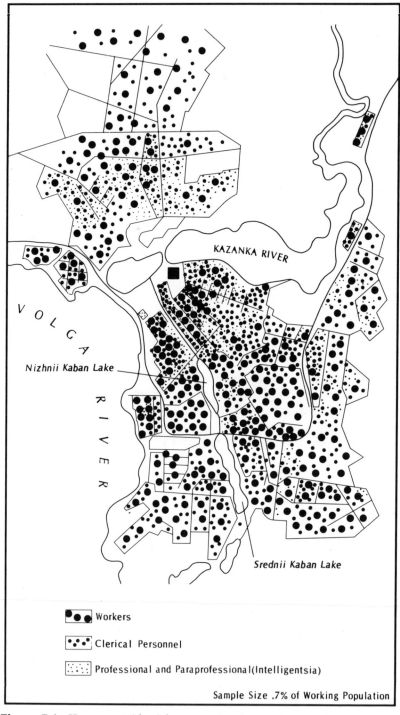

Figure 7.6 Kazan – residential: segregation by socioeconomic group (after Rukavishnikov 1978, p. 70).

inhabitants on the Angara River in central Siberia, what was to have been a unified settlement has developed into a system of noncontiguous single-industry or company towns built by particular ministries and focused on the hydro power station's cheap electricity (Bater 1978b). A peculiar kind of occupational segregation has ensued. Indeed, Padunskiy, the original town builders' settlement, lacks a modern industrial base, and has a less skilled workforce in consequence. The persistence of a departmentalist approach to new-town development elsewhere in Siberia is creating similar built environments and sociological conditions.

Over the years, notwithstanding official Soviet proclamations, and town-planning principles, one form or another of privatism and privilege has come to shape urban cultural values in subtle ways, and to shape some parts of the Soviet city itself (Plate 7.6). It has been argued that privatism and privilege must be tolerated, as they constitute a necessary but ephemeral stage in the process of building socialist society during a period when all material needs have not yet been satiated (Lukes 1977, p. 87). Given the current state of the Soviet economy, with its ever-greater need for more effective participation on the part of the labor force, it seems unlikely that the system of privileges will be disbanded in the near future. For a growing number of what Dunham has characterized as the Soviet 'meshchanstvo,' the ownership of an automobile is perhaps the ultimate symbol of privilege, a symbol which can be paraded publicly far more easily than can the ownership of a dacha (Plate 7.7), or access to special shops catering to the perceived requirements of an élite. On a more personal level, a recent press campaign has singled out the widespread preoccupation with gold jewelry and, sometimes, gold teeth, as a socially undesirable manifestation of certain people's concern with publicly pro-claiming their wealth, if not position, in society (Lesoto 1980).[6] The dilemma for the state is obvious: to remove all forms of privatism and privilege could well undermine incentive to excel. Indeed, current prob-lems with flagging labor productivity may necessitate more privilege, not less. The Soviet city cannot fail to be influenced in consequence.

Summary

In the evolution of urban culture in general, and of privilege and place in particular, four broad periods can be identified from the late 19th century. In the later imperial era, the relationship between the city and the state was shaped by the precepts of an absolute autocracy, and the essentially rural cultural values of society in general. Cities were the center of cultural change, and change invited the possibility of challenge to authority. Thus, with ever-less success, the state attempted to control and monitor urban growth. Rapid urban-industrialization did not necessarily mean that all who flocked to the city were automatically transformed into urbanites. The ties with the land remained strong right up to World War I, and not just for the peasantry, who by then comprised the largest share of the urban population. For all socioeconomic groups, transience was a deeply ingrained social phenomenon, and one which helped to shape the built environment. For the urban élites, place in society was as often conveyed in a personal way as it was through exclusive claim to territory within the city. Thus, residential segregation was weakly developed. By the eve of World War I, however, reliance on personal manifestations of place in society no longer assured a deferential response from the masses, who were increasingly sensitized to the inequalities of the *status quo*. Élites had reason to withdraw from personalized symbols of position in society into more exclusive territorial enclaves. But the technological underpinnings for such a transition were only weakly developed, and, in any case, world war, and ultimately revolution, submerged what momentum in this direction there might have been.

The second broad period is that from the revolution of 1917 through the 1920s. This was a time of enormous intellectual activity – a time of cultural revolution in the full sense of the word. With only the most general guidelines for the creation of a socialist society, the prospects for the new Soviet socialist city were as exciting as they were uncertain. On the whole, the state tolerated, if it did not endorse, most of the ideas put forward at this time. By definition, urban culture was good. The reality of urban life was quite another matter, however. The massive urban–rural migration, which revolution and civil war occasioned, was only reversed in the early 1920s. But thereafter, unemployment and severe privation were the lot of many who sought a better life in the city. As yet, there was little to be shared amongst those who comprised the privileged in the new society. For all the theorizing about the future Soviet socialist city, the unsettled conditions meant that little was actually built. With the onset of the Stalin era, the fluidity of ideas in particular, and personal freedoms in general, were steadily checked.

Under Stalin, public proclamation about the leading rôle of the city and its proletariat in shaping culture went hand in hand with a program of coopting privatism in a variety of forms, and legally sanctioning them, on the part of the state. It was in this third period, a period of retrenchment in many ways, that the ground was prepared for the emergence of a middle class, something which had not fully developed during the imperial era. While privilege in the form of housing perks was sanctioned, it is debatable whether it materially altered the form and fabric of the city. Given the continuing acute shortage of housing, it is more likely that, as in the era of autocracy, place in society continued to be proclaimed in personal ways rather than through territorial exclusivity.

The economic reform of 1965 initiated a fourth period in which the material needs of the Soviet population have been accorded unprecedented attention. Notwithstanding the continued shortage of many consumer durables, for those who are consciously successful, or perhaps simply lucky, the opportunities for acquiring the trappings of Soviet middle-class materialism have increased enormously. From the ownership of an automobile to possession of a cooperative apartment, the rewards for participation in the system have never before been in such abundant display. Of course, this is a relative change and seemingly not always necessarily a welcome one. Since the 1960s, the tensions and anomalies of contemporary Soviet urban life have become almost as evident as the improvements in material wellbeing. From the pens of sociologists and the *literati* has issued a stream of statistics and stories suggesting that urban cultural values have not always evolved in the manner intended. But then the Soviet city both as an agent, and as an example, of cultural change has not always evolved according to town-planning principle either.

Clearly the phenomenal urban growth in the Soviet Union since the 1920s testifies to the attraction of city life. However, despite bureaucratic controls for guiding population movement, the state has been unable either to stem, or to direct spatially, this human tide according to planning principles. This has been especially so during the past 20 years. In both the imperial and Soviet eras, however, the successful realization of state policy concerning the city and society has depended upon the effectiveness of these controls. As the state's ability to direct internal migration diminished, so the goal of ordered urbanization, of an ordered, if not ideal, urban environment, has slipped from grasp. In intentionally emphasizing historical continuity as much as, or perhaps even more than, historical change, I do not wish to imply that what occurred in 1917 was unimportant or inconsequential. Rather, I am suggesting that there is some basis for arguing that urban culture, that human behavior, has been rather less easily modified by decree than have the apparatus and policies of government.

'One of the compelling ironies of urban existence is the great gap between the promise of modernity, the vision of abundance and equality, and its fulfillment by the cities which are its agents' (Dyos 1973, p. 5). In penning these words, that percipient urban historian, H. J. Dyos, was thinking of the course of urban development to the end of the 19th century. Had he extended his purview to include the 20th century, it would seem that the history of urban development in the Soviet Union would not have caused him to alter this judgment substantially.

Notes

1 In 1910, these three estates in the empire's largest city (the capital St Petersburg) comprised 20.3 percent of the 1.9 million inhabitants (*Petrograd* 1914, pp. 12–13)
2 For a brief overview of the Westernizer and slavophile ideologies, see Spector (1952, pp. 56–7 & 159–61).
3 As Olsen has noted in the context of London: 'What the Victorians desired was privacy for the middle classes, publicity for the working classes, and segregation for both.' (Olsen 1974).
4 For a pertinent contemporary model of the urban social-class structure proposed by a contemporary observer (one who was, in fact, resident in St. Petersburg during the 1830s, and who had noted the spatial heterogeneity of classes there), see Kohl (1841, pp. 181–5) and Kohl (1852, p. 10).
5 For a detailed account of the resultant differences in living standards at this time, see Barber (1980).
6 This is scarcely a new phenomenon, of course. It is interesting in this connection that even during times of real hardship, unemployment, and poverty, such as in the early 1920s, jobs in which some type of uniform was provided were especially popular. As in some contemporary situations, how one appeared was sometimes of greater import than the job itself, and even than the remuneration.

References

Barber, J. 1980. *The standard of living of Soviet industrial workers 1924–1941.* Informal working paper. Birmingham: Centre for Russian and East European Studies, University of Birmingham.

Bater, J. H. 1976. *St. Petersburg: industrialization and change.* London: Edward Arnold.

Bater, J. H. 1978a. Some dimensions of urbanization and the response of municipal government: Moscow and St. Petersburg. *Russ. Hist./Histoire Russe* **5**(1), 46–63.

Bater, J. H. 1978b. Planning problems in Siberian new towns. *Bloomsbury Geog.* **8**, 55–62.

Bater, J. H. 1980a. Transience, residential persistence and mobility in Moscow and St. Petersburg, 1900–1914. *Slavic Rev.* **39**(2), 239–54.

Bater, J. H. 1980b. *The Soviet city.* Beverly Hills: Sage.

Bater, J. H. 1981. *The social geography of St. Petersburg on the eve of the Great War.* Paper presented at the social history of Leningrad conference, University of Essex.

Blackwell, W. L. 1983. The historical geography of industry in Tsarist Russia. In *Studies in Russian historical geography.* Vol. 2. J. H. Bater and R. A. French (eds.), 387–422. London: Academic Press.

Donskov, A. 1972. *The changing image of the peasant in nineteenth century Russian drama.* Helsinki: Suomalainen Tiedeakatemia.

Dunham, V. 1976. *In Stalin's time. Middle-class values in Soviet fiction.* Cambridge: Cambridge University Press.

Dyos, H. J. 1973. *Urbanity and suburbanity. An inaugural lecture.* Leicester: Leicester University Press.

Fedor, T. S. 1975. *Patterns of urban growth in the Russian empire during the nineteenth century.* Department of Geography, University of Chicago.

French, R. A. 1965. Recent population trends in the USSR. *St. Antony's Papers* **19**, 72, 75.

Frolic, B. M. 1970. *Soviet urban politics*, p. 322. Unpubl. PhD thesis, Cornell University.

Giese, E. 1979. Transformation of Islamic cities in Soviet Middle Asia into socialist cities. In *The socialist city*, R. A. French and F. E. I. Hamilton (eds.), 145–65. New York: Wiley.

Hamm, M. J. (ed.) 1976. The breakdown of urban modernization: A prelude to the Revolution of 1917. In *The city in Russian history*, 182–200. Lexington: University Press of Kentucky.

Hosking, G. 1980. *Beyond socialist realism*. London: Holmes & Meier.

Jacobs, E. M. 1975. Urban housing in the Soviet Union. In *Economic aspects of life in the USSR*, 65–90. Brussels: NATO.

Johnson, R. E. 1979. *Peasant and proletarian*. New Brunswick, NJ: Rutgers University Press.

Kohl, J. G. 1841. *Der Verkehr und die Ansiedelung der Menschen in ihrer Abhangigkeit von der Gestaltung der Erdoberflache*. Leipzig: Arnoldische Buchhandlung.

Kohl, J. G. 1852. *Panorama of St. Petersburg*. London: Simms and McIntyre.

Kravchuk, Ya. T. 1973. *Formirovaniye Novykh Gorodov*. Moscow: Izadatel'stvo Literatury po Stroitel'stvu.

Lesoto, Ye. 1980. Craze for costly gold jewelry deplored. *Komsomolskaya Pravda* p. 4. Translated in *The Current Digest of the Soviet Press* **32**, No. 33, 8.

Lewin, M. 1979. An open depiction of Soviet Society (a review of B. Kerblay). *La Societé Sovietique Contemporaire, Soviet Studies* **31**(1), 119.

Lissitzky, El. 1970. *Russia: an architecture for a world revolution*, translated by E. Lauhosch. Cambridge, Mass.: MIT Press.

Lofland, L. H. 1973. *A world of strangers: order and action in urban public space*. New York: Basic Books.

Lukes, S. 1977. Socialism and equality. In *The socialist idea: a reappraisal*, I. Kolakowski and S. Hampshire (eds.), 74–95. London: Quartet.

Luppov, S. P. 1957. *Istoriya Stroitel'stva Peterburga v Pervoy Chetverti XVIII Veka*. Moscow: Izdatel'stvo Akademii Nauk SSSR.

Matthews, M. 1978. *Privilege in the Soviet Union*. London: George Allen & Unwin.

Matthews, M. 1979. Social dimensions in Soviet urban housing. In *The socialist city*, R. A. French and F. E. I. Hamilton (eds.), 105–18. New York: Wiley.

Miliutin, N. A. 1974. *Sotsgorod – the problems of building socialist cities*, translated by A. Sprague. Cambridge, Mass.: MIT Press.

Morton, M. W. 1980. Who gets what, when and how? Housing in the Soviet Union, *Sov. Stud.* **32**(2) 235–59.

Narodnoye Khozyaystvo SSSR v 1977 1978. Moscow.

Narodnoye Khozyaystvo SSSR 3a 60 Let. 1978. Moscow.

Narodnoye Khozyaystvo SSSR v 1979g 1980. Moscow Statistika.

Olsen, D. J. 1974. Victorian London: segregation, and privacy. *Vict. Stud.* **17**(3), 265–78.

Parkins, F. 1953. *City planning in Soviet Russia*. Chicago: University of Chicago Press.

Petrograd po Perepisi 15 Dekabrya 1910 Goda 1914. Part 1, Section 2. Petrograd.

Rukavishnikov, V. O. 1978. Ethnosocial aspects of population distribution in cities of Tataria. *Sov. Sociol.* **8**(2), 59–79.

Rukavishnikov, V. O. 1980. *Naseleniye Goroda*. Moscow: Statistika.

Sennett, R. 1977. *The fall of public man*. New York: Knopf.

Shkvarikov, V. 1954. *Ocherk Istorii Planirovki i Zastroyki Russkikh Gorodov*. Moscow: Izdatel'stvo po Stroitel'stvu Arkhitektura.

Shneidman, N. N. 1979. *Soviet literature in the 1970s: artistic diversity and ideological conformity*. Toronto: University of Toronto Press.

Spector, I. 1952. *The golden age of Russian literature*. Caldwell, Idaho: Caxton Printers.

Starr, S. F. 1978. Visionary town planning during the cultural revolution. In *Cultural revolution in Russia, 1928–1931*, S. Fitzpatrick (ed.), 207–240. Bloomington: Indiana University Press.

Strumilin, S. 1961. Family and community in the society of the future. *Sov. Rev.* **2**, 3–24.

Thurston, R. W. 1980. Police and people in Moscow, 1906–1914. *Russ. Rev.* **39**(3), 320–38.

Trifonov, Y. 1969. Obmen. *Novyy Mir* **12**, 29–65.

Voyce, A. 1948. *Russian architecture. Trends in nationalism and modernism*. New York: Philosophical Library.

Warner, S. B. Jr 1962. *Streetcar suburbs: the process of growth in Boston, 1870–1900*. Cambridge, Mass.: Harvard University Press.

Zelnik, R. 1971. *Labor and society in tsarist Russia, the factory workers of St. Petersburg, 1855–1870*. Stanford, Calif.: Stanford University Press.

8 *Japanese urban society and its cultural context*

GARY D. ALLINSON

Culture does make a difference. Despite common technology, similar construction, expanding commerce, and rising affluence, cities throughout the world retain features that emanate from distinctive cultural traditions. Other essays confirm this observation. Chinese cities, for example, display persisting indigenous qualities, fostered by the insularity of that massive nation. Middle Eastern cities, too, retain traditional features while assuming new ones, owing to the instability of international markets. Insularity and instability have also shaped the evolution of Japanese culture, as well as Japan's cities, which remain distinguishable from those of Japan's cultural cousins in both the Far and the Middle East.

But one can speak too glibly about culture. To avert that risk, it is necessary to reduce some of the ambiguity that surrounds the concept by offering the outlines of a definition. In the essay to follow, the term culture will be used in a rather arbitrary fashion: it will be defined as the cumulative product of the Japanese people's experience since the Meiji Restoration of 1868. In that year, a small group of young reformers removed from power the old régime and established the foundations of a centralized nation–state that has persisted to the present. Out of the restoration arose a grand design for the new Japan, one focused on the pursuits of military security and economic power. The outlines of that grand design have continued ever since to constitute a basic blueprint within which one can depict the more detailed features of an evolving Japanese culture.

Given this conception, the grand design can be viewed as a national vision to be implemented through political, military, diplomatic, economic, social, educational, and artistic policies. The vision, however, has been constantly and intrusively influenced by events outside the country, and by Japan's perception of those events. Defined in this way, Japan's culture is a dynamic aggregation of effects arising both from internal and external causes. These effects have shaped the evolution of a cumulative cultural product that is essentially unique. And the uniqueness of this product has in turn shaped the distinctive character of urban Japan.

I would be the first to concede the provisional and highly arbitrary nature of this definition of culture. Rather than a definition, it is better labeled a declamatory posture. It offers a perspective from which we can examine how some of the political and economic experiences of the past century have contributed to the evolution of Japan's contemporary cities. Nonetheless, my perspective seems to accord with that adopted by other authors in this collection. Both Abu-Lughod's review of the Middle East and North Africa, and Walton's study of Mexico, confirm the essential importance of international economic and political forces to the evolution of cities in particular societies. Although we may be able to appreciate those cities as distinctive artifacts, we must acknowledge that external forces have been as important in shaping their evolution as internal forces have been. This is as true of Tokyo as it is of Riyadh, Tunis, or Guadalajara.

In asserting the distinctiveness of Japanese urban society, this essay will devote considerable attention to the intangible features of urban life that are revealed in the texture and the feel of individual cities. To proceed this way is to ignore some current fashions in the social sciences, which stress systematic and empirical techniques. Certainly, these must be honored, and this paper does make slight bows in their direction. But, having used such techniques to analyze the universals, the perhaps more subtle and significant task of highlighting the particulars still remains. It is the particulars on which this essay will focus, because they are the source of what is fascinating, illuminating, and even annoying about Japan's cities.

To elucidate more fully my conception of culture – the product of the grand design that has shaped Japan's political and economic history since 1868 – the next section of the essay offers a synthetic overview of modern Japanese history. That analysis confines itself to a few factors that have been instrumental in conditioning Japan's urban environment. A third section relates these factors to the city in Japan with a description of social aspects of contemporary Tokyo, which recommends itself for several reasons. It is, first of all, Japan's largest metropolitan region. In addition, although it is not a typical case, by virtue of its size and importance Tokyo does in many ways symbolize urban Japan. Moreover, it is the Japanese city that foreign observers are most likely to encounter or visit. Finally, it is an area that I have lived in for several years and studied for many. Since my comments are often impressionistic, these experiences will, I hope, lend authority to my claims. The paper concludes with a brief, summarizing statement.

The political and economic determinants

The overriding objectives of the Meiji Restoration were to achieve military security and economic power. Thoughtful Japanese had begun to worry about their security as early as the turn of the 19th century, when

Russian expansion and Western aggression stirred their fears. Their worries grew steadily while they watched the consistent erosion of China's political sovereignty after the 1840s. They finally reached crisis proportion when Western intruders arrived at Japan's own doorstep in the 1850s. The Tokugawa régime that ruled Japan struggled valiantly to deal with the drastic changes that Perry's arrival, and a subsequent commercial treaty, caused. But it finally had to cede its authority to a new governing coalition that carried out sweeping reforms between 1868 and 1890 in order to consolidate power.[1]

The new government turned to military reform with a sense of profound urgency. Abandoning the old military organization based on a hereditary warrior class, the reformers established a conscript army and navy which drew most of their lower ranking recruits from the peasantry and relied on the old warrior class to staff the officer corps. The success of this organization was affirmed in the late 1870s, when the new army defeated the last of the dissidents opposed to the Meiji government. Thereafter, threats to domestic security from internal sources virtually disappeared, owing both to the effectiveness of the new military, and to the intrusive power of domestic police forces.

Confident of its internal position, the new government and its military leaders soon began to equate national security with foreign conquest. Emulating the Western powers, Japan began to develop its own colonial empire in the 1890s. Taiwan was the first to fall into Japan's net, following a brief skirmish with China in 1894 and 1895. In quick succession, Japan won a foothold on the Chinese mainland, assumed control of Korean affairs, and seized the expansive Manchurian area. Swept along by the events of the 1930s, Japan eventually overreached its resources, attacked the wrong enemies, and fell victim to its excessive ambitions. The price it paid was a devastating defeat in 1945.

That defeat, however, has led to a paradoxical solution to the perennial problem of national security. Although Japan has continued to maintain its own military forces, they are comparatively weaker than before the war, because Japan has relied since the war on a proxy benefactor to provide her defense. Under the terms of a treaty concluded in 1952, and renewed in 1960 and 1970, the USA agrees to protect Japan under its nuclear umbrella. The persistence of this alliance has assured for Japan the military security that its people have sought with such anxiety since the Meiji Restoration. At the same time, it has provided valuable, indirect benefits highly conducive to Japan's economic expansion.

Worry over military security, that arose so prominently in the 1860s and after, was not only rooted in anxieties about political sovereignty. Many (though not all) Japanese, from the most powerful statesman to the most poverty-stricken peasant, also harbored deep concerns about the threat to cultural autonomy and ethnic integrity, posed by the threat of foreign influence, control, or invasion. Between 1858 and 1899, these fears took on special weight, because foreigners enjoying the right of extraterritoriality were numerous in Tokyo, Yokohama, and Kobe. But the concern with cultural autonomy has remained a persisting theme in Japan's history, and has manifested itself in various guises since 1868.

In the late 1800s, Japan initially sought cultural autonomy with a military defense adequate to protect the nation from external attack. When assured of its own defensive capability, Japan assumed a different posture. It adopted the patronizing rôle of protector of the yellow peoples of Asia against the aggressive caucasian nations of the West. Japan played out that rôle in quite unconvincing fashion during World War II. But even in the more liberal postwar world, Japan has still evidenced traces of its concern for cultural autonomy, or ethnic integrity, in a range of policies affecting trade, capital investment, immigration, and so on. How these anxieties, and the policies that they spawned, have influenced the evolution of urban Japan is an issue that will be treated in the following section.

In tandem with its aspirations for military security, the new Meiji government, and nearly all of its successors, have been preoccupied with Japan's rôle as an economic power. It is perfectly understandable why this was the case in 1868. Essentially closed off from foreign intercourse during the Tokugawa period (1600–1868), Japan's technical and productive capabilities in 1868 ranked well below those of the industrializing nations of Europe and the USA. Although standards of hygiene, nutrition, and mortality may have compared favorably with the most advanced European nations, Japan's manufacturing and transportation facilities were far behind. At a time when national strength was measured in terms of foreign exports, steel capacity, and shipping tonnage, this was a cause for deep concern, and a reason for national mobilization.

In the late 1800s, governmental, as well as private, interests turned to economic development with the same avidity shown for military reform. Reformers directed early efforts toward improvements in agriculture, finance, manufacturing, and transportation. By the turn of the 20th century, they enjoyed the affluence and resources to turn to more ambitious projects in steel, electricity, and chemicals. Although initial efforts in heavy industry occurred before dramatic military expansion in the 1930s, that expansion spurred much higher rates of growth in steel, electrical goods, and chemicals, as well as aircrafts and vehicles. Wartime destruction and postwar depression placed a moratorium on Japan's economic development. But, by the late 1950s, the nation had returned with a vengeance to the goal of making itself an economic power. Having had to sublimate its military urges, Japan has seemed to invest almost double energy since then in its economic pursuits, whose successes need not be chronicled here (Okhawa & Rosovsky 1973).

However, it must be noted that the twin goals of military security and economic power have played a decisive rôle in shaping the pattern of urban development in Japan since 1868. The new military forces were garrisoned in a group of battalion headquarter towns, giving a new lease on life to many old castle-towns whose fortunes waned with the demise of the Tokugawa régime. In addition, the emergence of a new navy stimulated the need for ports, arsenals, and shipyards, that grew after 1868, sometimes in old cities, and sometimes in entirely new ones.

Japan's pursuit of economic status also stimulated the expansion of old cities and the appearance of new ones. Many early textile mills were built in former castle-towns, with the purpose of reviving their flagging economies and rescuing the old warrior class. Later, however, mills were often built in rural towns, which became diversified industrial and commercial centers. In similar fashion, some of the new heavy industries also rose from modest beginnings in rural places. Their growth has fostered the emergence of large regional cities dominated by single firms or industries (see, for example, Allinson 1975). And, of course, many new firms, industries, and cities grew on the edge of Japan's historic manufacturing quarters in Tokyo and Osaka. In all these ways, the grand design for military security and economic power played a decisive rôle in laying out Japan's contemporary system of cities (Allinson 1978).

The grand design produced ancillary effects that have also influenced the development of Japan's urban system. The urge to centralize control was strong in the Meiji government. Fostering this urge was a legacy of more than 270 years of quasi-feudal authority, when the country had been divided into over 200 small, regional, semi-autonomous baronies. Within five years of its ascent, the new government eliminated the old administrative structure, and organized a new one. The focal point of the system was the capital city of Tokyo. It became the headquarters for the new government. It also became the residence of the emperor himself, who was obliged to move from the former capital of Kyoto, where his ancestors had resided for more than a millennium. Beyond Tokyo were the 47 prefectural capitals through which bureaucratic appointees of the central government ruled the new administrative units of the country. Each of these prefectural cities automatically became a center of commerce and administration, thereby boosting the fortunes of older cities that had declined in the immediate wake of the Restoration.

In addition to centralization, colonization also played a rôle in developing the nationwide system of cities after 1868. Japan's northernmost island of Hokkaido had never been fully integrated into the life of the nation. During the Tokugawa period, it was populated by sparse settlements of Ainu tribesmen, and by two small settlements of native Japanese. The Meiji government declared Hokkaido a target for colonial settlement and agricultural development. Experiencing sporadic success,

Hokkaido began to grow more rapidly when coal and iron ore were found, spawning the emergence of an industrial economy based on scattered mining and manufacturing settlements. With their appearance, the administrative center of Sapporo took on greater importance, as did the island's port cities. Out of Hokkaido's development has emerged a new urban zone that complements development on the main islands while retaining its own character.

A final element in the compound of national policies that fostered Japan's military and economic expansion was the internal system of transport. Japan had no modern railways when Perry arrived in 1853, and few harbors capable of accepting large, ocean-going vessels. Both public and private initiatives helped to resolve the former problem; by the turn of the 20th century, Japan had more than 5000 miles of railways. The new rail system, like the growing industrial sector, breathed life into old cities, and stimulated the rise of new ones that served as rail heads and repair yards. Dependent on ocean transport for the import of raw materials and the export of industrial products, Japan also turned to the construction of better ports and harbors. Out of this effort have emerged two of the country's largest cities, Yokohama and Kobe, as well as a spate of smaller transport entrepôts that serve the nation's economic needs.

This altogether too schematic survey has stressed the significance of anxiety about military security and desire for economic power as two driving forces in Japan's recent history. Of course other nations have also been preoccupied with the same issues; but what sets Japan apart is the remarkable dedication with which it has pursued these goals, the relative success with which it has attained them, and the distinctive culture that has emerged as a result. By contrast with many other nations that once experienced the problems Japan faced in 1868, Japan has been able to protect its domestic security, and to pursue its economic goals, in large measure at its own initiative. Such retention of political integrity, fed by a need for cultural autonomy, has also imposed distinctive marks on the character of Japan's cities.

Japanese urban society: aspects of life in Tokyo

To illustrate the character of Japan's cities, this section will analyze social aspects of contemporary Tokyo. Although it is a designation with a familiar ring, 'Tokyo' is nonetheless a term that requires a moment's attention, because there is no city of Tokyo.

Since 1943, the term Tokyo has been used to designate a metropolitan prefecture (*to*). Japan has 47 prefectures, which embody dual (and sometimes contradictory) rôles as both autonomous units of local government, and subordinate agencies of national administration. Like Japan's other

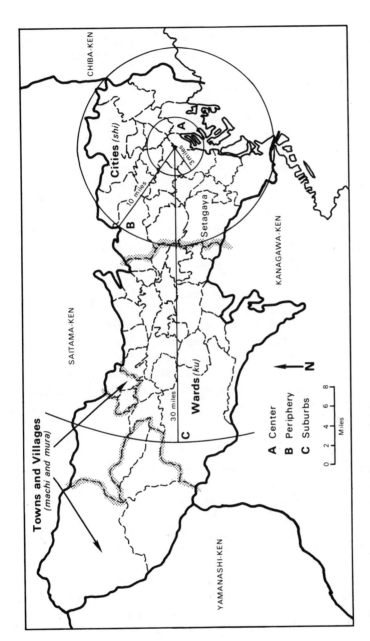

Figure 8.1 Tokyo metropolitan prefecture.

prefectures, Tokyo Metropolitan Prefecture governs many of its own affairs, through the authority of an elected governor (*to chiji*), and legislative assembly, but it does so under the watchful eye and intrusive control of the central government.

Within the prefecture are two distinguishable parts (Fig. 8.1). Its eastern third is comprised of 23 wards (*ku*), each with an elected executive (*kuchō*), and legislature. The wards have a population exceeding 8 million. The western two-thirds of the prefecture is divided into 32 separate municipalities (*shichōson*). They have their own elected executives (*chō*), and assemblies, and a total population approaching 4 million. In its formal designation, therefore, 'Tokyo' refers to the metropolitan prefecture with its numerous administrative subdivisions that today embrace 10 percent of the nation's population.[2]

In a broader sense, however, 'Tokyo' refers to much more than this metropolitan prefecture. The concept must be stretched to encompass most of the adjacent prefectures of Saitama, Chiba, and Kanagawa. From this perspective, one can envision Tokyo as a series of three concentric circles, including a center, a periphery, and a suburban ring. The center has a radius of about 3 miles, and encompasses 8 of the 23 wards. The governmental, commercial, and financial facilities situated in the center act like magnets to attract millions of commuting workers, shoppers, and others each day from the periphery and suburbs. We can think of the periphery as the 'outer city;' it is devoted mainly to residential use, but it also has extensive commercial and industrial districts within it. It stretches to a distance of about 10 miles from the center, thus embracing the remainder of the 23 wards. If there were a city of Tokyo, casual logic would recommend that it encompass these two circles within the metropolis – the center, and the periphery. The third and final circle in the Tokyo metropolis is the suburban ring. It stretches to a distance of 30 miles (and, increasingly, beyond), and reaches out to embrace not only the western two-thirds of Tokyo Metropolitan Prefecture, but also large parts of Saitama, Chiba, and Kanagawa prefectures. Adding the population of the suburbs to those of the center and periphery produces a total of more than 27 million metropolitan Tokyo residents.

The following discussion will deal with this metropolitan area in its entirety. When appropriate, reference will be made to the various subareas within it, in particular the center or downtown business district, the periphery or outer city, and the suburban residential ring. The discussion will focus on conditions since the 1970s, and will address the following topics: functional concentration, rhythms of urban life, patterns of work, status and space, models of retreat, and urban pathologies.

Functional concentration The 27 million residents of the Tokyo region provide the first, and most visible, evidence of concentration. They comprise one-quarter of the nation's population, all living in an area about one-half the size of Connecticut. Such ratios of concentration are familiar in the so-called primate cities of developing countries, but they are less common in highly developed industrial societies, so we shall examine in due course some of the causes and consequences of this phenomenon in Japan. High population densities attend such concentration. For the entire metropolis, densities are similar to those in crowded American cities such as Pittsburgh and St Louis; they approach 10 000 persons per square mile. Closer to the center, densities rise sharply. Within the 23 wards, they are half again as high as the New York City; in the most crowded wards, they are nearly double the New York City level, and approach 50 000 persons per square mile. This fact is the more remarkable when we consider that large amounts of residential space in Tokyo, even in the center, are still constructed in only two- or three-storied dwellings, not in high-rise buildings. Although we might expect to associate such high densities with some predictable urban pathologies, this is not the case (as will be seen later).

The demographic and functional concentration that characterizes Tokyo is, to a large extent, the product of a national urge toward centralization since the Meiji Restoration, especially in government and political life. Tokyo had been the site of the shogun's headquarters during the Tokugawa period (when it was known as Edo), but only in 1868 did the emperor also move to the area and make it the center of both nominal and actual political authority. As the ministries of the new government expanded, they put up their stately structures in Tokyo. So, too, did the national legislature when it was formed in 1890. And the many research institutes, special agencies, and quasi-public bodies that grew in step with Japan's military and economic development also often settled in Tokyo. By the 1960s, nearly 0.5 million officials worked for the national government alone, most in Tokyo; and an indeterminate number of others were funded, directly or indirectly, by the national treasury. Since the 1970s, the government has striven to reduce concentration somewhat, by siting new research facilities at a planned city a two hour train ride to the north. But this modest dispersion has done little to diminish Tokyo's fundamental importance as the center of the nation's governmental and political life.

Because Japan's central government has employed its administrative and political influence extensively in promoting the nation's economic development, private concerns found themselves obliged to situate in Tokyo. Old family enterprises (like Mitsui), and new ones (such as Mitsubishi), demonstrated the values of this arrangement during the late 1800s. They bought land in central Tokyo near the headquarters of the new government, and benefited handsomely from their proximity to the régime. Other firms in manufacturing, commerce, and finance were quick to learn the lesson. Even if their major facilities were not situated in

Tokyo, they needed at least a liaison officer there, if not a headquarters building. The events of the war, and the consolidation and concentration that it promoted, helped to draw more firms to the Tokyo area. Today, it is virtually impossible for any major business organization to function without substantial representation in Tokyo. As a consequence, nearly one-third of Japan's private corporations are located in the four prefectures of the Tokyo metropolitan region.[3]

A metropolis in which both government and business were so heavily concentrated proved a special lure for educational institutions. Government itself sought to create a public system of higher education, making the University of Tokyo a national model with international aspirations. It also tried to monitor and control the emergence of a private system of higher education. The men who initiated this system, often outspoken opponents of the Meiji government, succeeded in making their universities some of the best in the country. Proximity to government and business, the quality of the institutions themselves, and the appeal of the metropolis all helped to promote the development of an extensive body of educational institutions in Tokyo. By the late 1970s, 20 percent of the nation's post-secondary schools were situated in Tokyo Metropolitan Prefecture alone, and they were training a full one-third of the nation's college and university students. Among cities in the advanced capitalist societies, only Paris can perhaps rival Tokyo as the pre-eminent national center of university life and student culture. Higher education and the arts are also Tokyo's special preserve. Nearly one-third of the nation's college and university teachers reside in the metropolis. They are essential producers for a huge publishing industry that relies heavily on the still-respected *sensei*, or teacher, to write for the daily newspapers, weekly magazines, and monthly journals that make Tokyo the center of the nation's print media. Tokyo is also the site of the nation's major libraries, museums, symphonies, theaters, and (that latecomer to the entertainment scene) television studios. Although Kyoto and Osaka still preserve the major traditional arts, such as the tea ceremony, the Noh drama, and *bunraku*, or puppet theater, Tokyo has long been the point of entry for literary and artistic productions from abroad. Whether as innovator or conservator, however, Tokyo brooks few challenges from other cities, and occupies the dominant position as Japan's fine arts and intellectual center.

Rhythms of urban life   The vibrant rhythms of Tokyo's urban life are a product of its concentrations of people, government, business, industry, education, and the arts. To develop a feel for those rhythms, let us accompany a typical white-collar suburbanite through his daily routine.

The commute from home to work issues his first challenge of the day. Let us assume that ours is a young commuter in his thirties, with a wife and young children, who lives in a rented apartment that is likely to be an hour or more from his place of work. He probably rises early to gulp down a breakfast. A rapid hike of 10 to 20 minutes will bring him to a major transport point, where he will board a bus, subway, or electric train that will carry him most of the distance to the center. Often operated by public bodies, these conveyances are clean, punctual, and efficient. During the early morning rush, they are also crowded. He will find himself jammed in among hundreds of others like him, with space only to hold up a small, inexpensive weekly magazine he has grabbed at the station to occupy his thoughts during the long, tedious trip. Even though many other young commuters may live in his own apartment dwelling and make a similar journey each morning, he is unlikely to travel with a companion. He spends so little time at home that he knows few of his neighbors. And, since he assumes he will be moving shortly into his own home, he sees little reason to strike up friendships on the walk to the station or the ride to work.

Although our young worker travels singly, he is by no means alone on his commute into the center. In the early 1980s, some 4 million persons move daily from the suburbs and periphery into the central districts of Tokyo. Some are students, others are shoppers, but most are workers. High land prices and scarce housing in the central districts necessitate their long journeys. The buses, trains, and subways on which they ride are routinely filled at three times capacity during the hours from seven to ten. As the crush of commuters descends on the center each morning, Tokyo comes to life. Students, shoppers, and workers form a human procession as they rush to their destinations. Daylight hours witness a continuing buzz of activity within the center sections, which only begins to wane in the early evening, when the droves of commuters gradually retreat to their homes for the night.

During the lengthy day that our young man spends in the center, he would find himself occupied with a variety of work and diversion demanding something less than exhausting effort on his part. He would find time for a break at least once during the morning, and again in the afternoon, when young women from his office would be called on to serve him tea or coffee. He would also have time to accompany some fellow workers to a midday lunch. They would probably find a small spot stuffed in an alley or hidden in a basement, of the kind that serves cheap lunches to the daily working crowds. The crush of business at such establishments would oblige them to wolf down a meal of fish and rice, or a bowl of noodles, and they could stroll about for a smoke before having to return to work. In the office itself, they might be lucky enough to delegate the most stressful work to subordinates, or to young women who, as in banks, are often placed at the point of contact to deal with the steady flow of customers. Protected behind barricades of secretaries, that grow deeper as one moves up the hierarchy, many male white-collar workers in Tokyo's offices seem to enjoy considerable discretion in setting the pace of the typical workday.

By the 1970s, the formal workday drew to a close at five in the afternoon, but it seldom actually stopped until six or seven in the evening. Quitting time depended on many things, including tasks, rank, day, and season, but for most it came in the wake of some nine or ten hours on the job. Leaving work, however, would not bring office associations to an end. For our commuter would be very likely to leave his building with a subordinate in tow, following at a respectful distance behind his supervisor. They could well spend the next two to three hours together easing the tensions of the day at a beer hall, sake bar, or small restaurant in an entertainment quarter near their office, perhaps in company with a hostess or two, remarkably skilful at burnishing male egos. Dedicated to the leisure and social wellbeing of the salary man, these establishments dot the map of the Tokyo region. They concentrate near downtown business districts, or at transportation junctions where subways and trains meet to carry the workers into the suburbs at night. If our young man feels especially flush, or if there is business to conduct through the informal channels that this kind of social lubrication offers, he may not get on his train to go home until nine or ten in the evening.

By the time he reaches home, his children will long since have retired for the day, and his wife will wait only long enough to feed him a late meal, prepare a bath, and greet him before she turns in, if she has not done so already. His time at home during the week is given over mainly to eating a hasty meal late at night, taking a leisurely bath, viewing a little television, sleeping through the night, gulping down breakfast, and moving off to pursue the same routine once more the next day. Through the early 1970s, he did this six days a week, but since the economic recession of the 1970s, most workers in Tokyo's offices have pursued only a five-day week. Under these circumstances, the typical white-collar suburbanite has shallow roots in his neighborhood and community, finds himself preoccupied with work and career, and sees little of his wife and children.

His wife, like most of the other middle-class urban women with whom he is likely to come into contact, lives a sexually segregated existence, with its own rhythms that differ from his and those of his male associates. She is, to a large extent, confined in the suburban home and its immediate environment, owing to a firm division of labor by gender that is deeply embedded both in the institutional structure of Japanese society, and the cultural consciousness of its citizenry. From the moment of marriage, and certainly from the onset of pregnancy, middle-class urban women are expected to devote their energies to homemaking, in accordance with a feminine ideal that first appeared in the 1910s and 1920s. The wife sees that the children get to school and do their homework; she represents the family on the PTA; she serves when the school needs 'volunteers;' she does the shopping, the cleaning, the bookkeeping; and she is the family's diplomat in the neighborhood and the community. As inflation has driven more women back into the labor force, and as young women have insisted on pursuing their own careers, changes have begun to take place in what must seem a stereotyped portrait. But to a very large extent, a strict, gender-based division of labor, opportunities, expectations, and rewards prevails as a societal norm in urban Japan. It has, perhaps, facilitated the productivity that emerges out of Japan's work patterns, by essentially releasing husbands from the responsibilities that attend household management and the anxieties that accompany child rearing.[4]

Patterns of work   The drive for economic power has been a controling theme in Japan's history since the Restoration of 1868. It has taken on added impetus in the postwar era, when the need to sublimate military aspirations has provided surplus energy for economic endeavors. Japan has pursued its economic goals through a variety of policies that have evolved to adapt effectively to changing internal and external circumstances. But among all the economic policies pursued, few have been as consistent as those aimed at controling the labor force. Both government and private management have striven to create labor policies that will assure stable supplies of capable, dedicated, and acquiescent workers.

The contemporary outcome of this effort is a pattern of work relations that is distinctive among the advanced industrial societies, at least in those sectors of the Japanese economy where it prevails (Dore 1973). Although controversy surrounds estimates of the extent of the system, we might safely assume that about one-third of the salaried labor force is subject to this pattern of relations in the nation as a whole, and perhaps closer to one-half the Tokyo labor force. The essential features of the system are firm- or enterprise-based labor markets, in which employers elicit high measures of loyalty from their workers through customary grants of lifetime employment, payments of seniority wage increases, and provisions of substantial ancillary benefits.

In firms that respect these practices, workers are hired when they leave school. Production workers usually enter the labor force after completing a high-school degree, white-collar workers after graduation from college. Following a short probationary period, when new recruits are subjected to an intensive training program that emphasizes spiritual training as much as technical, the new entrants become regular employees. It is assumed, largely on customary grounds, that they will remain with the firm until retirement. This commitment represents a vow of loyalty on the part of the worker. In return, he can expect to receive many tangible and intangible benefits.[5]

Tangible benefits include virtually guaranteed wage increases that rise with length of service, inexpensive housing, or low-interest home loans, and a lump-sum severance bonus on retirement. In addition, his firm will provide medical facilities, and a wide range of social and recreational benefits. These could include everything from after-work softball games on the company's own nearby fields, to group outings at the company-owned ski lodge in the mountains. During his working career, the typical employee will often spend his weekends and holidays with his work associates, seeking them out in preference to friends outside the company. And even his wife and children will find themselves growing old in association with other wives and children from the firm. To an American, it will seem suffocating and claustrophobic. But to the conventional Japanese company man, this pattern of work and leisure relations provides a warm, secure setting in which to carry on a life dedicated to the wellbeing of his firm – and, to some extent also, of the nation.

This pattern of relations has had one profound effect on Japan's social structure, and therefore on its urban society. It has demonstrably dulled class consciousness and visibly restricted class cleavages. One small, but significant, bit of evidence must suffice to substantiate this claim. The organized labor movement in Japan is highly segmented along several lines of partisan division. The largest national federation embraces about 4 million workers, or some 30 percent of all those organized, but only 11 percent of all salaried employees. Most of the members of this federation are public employees who support left-socialist candidates. However, the next largest federation, with about 2 million members, almost exclusively organizes workers in private enterprises. Although this federation is allied with the right-socialists, it has itself pursued policies that are barely distinguishable from those of the conservatives who have ruled Japan since 1955. In short, enterprise-based labor markets have fostered enterprise unions that stymie class consciousness and obstruct working-class organization. This has divided the labor movement along partisan lines, weakened the collective political influence of organized workers, and contributed to the persistence of conservative power in Japan. The bureaucratic and managerial desire to exercise strict regulation and control over labor has manifested itself in another outcome that highlights a crucial distinction between Japan and other nations, especially those of the contemporary Middle East. Japan has not relied on immigrant laborers or guest workers to staff its factories – with the exception of a brief period during the Pacific War (1937–45), when it imported laborers from its Korean colony to toil in mines and factories in the home islands. Many of those Korean immigrants have remained in Japan; they usually occupy low-status jobs in the manufacturing and service sectors. But, and this is the point to note here, they number only about 650 000. When all non-native residents of Japan are counted, the total is only about 770 000, or less than 1 percent of the nation's populace (*Nihon no tōkei* 1978, p. 25). The virtual absence of foreign residents attests to Japan's success at achieving its aspirations for ethnic integrity, and it clearly distinguishes labor conditions and urban society in Japan from those in most other societies.

Status and space   Intimately related to the features of class and ethnicity just discussed are the patterns of status and spatial development in urban Japan. Spatial segregation according to socioeconomic and ethnic criteria is an urban phenomenon that dates from time immemorial. But it may have reached an apogee in the contemporary world. One thinks, for example, of the subtle gradations of status in the suburbs of contemporary America, and of the brazen and unusual cities of the petroleum-rich Middle East. Japan, however, seems to confound this general expectation, because its cities have few districts sharply defined by the status and ethnicity of their residents.

Having said that, we must nonetheless begin with a few disclaimers, drawing our evidence from the Tokyo metropolis. First, speaking in general terms, there are areas in Tokyo which have always been more desirable than others. Since the Tokugawa period, when the regional barons (*daimyō*) were required to maintain residences near the shogun, the residential quarters situated on the higher lands to the west of the central districts have attracted those with the highest incomes and greater status. As Tokyo spread outward, its western and southwestern districts retained their attractions for the wealthy, owing to their accessibility to the center, the breezes their heights attracted, and a generally more appealing topography. By contrast, the area to the east of the central district holds fewer appeals for the well-to-do. It is situated, for the most part, in low-lying delta lands, or it is based on land-fill built into the bay. As a result, its topography is flat and drab, its temperatures are high, its breezes are infrequent, and its desirability for residential purposes is low. As a general rule, therefore, western Tokyo enjoys a higher status than eastern, and empirical evidence confirms that perceptions are underlain by actual differences in income of residents, quality of housing, and degree of congestion.

Secondly, Tokyo does not have very many exclusive enclaves, but it does have some. In the United States, one can find entire communities (Grosse Point Farms comes to mind) where virtually everyone is obliged to own an acre or more of land, and to put up a dwelling that does justice to the property and to that of one's neighbors. There is no location precisely like this in Tokyo. However, there are a few concentrated districts in which an unusually high proportion of wealthy residents have built expensive homes with some land around them. One of these is a planned garden community, built in the 1920s, and focused on a prestigious private academy south-west of the center. It persists today as the Seijō District of Setagaya Ward, where one also finds other enclaves of large dwellings for the wealthy. But the exclusive, socially, and perhaps ethnically, homogeneous suburb of North America has features that, by and large, are not replicated in Tokyo, for a variety of reasons.

Technical constraints, embodied by the transportation network, have promoted dense settlement in mixed districts. During its period of most dramatic expansion, Tokyo relied primarily on electric trolleys, buses, above-ground railways, and subways to carry its residents about the metropolis. Autos appeared on the scene in quantity only after the 1960s, by which time most of the physical structure of the metropolis had been defined. Its definition took the form of a series of points along lines created by railways and subways, especially in the periphery and suburbs: the points were transfer stations where buses and trolleys dropped commuters, who then boarded railways, or perhaps other buses, to make the trek into the more distant regions. These transfer points nearly always grew to become centers of commerce. They attracted department stores, retail shops, service outlets, restaurants, bars, office buildings, and a melange of urban establishments to serve residents and commuters alike. New residential quarters then grew on the edge of these commercial nodes, because they provided convenient shopping for wives and easy transportation access for husbands. Therefore, the desire to reduce commuting costs fostered the emergence of a concentrated pattern of development, by contrast with the expansive, long-distance commuting that the automobile encouraged in postwar America.

A second factor promoting mixed residential siting in Tokyo has been the virtual absence of concentrated ethnic groups. By sharp contrast with the United States, Japan (and Tokyo in particular) has simply not had large groups of immigrants who were driven together by their own need for cooperation and by the nativist demand for separation. The Korean population has always been too small, and too dispersed in several cities, to pose the conspicuous problem of ethnic assimilation that American cities have faced, or that Middle Eastern cities now face. The absence of this goad seems to have dulled the salience of residential separation in the mind of the Japanese urbanite.

Third, we have noted above that class consciousness, too, has been relatively weak among Japanese urbanites. The combination of speech, dress, manners, and style, that drove a strong wedge between the English worker and his social betters, for example, did not operate with the same efficacy in Japan. The refined obsequiousness inherent in the Japanese language probably impeded the development of some differences. What language did not obstruct, the peculiar consciousness that emerged out of the employment system may have. Rather than seeing each other as implacable enemies, the most urbane manager and the lowest production worker seemed to elevate their common bonds as enterprise members (and Japanese subjects?) to a higher plane that overcame their class, if not their status, differences. As a consequence, the manager did not come to feel that he could only survive in the residential company of other managers, and the worker was not obliged to think that he was good enough only to live among his mates. Many seem to have adopted a far more pragmatic tack. They just settled where they could find affordable housing, unfettered, at least to some extent, by the weight of class concern.

Perhaps for some of the reasons already noted, the lack of rigorous city planning is a fourth reason for the mixed character of spatial use in Tokyo. There were occasions when enlightened civic reformers sought to adopt European plans in the development of Tokyo and other Japanese cities. The efforts of Gotō Shimpei in the wake of the 1923 earthquake are just one example. But the kind of planning that produced segregated residential districts in Europe and North America did not take root in Japan until very recently. This is perhaps attributable to the low salience of the issue in the popular mind. Since the issue never seems to have been forcefully articulated, it is not surprising that the desire for socially segregated housing areas was never widely met.

On a wholly speculative note, we might identify a fifth reason for the lack of emphasis on social segregation in urban Japan. Refined understatement is one of the enduring esthetic values in Japan. It is expressed, for example, in an appreciation for things that are *shibui*: defined, somewhat subjectively, as the sensation one derives from tasting a persimmon. Things *shibui* are spare, plain, almost rustic, but nonetheless elegant in an understated way. Moved by such attitudes, the wealthy industrialist was not obliged to advertize his fortune with a rococco mansion on the corner. He could seek quiet satisfaction in a rock garden hidden behind a stucco wall down the street from his workers' apartments, and some of them did just that. It was the owner's interior appreciation for the object itself that counted, not the statement that it blared to the outside world. By contrast, therefore, with the conspicuous consumption that has usually signaled the rise to status in the West, the Japanese (sometimes, though by no means always) have emphasized inconspicuous display.

For all these reasons, the Western observer will be surprised by the highly mixed nature of land use in Tokyo and other Japanese cities. It is not at all uncommon to find people from different socioeconomic statuses living cheek-by-jowl. A fitting example concerns the heir to one of Japan's postwar electronics fortunes. He has built, in a western suburb, an opulent home that could easily be mistaken for a small, modern cathedral. On the western edge of his property sits a dormitory for single men who work in a downtown bank. On the south are several small homes owned by middle-level white-collar workers. On the east is a building used as a *kendō* (mock sword-fighting) hall by students from a local university. And on the north, beyond a parking lot awaiting development, sits a spanking new drive-in restaurant. Apparently, the eclectic features of his neighborhood are of minor consequence to this Japanese industrialist, but they make you wonder if the president of Texas Instruments would abide the situation.

Modes of retreat   Enough has been said by this point to provoke questions about how the Japanese get away from it all. Here are millions of people living in small dwellings, situated in congested districts. They constantly bump up against others from all walks of life, not only on crowded subways, but even in their own neighborhoods. And all this at the end of 10- to 16-hour workdays. How do Japanese retreat from the pressures of urban life?

One recourse is to go where the crowds are. Recall that our young commuter sought to unwind from his day at the office by accompanying associates to a beer hall, sake bar, or restaurant. Usually, these are situated in congested districts, teeming with people between the hours of six and ten at night. Indeed, the louder the noise, the greater the crowds, and the more pressing the crush, the better it is for many. Districts that succeed in combining these elements in an indefinable, yet not excessive, fashion are the ones that lure most night-time revelers.

Our man of the house is not the only one who might find retreat by seeking out crowds. His wife, left at home alone while the children are at school, may join a companion or two to seek out their own crowds. They will probably find them in a nearby shopping district, or perhaps near a train station where several large department stores display their wares. Once again, the wife and her companions will be attracted most avidly to those places that combine an indefinable but appealing measure of noise, frenzy, and crowding. Contributors will include milling coveys of shoppers, hawking salesmen at storefronts, and shouting greengrocers and fruit dealers. Too little of this noise and bustle operates like a mute warning signal to drive people away; too much is a limit that few seem ever to reach.

We now have descriptions of Japanese who sanction the esthetic values of understatement and inconspicuous display, yet retreat from the trials of urban life by seeking out noisy crowds. Is such behavior not openly contradictory? Yes, and to many it seems not to matter. We can resolve the contradiction somewhat by noting that all of us develop moods that call for solitude on some occasions and camaraderie on others. The Japanese urbanite is no different in this regard. A tired executive might opt for a cup of tea while gazing at his garden following a hectic day, and a night out with associates on another. But in his case, there may be more at work than the requirements of a proper mood.

Most Japanese pride themselves on their ability to close themselves off from their immediate surroundings. In some respects, this is an absolutely essential defensive mechanism conducive to survival in Tokyo. If one is trying to write an essay while a dog barks across the street, a neighbor's daughter practises her piano, and a pile driver works away at the corner, one either learns to adapt (since a move is seldom possible), or one goes crazy (as a few actually do, sometimes eliminating the budding pianist in the bargain).

For the harried journalist, or the overburdened *sensei* behind in his deadline, there is an institutionalized form for closing people off. It is called *kanzume*, or being canned. The desperate publisher puts up the money to ensconce the negligent author in a secluded hotel room for three nights and three days, or however long it requires for him to complete his assignment. This carries confinement to an extreme, and it is a mite involuntary, but it suggests one mechanism for dealing with the distracting bustle of urban life.

One sees the same, or similar, mechanisms being employed in other places under different circumstances. Quiet, secluded areas are rare in Tokyo's commercial districts. Someone seeking a few minutes of respite, while assembling energies for the next challenge, will likely repair to a *kissa*, or coffee shop, to do so. More often than not, noisy music will be blaring over loudspeakers, and other patrons will also be raising a bit of a ruckus. But people think, read, even write under such circumstances. Some of the few secluded areas that do exist are on the grounds of Buddhist temples or Shinto shrines, often situated in the midst of very busy commercial districts. Once inside, it is possible to feel wholly separated from the material world beyond – unless a herd of visiting students arrives to threaten one's solitude. People can nonetheless sit obliviously through the racket such students create, apparently untouched by their clamor. Some might attribute their stoicism to the Buddhist ability to eschew this-worldly things, but we may not want to dismiss the possibility that it is also a determined insouciance devised to face minor catastrophes. Life in Tokyo hones such skills.

Urban pathologies Hints have appeared throughout this chapter to suggest that Japan's cities may not be victimized by the urban pathologies that are so common in other contemporary societies. Turning to address this issue directly, we can assert that Japan does not experience the same problems of urban poverty, unemployment, slum life, crime, discrimination, and ethnic conflict that so many other nations now do.

The national commitment to economic power, and the success with which the goal has been achieved in the postwar period, have both restricted unemployment in Japan to exceptionally low levels. Throughout the 1960s, when the economy was growing at real rates that often exceeded 10 percent per annum, the official national unemployment rate hovered at around 1 percent. In the wake of the international economic uncertainties that arose after 1973, unemployment rose somewhat, but it has seldom gone beyond the 2 percent mark. Perhaps as important to the issue of urban pathology as the rate of unemployment, is the effect of unemployment on age groups. In Japan, young workers are likely to be the first hired, so adolescent unemployment is virtually nonexistent. Those who lose their jobs are most likely to be older workers with experience, and, if they are fortunate, some private resources to see them through the worst of times. Consequently, Japan simply does not have the massive pockets of unemployment among volatile groups of younger males that so plague urban society in the United States.

A high rate of employment is just one reason why Japan has very low crime rates. Other reasons include the efficient operation of an extensive domestic security force, a cooperative rather than adversarial relationship between the police and society, patterns of social relationships that constrain deviants before they become a public menace, and strict laws (including gun-control legislation) that still elicit widespread compliance (Bayley 1976, Ames 1981). The consequence of these habits and practices is a crime rate that is among the lowest in the world for a nation with cities so populous. This makes it possible for people to stroll safely at night through the streets of central Tokyo without fear of attack or assault. The worst offense a woman returning home alone late at night might (ordinarily) expect to encounter would be a lewd sneer and a verbal fantasy from a tipsy clerk staggering to make the last train.

Broad swaths of American cities are now scarred by dismal areas given over to empty lots, burned-out buildings, and decripit housing where thousands of people are forced to survive. One finds no counterpart to such devastation in a Japanese city. In part, the land would be too valuable to so misuse it. But beyond this, the racial discrimination and income inequalities that are so much a stimulus to slum conditions in the United States are comparatively absent from the Japanese scene. We have seen that non-native groups comprise less than 1 percent of the resident populace, thus drastically limiting the potential for ethnic-based discrimination. Although there are obvious inequities in the distribution of income, some current statistics suggest that they are not as wide as those in the United States, for example (Schnitzer 1973, pp. 222–9). Moreover, given the low rates of unemployment and a still operative system of family-based social welfare, even those who are the worst off are fewer and less conspicuous in Japan than in many other countries of the world.

But this glowing portrait does have some blemishes. The Korean minority has already been mentioned. One has only to talk briefly with Korean immigrants to understand that, public rhetoric to the contrary, they suffer visible discrimination at the hands of the Japanese majority.

They are shunted into the least desirable jobs, they often eke out tenuous livings, and they suffer a low social status (Lee & DeVos 1981).

Another minority group afflicted with similar disabilities is the *burakumin*. *Burakumin* do not differ ethnically or physically from the majority Japanese. They are a segregated minority because their ancestors once pursued occupations proscribed by Buddhist law, such as tanning, butchering, and undertaking. For more than a millennium, political practice and social customs have sustained their segregation, and they continue to suffer social, educational, political, and economic discrimination today. They live in *burakumin* ghettos, speak (in many cases) a distinct form of Japanese, work at low-status occupations, and generally suffer acute deprivation. Because their numbers are relatively small (estimates range from 2 to 3 million) and because their communities are dispersed in many urban and rural areas, the *burakumin* have found it difficult to press their case politically. But in recent years they have won a hearing among progressive governments in the largest cities, and some of their worst problems are now being addressed effectively for the first time (Wagatsuma & DeVos 1966).

Finally, every major Japanese city does have a few pockets of abject poverty. In some cases, these provide a home for those who are chronically down and out. In other cases, they are the vanishing remnants of communities established by wartime survivors who were never able to resume productive lives in the majority society. As is often the case in so-called cultures of poverty, these communities are frequently orderly enclaves of disadvantaged persons. Their residents are able to eke out a meager living in casual labor markets, or by dint of individual efforts. And they possess a measure of social cohesiveness that partly sustains them in the face of obvious misfortune.

Conclusion

The evidence presented above illustrates that Japan and its principal metropolis are possibly anomalies among contemporary urban societies. We have sought an explanation for this condition in Japan's political and economic history since 1868. The Meiji Restoration of that year was animated by two overriding goals: military security, and economic power. Moreover, those goals were pursued in an ideological context, and with political purposes that sought to preserve Japan's cultural autonomy and its ethnic integrity. Since then, strong state administration has been almost consistently successful in realizing the goals first articulated in the late 1800s.

The product of this experience is a distinctive national character that is reflected in an equally distinctive urban society. Symbolizing Japan's cities is a huge metropolis with an unusually high concentration of people, government, business, industry, education, and the arts. The metropolis is a daily witness to a familiar, yet distinctive, set of rhythms that pace the life of its residents. Drawing inspiration both from the Japanese past and from the external world, these rhythms reflect a synthesis that influences the organization of work life, shapes perceptions of status, affects modes of retreat, and regulates social pathologies. Out of this constantly evolving synthesis have emerged some 650 cities that are, like the Tokyo region, vital, stimulating, prosperous, and safe. In comparison with other societies, it is a remarkable – perhaps even enviable – achievement.

Notes

The author would like to express his appreciation to the Japan Foundation and the United States Educational Commission in Japan for fellowship support that facilitated the writing of this essay. This work is in no way associated with the University Centre for International Studies or the Asian Studies Program of the University of Pittsburgh.

1 Two major sources that examine this period and its changes are Beasley (1972) and Norman (1940).
2 The one monograph now available on Tokyo treats its western suburbs (see Allinson 1979).
3 Statistical data cited in this essay are drawn from *Nihon no tōkei* (1978). For this citation, see pp. 40–41.
4 A recent study of women in Japan is detailed in Pharr (1981).
5 For an insightful analysis of the rôle of spiritual training, and the function of loyalty in a Japanese firm, see Rohlen (1974).

References

Allinson, G. D. 1975. *Japanese urbanism: industry and politics in Kariya, 1872–1972.* Berkeley, Calif.: University of California Press.
Allinson, G .D. 1978. Japanese cities in the industrial era. *J. Urban Hist.* 4(4), 443–76.
Allinson, G. D. 1979. *Suburban Tokyo.* Berkeley, Calif.: University of California Press.
Ames, W. L. 1981. *Police and community in Japan.* Berkeley, Calif.: University of California Press.
Bayley, D. H. 1976. *Forces of order: police behavior in Japan and the United States.* Berkeley, Calif.: University of California Press.
Beasley, W. 1972. *The Meiji Restoration.* Stanford, Calif.: Stanford University Press.
Dore, R. P. 1973. *British factory, Japanese factory.* Berkeley, Calif.: University of California Press.
Lee, C. and G. DeVos (eds.) 1981. *Koreans in Japan: ethnic conflict and accommodation.* Berkeley, Calif.: University of California Press.

Nihon no tōkei, 1978 [Statistics of Japan]. Tokyo: Ministry of Finance Printing Office.

Norman, E. H. 1940. *Japan's emergence as a modern state.* New York: International Secretariat, Institute of Pacific Relations.

Okhawa, K. and H. Rosovsky 1973. *Japanese economic growth.* Stanford, Calif.: Stanford University Press.

Pharr, S. J. 1981. *Political women in Japan: the search for a place in political life.* Berkeley, Calif.: University of California Press.

Rohlen, T. 1974. *For harmony and strength.* Berkeley, Calif.: University of California Press.

Schnitzer, M. 1974. *Income distribution: a comparative study of the United States, Sweden, West Germany, East Germany, the United Kingdom and Japan.* New York: Praeger.

Wagatsuma, H. and G. DeVos (eds.) 1966. *Japan's invisible race: caste in culture and personality.* Berkeley, Calif.: University of California Press.

9 City as a mirror of society: China, tradition and transformation

RHOADS MURPHEY

The city in cultural context is truly a seminal theme. Our word *city* is derived from the same Latin root which also yields our word *civilization*. Even in casual speech, we often equate 'civilization' with urban culture and its overtones. Since the origins of what we call civilization, perhaps as long ago as the fifth or sixth millennium BC, with the appearance of the first cities, each successive culture has built cities which reflect, symbolize, and affirm its character, its values, and its distinctive set of solutions, or nonsolutions, to common human problems. The city is thus both a convenient and a revealing key to culture, the clearest, most concentrated, most significant imprint which a culture produces on the geographic landscape, and on the diverse record of the human experience as a whole. It is, of course, a key which works both ways: one may read a culture through the cities it builds, and one may also read a city through the lens of the culture which builds it. It is a key which greatly enhances the study of both regional and temporal variations in culture, as might be illustrated by the significance of the many-sided differences between a cathedral town of medieval Europe and the very different cities of, say, southern California. Spatial form, architecture, street patterns, interaction patterns, iconography, and function, among a host of other urban characteristics, are all revealingly different in each of these cases, and speak eloquently, to the attuned observer, of the different cultures which produced each distinctive urban expression.

The Chinese case is a special one only in that it has the longest and largest continuous history of cities produced by a culture which remained, at least in consciousness, essentially the same for well over two millennia, largely free of significant cultural admixtures of foreign origin, and within a context of political–administrative continuity as well. However, this 2000-year experience was built on a period of about the same length preceding it, during which cities, of a somewhat different (though related) character, arose, evolved, and were ultimately replaced by what we may call the traditional/imperial model, beginning in the third century BC with the rise of the first great territorial empires of the Ch'in and Han (221

BC–AD 220).[1] Given China's immense size, in both area and population, and the great age of its civilization, there have probably been more cities and more city dwellers in China than in all of the rest of human experience. Even now, despite a relatively low level of urbanization as compared with industrialized countries, there is a larger total of urban population in China than in the United States.[2] Until some two or three centuries ago (only a brief interval in Chinese history), the level of economic, commercial, administrative, and technical development in China was higher than anywhere else in the world; this was accompanied and manifested by a larger number of cities, many of them bigger than any in the West until the recent advent of industrialization. Sian, Kaifeng, Hangchow, Nanking, and Peking have each in their time been the largest city in the world, with populations of about a million a thousand or more years ago, larger still in more recent centuries.

So much for scale. It is nevertheless a point worth making. China's urban experience, like the civilization of which it was and is an expression, is not a curious piece of exoticism, a sort of lunar landscape as viewed from the self-satisfied and culture-bound perspective of the modern West. China has too often been seen by arrogant, provincial, and ignorant Westerners, themselves a minority only recently 'arrived,' as that remote corner on the other side of the globe where everything is 'backward' (in both senses of the word), where behavior and institutions are 'inscrutable,' but nothing is really important or relevant for the rest of 'normal' mankind, except to the odd curiosity seeker. Others, more concerned with 'global' explanations of society, and hence perhaps even more arrogant, gloss over, with little apology, their profound ignorance of the Chinese quarter or third of the human experience in constructing 'systems' or theories which the massive Chinese segment of the world, had they troubled to examine it, frequently made nonsensical. As G. W. Skinner (1964) put it, they 'studied Western man and spoke of mankind.' Still others, failing to heed the wise precaution that 'a little learning is a dangerous thing,' have recognized the obvious, that Asia (half the world) is different from the West, but then write as if all Asia were the same, or generalize about it from Middle Eastern or other small particularistic samples, with disastrous results for the understanding of the far greater whole, let alone its largest component, China. China scholars run the risk of becoming tiresome with their continued insistence on the age, scale, and achievements of the culture whose study earns them their bread; and we are all, I am sure, tired of being reminded that the Chinese invented practically everything, eons before anyone else thought of it. But the centrality, the relevance, the normative credentials of the Chinese experience, because of its immense scale as by far the largest single chunk of the human experience (including its urban component), as well as because of its general level of sophistication, are points which, however tiresomely, do still need to be harped on, until the rest of the world accepts them as axiomatic. Judging from the way people in general, and certain scholars in particular, continue to ignore it, we China types will have to go on boring you for some time.

The traditional Chinese city

However, this volume is presumably concerned with the city as a mirror – *the* mirror – of the society which builds it. The traditional–imperial Chinese city, which we know far better than its pre-Ch'in/Han predecessor of the Shang and Chou periods, is the model to be examined here as a mirror of the traditional society. It lasted in fact, essentially unchanged, well into the present century in many parts of the country; many of its outlines are thus still observable, in Peking, of course, but also in former capitals such as Sian, in other provincial centers which were never part of the treaty-port system (for example, Chengtu, Kunming, Taiyuan), and even in most of China's other cities, where the foreign treaty-port imprint was merely grafted onto a traditional urban base which continued to function as before. These traditional cities were primarily centers of imperial authority imposed in a uniform plan on a varied landscape, symbolic monuments of the power and majesty of the Chinese state and of Chinese culture over which it presided. Functionally, they were in most cases predominantly agents of the imperial bureaucracy; directly or indirectly, the largest sector of the urban workforce was employed in that administrative enterprise. This workforce included officials, clerks, scribes, garrison troops, teachers of the classics to aspirant generations of examination candidates, merchants employed by the state in the management of official monopolies of trade or manufacture, artisans whose output went predominantly to the offices and households of all the foregoing, and the vaster army of shopkeepers, coolies, servants, transport workers, butchers, bakers, and candlestick makers, whose service livelihood depended on the city's basic industry, which was most importantly administration. All of these cities included also a commercial and a manufacturing function, apart from the official and state-run monopolies in salt, iron, copper, weapons, tax or tribute grain, and foreign trade. In a few, these functions were more important than official and administrative functions, but in none above the level of local market town was the hand of the state not apparent, or its business not prominent.

The imperial bureaucratic imprint reached down the urban hierarchy to the level of the county seat (or its equivalent) – the capital of the administrative district, called the *hsien*; the population of the *hsien* as a whole averaged (very roughly) about 200 000 (with considerable temporal and regional variations), while that of the *hsien* capital city might average perhaps 10 000–15 000.[3] In most *hsien*, the capital would be the only real city; in other, more commercialized, parts of the country (for example the lower Yangtze valley), there might be one or more as well. But the *hsien* capital was nearly always the largest, and the only base for the official bureaucracy. There the imperial magistrate, through his court and assistants, was officially responsible for everyone and everything in the *hsien*, but in practice it was not possible to carry out close administration of so large a population, the great majority of it rural–agricultural, in an area (again a possibly misleading average) roughly equivalent to an eastern American county. Unofficial, but often powerful, local gentry and peasant village elders or clans managed the bulk of rural, and hence of *hsien*, affairs. It was a closely ordered society, but not as any direct result of intervention by the bureaucratic state. Although 'the emperor (was) far away,' in the traditional peasant assertion of independence from imperial control, as, for all practical purposes, was his vicar, the magistrate, in the *hsien* capital, the combined force of family, clan, gentry, and nearly universally accepted Confucian morality kept order remarkably well in what we may call a largely self-regulating society.

But the *hsien* capital played a crucial *symbolic* rôle in insuring such an outcome, not least through its institutional and inconographic assertion of the Confucian virtues of order, and its manifestation of the state power which, however symbolically, supported that order. All *hsien* capitals were walled, the feature which instantly distinguished them from other lesser urban centers, and were planned in detail. The walls were as imposing as the rank and size of the city dictated, but in every case were designed to awe and affirm, only secondarily to defend, although of course they might be useful in troubled times. The Chinese word for *city* means also *wall*, further underlining the urban function as a symbol of power and of the concentration of authority. City walls were built in a regular and consistent pattern, with great gates at each of the cardinal compass points from which broad, straight avenues led to the opposite gate. These, of course, intersected in the middle of the city, where there was a ceremonial center with a plaza, a drum tower, a cluster of official buildings (including the magistrate's offices and court), or a Confucian temple. The major streets, fixing the main axes of the gridiron pattern, divided the city into major quarters, which were sometimes also enclosed by their own walls, whose gates, like the city's main gates, were closed at night. Each quarter tended to be functionally specific: transport termini, warehouses, and commercial offices or banks in one sector, retailing (often segregated by street according to commodities) in another, manu-facturing in another, and others for academies, universities, booksellers, theaters, the military establishment and its garrison troops, public food markets, and so on. Most people lived in the same structures which housed their work activities, and within each quarter there were regular lanes organized into neighborhoods, a system often used for the control of urban populations. The emphasis, as in the ideology of the Confucian state, was on order and on planned management.

Most cities were founded explicitly by the state, as centers of imperial control, although occasionally (especially in the early imperial period under the Han), a pre-existing urban center of trade might be designated as an administrative center, and provided with the planned monumental accoutrements. But the imperial imprint was unmistakable in all walled cities, and in their striking uniformity as part of a master plan, imposed on the landscape for the creation of order. One can chart (in a fascinating exercise pioneered by S. D. Chang 1963) the southward migration of Chinese civilization from its early northern base by noting and mapping the successive founding of *hsien* cities to control and administer newly occupied territory, the multiplication of their number as population increased, and the routes followed by the expansion. While the *hsien* city was, of course, the commonest, it reflected, on a smaller scale, the superior hierarchical models of the provincial and national capitals, whose managerial and cosmic rôles were exercised over progressively larger spheres, until, in the case of the imperial capital, it encompassed 'all under heaven,' the name by which the Chinese called their empire and its surrounding, but far lesser, tributary states. Within each *hsien*, the capital city was usually located near the middle of the territory, whose areal size varied (naturally enough) inversely with the density of population, but which was ideally designed as much as possible so as to constitute a coherent geographic region of trade, production, and movement. Where the physical landscape and population density permitted, this might be a stream watershed or confluence region, or a basin surrounded by hills. The capital city was responsible for the defense as well as administration of the *hsien* as a whole, and not merely with the defense of its own walled base. It was truly a *center*, not an isolated or discrete intrusion.

This, in turn, was related to the perceived relationship between city and countryside. Traditional China was an overwhelmingly agrarian society; there was no question as to what the source of wealth was, including the means for the support of the state and its apparatus. Cities were designed to control and tax the countryside, but more importantly to serve it, as the basic reason and sustenance of their existence. Trade and merchants flourished in all Chinese cities, but most commodities were of agricultural or rural origin. The primary responsibility of officials was to ensure the productivity as well as the orderliness of the agricultural countryside, since it was this which sustained the empire, its power, its cultural grandeur, and its bureaucratic structures. This was true most immediately for the *hsien* magistrate, the official closest to rural areas, but true also for the emperor himself, at the head of the pyramid; each year, to mark the beginning of the new agricultural season, he plowed a ceremonial furrow in the grounds of the Temple of Heaven at the imperial capital, and interceded with heaven for good harvests. His and the city magistrate's first concern was the well-being of the agricultural sector and the serving of its needs: order, productivity, and protection. The close interdependence of city and countryside was far more explicitly recognized, and indeed welcomed, in China than elsewhere. In the West, in particular, when commerce and later manufacturing became proportionately important, the symbiotic tie between rural and urban worlds tended to be obscured, or even forgotten. New classes arose in cities – which, of course, is what the word *bourgeoisie* means; they and the new class of urban proletariat became divorced from the rural context, as different kinds of people with different goals and values. They often scorned rural people as 'hicks,' or regarded them merely as servants of the city, providers of food, raw materials, or cheap labor. The city, as our word for it suggests, *was* civilization, the mover and shaker – the maker of the modern world.

In China, there was no such split between urban and rural worlds, and no place in either traditional or contemporary China (despite its avowed Marxism) for Marx's mirroring of Western attitudes in his contempt for 'the idiocy of rural life.' Urban élites may often have exploited the rural sector, but it was universally recognized that the city's chief function concerned the services it provided for the good ordering and productivity of the countryside which fed it, both literally and metaphorically. The state's predominant source of revenue, the land-and-grain tax, was in effect sustained by urban-based élite investment, and management of irrigation and water-control projects, roads and waterways, the dissemination of improved techniques, and the protection of rural areas from disorder. The intensive hand agriculture of traditional China, especially wet-rice agriculture with its heavy cumulative investment in dikes, terraces, and irrigation projects, required consistent order, and organization, to remain as highly productive as it was. The same was true of the social system, with its orderly stress on 'right relations' throughout its hierarchy, and on the companion Confucian precept of model behavior. Disorder – chaos, absence of officially sanctioned and enforced rules (all incorporated in the Chinese word *luan*) – was seen as the greatest evil to be prevented, an effort in which urban and rural areas worked together for a recognizable common good.

Urban élites were drawn in the first instance, in each new generation, as much from the countryside as from the cities, and retained close ties with their rural origins. There was a continuous flow of people moving in both directions, officials in the course of their duties or on furlough or retirement, and rural recruits moving into the commercial or bureaucratic world of the city. There was no denigration of rural circumstances and values, but rather, on the part of many of the urban élite, a longing for the countryside, to which they would retreat whenever they could, and to which they almost invariably retired – a theme prominent in Chinese poetry, as in these lines from the Sung poet-official Su Tung-p'o (although, in this version, really from Arthur Waley):

> Layered blue hills make a ring where the brook runs east.
> On a white moonlit sandy shore a long legged heron roosts;
> And this is a place where no dust comes.
> [Dust was the accepted symbol of cities and bureaucracy.]

> An old man of the stream says to himself:
> What is your little reason for wanting so much to be a bureaucrat?
> You have plenty of wine and land –
> Go on home to your district, enjoy your share of leisure.

The rural sector was recognized as the source of at least as much wisdom and virtue as the city: Su Tung-p'o was by no means alone in his view, nor was it limited simply to the admiration of nature. The Chinese record is full of conscientious officials or members of the rural gentry, whose careers centered on maintaining and enhancing rural prosperity, and who found rural virtues more important than urban. As an imperial official in the mid-17th century put it (Tsu-chun 1954, p. 54):

> Goodness develops only in the village, evil in the city. The city is the place of commerce and trade. People relate to one another only with the aim of making profits. They are superficial and pretentious. As a result, the city is a sink of iniquities. The village is different. These people are self-reliant and have deep emotional ties with each other.

Rural people were better attuned to the world of nature and its rhythms, and therefore better understood the universe and man's place in it. Especially in Confucian logic, this gave them a better moral character and a simple goodness. In the cities, where people disregarded nature, truth was clouded and virtue weakened. Only the continual interchange with the countryside kept the city viable. The great sages did not live in cities, nor did the happiest people. The Chinese version of the good and the true had a strongly rural, even anti-urban, bias. Admittedly, our perception of that vision is dependent entirely on what the mainly urban-based élite left behind, in writing or in art; some of it was no doubt produced for effect, or to conform to normative values, and most of them did, after all, whatever they wrote, live most of their working lives in cities and, one may presume, enjoyed many things which only cities can provide; few of them were sages or self-denying philosophers. But much of their other action was, in fact, consistent with what they preached. The remarkably high degree of social mobility characteristic of traditional China, whereby something like a third of the gentry-literati group in each new generation were people from originally humble (dominantly rural) origins who had passed the imperial examinations, continued to inject rural people and rural values into the urban world. Rank could not be inherited; the openness of the system had no doubt a lot to do with its long survival, and, for the present point, with its continued reaffirmation of the importance of the rural base for all cities.

Change was not, of course, absent in the long span of 2000 years of imperial Chinese history. But, especially after about the 12th century, it was not primarily focused in cities, which instead were seen as presiding over the 'Great Harmony,' a persistent Chinese ideal in which disruptive change was to be minimized, all groups worked together for the common good, and cities served the countryside as part of a single symbiotic order. What pressures there were for change came far more often from rural areas, as protests against arbitrary city-based power, or the exploitative accumulation of urban wealth at the expense of peasants, as corruption and self-seeking become more prominent in the last decades of each dynasty. The rural areas were often seen as the base for correcting the excesses of the city, including the overthrow of urban-based power which marked the collapse of a dynasty, to be succeeded by a new dynasty which often had significant peasant or rural origins. Urban merchants, the spearhead of change in the early modern West, were, in traditional China, too closely involved with and nurtured by the official system to fight against it. They had little to gain (unlike their Western counterparts) by upsetting the apple cart, either by changing the rules or by putting a new group in power. Most of the big merchants were from urban gentry families; many were, in effect, officials involved in one or another of the many state trade monopolies, but all depended on some form of official connection or patronage. If that were lost, as of course happened from time to time to individuals, and to all when the dynasty or government fell, the result was total ruin.

Cities were centers of action in great variety, but in general not of institutional change, which indeed their major efforts were directed toward preventing. They were splendid places, probably the most splendid in the world, as well as the largest and richest, as Marco Polo tried to persuade an unbelieving Europe, who nicknamed him 'Millione,' a Venetian Baron Munchausen. By the 19th century, when Westerners could again travel more or less freely around China (and were able to confirm what were reported to be Polo's dying words to a confessor when he was anxious to relieve his soul of the burden of all those 'lies:' 'I have not told the half of what I saw,'), China's now more tarnished cities were no longer so impressive in the heady context of Western industrialization and the booming, though different, splendor of merchant capitals in London, Paris, Berlin, Hamburg, and New York. By then, the whole of the traditional Chinese system was in deep trouble. Cities increasingly became targets of rural outrage, as in the great Taiping Rebellion from 1850 to 1864, which nearly toppled the dynasty, and in many subsequent uprisings. The cities were no longer able to keep agricultural output in pace with population increases, nor to maintain order as China was caught in a 'high-level equilibrium trap' (Elvin 1973). Trade and, later, manufacturing increased their proportional shares of the economy, and created some new rich, based in now rapidly growing cities, including the new treaty ports, but the lot of peasants and rural areas deteriorated, until, by the 20th century, there were many areas of severe suffering, chronic disorder, and periodically catastrophic famine.

The Western presence

The almost 40 years which have elapsed since the Pacific War, the end of Western colonialism in East Asia, and the rise of a new, dynamic, and unmistakably Chinese revolutionary order, have given us new perspectives on the short period of Western dominance in Asia. Briefly, it no longer seems so important, in the context of the modern world or that of the far longer span of Chinese history. As we can now (with the wisdom of hindsight) survey the scant century of the China treaty ports, they appear more clearly as specks on the far water, and, far more significant, Chinese landscape. As I have suggested in greater detail elsewhere (Murphey 1977), the treaty ports were seen by their Western masters as beachheads, agents of the transformation of China into a Western likeness through the yeasty power of the commercial and industrial revolutions which had made the West the arbiter of the modern world. The treaty ports were indeed explicitly referred to as 'model settlements,' and it was expected that their example would of itself convince China to follow the Western path toward wealth and power, rejecting its own clearly inferior and 'backward' tradition. Surely no one would *choose* to remain 'backward' once he had been exposed to the advantages of railways, power-driven factories, joint stock companies, modern banking, Western medicine, Western learning – and, of course, Christian/Victorian morality, whose superior virtues were plain in their association with the unquestionably superior *success* of the post-1850 West. All of this was consciously encapsulated in the treaty ports. Altogether, about 100 Chinese cities were classified as treaty ports, although less than a dozen (primarily, of course, the biggest coastal or riverine ports) were or became major centers of foreign trade or of foreign involvement and presence. They did acquire the dominant share of China's expanding foreign trade, and of the newly developing industrial sector, and they also attracted as they grew large numbers of Chinese, who remained the overwhelmingly dominant inhabitants of all the treaty ports.

The foreigners hoped that these included a new kind of Chinese, quick to follow Western ways (as the Meiji Japanese had been), and hence to fulfil the treaty-port goal of transforming China in the Western image. These treaty-port Chinese, although a tiny minority within the country, were indeed apt pupils. By the 20th century, they owned the largest share of treaty-port factories, founded Western-style banks and steamship lines, lived (many of them) in Western style, and formed the most important wing of the new Nationalist Party, the Kuomintang, which at least in part was committed to more such Western-style modernization. Foreign control in the treaty ports also meant that many dissident Chinese, including outright revolutionaries, fled there for refuge from official persecution, and these cities became the main centers of new intellectual ferment. Those who lived in the treaty ports, and were most directly exposed to this challenge to China, were concerned about their country's weakness, its inability to resist foreign pressures, and its technological underdevelopment compared with the modern West or Japan. In the political sanctuary of the treaty ports, they groped for solutions, goaded by the arrogant example of Western success; it was there that the ultimately successful movement was founded for the overthrow of the old dynasty in 1911, and there that Chinese nationalism, in the Western sense, was born, primarily as a reaction to the humiliation of foreign imperialism. The Chinese Communist Party was founded in Shanghai, the biggest treaty port, in 1921, by a group of revolutionaries convinced that China could never be strong again without radical change, but also determined to resist, and eventually to expel, the foreign model in the treaty ports and all it stood for.

The treaty ports offered an alternative model, as Western-style commercial/industrial centers totally different from traditional Chinese cities, where private enterprise and property protected from state control were enshrined, and where traditional Chinese values were stood on their heads. It was a positive model for its demonstration of new technological power, and of wealth for a few, but a deeply negative and bitter one in its affront to Chinese pride. Most of the treaty-port Chinese were not wealthy entrepreneurs, but poor and exploited workers; all treaty-port Chinese were subjected to foreign racism and discrimination – in their own country. Those who profited from the new business conditions in the treaty ports were cut off by their own careers from their traditional roots, and committed to a new and foreign kind of world. Conservatives and radicals alike called them simply traitors, running dog collaborators with the alien forces who were destroying the soul and nibbling at the body of China. The treaty ports never built effective ties with the vast rural hinterland of China, most of which was negligibly affected, except to drain a few goods from it for export abroad, to foreign profit. As separate places, enclave/exclave economies belonging to a separate world and controlled by outsiders, they were the more easily rejected as alien, and their commercial and industrial success resented as exploitative. In sharp distinction to traditional Chinese cities, with their inward-facing concern for their rural hinterlands, the treaty ports were outward facing, concerned far more with the wider world overseas than with China. London and New York stock reports and commodity prices were more important in Shanghai than news of what was happening in Szechuan or Hunan. These cities meant alienation, humiliation, slums, pollution, a new group of urban poor, and foreign control, not 'progress.' Most of China was materially unchanged by a century of vigorous treaty-port efforts and increasingly shrill preaching: in part because its rural mass, larger than Europe or the United States, was simply too huge to be moved by marginal foreign contact in a few spots on the coast; and partly because the treaty-port formula, born and bred in the urban-commercial West, was profoundly unsuited to China's very different circumstances and needs; most of all perhaps, it was *foreign*, and the deep Chinese pride, buttressed by millennia when China led the world, could not and did not accept it.

The Communist revolution and after

China remained, as it has always been and still is, a peasant country. Its body, if not its soul, was now seriously sick, but any successful treatment would have to recognize that most of that body was rural, to identify the main problems and find solutions to them there. The treaty ports were important only as a goad – and as a counter-example. China now badly needed new technology, but not through their agency or through their kind of city. In the end, it was a *peasant* revolution, based in the countryside and reaffirming peasant and rural virtues, values, needs, and goals, whose peasant armies won power *against* the cities, and celebrated their victory in Shanghai as in Peking in 1949. Communist-led uprisings in several cities in the 1920s had failed, wiped out by the superior forces of the Kuomintang, whose major bases were in the treaty ports. The industrial proletariat, key to revolution in the Soviet model which the Party tried to follow, were too few, but in any case were unwilling to join the struggle, apparently corrupted beyond redemption by the bourgeois setting of the treaty ports, or with their supposed revolutionary vision blurred by that contamination. Defeated, almost annihilated, in the cities, the communists retreated to the countryside, where, under Mao's leadership, they built a political base among the peasants, who had not been exposed to the corruption of cities or treaty ports. Here was the *real* China, largely untouched by alien influences. Only in the countryside could a genuinely *Chinese* answer to the Western challenge, and a *Chinese* solution to the country's problems, be generated. The formula was announced as early as 1939 (Long live the victory of people's war 1965):

> To rely on the peasants, build rural base areas and use the countryside to encircle and finally capture the cities – such is the way to victory in the Chinese revolution . . . The countryside and the countryside alone can provide the revolutionary bases from which the revolutionaries can go forward to final victory . . . The contemporary world revolution also presents a picture of the encirclement of the cities by the rural areas.

Having won political power, with so clear and bitter an anti-urban legacy, the new government's early efforts were directed to de-emphasizing the cities – especially the former treaty ports which accounted for nearly all of the large cities – attempting to reduce their size, and to remake them in the socialist image. But the chief drive for the development which China urgently needed was to be based in the vast hinterland, and as much as possible in rural areas. It was easy to criticize the treaty ports, and China's overall urban pattern by the 1940s, as unreasonably peripheral to the main body of the country, and as far too little involved with the service and development of China as a whole, directly counter to the long-standing traditional model. The treaty ports had virtually monopolized what modern manufacturing and commercial enterprise had developed in China, much of it under foreign control, and yet were limited to a few scattered spots along the coastal edge of the country and the navigable Yangtze River, where they could the more easily drain China's wealth abroad. The treaty ports contained over 90 percent of the pre-1949 industrial plant, a heavily lopsided pattern within any national context. Over a third of China's 'modern' industrial investment, labor force, and output were in Shanghai alone; nearly all the rest was in the Liao River valley of south-central Manchuria, the Tientsin area on the northern coast, the Wuhan area on the Yangtze, and a few other major treaty ports also accessible to ocean shipping. These cities (inherited from colonialism) had to be transformed so as to serve the nation as a whole, and to change their character accordingly. At the same time, new cities, of the approved sort, had to be built in the rest of the country as necessary bases for the urgently needed economic and technological development of China, most of which had been touched hardly at all by what had happened in the treaty ports.

How well has a revolutionary China succeeded with these goals? In the first flush of revolutionary success, there was talk of actually dismantling much of the industrial structure of Shanghai, and other major treaty ports, so as to build new inland centers, but it was soon realized that development depended on the fullest and most efficient use of the existing base.

The development of inland and rural China, and the construction of new industrial cities there, could come only with the help of the former treaty ports, and it made little sense to dismantle them, or to starve them of new investment. However, the largest share of new investment went to the growth of industrial centers in the formerly neglected inland areas, some of them older cities which were now transformed (Loyang, Sian, Lanchow, Chungking, Kunming, all in the neglected west), some wholly new establishments keyed to newly discovered local resources: the steel city at Pao T'ou in Inner Mongolia, the oil city of Ta Ch'ing in northern Manchuria, or the industrial complex at Urumchi in distant Sinkiang. These, and especially the new centers, were extolled as models, socialist cities of socialist man. At the same time, the former treaty ports were used to provide the skilled labor technicians and much of the equipment and high-technology components for these new cities, while their own growth was restricted. Shanghai, by far the largest city, was apparently actually reduced in size, through controls on in-migration and the assignment of Shanghai workers to rural or inland urban jobs. Although all other older cities have grown, and especially Peking, as the national capital, with its immense new administrative responsibilities in this planned economy, there has been some success in controlling urban 'giantism,' as it is called. In a country of about a billion people, there are probably only about 25 million-class cities, and probably only six of those are over 2 million,[4] all, except for Peking, major former treaty ports: Shanghai, Tientsin, Shenyang (Mukden), Wuhan, and Canton.

If it has thus not proved possible to reduce the *absolute* size of these and other former treaty ports (except for Shanghai), their *relative* urban dominance has certainly been reduced as inland centers have grown disproportionately, and have at least begun to correct the lopsided spatial pattern of manufacturing. And if this must be judged only a qualified success in terms of early goals, it looks far more impressive in the context of urbanization in the developing world as a whole. There, in India, South-east Asia, Africa, the Middle East, and Latin America, the growing pains of urban-centered change seem mirrored most sharply in what is often called 'over-urbanization,' a term poorly defined and quite possibly misleading, but clear enough in its commentary on the urban scene: gross overcrowding, high unemployment, inadequate housing, sewage facilities, transport, water supply, schooling, health services, and other basic minimum support for millions who live in shanty towns or slums, on the edge of an urban promised land to which they are still denied entry. Nevertheless, they continue to flood into the cities, not only because life in the villages is hard, but because however miserable urban slums may be, the city offers the promise of upward mobility, away from peasant toil but also into a wider world of stimulus, excitement, and variety which the village can never match. The lucky and persistent among the new migrants will make it into that world, sometimes with occasional nostalgic glances back to their rural origins, but rarely, even among the failures, a permanent return to the comparatively limited world of the village. This was, after all, the nature of urbanization in the developed world too, in the course of the 19th and early 20th centuries, and there is nothing surprising about it. We forget, with the short historical memories of Americans in particular, what life in New York and Chicago in the 1880s was like for most of their inhabitants, even if we still understand their attraction nevertheless for farm boys from Vermont or Iowa. Urban conditions were probably worse then than in contemporary Calcutta, Djakarta, Lagos, or Lima, judging from accounts of each or from life-expectancy figures. But the waste and suffering of humanity in the often squalid cities of the modern developing world now are undeniable. China has paid a heavy price in minimizing such problems through controlling the growth of its cities;[5] perhaps it has been worth it? One cannot measure the human cost of the controls on travel, employment, housing, and consumer goods which have kept Chinese cities from the extremes of unplanned growth.

What one can see more clearly, especially now that some of the control measures have been eased a little, is that most Chinese too, despite the official extolling of rural and peasant virtues and priorities, would choose the urban alternative. Those 'sent down' earlier from cities to the countryside are massively unhappy and try to use any means to return. It is all very distressing to those, Chinese and outsiders, who found and still find the Maoist vision inspiring: build the new China squarely on its peasant base, get rid of the poison of the cities, 'take agriculture as the foundation,' and transform the rural body of China through diffusing new industrial technology to it, in the service of the great rural majority. This was to be done not only by dispersing urban industrial centers through each province (as has largely been accomplished), but by bringing modernization and industrialization to the countryside, in small-scale local production units on the rural communes. It was an idea which many people found appealing, an alternative to the undoubted evils of the Western model of industrial concentration in a few big cities with their special privilege, corruption, alienation, pollution, de-humanization, and drearification of life. Instead of depending on technical and professional élites in the big cities, and the unsatisfactory process of 'trickle-down,' especially for a country as huge and as rural as China, get rid of élitism (something which traditional China had notoriously suffered from), and let the peasants be their own modernizers, technicians, and industrialists. This would also produce development immediately where it was most needed, rather than continuing to concentrate it in the already developed cities. Such a minutely dispersed pattern would also avoid the problems of cities, the pollution, the alienation, the particularism and selfishness, and would at the same time achieve the twin Maoist goals: remove the differences between city and countryside, and between mental and manual labor, peasants and urbanites.

However inspiring this vision, it has run into increasing practical trouble. The problems of economic development are tough, much the same everywhere, and cannot really be solved by slogans or revolutionary fervor. The small-scale rural industrial plants, which at one time produced perhaps half of China's cement and fertilizer and important shares of total output of iron and steel, electric power, and consumer goods, proved, in nearly all cases, to be far more expensive in unit costs than large urban-based plants, and also made much less efficient use of scarce materials. In the end it seems to have been recognized, as now, that China simply cannot afford high-cost development strategies, whatever their political, revolutionary, or just plain human appeal. Small-scale commune-based industry will probably remain, but as a shrinking proportion of national industrial output and increasingly as a symbolic gesture. Agriculture is still (rightly) given priority, but it will have to depend on large urban-based factories for fertilizers, pumps, cement, tools, and equipment – as it will have to depend on urban-based research centers and agro-technicians ('experts') to develop and diffuse the improved crop strains which form the other vital component of the drive to raise output. Far from eliminating the élite, or putting more stress on 'redness' than on 'expertness,' China is now obliged to acknowledge, increasingly openly, that urban élites and experts are essential to successful development, as to planning and management. As Teng Hsiao-p'ing put it while he was still under attack before the fall of the 'Gang of Four;' 'I don't care what color a cat is so long as it catches mice.' China is a poor country, and the urgency of development for a billion people is too great to permit the luxury of any other goals which work against maximum economic rationality, as the Maoist vision, however inspiring, clearly does. Perhaps such goals are worth it, worth more than mere economics; we may say so, from our far more economically secure position; China's present leaders cannot.

Nor does the implanting of modern industrialization on the commune, and the development of new peasant 'experts,' remove the differences between city and countryside. Rural work is still hard, and the excitement and variety of urban life are missing. There is just no way to create on the communes the equivalent of the city's world. Even in immediately practical terms, rural wages are about half the urban average, and living standards, including health and education facilities, correspondingly lower. In the cities, there is a far wider range of career opportunities, and the possibility of upward mobility which is, it seems, as appealing to Chinese, despite the Maoist vision, as to anyone else. There are as many would-be experts or élites there as in the rest of the urban world, and a long tradition of upward mobility through education, and the acquisition of essentially urban-based skills. These are all more than sufficient reasons for the pressures for urban migration long held in check by controls, and for the efforts especially of urban youth to avoid rural assignment. With the degree of political relaxation since 1978 (far from complete), more and increasingly vigorous protests against these and other devices to limit upward and centripetal mobility have been voiced. In these terms, China is sitting on a powder keg, re-encouraging education and post-high-school training with one hand, with its built-in expectations of upward mobility in an urban focus, and with the other trying still to prevent runaway urban growth and to curb the manifestations of new expert-based and urban-centered élitism. It is not enough merely to control the growth of Shanghai or the other major ex-treaty ports. Even new socialist cities in formerly remote areas can and do generate experts, élites, and élitism – and the other undesirable characteristics of cities, especially industrial cities, every-where. And it is city people, in a revolutionary China, who, perhaps predictably, stand out as the complainers, cynics, and self-seeking grab-bers of privilege and scarce goods, reconfirming, in their bourgeois character, traditional Chinese images of the moral corruption of cities.

What can be salvaged of the original vision? Will China's growing cities become just like those in the West, or in the rest of the devoping world? That is surely too pessimistic. There may be no cheap or quick rural-based alternative to the Western model of industrial development concentrated in cities, for all its dreadful flaws, but, for a long time to come, China will remain a dominantly peasant society, and a genuinely revolutionary one, even as the sharp edges of radicalism soften or are adjusted to pressing economic realities. The Maoist vision will continue to inspire, and, even as symbol or lip service, will go on affecting policy and behavior. Its formula for China is too apt, too closely rooted in China's history and circum-stances, and too ideologically appealing to even a nominally revolutionary country, to be wholly discarded or ignored. There is little attraction for China especially, with its immense traditional and now revolutionary pride, in becoming merely a second-class and belated follower after a flawed Western model. If China can no longer lead the world as it did for so long, at least it can offer a distinctive new path, one forged in the Chinese context, perhaps a model for other developing societies, but in any case never just an inferior echo of the West. Technology can be de-cultured, but its application and its urban bases must fit both China's circumstances and her ideological goals. At the least, those goals, changing over time as they may, but necessarily different from those of other societies, are certain to make an impact on policy, planning, and implementation, especially in so politically conscious and controlled a society as China's. There seems no chance that 'free enterprise' Western style will, in the foreseeable future, play any major rôle in shaping China's development, as opposed to planning in a socialist context.

The cities will play a far more important rôle in that development than the Maoist formula provided, and the greatest challenge may therefore be changing and controlling their *nature*, limiting their bourgeois character, preventing at least the excesses of élitism, ensuring that their growth and functions serve the needs of the country as a whole (primarily rural), and curbing the other evils of urban concentration (pollution, overcrowding, alienation, and so on) by continued careful management. It seems likely that, with the new emphasis on economic growth and the de-emphasis of radical policies, cities will now grow much faster. Part of the price of that strategy, as the rest of the developing world has found, will surely be more overcrowding, more inadequate urban housing and services, more problems with urban pollution, and probably more urban unemployment, although controls and planning will probably make each of these problems somewhat less severe than in most of the rest of the developing world. There is not space here to discuss the details of urban planning in China, or the partially successful efforts at spatial re-ordering and rationalization of both older and new cities, but enough has been accomplished to suggest, that, in these respects too, Chinese cities will remain distinctive, and that the effort will continue to make them into cities for 'socialist man'.

However, the greatest problem may well be what happens to people and their values, as more of them live in cities, and as urban-centered development gathers momentum. Mao was right to identify what he saw as the corrupting qualities of cities and of urban-based élitism as the greatest of all threats to his revolutionary vision. Already, urban people, a privileged minority, live better than rural people, the peasant heroes of revolution who comprise 80 percent of the population. Urbanites use 'connections' to advance their status, and to ensure status opportunities for their children. They are in the forefront of the new consumerism, perhaps the greatest single contradiction to revolutionary goals. Urban department stores (but not rural communes) sell a wide variety of consumer goods, many of them nonessential luxuries – watches, cameras, radios, even TV sets; demand far outruns supply, and status is increasingly demonstrated by possession of scarce consumer items. Now there are even hairdressing establishments and fancy clothing stores in the bigger cities. Can the revolution survive such trends? In the face of them, how far can the state continue to hold the lid on migration to the cities? Americans are the *last* people to comment critically on other people's addiction to consumerism, and one must recognize that people everywhere are pretty much the same: they want a better life, and they tend to define that mainly in terms of more goods and services – in some ways, the more nonessential, the better to demonstrate their material success. Urban Chinese are now behaving in these respects like the rest of us, and like upwardly mobile urban Indians, or Africans, or Latin Americans.

But Chinese society will remain distinctive, and so will the cities it builds and shapes. The forces generated by economic change, and the urgency of development, are indeed in many respects in conflict with China's revolutionary or ideological goals. But is there a society anywhere which is not ridden with such conflicts, or where economic forces are not frequently at war with supposed political or moral values or objectives? Of course not, but this does not mean that all societies are the same in other respects. China's cities will, as cities everywhere have always done, reflect the forces at work in the larger society of which they are the expression. As the society moves along the time spectrum of development from its peasant–rural base toward an increasingly urban emphasis, and as its ideological goals continue to adjust to the realities and needs of that development, its cities will mirror those changes, as the traditional city mirrored the values and the grandeur of imperial China.

Notes

1 The first real cities in China (as opposed to villages or towns) may be said to have emerged by about 2000 BC. The clearest case, in a period where our knowledge is limited, is the early Shang capital of Ao (near modern Changchow), with walls 9 metres (30 feet) high and 18 metres (60 feet) wide extending for some 4.5 miles around the central administrative–ceremonial area only, and dated within a few years of 2000 BC.
2 All figures pertaining to China's population must remain approximations at best until the release of data from the census now scheduled for 1982. Official figures as of 1980 suggest a total population of about 1 billion, of which 20 percent are said to be urban. The 1980 census figures for the United States show a total population of 226.5 million, of which we may call roughly 80 percent urban in order to make this distinction better comparable with the generally poorly defined Chinese 'urban' category.
3 Averages are, as usual, misleading, and especially for a country the size of China over a 2000-year period, not to mention the grossly approximate nature of the population data, but it may be worth giving these estimates as at least a gesture toward fixing a scale. The average *hsien* population in Han times was probably closer to 50 000, and, by late Ch'ing, with a national total three or four times greater, about 300 000.
4 See note 2 above.
5 Hardly preventing; they are present in Chinese cities too.

References

Chang, S. D. 1963. The historical trend of Chinese urbanization. *Ann. Assoc. Am. Geogs.* **53**, 109–43.

Elvin, M. 1973. *The pattern of the Chinese past.* Stanford, Calif.: Stanford University Press.

Long live the victory of people's war. *Peking Rev.* Sept. 3, 1965; based on Mao Tse-tung, *The Chinese revolution and the Chinese communist party*, written in 1939.

Murphey, R. 1977. *The outsiders: the Western experience in India and China.* Ann Arbor: University of Michigan Press.

Skinner, G. W. 1964. What the study of China can do for social science. *J. Asian Studs.* **23**, 517–22.

Tsu-chun, L. 1954. *Ch'ao-lien hsiang-chih* [Village Gazetteer of Ch'ao-lien] (Kwangtung); statement attributed to Ku Yen-wu (1616–82). Hong Kong: Lu–Kuang Hsin-hui Ch'ao-lien t'ung-hsiang hui.

10 *Autonomous and directed cultural change: South African urbanization*

JOHN WESTERN

Beneath this central thesis – that two-thirds of a nation's population is only tolerated as an economic resource – has evolved probably the most complex system of human control in the world (the Soviet bloc not excepted). *The Economist*, June 21, 1980.

South Africa represents a fascinating, if disquieting, laboratory for probing the interrelationships between cities and cultures. Here, European conquest has imposed the idea of the city upon indigenous peoples lacking an urban tradition. But it is a particular *variant* of the 'Western' city idea which has evolved in South Africa, and it has to be seen in the context of the White power-holders' perceptions of the cultural gulf between themselves and local peoples. Such perceptions have been fundamental in molding the cities of the country, whose form today is thus not fortuitous. At the same time, this form, most marked by strict *de jure* residential segregation, has, in turn strongly, influenced (and, again, not at all fortuitously) the nature of the culture(s) of present South African cities.

Yet it is not only culture per se and the perceptions thereof that are basic to an understanding of the social engineering practised in South Africa; there is also the intertwined strand of the nature of capitalist industrialization which has so rapidly occurred there. What cultural changes might *this* transformation be expected to bring in its train, to which groups? These latter changes I presume to classify as 'autonomous.' This is not because I feel such changes (whatever they may be) to be wholly self-generated, but because I think that the human agents of industrialization and the attendant urbanization did not have among their primary aims the achievement of cultural mutations; rather, they sought financial gain. Conversely, since Union (self-government) in 1910, and especially since Afrikaner Nationalist control in 1948, certain other human agents – those wielding White settler political power – have *wittingly* attempted various modifications of culture; hence the classification of 'directed.' The interplay between 'autonomous' and 'directed' cultural modification is of the greatest moment for both the uneasy present, and the probably even more conflict-ridden urban future.

Retrospect

Basic to an understanding of South African cities is an appreciation of their recency. All save one of the major urban centers of the Republic are, in essence, creations of the last 160 years. Indeed, the greatest urban agglomeration in sub-Saharan Africa, the Witwatersrand, centered upon Johannesburg, is less than 100 years old, with cities such as Witbank or Welkom more recent still. Cape Town is atypical. Its 330-year history rendered the 'Mother City's' sociocultural geography prior to apartheid (and even in remnants today) a much more ambiguous and subtly drawn palimpsest of changing social structures, cultural influences, and moral beliefs. If the broad parallels for Cape Town are to be found in cities like New Orleans or Rio de Janeiro, those for the more 'typical' South African city are to be found in Nairobi or Lubumbashi: cities whose origin is totally that of late 19th-century European colonial exploitation.

What was the nature of the South African economy, and of the various cultures found there, in the second half of the 19th century, when industrialization and urbanization commenced in earnest? First, those European farmers (Boers) nearer to Cape Town were part of a rather poorly articulated export economy, in, for example, wine and wheat, plus the victualling of shipping. However, many others of European origin were basically subsistence farmers or stock-raisers (Guelke 1976). From Dutch, and some Huguenot, ethnic roots, the *trekboeren* especially seem to have established a much-simplified version of the European culture from which they had sprung.

The rustic life, as practised, lent itself to affectionate retrospective portrayal once industrialization began ineluctably to erode it (see, for example, Bosman – 1963, 1969 – or Schreiner – 1923). Despite the apparent timelessness of Boer agrarian life conveyed in these portrayals, change was continually occurring: the gradual closure of the frontier, hence a rising population and stock density; agricultural innovations, one of the most important being the introduction of the merino sheep in the mid-19th century; encounters with different Black African peoples, not so easily shouldered aside as the Khoikhoi and San; changes in the policies; and the increasing effectiveness and reach of the Cape Town-based administration, British (not Dutch), after 1806. This is a vivid example of the need to beware of that once common pitfall apparent when Western scholars described the impact of what they termed 'modernization' upon 'traditional' societies. They assumed that these societies were unchanging, set in stone, and that the sudden experience of the West's more sophisticated technologies could only be rudely disintegrative of local cultures, which were presumed to be incapable of effective, creative adaptation.

Such a viewpoint was certainly long held concerning the indigenous peoples who had been practising subsistence economies in southern

Africa. Indeed, the Cape's Khoikhoi (once dubbed 'Hottentots' by Europeans), and San (likewise 'Bushmen'), *were* gradually overwhelmed, much as were the East Coast North American Indians – by wars, disease, starvation sequent upon the Whites' appropriation of their territorial resources, and by miscegenation of the remnant. What shattered the Khoisan peoples was competition for their land from stronger agrarian groups: the Boers moving from the south-west; the Bantu-speaking Black African tribespeoples moving from the north-east – the Khoisan were caught between the hammer and the anvil.

To consider the impact of 'modernization' and urbanization upon South Africa, we see, in broad terms, British imperialism as the primary agent, and those who had to adapt were the Boers (latterly 'Afrikaners'), their appendages the Coloureds (emancipated from slavery in 1834–8), and the Black African peoples. The natures of the urbanization of each of these groups will be dealt with in turn, observing the degree to which autonomy or directedness of cultural change has occurred at differing periods. I shall discuss Black African urbanization first, and at far greater length than either Afrikaner or Coloured (and Indian) urbanization, because the former is numerically much the most important, and because it is the central feature of the whole South African situation. It would, of course, be possible to study urbanization of all the above population groups from a different perspective, viewing them in relation to capital, as all members of a developing industrial proletariat. I choose not to do this here, not because of some in-built predilection for 'vulgar pluralism,' but because the cultural differences (real or perceived) among the above-mentioned groups have been used by White rulers as bases upon which to erect bureaucratic structures to canalize urbanization. These structures have either facilitated (in the case of the Afrikaners), or held back (in the case of the Black Africans, or, much less so, in the case of the Coloureds, or, in different manner again, in the case of the Indians) the transition to urban life. This transition has thereby been rendered objectively different for the various groups as the ruling Whites have chosen to define them.

Majority urbanization

Overview   Black African urbanization began at the same time as the final wars of subjugation by Whites. The opening up of the diamond fields at Kimberley from 1867, the gold fields of the eastern Transvaal in 1884, and, most important, those of the Witwatersrand from 1886, are contemporary with concluding large-scale military actions against the Xhosa (1877), the Zulu (1879), and the Sotho (1880). Many Europeans, viewing their newly established settlements on the previously open veld as incontestably 'the White man's creation,' perceived the Black African laborers coming to the mines as enemies, or, certainly, as members of 'savage,' newly defeated peoples; they could hardly be looked upon as partners, actual or potential, in a common enterprise of building up a nonracial South African economy or society (if this was ever the vision). But their labor was needed. Immigration from Britain or elsewhere in Europe could not meet the demand. And, indeed, DeKiewiet (1941) conveys the situation neatly when, posing the question as to why there was so little immigration (relative to that to, say, Australia, Canada, or the United States) into the burgeoning mineral centers of South Africa, he reminds the reader that, of course, there *was* large-scale immigration: it was *Black African* immigration from their circumadjacent conquered territories, providing labor cheaper than that of immigrant Whites.

This is at the real nub of the South African political economy, as the epigraph to this chapter indicates. Rather than erase the Black Africans in the subcontinent (the way North American Indians were erased), it seemed more attractive to use their cheap labor instead. But, in the long run, given a base of greater Black African numbers and differential fertility rates, the White operators of this efficiently exploitative economic system became increasingly outnumbered by those whom they are exploiting – a situation of which the latter are becoming more and more aware. In the country as a whole, Whites were outnumbered by 'Non-whites' in the ratio of 1 to 3.6 in 1921, 1 to 4.2 in 1960, 1 to 5.2 in 1977. Even in the cities, Whites have become increasingly outnumbered since then, and feel themselves to be at a potential strategic disadvantage.

Yet the Black Africans cannot simply be removed, for the modern economy, yielding high living standards for Whites, is dependent on their labor. They are thus needed as *units of labor*, but not as anything else – certainly not as a settled city-dwelling working-class, demanding equal, democratic rights, whereby their greater numbers would mean they could outbid the Whites and gain power in any common constitutional structure. So the whole edifice of the 'Native Reserves,' and its direct descendant, 'Grand Apartheid' – with all the concomitants of pass laws, contract migrant labor, industrial color bars, the restriction of many facilities for Black Africans to the homelands, residential segregation in the cities (both between the races and among the Blacks), all those elements which have conditioned the cultures that exist in South African cities – can be seen as a concerted attempt to resolve the basic paradox: the ruling Whites need and will treat the Black Africans only as units of labor; whereas the Black Africans, coming from their impoverished overpopulated reserves, need the urban employment, but are also increasingly demanding that they be treated not only as mere replicable units of productive energy, but as people with certain rights: to family life and to a political voice, for example. Furthermore, they demand the exercise of these rights in the cities to whose growth they have contributed from the very beginning.

The first large-scale mineral finds were at Kimberley, and the first Black Africans who migrated to work there were 'target-workers,' not intending to change their life-style permanently to that of the urbanite, but aiming to return home to the kraals once the target sum of money had been made. Welsh (1971a) reports that many of the circumscriptions which have come to be indissolubly associated with the South African labor system originated in Kimberley, such as migrant labor, and closed compounds for male-only workers (for ease of policing, and also enabling greater profit to be extracted with company-only stores within the compound). As further mineral finds in the last quarter of the century occurred, the Glen Grey Act of 1894 was imposed in Cape Colony, providing for the monetary taxing of Black Africans, and therefore propelling them into nonsubsistence employment for cash reward – that is, stimulating the labor supply for White farmers and mine operators. A few years later, the mining industry was very influential in the setting up of pass laws, in the Transvaal in 1896, and the Cape in 1902, whereby, at any time, Black Africans might be checked on by police demanding to see the 'pass' which permitted them to be in the particular urban area, and which obliged them to remain at their contracted place of employment.

At the same time, White townspeople viewed the Black African urban presence with some misgivings. To be sure, the industries needed their muscle-power, White traders might make money from their custom (and therefore tended to oppose the closed-compound system), and female Black Africans would provide cheap domestic service; but was it *safe*? In 1887, the mayoral minutes from Durban report that, after a discussion of the assaults and other crimes that Black Africans had apparently been committing, there was a request that a Black African "location" be established 'at a convenient distance' from the town (Kuper *et al.* 1958). Similarly, in what is today Woodstock in inner-city Cape Town: 'by 1881 there was again a sizeable African population in Papendorp – such that Whites began to talk of the need to establish an official "Kafir location" for it' (Saunders 1980). 'Let them understand' intoned a government position-paper in 1904, 'that the towns of the Colony are the special places of abode for the White men, who are the governing race.' The hope of permanent residence should be 'distinctly discouraged' for most Black Africans, who were to be 'mere visitors' (quoted by Welsh 1971a).

This last has been a continuing theme in official South African labor regulatory policy: in 1921, 'It should be understood that the town is a European area in which there is no place for the redundant native who neither works nor serves his or her people' (quoted by Fredrickson 1981); 55 years later, '. . . Mr. M. C. Botha [Minister of Bantu Administration] said in a speech in Port Elizabeth that the basis on which Blacks were present in White areas was "to sell their labor and for nothing else."' (South African Institute of Race Relations 1977). The fact that Black

Africans were, until 1978, *officially* deemed 'temporary sojourners' in the cities of South Africa is seen, for example, in the glaring lack of recreational or social facilities provided for them by White rulers. (Such attitudes were precisely congruent with those in cities of colonial British East Africa, as Furedi (1973) and Fair and Davies (1976) have shown.)

Yet, whatever the official constraints, urbanization of Black Africans continued. From 1936 to 1946, with the World War II industrial spurt, the official number of urban Black Africans rose by 57.16 percent (doubtless an underestimate). Then, from 1951 to 1970, their numbers more than doubled (and the 5 million officially enumerated in the latter year does not include those deemed 'migrant' workers, who spent 49 of the 52 weeks of that year in the cities, see below). The past decade has seen further increases.

The Black African has for ever become part of the South African city scene. This is, for example, reflected in literature. In 1926, William Plomer wrote a long story (*Ula Masondo*) about a young man from the rural reserves who comes to work on the mines, and of the knocks which transform him from hayseed to street-wise survivor. So common did this theme subsequently become (used, for example, in what must be the most well known South African novel, Alan Paton's *Cry, the beloved country* of 1944) that it was simply referred to in London literary circles as 'the South African plot.' And a South African government Department of Information tract in 1973 asserts 'Most Bantu authors . . . are concerned mainly with conflict between the old and the new, with social changes that are often synonymous with social decline, and with the problems created by contact with new cultures.' Observe the *leitmotif* of negativity in this last quotation. The impression is purposively given that 'the Bantu' are not truly fitted for town life, that cultural disintegration lurks there, and that rather (it seems to be intimated) they would be happier staying in the traditional countryside than in the cities which, after all, are really the province of the White man. This, of course, dovetails neatly with the long-standing (and self-serving) cultural perceptions of urban Whites, as a choice quotation unearthed by Welsh (1971a) from a claim-owner in Kimberley's early days reveals:

> The raw, untutored, unclad Kafirs, fresh from their 'kraals' up the mountains are by far the best and most trustworthy workmen. The contact of civilization seems to be almost invariably pernicious and demoralizing to the peculiar organization of our Kafir friends. Above all things, mistrust a Kafir who speaks English and wears trousers.

The townsmen–tribesmen dimension   A supply of muscle-power from those Black Africans who were 'fresh from their kraals up the mountains' was long preferred by the White rulers, who devised policies to perpetuate it.

There are also cultural implications here, which likewise have been subject to attempts at manipulation by government for its particular ends. These attempts have generated a split between the urbanites and the migrants among city-employed Black Africans. On the one hand, there are those who are committed to an urban way of life, and, on the other, those who work in the city but who either *choose* that their aspirations and loyalties be still rural aligned or who are *forced* into this state by being deemed only 'contract laborers.'

Something approaching 60 percent of Black Africans in South Africa today live in the cities or on the farms of 'White South Africa.' Only 40 percent ordinarily reside in the homelands (formerly 'Native Reserves,' later 'Bantustans'), which comprise 13 percent of the total area of the Republic. (I am including the Transkei, Bophuthatswana, Venda, and, from December 1981, the Ciskei in the Republic; their 'independence' is fictive.) Grand apartheid (i.e. the homelands policy) proposed that Black Africans, whether in or out of the homelands, should exercise their political rights only in that homeland to which their ethnic roots are adjudged to go back.

A number of points arise. First, the extent of the homelands is considerably smaller than was the original home territory at the time of European contact, whatever the tribal group. Secondly, the homelands are incapable of supporting their inhabitants, due to rapid population increase, in turn bringing extensive ecological damage and loss of agricultural productivity. This incapacity is also due to the present government's policy of 'resettlement:' over the last score of years, the moving in of at least *3.5 million* Black Africans, surplus to present labor requirements, mainly from 'White' farmlands, to rural dumping-grounds in the homelands (Maré 1980, United Nations 1982). Therefore, to survive, persons *must* leave the homelands to find jobs in 'White South Africa,' on its farms or in its cities, whence they may send home remittances. Thirdly, even those Black Africans who may be third-generation city born, or third-generation 'White farmland' born, and who (especially the former) may have no contact or cultural empathy for 'their unilaterally declared homeland,' are expected to direct their political aspirations to that homeland only.

Note that, in theory, this concept addresses the White government's 'urban Black African dilemma' rather nicely: their labor is retained; their political clout deflected to a relatively harmless backwater. And, for purposes of overseas misinformation, it can be claimed that in South Africa's 'plural democracy,' the same rights as the White 'nation' enjoys in 'its' homeland (87 percent of South Africa) are enjoyed by the various Black African 'nations' in '*their*' homelands. (I shall consider the significance to the government of what it terms 'ethnic' or 'national' – i.e. tribal – differences among the Black Africans below, p. 216.) As former Prime

Minister Vorster once memorably put it, 'If I were to wake up one morning and find myself a Black man, the only major difference would be geographical' (*Star*, April 3, 1973).

A geographical difference representative of that to which Vorster was referring would be, let us say, between a homeland in northern Natal versus a city on the Rand, a distance of 250 miles or so. But there was a juncture at which this could have been made enormously greater. In advance of the Afrikaner Nationalist government winning power in 1948, the SABRA[1] committee of apartheid planners, in significant part academicians at Stellenbosch (the leading center of Afrikaner intellectual life), was toying with the idea of a truly large-scale geographical re-organization of Black Africans – rather like Andrew Jackson expelling the Cherokee to west of the Mississippi. Of their deliberations, which created much of the present 'grand apartheid,' Walker (1957) reports: 'Some of its members realised that the Reserves were inadequate; indeed [Professor Werner] Eiselen and [Professor Andries] Cilliers proposed that the Union's [of South Africa] eight million Africans should be pushed bodily northward of the Limpopo river, though they did not say whether this should be into Southern Rhodesia or the Belgian Congo.' The advantages that such a system of control would have offered the Whites are evident. The Black Africans, migrant workers only (mostly male), are 'foreign' units of labor, inhabiting the jurisdiction of another state. Thus, one may permit the entry of *only* those who production requires at any given moment – thereby keeping down numbers – and can repatriate any 'surplus' *gastarbeiter* whenever expedient; one has few obligations towards them in terms of social security expenses, and *no* obligations in the area of political rights. The scheme was not taken up because of its imprac-ticability, but the granting of 'independence' to the peripheral homelands is a less ambitious attempt to achieve identical ends.

These efforts at controling Black African urbanization are not only concerned with numbers per se. It is also a question of maintaining an unwelcoming climate of impermanence for Black Africans in 'the White man's cities;' of inhibiting those sociocultural changes that might bring immigrants to realize subsequently that they 'have moved in some pro-founder sense than the mere physical change of abode' (Mayer 1971) – that they have become urbanites. The afore-mentioned edifice of pass laws, segregated Black African townships on the outskirts of 'White South Africa's' cities, the lack of social facilities there (but purportedly available in the homelands), the lack of political rights there (but purportedly avail-able in the homelands), the lack of higher (e.g. university) education there (but available in one's homeland), the law's preference for single male contract workers as opposed to accompanying families ('superfluous appendages') in train, all these underline the officially desired, supposed impermanence of Black Africans in 'White South Africa.'

Yet, as the economy has become more sophisticated, less based on mineral extraction, so does the demand for workers of greater skill and education grow, a demand that cannot be met by the relatively small numbers of Whites or by White immigration. Thus, despite all the official inhibitions, a settled, family-living Black African urban proletariat has been long apparent: 'perhaps the most "westernized" Black population in Africa, and the most highly attuned to the institutions of an advanced industrial society' (Mayer 1975). The government is finally rather grudgingly admitting that these persons are now inevitably permanent urbanites, for example by the permitting of 30-year, and now 99-year, leaseholds on properties in the segregated townships (where *all* land is owned by the government's Black African administration apparatus). And it is between these urbanites, and those who will be permitted only as contract migrant workers from the homelands – respectively 'urban insiders' and 'urban outsiders' in Francis Wilson's (1975) terms – that government policy attempts to drive a wedge.

The proportion of single migrant workers in the total Black African urban population varies from city to city: in Port Elizabeth, it is only 20 percent; on most of the Witwatersrand, and in Durban, it appears to be about 50 percent; in Cape Town, the most distant of the large cities from any homeland, and where regulations favor Coloured over Black African employment, the proportion is as high as 85 percent. This last figure is, to a degree, misleading, because many who work in Cape Town for 49 of the 52 weeks of the year go 'home' at Christmas, and who then return via the 'call-in card' system to the self-same job, are officially considered migrant contract workers.

Section 10 of the revised Bantu (Urban Areas) Act, the pass law which has been conditioning Black African urban residence over the last 35 years, reads:

No Bantu shall remain for more than 72 hours in a prescribed area unless he produces proof in the manner prescribed [that is, a pass] that –

(a)   he has, since birth, resided continuously in such area; or
(b)   he has worked continuously in such area for one employer for a period of not less than ten years or has lawfully resided continuously in such area for a period of not less than fifteen years and has thereafter continued to reside in such area and is not employed outside such area and has not during either period or thereafter been sentenced to a fine exceeding one hundred rand or to imprisonment for a period exceeding six months; or
(c)   such a Bantu is the wife, unmarried daughter or son . . . of any Bantu mentioned in paragraphs (a) or (b) of the sub-section and

after lawful entry into such prescribed area, ordinarily resides
with that Bantu in such area.

It is clear that permanent legal urban residence is attainable either by the
good fortune of being a 'borner' [10(a)], or by a long, law-abiding spell in
one city [10)b)]. But, even in the context of these laws, the government can
redefine meanings to keep Black African numbers down. In Cape Town,
for example, from 1968 all males were declared to be on one-year contracts. So even if one were to come back, after three weeks' vacation in the
Transkei 'homeland,' to the same job year after year, those years could *not*
be summed in order eventually to total 10, or 15, years as per Section 10(b);
so it is now impossible to gain permanent residence rights here. Similarly,
in Section 10(c), concerning women and children of urban workers, there
is the apparently innocuous phrase 'after lawful entry.' But this does not
simply mean dutifully recording one's arrival with township officials. In
order to enter *lawfully*, Black African family accommodation must be
available. And, as the government's apparatus for the administration of
Black Africans has a monopoly on the land and on the provision of family
housing in the townships, it can simply decline to provide any such
housing, thereby rendering 'lawful entry' impossible. Thus, despite an
official shortage of 1440 dwellings for legally entered families *already in* the
Cape Town townships, not one new house was constructed from 1972 to
1978. Not surprisingly, one response is to 'squat' in a shantytown peripheral to the city (Ellis *et al.* 1977).

The pass law is currently being revamped, sequent upon the 1977
Riekert Commission, whose report *The Economist* – a journal not noted for
hyperbole – termed 'one of the most cold-blooded accounts of the operation of apartheid in existence.' Although claimed to be advancing 'liberal-
izing' neo-apartheid measures, representing a 'new deal' for urban Black
Africans, many observers see the new bills as a streamlining and a tight-
ening of grand apartheid. For example, the politically liberal South African
Institute of Race Relations (SAIRR) stated (*Race Relations News*, January/
February 1981):

> . . . that Africans be permitted to live in urban areas only on the basis of
> approved accommodation and employment, represents a significant
> hardening of influx control regulations . . . this legislation appears to
> envisage the creation of an urban élite, while poverty continues to be
> rampant in rural areas . . . The negative aspects are : 1) With the aboli-
> tion of the Urban Areas Act 25 of 1945 all rights to remain in the urban
> areas have been removed. 2) Persons born and working for a long time
> in the urban areas will no longer be in a protected position. 3) The
> hardening of the whole citizenship issue and the widening of the use of
> the phraseology 'prohibited immigrants'. . .

This last point concerns the unilateral attribution, by the government, of homeland 'citizenship' to Black Africans living in the 'White' cities. One may be a third-generation 'borner' in Cape Town, but if one's ethnic roots go back to, say, the Pondo tribe in the eastern Transkei, one is liable to be declared a 'Transkei citizen' (even though, maybe, unable to speak one's supposed 'mother-tongue'). And thereby all claim is lost to South African citizenship. This can happen equally to Zulu or to Tswana or to Venda, each being made 'foreigners in the land of their birth.'

This cleavage, then, between townspeople and tribespeople – with the government trying to nudge as many as possible of the contract laborers in the latter cultural and political direction – is the one which is the most fundamental among Black Africans. In a sense, it represents the interface between, respectively, the First and the Third Worlds. Mayer (1975) states that, 'a sharp dichotomy between the migrant and the residents has replaced former gradual transition between them.'[2] This enhancing of the rural–urban dichotomy by the government is a conscious attempt at 'directed' cultural change. From an appreciation of this flow the deep suspicions held by many urban Black Africans concerning certain incidents in the Soweto civil unrest of June–August 1976, and that in Cape Town at Christmas of the same year. Fierce fighting broke out when migrant contract workers sallied forth from their barrack-like hostels, armed with clubs and machetes, looking for trouble with the Black African 'permanent' urbanites whom they resented (P. Magubane 1978), especially the politicized high-school students trying to promote stay-aways from work. Many were beaten to death by these groups, and widespread allegations (many from respectably conservative Black Africans) that the South African police aided and abetted the migrants have refused to die down (SAIRR 1978). These actions are seen as evidence for a divide-and-rule policy.

If, then, the government can convince the *urban* Black Africans to accept a separate peace, with some of the material comforts of industrial civilization increasingly available, and let their homeland-dwelling fellows fend for themselves in powerless peripheral poverty, the government has thereby effected an advantageous split in its opponents' camp. This is a possible strategem which has long been pondered. For example, Leo Kuper (1965, 1971) has depicted the lack of solidarity between the urban 'bourgeoisie' and the lower-status contract workers. Of Durban and the immediately adjoining KwaZulu homeland, Schlemmer and Muil (1975) write: 'It is not yet clear that middle-class Africans will lead rank-and-file Africans.' Many others have made similar observations, among them Doris Lessing (1957), who provides a southern Rhodesian example from the 1920s: 'I remember hearing Lord Malvern, then Dr. Huggins, addressing a farmers' meeting in Lomagundi when I was a little girl. He said that the white people must create a class of privileged blacks to act as a bulwark against revolt.' The same theme underlies the 1980 plea to the South African government of a Bantustan leader, requesting for homelanders that which 'urban insiders' are already being accorded: 'Give our people something to lose!'

Yet attempts to manipulate society and its culture frequently have a way of rebounding on the would-be manipulator. So, in the very report in which he asserts the appearance of the 'sharp dichotomy' between migrant and resident, Mayer (1975) later writes, from the same Sowetan data, that:

> Indeed, all the major policies meant to protect the White character of South African cities are having one important unintended consequence: they are all helping to blur the division between urban and rural Blacks. Homeland citizenship for Blacks in white cities, growing armies of contract laborers, mass deportation of urban 'surplus' populations to homeland areas, the reclassification of urban workers' suburbs as homeland towns, and even border industry development seem almost custom-built for helping Blacks over the town–country divide that has been such a powerful obstacle to their political mobilization. 'We can achieve black solidary,' writes Chief Buthelezi, 'even through structures meant to destroy it, like ethnic legislatures and ethnic urban boards.'

The intertribal dimension   Buthelezi's assertion brings us to a second cleavage within the Black African population, one which provides a remarkable example of attempts at 'directed' cultural change by the White government. This is the ethnic/tribal basis chosen for the administration of city-dwelling Black Africans. One way of viewing this policy is that it simply seemed to bring order to, and to offer ease of administration to White overseers of, urban Black Africans. Just as Furedi (1973) tells us that, in Nairobi in the early 20th century, British policy encouraged urban associations to be founded on administrative districts of origin, so in South Africa it would *prima facie* seem practical to segregate Black Africans internally according to language, for ease of interpretation or policing, for example. There are deeper reasons, however. The Under-Secretary for Native Affairs in Natal warned (1906–07): 'National and tribal disintegration would quickly be followed by racial amalgamation. There was evidence of this process and this result in the towns. Let us stem back and keep off the process of disintegration, both in ours as well as in the interests of the natives themselves . . .' (quoted by Welsh 1971a). Forty years later, 'the interests of the natives themselves' were more explicitly, unilaterally defined for them as pertaining to tribal culture. Fredrickson (1981) reports that, 'Building on their own traditions of cultural nationalism, Afrikaner theorists of apartheid applied the notion of a separate and God-given destiny for each *volk* or "nation" to every nonwhite group to which it could assign a distinctive ethnic or tribal origin.'

Thus the afore-mentioned Department of Information production of 1973 states its view unambiguously: 'The Bantu consist of several distinct nations, each with its own customs and traditions. There are ten different Bantu languages ...' This position is illustrated by a list of the 1970 populations of the ten principal cities: 'Cape Town: total 1 096 597; Whites, 378 505; Coloureds, 598 952; Asians, 11 263; Xhosa, 100 947; Zulu, 1378; Swazi, 103; Sepedi (North Sotho), 315; North Ndebele, 19; South Ndebele, 44; Tswana, 684; Seshoeshoe (South Sotho), 2428; Shangaan, 82; Venda, 39; other Bantu, 1838.' Each other city is painstakingly enumerated likewise, down to the seven 'Venda' in Port Elizabeth, the solitary 'Asian' in Bloemfontein, and the zero 'North Ndebele' in East London!

Similarly, the government-supporting segment of the press occasionally celebrates such occupational specialization as can be found that varies according to Black African ethnicity – for example, that the Bhaca from the eastern Transkei seem to have a particular niche in trash collection. The assertion is undisguisedly made that this is somehow a result of their 'traditional culture.' Whatever reasons may stem from the severely curtailed opportunity structure for migrant male Bhaca in Cape Town go unmentioned. Similarly again, violent 'faction fights' are not infrequently reported in the South African Press, between different ethnic groups of migrant laborers, often in their mine compounds. The 'explanation' for such occurrences is invariably couched in terms which suggest that such conflicts inevitably stem from immutable cultural pluralism among Black Africans. Alternative attempts at explanation, which address the highly plausible angle of competition for scarce economic rewards in a White-manipulated labor market, go unmentioned. (See, for example, Phimister & van Onselen 1979.)

There is no doubt that many of those Whites who had a hand in the apartheid plans that flowed from such precepts of 'Nonwhite' cultural pluralism were sincere in their beliefs that under such a system 'greater scope for more effective self-determination' would be the desirable result. One such, the author of that last phrase quoted, has been Professor Erika Theron, a sociologist at the Afrikaners' premier university, Stellenbosch, who now feels that she was mistakenly 'naïve' in such a belief (*Christian Science Monitor*, April 13, 1981). For it is *not* simply the Afrikaners' belief in cultural nationalism that is involved here. Adam (1971), without committing himself openly, reveals another possible motive:

Whether the Afrikaner past with its former progressive nationalism is projected onto the other groups, or whether Apartheid is merely a witting device of *divide et impera*, is hardly significant compared with the fact that obviously a widespread ethnic narcissism in all groups responds to such offers. That for which minorities in other parts of the world struggle – the right to keep their cultural identity – is granted readily in South Africa.

Leo Kuper (1965) is more decided; he feels divide-and-rule is definitely involved here:

> The tribal enterprise of the Government is not altogether fantastic. It calls for a restructuring of urban African relations . . . The technique is that of tribal segregation (or segregation of linguistic groups). This the Government can enforce in residence and education, over which it has effective power, but not in worship, play, or voluntary association, and probably not even in employment . . . [but] perhaps it is not necessary . . . that it should be complete . . . If their combined effect is to dilute the perspectives of African nationalism, and to fragment and confuse African political purpose, then the Government's strategy will have succeeded.

Six years later, Kuper opined that such cultural manipulation by the government had doubtless had some success in eroding both 'Nonwhite' and Black African solidarity, and in enhancing pluralism. Or, as Whisson wrote in the same year (1971): 'The policy of apartheid has been successful in creating self-sustaining barriers which make group attitudes of suspicion more likely and individual nonracist attitudes less likely.'

The hostile views of an intellectual spokesman, Mphahlele (1974), are clear:

> Today the Boer government is forcing our people to accept institutions of its own fabrication which it advertizes as 'Bantu culture.' This is a technique of oppression. We know where we stand culturally, but the whites are out to confuse our people by making them believe that fragmented tribal cultures are the ultimate in our black consciousness. The whites know very well that they are safe as long as our cultural development is fragmented into tribal compartments. They fear the day when we will take things in hand as the majority race and direct our own cultural destiny, mightier than their own miserable dead-end racism will ever attain.

Mayer (1975) insists that similar sentiments were found right down to the rank-and-file (as he puts it) in Soweto: 'The motive behind this policy is to kill the spirit which was gradually growing among these different tribes – the spirit of African nationalism. If one makes the small nations to clash among themselves, they will somehow forget about the major enemy;' and Patricios (1975) found strong sentiments against ethnically segregated housing among ('rank-and-file') miners in Carletonville (west Witwatersrand).

So, Black Africans are indeed aware of the attempt to manipulate them by 'directed' cultural change, via residential and educational ethnic segregation, or via the themes concentrated upon by government-directed communications media. Radio Bantu, broadcasting in the various Black African mother-tongues, is, for example, valued as a source of information by 60 percent of a sample of Durban Black Africans; but the other 40 percent see it as the propaganda arm of the government (Schlemmer & Muil 1975). Much more decidedly, Sowetans see the emphasis on mother-tongues as mediums of instruction in the schools of the Department of Bantu Education as consciously fostering tribalist perspectives, and 'holding back the African nation.' Then there is the tribally segregated housing, so undesired by Sowetans. A most illuminating parallel to this comes from the British colonial administration's chosen policy in response to the upsurge of the 'Mau Mau Emergency' in Kenya in April 1954: 24 000 Kikuyu, Embu, and Meru (members of the ethnic groups most deeply embroiled) were simply removed from Nairobi; pass books were issued to Black Africans in the city; *and Black African housing was reorganized in the locations on a tribal basis.*

Black–white contact: cultural ramifications We have observed the 'townsmen–tribesmen,' and then the 'ethnic' cleavages among Black African cultures during a continuing process of urbanization, and seen how government has attempted to orchestrate and canalize these cleavages. Yet such attempts at canalizing, at *directing* cultural change have been only partially successful. At the same time, *autonomous* cultural changes among Black Africans have been occurring in the urban industrial milieu. Thus, the status of women has invariably risen in the cities, according to Welsh (1971a). Many and varied have been the voluntary associations formed in the townships, and not necessarily based on ethnic home-area criteria at all. English has come to be claimed as the 'Black man's *lingua franca*,' and an Afrikaans-based *Tsotsi taal* is widely spoken also (Mayer 1975). Black African writers like Nkosi (1965), Mphahlele (1959) and Modisane (1963) have made English their own in their descriptions of urban Black Africa's Witwatersrand: its zestful vitality, the crime, police raids, squalor, violence, humor, and endurance apparently integral to life in *eGoli,* 'the place of gold.' Here, ethnic identity has been becoming submerged under an autonomous 'Westernization,' a process which the government (as we have seen) has been trying to inhibit. There is absolutely no doubt, claims Mayer, that Sowetans put ethnicity in the background. Most feel that a 'melting-pot' situation obtains among Black Africans there, and that they are 'settling down into a common Black identity.' In social relations, there are two things that matter much more to them than ethnicity: their own status within the universe of Black African city dwellers; and race, i.e. their relationship to the ruling Whites.

This last point brings us to one final consideration in the culture changes that have occurred concomitant with Black African urbanization. The dominant, incoming culture, to which accommodation has been made, is foreign and, at origin, British. Thus, according to Mayer (1975) 'Soweto people ... see [their common Black] identity as belonging within the family of Western (industrial–urban) cultures,' a view supported by Leo Kuper (1971). The material advantages, especially of Western consumer society, are desired, as is the opening up of a world of knowledge that Western education in a universal language promises; therefore, English is greatly preferred to Afrikaans, which, additionally, is more self-evidently 'the language of our oppressor.'

It is an intriguing, but impossibly complex and nebulous, area of speculation that one skirts here. To what degree is any supposed Western 'cultural imperialism' impressing its mold upon Africanity under this oppressive apartheid system? To what degree, conversely, does any supposed vitality in Black African culture make it possible 'freely,' 'autonomously,' to choose which Western traits to adopt, which to eschew, which to modify? Of 20 years ago, Leo Kuper (1965) wrote:

> Among the educated in particular, there is a strong repugnance for tribal society, a sense of cultural shame, a feeling that tribalism is a return to the past, to barbarism, to the primitive. The cultural shame derives from the teachings of missionaries, from formal education, and from exposure to Western civilization. And antipathy for the tribal society is now heightened by the Government's policy of retribalization. Latterly, there are signs of a revaluation of the tribal past, a searching for historical pride. But it is highly selective.

Of ten years ago, Mayer (1975) wrote that Sowetans:

> would say that in their view the great mass of the permanent residents are 'civilized,' or 'Europeanized,' or 'follow the Western way of life.' They said it firmly and without regret or ambivalence.

They did not, however, want the White South African way of life – with its perceived lack of *ubuntu*, for example – as a package, whole and indivisible. Mayer claims that Sowetans were clearly able to separate the Western way of life in a general world context, from its White South African variant. But they also:

did see 'civilization' as having been diffused into South Africa historically by Whites. In this light they did claim to be sharing a European civilization . . . No wonder that some African intellectuals feel misgivings about it. The nascent Black consciousness movement in South Africa, while supporting radical antitribalism, has called for a 'consciousness of our cultural heritage' (Manganyi 1973). B. Magubane (1971) argues forcefully that 'A "Europeanised" African can never . . . aspire to an independent identity.'

A final quotation, which underlines the uncertainty that Black African intellectual leaders can feel in these matters, comes from Ezekiel Mphahlele (1974). He asks:

What is happening in this vast continent that bears the giant footprints or ruins or scars left behind by European occupation? I have seen the survival, in the most urbanized ghettos of South Africa, of the toughest of traditional traits: the sense of community, the rituals surrounding birth, marriage and death, the theater that surrounds life in general. But then we are fenced in. How much would this survive if we had the freedom to live where we wanted to? I have seen the new civil-service class in independent Africa fossilize as soon as they moved into suburbia, where towns had been structured to suit the white man. The new class began to visit by invitation or permission through the phone; something inside them died.

Mphahlele here has put his finger on the very distinction I have been trying to make between directed ('we are fenced in') and autonomous ('if we had the freedom') cultural change. And he continues: 'My speculation about South Africa would be idle if I did not take into consideration the fact that *political struggle interacts with cultural patterns.*' (My italics.)

Black-White contact: spatial ramifications For the geographer, there is, furthermore, the anticipation that both the political struggle *and* the cultural patterns will interact with *spatial* patterns, and that the very form of the South African city is both product and primer of sociocultural change. Since the first days of large-scale industrial urbanization a century or more ago, the Whites have wished to segregate Black Africans spatially for more effective control. The White fear of Black African crime, or less explicitly, of the perceived cultural gulf – the enormous social distance – gave rise to the desire for segregation noted previously. Until that time, Black Africans had been crowded into cheap, rented rooms near to their work in the city centers (for these were still mainly pedestrian-era cities), or in shanty-like accommodations on the cities' outskirts (outskirts which at the most were only 1.5 to 2 miles distant). In response to such fears in

Cape Town, in 1890 the city's first custom-built segregated Black African township, the Dock Native Location, was established. A dozen years later, another theme enters. Bubonic plague broke out among Black Africans, and fearful Capetonians demanded a *cordon sanitaire*, and a new 'government reserve' was established a considerable distance from the then edge of the city. In Port Elizabeth, in the same year, the same sequence of events occurred. However, such new 'locations' still left many Black Africans renting in the poorer inner-city areas, or living on their employers' premises, and, in 1918, the great influenza epidemic again drew attention to the slums.

Thus, in 1923 in Cape Town, for example, a new 'model township,' Langa, was established for Black Africans, way out of the city, on the sand dunes. In that same year the Natives (Urban Areas) Act was passed, the immediate forbear of the present pass laws. It restricted the Black Africans' entry into the cities of South Africa, legislated the forcible removal of those who were considered to be undesirable or habitually unemployed, and provided for the establishment by municipalities of totally segregated 'native locations.' The Act has often been amended and tightened, but nonetheless many, if not most, Black Africans in the cities did *not* live in the segregated locations at this period.

The major reason was the (White) local authorities, upon whom the onus rested, were not greatly exercised by the thought of planning for Black African urbanites, nor were they attracted by the time or cost this might entail. Rather did they in many instances pursue a policy of neglect – epitomized perhaps by the fact that in Johannesburg 'native locations' fell under the responsibilities of the *Parks* Department in the 1920s! Thus a liberal-minded White politician, Edgar Brookes, referring to the pre-apartheid years, said in Parliament in 1950:

> . . . Hon. members who have been on the Native Affairs Commission in this House will admit – that what you get for a native location in an urban area is a bit of land which nobody else wants. Just what is left. They know that. They know that is so all over the country.

The consequences of such neglect were exacerbated by the World War II industrial spurt; so many Black Africans had been drawn into the expanding employment market of the cities that they could not find accommodation. Nor was the government prepared to direct the enormous energies and resources necessary to provide reasonable housing for these people, who after all had no vote, no political clout. So vast shantytowns sprang up: Sophiatown in Johannesburg, Cato Manor in Durban, Windermere in Cape Town.

At this juncture, the Afrikaner Nationalists won the election of 1948, and determined to devote great *central* (not local) government energies to the removal of shantytowns, and to an effective apartheid 'solution' to the Black African presence in towns. Over the previous decade, the Whites had become outnumbered there, and now the most basic fear of all, that of 'swamping' by a vast urban *swart gevaar* ('black peril'), is clearly involved. The Urban Areas Act was tightened, with the time a jobless Black African was permitted in the 'White' city to find employment being reduced from 14 to 3 days. The apparatus for enforcing the pass laws – the police, the Bantu Administration courts – was beefed up. Shantytowns were demolished, and enormous new uniform housing tracts built: Soweto in essence dates from this period, as does Guguletu-Nyanga outside Cape Town. The strategic element is evident:

> The older non-White shanty towns with their maze of narrow, tortuous alleys were often located close to White residential or business districts; they are now systematically being razed as a major military hazard ... The new ghettos are typically situated several miles from the White towns, with a buffer zone between (Van den Berghe 1966, p. 411).

And Adam (1971, p. 123) considered that:

> The design and location of the African townships has been planned on the basis of strategic considerations. Within a short time such a location could be cordoned off, and in its open streets, any resistance could be easily smashed.

No longer was a Black African location simply on a bit of land that nobody else wanted, as Edgar Brookes had charged above. Careful geopolitical planning now gave forethought to which sector of the city should be Black African, at what distance, and in which direction it should expand.

However, despite the whole 'influx control'/urban residential segregation system, Black Africans continue to be drawn to the cities. Housing provision has not kept up. Tens of thousands lived in the late 1970s in peri-urban shantytowns near Durban and Cape Town. In the latter city, attempts to erase 'the squatting evil' (the government's term) at a particular encampment, Crossroads, have attracted worldwide attention – attempts were still being made late in 1981 (Andrew & Western 1979). *In toto*, these efforts to inhibit the evolution of a common urban society, and a common nonracial (working-class or, indeed, potentially middle-class) culture among all South Africans, have been to a degree 'successful.' There is no doubt that strict spatial segregation (the physical form of the city itself) has enhanced the separation in effect between Black African and White South African city dwellers, with negative consequences for the possibility of any future peaceful accommodation between them.

Minority urbanization

This survey of Afrikaner, Coloured, and Indian urbanization will, of necessity, be more brief. Its major purpose will be to point out the differences between their varying experiences and those of the Black Africans. The socio-cultural changes concomitant with urbanization have, in the cases of the Indians and (especially latterly) the Coloureds, been subject to White attempts at direction. Afrikaner urbanization, however, has been the closest to the 'autonomous' ideal type. Yet, government intervention has also occurred in Afrikaner urbanization – both in ill starred agricultural rehabilitation schemes to keep Afrikaners on the land, and in more important and more successful attempts to reserve relatively unskilled, but satisfactorily paying, urban jobs for poorer, previously rural Whites (nearly all Afrikaners), and so assist their urban adjustment. Because of these interventions, *all* of these groups have experienced 'directed' urbanization. The question therefore arises as to whether supposedly purely 'autonomous' cultural change through urbanization is a chimera. In fact, I admittedly am using the 'autonomous' notion merely to represent one pole of a hypothesized continuum, and as an illustrative device aimed at effecting a clearer contrast with the Black African experience. This last is viewed as being near the continuum's other, 'directed' pole, that of highly constrained change. Indians and Coloureds are seen as being between the two extremes, although the Indians have, over time, been nearer to the 'directed' pole than the Coloureds.

Afrikaners In 1910, the 25 percent of the total South African White population who lived in urban areas were almost all non-Afrikaner. By 1980, 88.9 percent of Whites were urbanized. An estimated 80 percent of the Afrikaners, of whom there are approximately 2.75 million, are now urbanized. This has been a rapid urbanization – taking just one lifetime. At the turn of the century, the quintessential element of Boer life was viewed as being the sturdy, if not truculent, self-reliance sprung from the isolated frontier quasi-subsistence economy: the generic *trekboer* image. But this agrarian system was already unstable. And the *coup de grâce* was given by the over two-and-a-half years of the Anglo-Boer War (1899–1902), which devastated the Afrikaner farming communities. Hence, many had to make the move to the town, to a milieu inevitably viewed as associated with an unwanted foreign ruler, the subjugating British.

Newly arrived Afrikaners had few skills of use in this culturally threatening urban setting – even their language was seen as inapt and to be derided. For a time, indeed, British policy was to 'anglicize' the Boers by forbidding the instruction of Dutch in schools, leading to the language's demise. Afrikaners took unskilled laborers' jobs, some, to their chagrin, finding themselves working alongside Black Africans and Coloureds for the same remuneration (although they were not, of course, subjected to pass laws). Coloureds, in fact, held *superior* positions to Afrikaners in many instances, as, for example, as artisans on the mines and in Cape Town (in the latter city a long tradition of skilled work – e.g. cabinet-making – as house slaves gave many Coloureds the edge). On the Witwatersrand, Afrikaners gravitated to posts where such lack of urban skills was less of a hindrance: the police, the railways, the lower grades in the civil service.

The 1910 Act of Union, however, brought distinct possibilities for the Boers, with the creation of a new state, the Union of South Africa. In it, the defeated Boer republics of the Transvaal and the Orange Free State were united with previously British Cape Colony and Natal, and *White rule was enshrined in the constitution's franchise*. The Boers, although a recently defeated people, thereby had the vote – which basically the Black Africans, Indians, and by far the larger part of the Coloured people did not. Therefore, unlike these other groups, they had an actual and potential bargaining card with the operators of the urban economic system. And, indeed, among the enfranchised (five-sixths of whom were White), it was not the English speakers but the Boers who were in the majority. Clearly, if the Boers were to unite according to cultural ethnicity, then they might gain power in the Union. The 1924 elections, which gave rise to General J. B. M. Hertzog's 'Pact' government, may be broadly seen as the start of this incorporation, and the 1948 election its culmination.

Rural depression had continued in many areas since the Anglo-Boer War, propelling Boers to the cities, and, by the start of the 1920s, a large 'poor White problem' was evident: un- or underemployed rural Boers were living in slum or frequently even in shantytown-like conditions in the cities. But now the Boer lever on political power in the Pact government was translated into economic power through the implementation of the 'Civilised Labour Policy' from 1924 onwards. It underwrote poor White advancement. at the expense of Coloureds and Black Africans. Basically, a certain proportion of jobs was reserved for those who could attain 'civilized' living standards. This was almost invariably interpreted (as it was meant to be) as being 'for Whites only.' Similarly, education and apprenticeships were other areas in which the dice might be loaded in the (poor) Whites' favor in the competition for the prizes of industrial urbanism. Far more *per capita* was spent by the government on White schooling than on that of Coloured, Indian, or Black African; and apprenticeships to skilled trades were in turn made dependent upon education.

In these ways the Boers were able to adapt their culture (with government help) to city life. At first, the city, built around the mines owned by the British and by English-speaking Jews, was alien and feared: 'As the original agent of the destruction of the Boer way of life, the gold-mining industry has always retained its diabolic character for the majority of Afrikaners' (Patterson 1957).   And:

> To Afrikaner leaders the danger was that poverty and demoralisation might lead to the Afrikaner townsman's losing his identity, or becoming 'de-nationalized.' Common life and poverty in multiracial slums would reduce the significance of racial and cultural differences. Moreover, being an Afrikaner in itself was a handicap in the alien world of the city: 'To thrive in the town, he must degenerate as an Afrikaner; to progress socially he must retrogress nationally' (Welsh 1971a p. 203).

Welsh goes on to show how Afrikaner leaders, and especially the Dutch Reformed Church, strived continually, and with eventual success, to alleviate the poor White problem, and to ensure that urbanization did not result in the Afrikaner's loss of his *volkslewe* (national cultural life).

One focus was the creation of a fully fledged 'new' language, Afrikaans, out of the previously existing patois. At first a defensive response to 'anglicization,' this soon became a vehicle of self-pride and cultural self-confidence: 'Raise the Afrikaans language to a written language, make it the bearer of our culture, our history, our national ideals, and you will thereby raise the people who speak this language,' claimed D. F. Malan in 1908, 40 years before he became the first South African Prime Minister from the present Afrikaner National party. Another focus was the foundation of Afrikaner-specific voluntary associations – social, cultural, and economic – to help ensure that urbanizing Afrikaners were kept within the ethnic fold: the Afrikaanse Sakekamer (Chamber of Commerce equivalent), the Voortrekkers (Boy Scouts equivalent), the Broederbond, the Reddingsdaadbond, etc. As du Toit (1975, pp. 26–7) has put it:

> . . . the necessary precondition for the mobilization and consolidation of a unitary Afrikaner nationalism in power is to be found in the development and diversification of the organizational substructure – which coincided with the processes of Afrikaner urbanization and modernization. The social and cultural consequences were also profound. The Afrikaner was not simply exposed to and assimilated by an alien urban environment. The wide range of separate Afrikaner institutions and organizations largely succeeded in isolating the Afrikaner from other groups so that in the towns he tends to live in a predominantly Afrikaner environment. David Welsh has aptly termed this process the 'encapsulating of the urban Afrikaner.'[3]

This helps explain how some Afrikaner apartheid ideologists could, from the successful experience of their own *volk*-based mobilization, claim to be projecting in a genuine spirit such cultural nationalism onto other South African 'groups' or 'nations.'

However, such ascription of a desirable cultural nationalism is not made with equal fervor for all non-Afrikaner groups. Although Afrikaners in their *voluntary* associations may choose culturo-ethnic exclusivity, they do not *impose* this upon the other Whites via government-controlled education, or via residential segregation. If Sotho and Shangaan are different Black African 'nations,' then surely by the same token Afrikaner, Portuguese, Jew, or English-speaking Christian Whites are too? Not so, says the Department of Information (Republic of South Africa 1973): 'the White South African nation ... today is a nation in its own right, with its own way of life, and not a random assortment of immigrants.' Furthermore, consider one of the foundation-stone apartheid laws, the Group Areas Act, which legislates who shall live where in the now-regimented South African city (the law applies to Whites, Indians, and Coloureds directly, to Black Africans rather more indirectly). This residential segregation Act provides for the subdivision, if necesary, of Indians and Coloureds into seven separate groups, and even has the clause written in to it (subsection 12[2]) that the state president can specify '... (d) any group of persons which is under subsection (2) declared to be a group.' There is an important point here which Leo Kuper (1956) does not let elude him; he comments with precision:

> The danger is in the numerical preponderance of the non-whites. It is a threat, hower, only if the non-whites are united ... The Group Areas Act (1950) gives the Governor-General [now the state president] the necessary power to subdivide Coloureds and natives but not Whites ... If my interpretation is rejected, then we must assume that it is sheer accident that the government has ... discriminated against the Whites by withholding from [them] the privilege of communal living.

It is clear then that unity (not necessarily cultural uniformity) is to be fostered by the government for the Whites; whereas the same law can lubricate disunity among Blacks (i.e. all 'Nonwhites') by promoting cultural heterogeneity: *divide et impera.*

Coloureds and Indians

COLOUREDS   The reference to the Group Areas Act brings us directly to a consideration of the sociocultural aspects of the urbanization of those often broadly viewed as being 'in the middle,' between the Whites and Black Africans: the Coloureds (approximately 2 600 000) and the Indians (approximately 800 000). The situation of the Coloureds gives the lie once more to the simple 'vulgar pluralism' line of some apartheid ideologists.

For, despite government references to 'a nation-in-the-making,' the Coloureds' culture, *impressed upon them* over the 176-years' experience of slavery and thereafter subordination, has basically been the same as that of the Whites, and in fact mainly that of the Afrikaners. When Adam Small, a well known Coloured poet and dramatist, termed himself a 'brown Afrikaner' in 1971, it made one sit up and take notice, so contrary was it to the official government cultural–pluralistic line. But 10 years later, one of the less conservative Afrikaans newspapers has come to the realization of 'the reality that . . . there is today no essential difference between educated Brown and White people in respect of the degree of civilization, way of life, language, culture and religion' (*Rapport*, June 7, 1981). If there is no difference, why then should apartheid, supposedly justly based on objective cultural differences, offer differential political incorporation to a 'group' that is not a 'separate nation?' It is evidently not on *culture* that the distinction is made, but on *color*. Yet even color is not per se a foolproof guide to who is ('fair-skinned') Coloured or who is (swarthy) White. This issue is fraught with ambiguity, as is the urban milieu which has been the principal theater of Coloured urbanization: Cape Town, in which metropolitan area now live one-third of all South Africa's Coloured people.

In so far as Coloured people are considered to be the products of racial amalgamation between Whites and/or Khoikhoi and/or slaves (the first imported in 1658), then the first 'half-castes' would have been born in Cape Town at the beginning of 1653. And, as the frontier expanded (with further miscegenation) so Coloureds continued as slaves for their Boer masters; some Khoikhoi and few San, losing their lands, also became 'apprenticed' farm laborers, which, *de facto*, meant serfdom. In Cape Town there were many house-slaves, especially those captured resisting the Dutch in the East Indies and then exiled to the Cape. These last brought Islam with them, now practiced by about 1 in 17 of all Coloured people ('Cape Malays'), this being arguably the only major cultural difference between (a minority of) Coloureds and the Whites. Otherwise, previous names and language were lost in large degree through the generations of slavery. Slave-names are common, like 'Januarie' for the month of the year in which the slave-baby was born, or 'Hendrickse,' implying that the baby came into the world as the property of a White master named Hendrick. Afrikaans is the mother tongue of about 90 percent of Coloureds (the rest speak English).

In 1828, Ordinance 50 of Cape Colony had permitted freedom of ownership of land and of movement to Khoikhoi, San, and those 'free persons of colour' who had been manumitted prior to general emancipation. When the latter occurred, from 1834 to 1838, these rights were extended to all the newly freed, although the Coloureds did remain at the bottom of the Western Cape's socioeconomic ladder, now as *de jure* 'free' servants and subordinate laborers. Nevertheless, a pass law has never been imposed on the Coloureds, facilitating their voluntary urbanization (although there existed a Masters and Servants Act which imposed criminal sanctions if servants broke contracts in order to, say, leave the farm of their master on the *platteland* [countryside] for the city).

Thus, as Cape Town and other much smaller Cape urban centers grew, so did their Coloured populations, forming the bulk of the poorer citizens, renting their accommodation, very few able to buy their housing, experiencing informal residential segregation at the hands of the power- and property-holding Whites. In 1939, after a good half century or more of industrial urbanization, during which Cape Town (by far the greatest magnet for Coloureds) had grown much faster than theretofore, Marais wrote that:

> those of the Coloured people who could pay for it purchased housing accommodation in the ordinary way. Though no municipality in the Cape [over 90 percent of Coloureds lived in Cape Province] had (or has) the power to compulsorily segregate its Coloured from its European inhabitants, the Coloured People quite naturally tended to live together in the poorer quarters of the towns. Some of them, however, live interspersed with the Europeans.

It was in these latter tracts – in Cape Town, such neighborhoods as lower Woodstock, Salt River, Maitland, and inner Gardens – in the interwar years that Afrikaans-speaking poor Whites intermingled with Coloureds and, in so far as material standards of living and culture were identical, fears grew among Afrikaner political leaders for the 'loss' of 'their own' into the mass of those of slightly darker hue.

This was one reason, among others,[4] for the imposition for the first time of *de jure* residential segregation upon Coloureds. The Group Areas Act (1950) was one of the first major measures put through by the Afrikaner Nationalist government after acceding to power in 1948: 'one of the cornerstones for preserving a White South Africa,' pronounced the Minister of the Interior, Dr Dönges. 'It is the essence of the apartheid policy which is embodied in the Bill,' said Prime Minister D. F. Malan in the same debate; and, Dr Dönges again:

> Hon. members will realise what it must mean to those groups, always to have to adopt an inferior attitude, an attitude of inferiority towards the Europeans, to stand back for the Europeans, where they live alongside the Europeans, but if we place them in separate residential areas, they will be able to give expression to their full cultural and soul life, and that is why we say that separate residential areas must be established.

This reads like empty hyperbole if one considers that the Coloureds' 'full cultural and soul life' is scarcely different from that of poorer Whites; the expressed reason is therefore invalid in large degree.

I shall not detail the drastic and widespread effects of the Group Areas Act in remodeling the cities of South Africa to socially distance Indians and Coloureds (see Western 1981). Suffice to say that in Cape Town the official figure is that by the end of 1980, 195 White families, 1506 Indian families, and 29 337 Coloured families had been forcibly moved to fit the segregative plan. The figure of 29 337 Coloured families implies over 200 000 Coloured people – not quite one in three of Coloured Cape-tonians, the metropolis' population (all races) being about 1 200 000. Culturally, such thorough-going resorting has not resulted in some separate Coloured nation with its 'own' way of life. And, politically, the effect may well have been the opposite of what the government desired. *Rapport* (June 7, 1981) puts it very gently when it says 'it is this very policy [apartheid] that has precluded Whites and Browns from knowing each other better.'

At one time, Coloureds, though probably resentful, seemed to be more-or-less docile, and content with their status as politically dismiss-able second-class appendages to the Whites. Though paternalistically condescended to (as in the Afrikaans usage *ons bruinmense* – *our* Coloured people), they did possess certain tangible advantages over the Black Africans, to whom most felt superior. But today, young Coloureds especially – raised in a system that has almost totally segregated them since birth from person-to-person contacts with Whites on an equal basis (as neighbors, for example) – are turning to political affiliation with Black Africans, making common cause against apartheid as 'Blacks.' The Group Areas Act may well have become, as Theron (1981) suggests, a threat to the security of that decreasing minority of South Africans who are White – witness the unprecedented rioting of 1976 and 1980 among Coloured people at the Cape.

INDIANS   The Indian people of South Africa, except for that small minority of them in Cape Province, were subject to greater inhibitions upon their urbanization prior to the Group Areas Act than were the Coloureds. From 1860 onwards, they were brought as very cheap indent-ured laborers from the British Indian Empire, to work on the sugar plantations of the British colony of Natal. Later, a considerable number came on their own initiative as 'passengers' (taking themselves to be of higher status than 'the coolies'), looking for business opportunities. The great majority of Indians have always resided in Natal. Some remained on the plantations, or later on nearby truck-farming smallholdings, but many moved to Durban and worked there as industrial laborers, or became successful traders. When the Witwatersrand gold fields were opening up, a number moved there to trade, but tight restrictions (1885) were placed upon them, and areas where they could live and own land were strictly limited by law. A 1908 ordinance specifically kept them from owning land in mining areas or entering into the mining industry. In the Orange Free State, *no* Indians were allowed to settle, an 1891 ordinance still in force. (Just *who* is the one Asian in Bloemfontein of p. 217, one wonders – the only one in the Free State?) Finally, a small number of Indians moved down to the Cape; virtually all those 12 000 in Cape Town are in trading.

In their predominant settlement, Durban (where a third of all Asians live), Indians began to raise their socioeconomic status, and so came to be perceived as a threat by the Whites. Thus, in 1922, a city ordinance reserved certain sections of the city for White residence only, and in the late 1930s and 1940s, focus on 'penetration' by Indians into White areas resulted in the 'Pegging' Act of 1943 and the 'Ghetto' Act of 1946 (Kuper *et al.* 1958). Solidly English-speaking Durban's city council cooperated with and freely aided the Afrikaner Nationalist planners of apartheid, whose Group Areas Act can be seen as simply a more thorough-going extrapolation of the previous anti-Indian manipulations of the city's social ecology by Durban's Whites.[5] The Group Areas Act in Durban has proportionately hit the Indians as hard as, if not harder than, it has the Coloureds in Cape Town.[6] In particular, it is those provisions in the Group Areas Act that oblige persons to trade only within Group Areas proclaimed for their 'own' population group that have destroyed Indian businesses, which catered to a city-wide multi-racial clientele. And it is, of course, generally the Whites who have benefited thereby.[7]

There are evident implications for culture in this highly constrained urbanization process. Apart from Durban, Indians have always been a tiny minority in the cities, usually hemmed in by hostile legislation. Their predominant occupation, trading – especially if carried on as in Cape Town in the less monied areas of the city (Scott 1955) – leaves them open to stereotyping by the poor as the corner-shop *babbie*, the 'Jew of Africa,' seen as avaricious or foreign. There has therefore been a degree of defensive keeping oneself to oneself culturally – which in turn has sometimes given rise to resentment. Indians were the subject of attacks by Black Africans in the bloody Durban riots of 1949, and, on a far smaller scale, of attacks by Coloureds in Reiger Park (East Rand) in May 1981. From the latter, the Afrikaans newspaper *Die Transvaler* chose to draw the anticipated cultural pluralism/appropriateness-of-apartheid moral: 'It illustrates the complexity of the South African national situation, for which there are no simple answers ... there are the differences and tensions between groups, which cannot be ignored and which require accommodation.' *Die Transvaler* chooses not to mention the severe housing shortage here, nor the fact that the Indians have an *apartheid-imposed* monopoly of trading in Reiger Park.

Yet, contrary to the various pressures toward isolation, the Indians – in the statistical sense the most highly urbanized of the legally defined population groups – have also, autonomously, become profoundly 'Westernized' by their generations of experience of South African city living: 'Western' dress is the norm, for example; the status of women has risen markedly. The former divisons between those of indentured versus those of passenger origin are eroding. Indian languages are no longer spoken except by the old, therefore the Gujarati versus Urdu-speaking cultural distinction weakens; English is the mother-tongue of most Indians today. By 1960, only 5.5 percent of Indians had been born outside South Africa, and there is little desire to return to India or Pakistan, despite these countries' independence of White rule. Yet a substantial segment of White South African opinion had always wished to 'repatriate' the Indians, the way that nearly all the Chinese brought to work in 1904 on the Witwatersrand gold fields were. Legislation of 1914 and 1927 promoted repatriation. Only in 1961 did the government recognize the Indians to be 'permanent' members of South African society, and only in 1975 was the legislation providing for assisted passages 'home' to the Indian subcontinent allowed to lapse.

Already, in 1957, Brookfield and Tatham were of the opinion that the Natal Indians were more 'Westernized' than any other overseas Indian community. Even if one focuses on one of the most profoundly felt elements of cultural distinctiveness, religion, we find that most of those of 'passenger' origins are Muslims, and therefore share, through the 'Cape Malay' minority among the Coloureds, a religion which has for over 300 years been part of South African life. Whites have viewed Hinduism (the original religion of approximately 70 percent of the Indians) as more foreign to South Africa. But, even here, as Lemon (1976) writes:

> . . . religion is not necessarily so significant a barrier to assimilation as it seems at first. Hinduism is singularly eclectic, and Western influences are particularly noticeable in the Arya Samaj (reform movement), in such features as the structure of the temple and the 'middle class decorum' preserved by worshippers. Religion is in any case a personal, private affair for both Hindus and Moslems, and as such it need impinge relatively little on everyday social relationships.

So, despite all the restrictions upon their urbanization – imposed, certainly, for basically economic rather than cultural reasons – the South African Indians have gradually, autonomously, realigned much of their culture to their basically Western urban milieu.

Conclusion

From the body of this chapter, a number of themes emerge. A first is that there is a lengthy lineage to the manipulation of culture by White rulers simultaneous to urbanization. The most evident forms of such manipulation have been various kinds of segregation, to ensure White domination. To be sure, apartheid represents the most draconian version of these efforts but, apart from the partial departure that is represented by the residential segregation forced upon Coloureds and Indians in Cape Province, it can clearly be seen to be a descendant of methods used in pre-Afrikaner Nationalist days.

The result is that in the cities of South Africa, everybody today lives in a ghetto; that of the Whites happens to be gilded, that of the Black Africans less so. This is a second theme: fellow-citizens know little of each others' lives; there is a curfew for Black Africans in the 'White' areas of the city, while Whites need a permit to visit the Black African locations at any time, day or night. As tensions rise owing to differential access to political and economic power, as the Whites become more fearful, 'normal' nonracial social intercourse tends to be squeezed out. One comes to inhabit what Nadine Gordimer characterized as *A world of strangers* (the title of her 1965 novel about Johannesburg life). This is common to all groups and thus, regrettably, this must be one of the common, diagnostic features of South African urban culture: an overriding tendency to eye everyone warily as a member of some conflicting population group or other.

The third theme, the distinction I have been trying to fashion as an illustrative device between 'directed' and 'autonomous' cultural change, is ambiguous here. Certainly, segregation has 'directed' the urban culture into its present mistrustful 'us' and 'them' mentality. Yet, the form that this is beginning now to assume – an apparently growing consciousness of common blackness among Black Africans and Coloureds, for example – is hardly that which the government planned. But neither is this an 'autonomous' change, automatic upon urbanization. Under different circumstances, one might have posited the growth – amongst poorer Whites (especially Afrikaners), Coloureds, and the highly urbanized segment of the Black African population – of a common *working-class*, not 'racial,' consciousness and culture. So the growing polarization of White against Black is, in part, the unintended consequence of attempts to direct cultural change. It is thus *neither* autonomous *nor* directed in any strict sense (if such there be).

In a critique of Nadine Gordimer's latest novel, *July's people* (1981), which depicts the end of White hegemony in Johannesburg, an anonymous reviewer writes:

The languages of South Africa have been consonant with race and

caste, owner and worker, citizen and servant, for so long that
language itself – the language one speaks and writes – is a weapon
there, quite apart from those details of identity and ideology with
which it happens to coincide . . . By now, to write in South Africa is
by definition political.

There are white citizens of South Africa but no 'citizens' of the land
itself any more. There are only claims on the landscape, made in
words too loaded to be shared beyond the circle of one's own kind,
one's own 'people.' (*New York Review of Books*, August 13, 1981.)

In the Republic of South Africa, then, culture, urbanization, political
power, and economic exploitation are all knotted together in an appalling
and unpredictable bond. The mode of resolution of the contradictory
strainings within this bond could well be violent. To confront the city in
cultural context in South Africa is therefore not simply some tangentially
relevant 'academic' exercise. Rather does it offer indispensable insights
into that troubled society.

Notes

1 The South African Bureau of Racial Affairs.
2 The gradual transition referred to, an ambiguity in urban or rural directedness, had been
   studied by Vilakazi (1957), Glass (1961), Kuper (1965), and notably by Mayer himself
   (1961).
3 Welsh's phrase is an allusion to Mayer's (1961) seminal use of the concept of 'incapsul-
   ation' in *Townsmen or tribesmen*. The 'Red' Xhosa (i.e tribespeople) *in* the city of East
   London were able to live a social life that was not *of* the city. Rather did they incapsulate
   themselves there and hold to rural ways (pp. 90–134, 286–93 [1971 revised edition]).
4 See Western (1978) for a more detailed analysis of the strategic and economic reasons
   behind the Group Areas Act's enforced segregation of Coloureds since 1950.
5 Similarly, 'grand apartheid' – the homelands system – can be seen to have its earliest roots
   in the first 'native reserves' of English-speaking Natal (Welsh 1971b).
6 Coloureds are a small minority in Durban, only 50 000 in a metropolis a trifle smaller
   than Greater Cape Town.
7 This legislation – having in large part achieved the removal of Indian traders – is now
   being allowed to fall away (1978–81).

References

Adam, H. 1971. *Modernizing racial domination*, Berkeley, Calif.: University of
   California Press.
Andrew, P. and J. Western 1979. *Crossroads: black shantytown and white government
   in South Africa*. Unpublished paper.
Bosman, H. C. 1963. *Unto dust*. Cape Town & Pretoria: Human & Rousseau.
Bosman, H. C. 1969. *Mafeking road*. Cape Town & Pretoria: Human & Rousseau.
Brookfield, H. C. and M. A. Tatham 1957. The distribution of racial groups in

Durban: the background of apartheid in a South African city. *Geog. Rev.* **47**(1), 44–65.

DeKiewiet, C. W. 1941. *A history of South Africa, social and economic.* Oxford: Oxford University Press.

Department of Information, Republic of South Africa 1973. *This is South Africa.* Pretoria: Government Printer.

Ellis, G., D. Hendrie, A. Kooy and J. Maree 1977. *The squatter problem in the Western Cape: some causes and remedies.* Johannesburg: South African Institute of Race Relations.

Fair, T. J. D. and R. J. Davies 1976. Constrained urbanization: white South Africa and black Africa compared. In *Urbanization and counter-urbanization*, B. J. L. Berry (ed.), 145–68. Beverly Hills, Calif.: Sage.

Fredrickson, G. M. 1981. *White supremacy: a comparative study in American and South African history.* New York and Oxford: Oxford University Press.

Furedi, F. 1973. The African crowd in Nairobi: popular movements and élite politics. *J. Afr. Hist.* **14**, 2, 275–90.

Glass, Y. 1961. *Industrial man in Southern Africa.* Johannesburg: Institute for the Study of Man in South Africa.

Guelke, L. 1976. Frontier settlement in early Dutch South Africa. *Ann. Assoc. Am. Geogs.* **66**, 25–42.

Kuper, L. 1956. Techniques of social control in South Africa. *The Listener* (London) May 31.

Kuper, L. 1965. *An African bourgeoisie.* New Haven: Yale University Press.

Kuper, L. 1971. African nationalism in South Africa, 1910–1964. In *The Oxford history of South Africa*, Vol. II, M. Wilson and L. Thompson (eds.), 424–76. Oxford: Clarendon Press.

Kuper, L., H. Watts and R. J. Davies 1958. *Durban: a study in racial ecology.* London: Jonathan Cape.

Lemon, A. 1976 *Apartheid: a geography of separation.* Farnborough: Saxon House.

Lessing, D. 1968. *Going home.* St Albans: Panther. (First published by Michael Joseph, 1957.)

Magubane, B. 1971. A critical look at indices used in the study of social change in colonial Africa. *Current Anthropology* **12**(4/5), 419–30.

Magubane, P. 1978. *Magubane's South Africa.* New York: Knopf.

Manganyi, N. C. 1973. *Being black in the world.* Johannesburg: SPROCAS/Ravan Press.

Marais, J. S. 1939. *The Cape coloured people, 1652–1937.* London: Longman.

Maré, G. 1980. *African population relocation in South Africa.* Johannesburg: South African Institute of Race Relations.

Mayer, P. 1971. *Townsmen or tribesmen*, 2nd edn. Cape Town: Oxford University Press.

Mayer, P. 1975. Class, status, and ethnicity as perceived by Johannesburg Africans. In *Change in contemporary South Africa*, L. Thompson and J. Butler (eds.), 138–67. Berkeley, Calif.: University of California Press.

Modisane, B. 1963. *Blame me on history.* London: Thames and Hudson; New York: Dutton.

Mphahlele, E. 1959. *Down Second Avenue.* London: Faber.

Mphahlele, E. 1974. *The African image*, New York & Washington: Praeger.

Nkosi, L. 1965. *Home and exile.* London: Longman.

Patricios, N. N. 1975. *A planning and design investigation into family housing for black mine–workers,* working report. Johannesburg: Department of Town and Regional Planning, University of the Witwatersrand.

Patterson, S. 1957. *The last trek.* London: Routledge & Kegan Paul.

Phimister, I. and C. van Onselen 1979. The political economy of tribal animosity: a case study of the 1929 Bulawayo location 'faction fight.' *J. Sthn. Afr. Studs.* **67**, 1–43.

Saunders, C. 1980. Not newcomers. *S. Afr. Outlook* **108** (1280) 29.

Schlemmer, L. and T. J. Muil 1975. Social and political change in the African areas: a case study of KwaZulu. In *Change in contemporary South Africa*, L. Thompson and J. Butler (eds.), 107–37. Berkeley, Calif.: University of California Press.

Schreiner, O. 1923. *Thoughts on South Africa.* London: T. Fisher Unwin.

Scott, P. 1955. Cape Town, a multi-racial city. *Geog. J.* **121**, 149–57.

South African Institute of Race Relations 1977. *A survey of race relations in South Africa, 1976.* Johannesburg: SAIRR.

South African Institute of Race Relations 1978. *South Africa in travail.* Johannesburg: SAIRR.

Theron, E. 1981. Foreword in South African edition of Western (1981).

du Toit, A. 1975. Ideological change, Afrikaner Nationalism, and pragmatic racial domination in South Africa. In *Change in contemporary South Africa*, L. Thompson and J. Butler (eds.), 19–50. Berkeley, Calif.: University of California Press.

United Nations 1982. *Mass removals of Africans in apartheid South Africa (1960–1979)*, Notes and Documents 9/82, March. New York: Department of Political and Security Council Affairs, Centre Against Apartheid.

Van den Berghe, P. L. 1966. Racial segregation in South Africa: degrees and kinds. *Cahiers d'Etudes Africaines* **6**(23), 408–18.

Vilakazi, A. 1957. A reserve from within. *African Studies* **16**, 98–9.

Walker, E. A. 1957. *A history of Southern Africa.* London: Longman.

Welsh, D. 1971a. The growth of towns. In *The Oxford history of South Africa*, M. Wilson and L. Thompson (eds.), 172–243. Oxford: Clarendon Press.

Welsh, D. 1971b. *The roots of segregation: native policy in colonial Natal, 1845–1910.* Cape Town: Oxford University Press.

Western, J. 1978. Knowing one's place: 'the coloured people' and the Group Areas Act in Cape Town. In *Humanistic geography: prospects and problems*, D. F. Ley and M. Samuels (eds.), 297–318. Chicago: Maaroufa.

Western, J. 1981. *Outcast Cape Town.* Cape Town: Human & Rousseau; London: George Allen & Unwin; Minneapolis: University of Minnesota Press.

Whisson, M. G. 1971. The coloured people. In *South Africa's minorities*, P. Randall (ed.), occasional paper No. 2. Johannesburg: Study Project on Christianity in Apartheid Society (SPROCAS).

Wilson, F. 1975. The political implications for blacks of economic changes now taking place in South Africa. In *Change in contemporary South Africa*, L. Thompson and J. Butler (eds.), 168–200. Berkeley, Calif.: University of California Press.

Wilson, M. and A. Mafeje 1963. *Langa: a study of social groups in an African township.* Cape Town: Oxford University Press.

11 *The built environment and cultural symbolism in post-colonial Madras*

SUSAN J. LEWANDOWSKI

Introduction

Amos Rapoport (1969), architect and anthropologist, has suggested in his writing that a feature of the human mind is to order the world by organizing and naming space. In the words of one of his followers, A. D. King (1980, p. 27):

> Built environments encode or give expression to a particular set of cultural rules and also influence both social and cognitive environments. How people build not only results from but also influences how people think.

Rapoport and others have argued that buildings (their size, location, and form) are the result not only of factors such as climate or topography, but are shaped by 'a society's ideas, its forms of economic and social organization, its distribution of resources and authority, its activities and the beliefs and values which prevail at any one period of time' (King 1980, p. 1). In fact, sociocultural criteria may be a great deal more important than factors such as climate and technology in affecting built form. It is essential to remember that even the simplest buildings 'are institutions, basic cultural phenomena' (Rapoport 1980, p. 285). As a system of nonverbal communication, the built environment must be decoded by those who use or observe it. In the course of time, as society changes, so does its built environment; new building forms may appear, and existing buildings may be used for new purposes. But the changes reflect a larger pattern emerging in society as a whole.

This chapter will argue that the interface between religion and culture, which has been a historical feature of the Indian subcontinent, continues to be reflected in the built environment of post-colonial India. In a city like New Delhi (the capital of the Indian nation), more emphasis on urban architecture has been placed on the composite nature of Indian culture, whereas, at the regional level, and particularly in parts of southern and eastern India, Hindu symbols and imagery are increasingly appearing in

the built environment. Why do I say this? Let us take a look at the city of
Madras, India's fourth largest city.

Madras: a case in point

A series of photographs of the city of Madras (founded by the British in
1639) reflect three different periods in the history of urban building in
South India: the pre-colonial period, the colonial period, and the post-
colonial period. It is clear from these photographs that the post-colonial
public buildings (since 1947) appear more distinctly Indian than the
colonial buildings, but less Indian than the structures that were built
during the pre-colonial period.

   Long before the founding of Madras along the southeastern coast of
India, there flourished, near the site of the present city (Fig. 11.1), the
town of Mylapore, whose center was the Kapalisvarar temple (Plate 11.1).
It was here that the famous Tamil author, Tiruvalluvar, lived at some time
in the first centuries after Christ, and composed the Tirukkural, a
collection of moral prescriptions. Although the original temple is no
longer in existence, the present structure, built about 300 years ago,
reflects many of the characteristics of Dravidian architecture. The outer
gopuram (or gateway), allowing access to the inner shrine, where the
figure of the presiding deity resides, is covered with carvings of Hindu
gods and goddesses. They are adorned like royalty, and some have special
mounts of birds or animals. Their success in battle against evil forces is
captured for all to see in stone, for: '. . . the craftsmen who fashioned the
temples and their sculptures depicted their gods as visible symbols of
power as it was manifest to them in real life' (Temples of India 1968, p. 8).

   When the British arrived along the southeastern coast of India in the
early 17th century, the temple-center of Mylapore was a prosperous
town. Since incorporated as a suburb of Madras, it remains the residence
of high-caste Hindus, who not only view the temple as an important focus
for their religious and cultural activities today, but who are actively
involved in the markets that have grown up around the temple (Plate
11.2). The original colonial core of Madras was the secular civil-cum-
military complex centering on Fort St George, a few miles to the north of
Mylapore (Plate 11.3). It contained a factory house, that functioned both
as an office and a governor's residence. In front of the building that now
houses the Secretariat are 20 granite columns that were originally part of a
colonnade constructed by Governor Pitt in 1732, stretching from the
seagate to the fort house. The adjacent buildings were distinctly European
in their esthetic designs, as were the houses and churches of the British
who initially resided in the vicinity of the fort. Although there is little that
is Indian about these structures, in the course of the 19th century, the

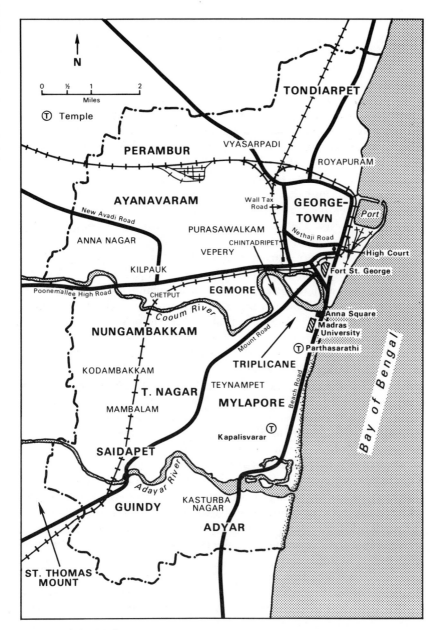

Figure 11.1 Madras.

British incorporated towers and domes borrowed from an Islamic tradition in the construction of public buildings such as the Madras High Court and the university (Plate 11.4). However, the court, like the fort, was a new institution whose architectural and spatial needs were basically imported from the West.

In contrast to the public buildings designed by European architects during the colonial period, which remain today as part of Madras, Plate 11.5 depicts part of a new cultural center, Valluvar Kottam, named after the Mylapore author, Tiruvalluvar, mentioned earlier. Built in Kodambakkam in 1976, Valluvar Kottam draws on a South Indian classical architectural tradition. The complex consists of two main structures, a modern auditorium that seats over 4000 people (one of the largest in Asia), and a temple car over 30 metres (100 feet) high (Plate 11.6) whose base has been carved in stone to depict scenes from the Tirukkural (Plate 11.7). The stone car is a replica of the traditional wooden cart used as a vehicle for the deity during temple festivals. Esthetically, this new building cannot compare with the temples constructed during the medieval period. Those who designed and assembled the building have neither the technical skill nor the artistic expertise of their earlier counterparts. Yet the building reaches back to the pre-colonial period for its architectural theme.

How can we make sense of this and other public buildings constructed in Madras during the post-colonial period? Should we aim for an esthetic analysis of architecture and space, or is there another approach that might help us discover the meaning of these buildings, and other changes in the built environment? What is striking about the post-colonial period is the conscious attempt on the part of state and national governments to integrate built forms culturally with the pre-colonial past. In looking first at Madras, it appears that the state government of Tamil Nadu has drawn on the cultural symbolism of the Hindu tradition to reinforce a Tamil identity, and, in so doing, is not only creating an urban landscape that meets the needs of its contemporary citizens, but is also contributing to its own political legitimation. Part of the process of change has involved the renaming of streets that symbolically reflect both the past and the present folk heroes of India, and the erecting of statues that honor writers in the classical Tamil language, and contemporary Tamil poets, who speak the language of the people.

If one strolls along the famous Beach Road (now renamed Kamaraj Salai), that runs along the Bay of Bengal and serves as the eastern boundary of the city (a place once frequented by the European population during the colonial period), one is struck not only by a change in street names from English to Tamil, but also by a series of statues along the walkway honoring famous classical Tamil authors. Now sculpted in stone is Kannaki, heroine of the famous Tamil epic of the first centuries

Plate 11.1
Kapalisvarar Temple, Mylapore, Madras City, 1957. The temple was built circa 16th century (photograph by David Sopher).

Plate 11.2
Kapalisvarar
Temple and shops,
Mylapore, Madras
City, 1977.

Plate 11.3 The Secretariat, Fort St. George, Madras City, 1977. The nucleus of
the building was constructed in 1694–5, with additions in 1825 and 1910.

11.4 Madras University (Hindu–Saracenic style) with statue of Queen ia, Madras City, 1977. The university was founded in 1857.

11.5 Valluvar Kottam Cultural Center, Nungambakkam, Madras City, The center was built in 1976 (photograph by Indira Peterson).

Plate 11.6 Valluvar Kottam temple car, Nungambakkam, Madras City, 1978 (photograph by Indira Peterson).

Plate 11.7 Valluvar Kottam, carved scenes from Tirukkurāl, Nungambakkam, Madras City, 1978 (photograph by Indira Peterson).

after Christ, and Silappadikaram, who tore her breast from her body in seeking retribution for the untimely death of her husband.

Anthony King (1976), in his analysis of colonial urban development in Delhi, points out that one can determine the way colonial streets were named in this city according to cultural–historical criteria that rank road networks by use. First in importance in New Delhi were the major thoroughfares, bearing names like Kingsway and Queensway. In Madras, a major thoroughfare like China Bazaar Road, connoting marketing activity in the heart of the central business district, has, since Independence, been renamed Nethaji Subhas Chandra Bose Road, after a nationalist revolutionary from Bengal in northern India. Mount Road, linking the center of Madras with the historic St. Thomas Mount (it was believed that St. Thomas the apostle died here in southern India), has been renamed Anna Road, after a Tamil regional political leader.

At first glance, this looks like a grass-roots indigenous attempt to link the city to its past which also involves reviving and renovating historic structures that connect the culture to its sacred roots. But perhaps it is important to ask who is investing in the buildings being constructed, and for what purpose, and what, in fact, is being encoded in the process of transformation taking place.

The historic roots of attempts at reshaping the urban landscape of Madras can be traced to the creation of the Dravida Munnetra Kazhagam (hereafter the DMK Party) founded in 1949, which ushered in a period of Tamil cultural nationalism. As in many Third World countries formerly under colonial rule, the rise of the DMK and its attendant nationalism was not directly rooted in anti-colonial sentiment, but was built on a foundation of opposition to the native élite who benefited from an enhanced status under the British, in this case the Brahman community. One of the antecedents of the DMK, the Justice Party, formed in 1916, was the backbone of the non-Brahman movement, which arose as a reaction against both the growing poverty of the lower classes during the 19th century, and the Brahman-dominated leadership of the nationalist movement in South India. It took the form of a 'cultural revolt' against what was perceived as North Indian and Aryan religious, social, and economic exploitation (Omvedt 1976, Ch. 1). At the time of Indian independence in 1947, one of the greatest fears of the non-Brahman leaders of South India was the assumption of Brahman political power from the colonizers. As early as 1939, a conference was held that called for the creation of a Dravidisthan, a separate state that would protect the needs of the Dravidian peoples of South India, and insure a non-Brahman leadership in Madras. A few years later, the Justice Party was reshaped to form the Dravida Kazhagam (Dravidian Federation), the direct antecedent of the DMK, a political party that emphasized the Tamil cultural heritage of this region of the south. The party played a major rôle in reviving Tamil language and literature, and popularizing the cultural traditions of the Tamil people through the structure of district and local party organization (Hardgrave 1965). During the 1950s, in building a larger following, the DMK Party increasingly turned away from its anti-Brahman stance, and instead focused on the common elements of the Tamil culture of South India that unite Brahman and non-Brahman alike. 'The opposition between Brahman and non-Brahman was,' then, 're-placed by the opposition between Tamils (Dravidians) and all others' (Barnett 1976, p, 267). In the 1960s and 1970s, the DMK party has attempted to appeal to the Brahman community as well as to the 'common man,' defined by the urban lower middle class and the educated unemployed. Issues such as rising food prices and jobs for Tamilians increasingly formed the rhetoric of party platform. The changes reflected above parallel the shift in party orientation as it became increasingly institutionalized as the ruling party of Tamil Nadu. In the process, I would argue, the culture of the Tamils has been very successfully manipulated by the DMK, in its attempt to legitimize itself politically.

One of the first symbolic moves made by the DMK when it came to power in 1967 was to change the name of the state from Madras, its British designation, to Tamil Nadu, 'the land of the Tamils.' This idea had originated in the early part of the decade, when it was suggested that the state be renamed for the purpose of interstate communication, and the capital be moved to Madurai – a city that had played a major rôle in the evolution of the Tamil literature, culture, and politics in the pre-British period. Following the renaming of the state on Tamil New Year's day (April 14), a neon light with the state emblem, a Hindu temple tower, was switched on over the Secretariat at Fort St. George, formerly the British colonial administrative center of Madras Presidency. Now the national motto of India was written in Tamil; excerpts from the Tamil epic, the Kural, along with a portrait of its author, appeared in buses run by the state, and the state government ordered Tamil name boards to be dis-played outside its offices. The Chief Minister also requested shopowners to exhibit Tamil name boards over their shops (Spratt 1970, p. 7). By renaming the urban landscape, the government was expressing 'a par-ticular set of cultural rules,' and in the process, was investing the city with a new symbolic meaning (King 1980, p. 27). Although the Secretariat buildings were a product of the colonial period, and would remain a part of the urban landscape, the DMK government was making a conscious attempt to divest this landscape of its colonial association, and to further a Tamil regional tradition. This pattern is also apparent in certain Western cities, for example those in Quebec, where French-Canadian cultural influences are playing an increasing rôle in defining the symbolic character of the city.

The emphasis on the Tamil language, reflected in the first symbolic moves made by the DMK after it assumed power, was translated into the Madras urban landscape during the same year. In the wake of a conference on Tamil language and literature held in 1966 in Kuala Lumpur, invitations were sent to scholars throughout the world to attend a World International Tamil Conference to be held in Madras City in the early part of 1968. As well as academic papers delivered on the merits of the Tamil cultural tradition, the government organized an exhibition at Madras University tracing the evolution of Tamil civilization, and, to mark the start of the conference, floats depicting scenes in Tamil literature and history were carried through the streets of the city.

It was at this point that statues were erected along Marina Beach honoring famous classical Tamil authors. But, simultaneous with the erection of these statues was the unveiling of a statue of the DMK chief minister, Annadurai, located at a road junction not far from a statue of his Congress party rival, Kamaraj, put up in 1962. Like its colonial predecessors, the DMK was using urban statues to reinforce its political legitimacy, and, in fact, during the post-colonial period, has removed statues of famous British civil and military administrators and replaced them with their Tamil counterparts, a very common pattern throughout the Third World today. At the same time, this activity reflects the tensions between different political parties in the post-colonial period as they vie for their own prominence in the urban landscape

The erecting of statues, and the renaming of streets and new suburbs after prominent Indian and Tamil political leaders, as well as historic figures in India's past, have gone hand in hand with new construction of public buildings sponsored by the state government. Tours of Madras, and the *Official Madras tourist handbook* (1977), now urge the visitor to view not only former colonial buildings such as Fort St. George, and the Madras High Court (built during the late 19th century by the British), but also Anna Square, located about a mile from the fort on the same road, housing the tomb of a former DMK chief minister. This building has drawn tourists from all over South India, and, in the words of one author, 'many of these approach the site with an attitude of religious pilgrimage' (Wiebe 1975, p. 108). Religious cultural symbolism has also been incorporated in an outdoor shrine honoring Mahatma Gandhi, a leader of the nationalist movement in India, and two local state leaders, Kamaraj and Rajaji. The style and architecture of the building, based on a model of classical South Indian Hindu temple design, and the description of the building in the guide book as 'a place for prayer and meditation,' reinforce both the sacred and secular imagery that surround contemporary political figures in India. Gandhi was perceived both as a nationalist leader and as a holy man upholding the religious values of Indian society; by association, the state's political leaders are invested with the same qualities.

These buildings were among the first projects undertaken by the trainees of the Sculpture Training Center, established in 1957 by the government of Tamil Nadu. The justification for founding the center was as follows. Although indigenous governments in South India were traditionally responsible for patronizing classical architecture and sculpture, under the British there was a deterioration in the quality of the classical arts which were 'on the verge of extinction at the time the country emerged independent' (Government of Tamil Nadu n.d., p. 1). In effect, what the state government was doing in this process was assuming the rôle of patron of the arts, a rôle played by Hindu kings throughout the history of pre-British South India.

Historically, gift giving as a kingly function grew out of the traditional rôle of the king as a sponsor of the religious sacrifice. As mentioned earlier, according to the Hindu world view, society is divided hierarchically into four varnas, or classes, with the priest–teacher holding the highest position, for he performs religious rites and sacrifices to the gods. Beneath him is the warrior–king, who is the ruler of lands and has secular power. It is he who endows the sacrifice. The third-ranked merchant–farmer has authority over material resources and animals. Fourthly, the laborer is dominated by those above him in the system; his duty is specifically to serve.

During the period immediately preceding the arrival of the Europeans on the coast of South India in the early 17th century, an elaborate system of royal endowments emerged as a kingly form of gift giving. In fact, in the course of medieval state formation (*circa* AD 900–1200) the Cholas, who became the leading dynastic house, used their vast revenues as a public display of sovereignty, and large-scale temples began to appear in the agrarian countryside, and subsequently in urban centers.

I have argued elsewhere that even as Madras City developed under the British, Indian merchants, who grew wealthy through their association with the British East India Company during the late 17th and the 18th centuries, built temples in the city as a way of raising their status in the urban environment, and exerting control over societal values and institutions.[1] In the course of the first 100 years of the Madras settlement, the small European community resided within the town of Fort St. George, and was spatially contained within a very small sector of the city. Black Town (later renamed Georgetown), where the bulk of merchant and artisan castes initially lived, developed to the north of the fort (see Fig. 11.1). It was here that the Hindu mercantile élite played a major rôle as urban builders, and, in the process, reaffirmed its political status within a traditional setting. Prior to the arrival of the British, there were already several thriving temple-towns that existed in the vicinity of the site of Madras, and today have been incorporated within the city limits. The most important of these were the Sri Kapalisvarar and Parthasarathi temples of Mylapore and Triplicane, dating from the 7th to the 10th centuries. The temples provided a central focus for settlement. They were surrounded by four streets (car streets), forming a mandala, or ritual square, and served as the major ceremonial route at the times of processions and on festival occasions.

The spatial form of these complexes, with the temple in the center, reflected a particular Hindu world view based on the concept of the microcosm (the world of men) paralleling the macrocosm (the universe). This principle was ritually enacted at the time of festivals, when the processional form of the deity (*utsavar*) was taken out of the temple and carried along the car streets, symbolic of its journey around the Universe (Lewandowski 1977). By organizing residential space in this way as a reflection of universal order, Hindus believed they could control chaotic cosmic forces. Thus, the construction of new temples in Madras promised a stable locale in which to live, and encouraged urban settlement.

The layout of the early town of Madraspatam was similar to that of the ancient ceremonial complexes of Mylapore and Triplicane in that the temple provided a focal point for activity. The streets were laid out in a grid pattern that formed a rectangle a little more than 1.5 miles in circumference, with the Chinna Kesava Temple (1648) located near the center. Close to the temple, in an adjacent street, was the town's vegetable market. As urban settlement stabilized in the vicinity of the temple, it performed several integrative functions for the neighborhood. It was in the temple compound that caste disputes were arbitrated, and cultural activities took place in the courtyard. Of particular interest were philosophical and literary discussions of Hindu texts, and the performance of classical South Indian music and dance, functions that temples still perform in Madras today.

By the late 17th century, as the population of Madras expanded, settlement began to take place in the suburbs to the north and west of Black Town, and new temples that provided the focus for residential activities were constructed. For example, in 1680, the chief merchant of the East India Company (Alangada Pillai) built Ekambareswarar Kovil, the principal temple of the suburb of Peddanaickenpet, located in the west of Black Town. In so doing, he enhanced his status as patron of the pettah, or locale.

Merchant castes in India, primarily nonlandowners who commanded considerable wealth, often attempted to combine their economic power with ritual purity as a way of raising their status. By endowing religious institutions and sponsoring festivals, merchants amassed religious merit, and hence were closer to the Hindu ideal of Brahmanic control over cosmic forces. Indian merchants involved in building temples in Madras were not only acquiring religious merit in their acts as donors, but were also legitimizing their political authority over the new neighborhoods they established.

The emulative model of kingship merchants employed in Madras was also a competitive one, and resulted in the creation of a number of rival temple centers in the city. The model chosen by the commercial élite to justify their new status, made possible by the commercial wealth of early Madras, was a traditional one. The two major ways of attaining status in Hindu India were political or landed power and ritual purity. Wealth alone was insufficient to command esteem, unless linked with one or the other criteria of status (Beck 1972, p. 267). As merchants acquired wealth through their association with the British East India Company, they were not only conforming to a classical pattern of ceremonial sponsorship by endowing temples, they were also combining their control over material resources with their control over men and over urban land, the major characteristics of a traditional model of kingship in pre-British India.[2]

Since temple construction was one of South India's foremost contributions to classical architectural development on the subcontinent, and since it is believed that the tradition of temple building has remained unbroken in this region of Tamil Nadu, the state government has chosen to concentrate, in the post-colonial period, on this unique art form by establishing the Sculpture Training Center. One of the most lavish projects sponsored by the government of Tamil Nadu in an attempt to give the city a new urban image has been the construction of Valluvar Kottam (the cultural center whose photograph appears earlier in this chapter). More than 500 craftsmen, with students from the Sculpture Training Center, were employed on the project. Prominently displayed at the entrance way to the temple car is a statue of C. N. Annadurai, a former chief minister of the DMK, and just inside the entrance is a plaque, stating in English that the center was declared open by the president of India, and the governor of Tamil Nadu, thus linking both the national and state governments in legitimizing the project. This is only one of a number of projects throughout India that members of the training center have worked on. Over the past decade, South-Indian-style temples have been constructed in New Delhi, Bombay, and Bhilai in Madhya Pradesh.

The government has also shaped a policy of temple renovation, and, by so doing, has cast itself as a guardian of sacred space, as its Tamil predecessors had done. Although, during the medieval period, the focus of temple-centered activity was the Tamil countryside, in the course of the 20th century such activity shifted to the urban areas (Lewandowski 1980b, p. 142). This is related both to the urbanization of South India since the 1920s, and to the political movements such as the non-Brahman movement of the 1920s, and 1930s, which sought to de-Brahmanize temple management. Such movements encouraged Brahmans, who were traditionally the priests and administrators of large temple-complexes of rural South India, to seek jobs in the major industrial cities of Salem, Coimbatore, and Madras. One author argues that, for these reasons, the larger

South Indian temples that date from the medieval period have lost their prestigious patronage, for investment has shifted with migration patterns (Kennedy 1974, pp. 275–7). In addition, with the increasing industrialization of South India that followed World War I, industry provided an alternative form of investment. It could not, however, replace the ritual status gained from temple donorship. The temple today remains an important ritual center for legitimizing newcomers, in this case the industrialists of the 20th century, as well as the DMK political leaders. In the past, it legitimized the pre-British rulers of South India and the merchant castes of early Madras, but the scale of surplus wealth today cannot compare with that of the pre-British or colonial period. In coming to terms with Hinduism and the Tamil cultural tradition of building and attending temples, in 1971 the DMK leader Karunanadhi stressed that the party supported Hinduism through the institution of the temple (Kennedy 1974, p. 285).

The DMK, in the course of the 1970s, has made attempts to Tamilize temples by ordering that temple rites be performed in Tamil, rather than Sanskrit (although the latter is not forbidden on request), and augmenting the number of non-Brahman priests in temples throughout the south. These steps reflect the growing rôle of the government in controling temple activities, and go hand in hand with increased government intervention in appointing temple trustees. The government has also played a major rôle in determining which temples should be renovated. As Richard Kennedy has pointed out, a pattern emerges in regard to those temples selected for renovation and receiving assistance from the state government. The majority of temples undergoing renovation in the early 1970s were dedicated to Tamil rather than Sanskritic deities. The DMK has not only emphasized the importance of Tamil cultural values, but is also shaping the direction of devotional worship in the future. The symbolic rôle of the government as protector of the temple is further illustrated by the ways in which members of the Hindu Religious and Charitable Endowments Commission (founded in 1959 to supervise temple activity throughout the state) participate in temple-centered activities. Representatives of the commission are often in attendance at temple festivals, and are honored during ceremonies and temple consecrations (Temple consecration after renovation 1977, p. 13).

If one asks which temples have the most support in Madras City today, what immediately becomes apparent is that the most popular temples are all located in the suburbs, rather than the heart of the city as was the case in the 19th century. Changes in the spatial and social location of a temple in relation to the neighborhood, are exemplified by the development of a new, privately endowed temple dedicated to Mahalakshmi, goddess of wealth.[3]

In 1971, the area where the Mahalakshmi temple is located (south of

Madras City) was an open beach, lined with fishing villages. There was a
small Catholic church, and a few, newly constructed flats for retired
government servants. The municipal bus depot was located several miles
away, in the suburb of Adyar. In 1977, a transformation had occurred in
this area: a bus depot was now located within 0.25 miles of the temple,
allowing pilgrims and devotees easy access to the temple, and, on Fridays
and Sundays, when the largest number of people attended the temple, the
buses were packed. Also, a paved road, traditionally called a Rajavedi (the
king's road) extended to the temple entrance, and was flanked by shops
selling all kinds of goods for temple puja, such as garlands of flowers,
bananas, coconuts, incense, and a variety of souvenirs, including pictures
of the deity. A further transformation was a housing colony, Mahalakshminagar, which has grown up near the temple, and here the head priest
resides. Thus, the temple has played an important rôle in helping to define
the neighborhood, a function historically associated with temples of
India.

The industrial development of Madras, as well as its suburban
expansion are essentially post World War II phenomena. After the war,
the government of Madras (which owned substantial land in the city)
encouraged the growth of cooperative housing societies in outlying areas,
some of which already housed industrial estates. This was a common
pattern in cities throughout South India. In this way, the area west and
north of Mahalakshminagar developed in the 1950s and 1960s, and today
its residents are either middle- and upper-middle-class employees of the
government, or retired professionals. Cooperative construction also characterized the building of neighborhood temples to meet the spiritual needs
of those living in the area, and families contributed a certain amount of
their income, drew up temple plans, and hired stapatis (traditional architects) to meet this end.

But the postwar period has also witnessed a tremendous population
growth in the city, as landless laborers have moved from the countryside
in search of factory jobs. Between 1941 and 1971, the population of
Madras rose from almost 800 000 to 2.5 million, and during the decade
from 1951 to 1961, 37 percent of the population growth could be
attributed to migration (*Census of India* 1961, pp. 46 & 53). As new
migrants entered the city, they brought their religious beliefs with them.
What is visually striking as one walks around the city of Madras is the
number of small street shrines that have grown up in recent decades. They
consist of a single small room where the deity resides, and usually a gate
that can be closed to protect the idol when puja is not being performed.
The prevalence of street shrines where popular deities can be worshipped
on the way to work, or where the poorer classes can maintain their
devotion to a village god or goddess, reflects a new mass form of urban
Hinduism.

The symbolic images that are now being projected by the government of Tamil Nadu reflect attempts to link public buildings with indigenous Tamil traditions of architecture, specifically through the medium of Hindu temple designs. That linkage is itself an important statement about the nature of urban culture in this part of South India, and the sacred roots of the tradition. Whereas, during the 19th and 20th centuries, the built environment of cities in Europe and the USA has increasingly become secularized, as religion has moved indoors and assumed a private rôle in people's lives, this is not a pattern that seems to be operative in South India and cities in other parts of the world (such as the Middle East). In building a new post-colonial urban image, the government of Tamil Nadu is not limiting itself to copying Tamil architectural forms in its public buildings, but is generating a new thought process with regard to modern urban architecture.

Indian urbanization in comparative perspective

In this chapter, I have been arguing that a conscious attempt has been made to politicize the culture in Tamil Nadu, and that this process can be seen in other parts of India as well. Here, I am stressing a concept of culture that is a product of social and political processes, manipulated to meet the ends of the party in power, to gain popular support for its policies. In legitimizing its power, the state government has interpreted its function as 'protector' of religious institutions and patron of the arts, drawing on a long historical tradition to defend its actions. Legitimation is seen as a way 'of ordering, of giving meaning and sanction to reality' (Larson 1978, p. 29). Although the linkage between the built environment and the process of legitimation may be articulated further in Tamil Nadu than in other regions of India, as new groups are rising to power in other states, comparable patterns are emerging. Businessmen and new élites have consistently attempted to overcome former power structures by sponsoring the construction of religious institutions. One interesting example is what is happening in the city of Bhubaneswar, today the state capital of Orissa in eastern India.

In contrast to the colonial city of Madras, Bhubaneswar was primarily a temple town and pilgrimage center when it was chosen in 1947 as a site for Orissa's new state capital. Over the past 30 years, it has expanded dramatically, with the construction of the new capital just to the north of the old town. Visually, the contrast between the two sectors of the city is a striking one, for settlement patterns are orientated around the temple in the old town, while government buildings, designed by a European architect (hired at the time of independence), provide the central design principle in the new capital.

Although one might expect there to be little relationship between the upper-middle-class civil servants and professional people living in the new capital and the old temple town adjacent to it, this is not the case. As in Madras, the patrons and sponsors of religious activities and festivals, and those responsible for building new monasteries and temples, are the very people who live in the administrative colony. It is today's government servants and state politicians who are the patrons of Oriya culture, and this culture is Hindu in its content. The assistant secretary of the Orissa Planning Department, and the development commissioner of Orissa, were responsible for donating the money and overseeing the building of a main residence for their Guru, or spiritual leader (Miller 1980, p. 91). In fact, more than one-third of the Hindu monasteries built in the old town (7 out of 22) date from the post-independence period, indicating increased patronage and new wealth flowing from the new to the old part of the city.

Similar patterns have emerged in the post-independence period in other cities in the state, such as Cuttack, an old commercial capital and formerly a princely city. Here, it is possible to trace shifts in patterns of patronage and new developments in Orissan culture as a result of political factors (Freeman & Preston 1980, pp. 101–106). Before Indian independence, Orissa included 26 princely states, which merged in 1948 with the districts formerly administered by the British to form a single political unit. Subsequently, the temples the Orissan rajas (or kings) had patronized lost their wealth and prestige, for they ceased to be centers of ritual activity and princely investment. However, in the years from 1951 to 1971, the urban population of Cuttack doubled, and, in the process, the commercial and business sector grew in size and wealth. The crisis of temple patronage that centered around the state's political reorganization led to the emergence of local merchants and government servants as the controllers of ritual performances and temple wealth in the city.

One final example, the city of New Delhi, illustrates a somewhat different, but related, pattern. Delhi is a culturally heterogeneous city. And, as the *capital of a multicultural nation*, the symbolism employed by the government has emphasized unity in diversity, and the composite nature of the Indian cultural tradition. When a former president of India (Rajendra Prasad) moved into the Rashtrapati Bhavan, (the official residence of the viceroy of India, under the British) he refurnished the interior, replacing the Western style of decor with rooms that each represented a different regional culture in the subcontinent. In so doing, all the states of the Indian Union were seen as a part of the whole, and 'a living symbol of India's culture' (Chopra 1970, p. 210).

The conurbation of Delhi is composed of the old medieval city, built by Mughal rulers, and New Delhi, founded by the British in 1912 as the capital of British India. Before the partition of India, and the creation of

Pakistan in 1947, an Indo-Islamic cultural tradition prevailed in Old Delhi (Shahjahanabad). Hindus dominated local trade and commerce, but the Muslim culture of the old Mughal Court was reflected in urban activities. Hindu festivals (such as Diwali and Holi), and Muslim festivals (such as Bakr-Id) were equally celebrated in the city, as they had formally been patronized by the Mughal Court, and Hindus participated in Mohurram ceremonies and processions as if they were a part of their own religious tradition (Jagmohan 1975, p. 12). With partition, the Muslim élite of Old Delhi migrated to Pakistan, and the city lost its poets, musicians, and cultural patrons. Those Muslims who remained (about 250 000 in 1971) belonged to a lower economic class (Jagmohan 1975, p. 34).

In place of those who migrated came Hindu and Sikh refugees from the Punjab in northwestern India, which had become a part of the Pakistani nation. Punjab refugees, in an attempt to preserve their regional cultural heritage and the religion of Sikhism (a mixture of Hindu and Muslim traditions), have been founding schools and associations in the old city. With the coming of refugees from the Punjab, the character of place names in Delhi's residential localities has also changed, reflecting the religious beliefs of the refugee population. Residential colonies named after the founder of the Sikh religion, Guru Nanak, are visible in the city, in the form of Guru Nanak Colony, or Guru Nanaknagar, and Nanak Pura (Jacob n.d.).

Since New Delhi is the residence and workplace of administrators and clerks from all over India, its regional enclaves reflect the nation's cultural diversity. The South Indian community of Ramakrishna Housing Colony, composed primarily of Tamil speakers, has built its own Hindu temple following a classical Dravidian style of architecture, and is now in the planning stages of constructing a South Indian college. Since Tamil scholars would be invited to teach on the faculty, Tamilians view the college as a focus for Tamil cultural activity in the community.

As indicated, the cultural symbolism that is being encoded in the city through new buildings, and the emergence of pan-Indian Festivals and cultural activities, also has sacred connotations. As some have argued, although India claims to be a secular state, 'it is a country filled with Hindu symbolism and dominated by a Hindu government' (*The Overseas Times* 1980, p. 2). A colleague of mine has recently suggested that a more Sanskritized Hindu culture is emerging in New Delhi under the guiding hand of Uttar Pradesh politicians of Hindu-speaking origin.[4] There has been an increased use of road signs in Hindu; more Sanskritized words are being used in the Delhi schools; and streets named after gods and goddesses are appearing in New Delhi housing colonies. Hindu religious literature is also providing data for place names, as the heroes of the great Hindu epic, Mahabharata, become immortalized in the urban landscape in the form of Arjun Nagar and Pandavpur. As in other parts of northern and eastern India, the Hindu festival in honor of the mother goddess Durga (Durga Puja) is being celebrated on a lavish scale in the city, and Hindu temples dedicated to the goddess are attracting larger and larger followings.

While it is likely that former colonial capitals built by European nations act 'as a dysfunctional model in the promotion of indigenous urban development' (King 1976, p. 285), since they were created specifically to reflect an imperialist hegemony, one could nevertheless argue that a politicization of culture is taking place in New Delhi, as in other parts of India. Where Delhi differs from the other cities of India is in its rôle as a showcase for the rest of the nation. Given its predominantly administrative and political functions, and its substantial Western population of diplomats and businessmen, it is not typical of other Indian cities. Yet its neighborhoods continue to be inhabited by migrants from particular linguistic and regional origins, and its culture is increasingly reflecting its Hindu majority.

Although the direct political imposition of building styles by European nations is no longer the case (the majority of Third World nations having gained independence in the 1950s), there is still a tendency to equate the material gains of the industrialized West with a process of development that has served as a model, and has brought with it changes in values, and cultural objectives. In fact, many Third World planners and architects have been educated in the West, and have brought home with them Western objectives and methods. By politicizing the culture, leaders in South Asia, and their counterparts in the Middle East, may be creating a consciousness among the people that may eventually lead to a greater indigenizing process. Based on the evidence presented, one could argue that much of the urban symbolism emerging in post-colonial India is drawing upon a religious, and, in particular, a Hindu tradition. In this case, the indigenizing process symbolically links religion, culture, and politics.

As I stressed in the opening part of this chapter, people build buildings that not only result from, but also influence, how they think. This raises a major question: 'On the basis of *whose* ideas, *whose* beliefs, *whose* values and *whose* view of the world are decisions based?' (King 1980, p. 31). The question challenges the assumptions of all of us, including designers and planners. Taking a look at a building alone is often a mistake. As this chapter has shown, one must examine buildings in the context of the larger socio-political and cultural environment of which they are a part.

Notes

1 The following analysis on 18th-century Madras is taken from Lewandowski (1980a).
2 For comparative data on Calcutta, see Sinha (1968).
3 This discussion of Mahalakshmi temple is from Lewandowski (1980b, pp. 144–5).
4 Conversation with Mary J. Jacob, Department of Geography, Mount Holyoke College, South Hadley, Mass.

References

Barnett, M. R. 1976. *The politics of cultural nationalism in South India*. Princeton, NJ: Princeton University Press.
Beck, B. E. F. 1972. *Peasant society in the Konku*. Vancouver: University of British Columbia Press.
Census of India 1961, Vol. IX: Madras, Part X-(I), Madras City Report. New Delhi: Manager of Publications.
Chopra, P. (ed.) 1970. *Delhi: history of places of interest*. Delhi: Gazetteer, Delhi Administration.
Freeman, J. M. and J. Preston 1980. Two urbanizing Orissan temples. In *The Transformation of a Sacred Town*, S. Seymour (ed.), 101–106. Boulder, Colorado: Westview Press.
Government of Tamil Nadu n.d. *A brief note on the Sculpture Training Centre*. Madras: Directorate of Technical Education.
Hardgrave, R. L. Jr. 1965. *The Dravidian movement*. Bombay: Popular Prakashan.
Jacob, M. J. n.d. Unpublished paper. Department of Geography, Mount Holyoke College.
Jagmohan 1975. *Rebuilding Shahjahanabad: the walled city of Delhi*. New Delhi: Vikas.
Kennedy, R. 1974. Status and control of temples in Tamilnadu. *Ind. Econ. Social Hist. Rev.* **11**, nos. 2 & 3 (June–September).
King, A. D. 1976. *Colonial urban development*. London: Routledge & Kegan Paul.
King, A. D. (ed.) 1980. *Buildings and society: essays in the social development of the built environment*. London: Routledge & Kegan Paul.
Larson, G. J. 1978. Modernization and religious legitimation in India: 1835–1885. In *Religion and the legitimation of power in South Asia*, B. L. Smith (ed.), 28–41. Leiden: E. J. Brill.
Lewandowski, S. J. 1977. Changing form and function in the ceremonial and the colonial port city in India: an historical analysis of Madurai and Madras. *Mod. Asian Stud.* **II**(2), 185–94.
Lewandowski, S. J. 1980a. *Merchants and kingship: an interpretation of Indian urban history*. Unpublished paper.
Lewandowski, S. J. 1980b. The Hindu temple in South India. In *Buildings and society: essays in the social development of the built environment*, A. D. King (ed.), 123–50. London: Routledge & Kegan Paul.
Miller, D. 1980. Religious institutions and political élites in Bhubaneswar. In *The transformation of a sacred town*, S. Seymour (ed.). Boulder, Colorado: Westview Press.

Omvedt, G. 1976. *Cultural revolt in a colonial society*. Bombay: Scientific Socialist Education Trust.
The Overseas Times 1980. **4**, no. 12, August 22.

Rapoport, A. 1969. *House form and culture*. Englewood Cliffs, NJ: Prentice-Hall.
Rapoport, A. 1980. Cultural determinants of form. In King (1980), 283–305.

Sinha, P. 1968. Approaches to urban history: Calcutta (1750–1850). In *Bengal Past and Present* **87** (January–June), 106–19.
Spratt, P. 1970. *D.M.K. in power*. Bombay: Nachiketa.

Temple consecration after renovation 1977. *The Hindu*, October 31.
Temples of India 1968. New Delhi: Government Publication Division.

Wiebe, P. D. 1975. *Social life in an Indian slum*. Delhi: Vikas.

12 A cultural analysis of urban residential landscapes in North America: the case of the anglophile élite

JAMES S. DUNCAN
NANCY G. DUNCAN

In this chapter, we present a cultural analysis of urban residential land-scapes in North America, illustrated by two case studies, one from Vancouver, Canada, and another from a suburb of New York. The approach emphasizes both the 'sentiment and symbolism' of landscapes, and the political–economic process by which they are produced and preserved. A number of authors – including Firey (1945), Seeley *et al.* (1963), Lowenthal and Prince (1965), Duncan (1973), Perin (1977), Duncan and Duncan (1980), Pratt (1981), and Rapoport (1981) – have argued that landscapes are a major repository of symbols of social status. The importance of the residential landscape as a symbol of individual or group identity varies cross-culturally (Rapoport 1981). In highly individualistic capitalist societies (such as the USA or Canada), where status is largely achieved rather than being ascribed by membership in a caste or kin group, a major means of communicating social identity is through private, 'conspicuous' consumption of objects (Agnew 1981). The dwelling, together with the status level of its locality, is one of the principal symbols of social status. Even within these societies, however, the meaning of the residential landscape and its rôle in communicating social identity vary. For example, Couper and Brindley (1975) distinguish two different English attitudes toward the house or residence: some see the house as an achievement and status symbol; while others believe that it is a right to be provided by the state.

In India, Duncan and Duncan (1976) identified groups whose social networks are relatively open and individualistic. Among these groups, individuals are socially mobile, and, as a consequence, the house and residential landscape provide an important marker of social identity. Among more traditional groups, on the other hand, this function of the residential landscape is less important because the social networks are largely closed, and social standing within the kinship group is well established by birth and intimate knowledge of one another. Within North America, one finds groups whose class or ethnic backgrounds are such that their social networks are also closed to a significant degree, and among whom, therefore, conspicuous consumption is not needed to establish personal status. The West Enders of Boston (Gans 1962), and the 'old' wealthy families of Vancouver (Pratt 1981), are but two examples of this kind. These contrast with, for example, members of the upper middle class of 'Crestwood Heights,' a fictitious name for a suburb of Toronto (Seeley *et al.* 1963), or some of the 'new' wealthy families of Vancouver (Pratt 1981), who utilize the house and its setting as a personal expression of the owner's identity.

A cultural analysis of urban landscapes requires a comment on our notion of culture. The culture concept, which has long been important to American anthropologists, has generated much debate among practitioners. This debate swirls around two antinomies: structure–action, and determinism–freedom. Should culture be considered a superorganic structure which determines action, and therefore explains it, or should culture be seen as a loosely structured system of behavior with little explanatory power?[1] In this chapter, following Geertz (1973), we will argue that culture is not an explanatory variable. On the contrary, it is what is to be explained or, less ambitiously, commented upon. Its complexity must be prised apart; one must not only discover the origins of various cultural elements, but also show what these elements mean to people, their relationship to group and individual identity, to what ends they are put, and the manner in which people struggle or fail to struggle to maintain or change them.

The two case studies we explore are of residential landscapes which signify the culture of two partly closed élite groups. These people are committed to a form of residential living which owes its origins to a particular version of 'English landscape taste.' As the élite, they have influenced landscape tastes, and have been imitated. To a degree, this landscape occurs in modified form, although often more conspicuously packaged, in other Canadian and American cities. The élite landscape is found in some older American and Canadian cities, and in western Canada. It is based on the ideal of an English country manor. As such, it can be viewed as one element in a whole cultural 'system' of practices and ideas. This system has been adapted to North America, and its popularity has spread beyond its original centers.

We shall show that the creation and preservation of these landscapes, which have both class and ethnic connotations, serve in part as a vehicle by which the integrity of a cultural group is maintained. Landscapes and other elements of a culture are used to define membership in a culture group through reaffirmation of members' values, and exclusion of non-members. The process not only involves conscious socio-political action, but also results from the unintended consequences of collective action based on unarticulated, 'taken-for-granted' values. A residential landscape helps in the reproduction of a class or status group because it is an important repository of symbols of social class and ethnic heritage. Increasingly subtle variations allow it to continue to serve this function for a particular cultural group, while certain elements of the model are adopted by members of the wider society.

Following further elaboration of the link between culture and landscape in the next section, we proceed to sketch the origins of the English country house ideal, and indicate why it is so dominant in English landscape development. With the desire of certain élites in Canada and the United States to emphasize their connections (directly in some cases, but, for most others, by association) to Britain (or, more specifically, England), this landscape is re-created in such different parts of North America as Westchester, New York, and Vancouver, British Columbia. The linkages are delineated, and the resultant landscapes are introduced in the third section.

Such residential districts with their signifying landscapes do not endure without effort on the part of the residents to safeguard the landscapes and their meanings. The struggle is political as the élites successfully use and manipulate land-use control instruments and public opinion; they also enlist the aid of sympathetic public officials to preserve these historic places. The struggle here is not so much with the masses of the working class or the upwardly mobile petty bourgeoisie, as with the *nouveau riche*. Members of this group have the economic ability to enter the élite preserves, but, lacking the anglophile culture, must either have their building intentions carefully controlled or be educated into emulating the old élite. The political issues arising from this attempt to impose the landscape of one group within a class upon others now in that same class are described and interpreted, both somewhat generally and with specific reference to Westchester and Vancouver.

A cultural approach to urban residential landscape

A culture is a complex but amorphous web of ideas and practices that forms the context of social action. It is a meaning system, an interpretive framework that is largely shaped by experience, but also by a continual interpretation of changing events. Within North America, there is a large amount of cultural variation (e.g. Canada–USA). Cultural analysis has tended to focus upon regional and ethnic differences. A less common approach has focused upon cultural variations between social classes. We view class in cultural terms, but pay particular attention to what Weber termed status group divisions within classes. Status groups are marked by specific patterns of consumption, or, more generally, style of life. Cultural analysis of classes and status groups is important because it firmly ties questions of identity to questions of social and political order.

As geographers, we are particularly concerned with the interaction of landscapes and culture. We want to see how objects within residential landscapes and associated meanings are conveyed from generation to generation, a point of particular interest as a self-conscious link to the past is one of the critical characteristics defining the groups we are studying. We also want to see how political action helps to maintain a particular kind of cultural landscape and, hence, the identity which that landscape symbolizes.

The residential landscapes of the upper-class groups considered here have their roots in a past time and place. It is unlikely that such élite groups are more than partly aware of or understand the historical symbolism of their landscapes. The meaning of many landscape elements has changed, adapted to the nature of late 20th-century North American societies. We will argue, however, that although the overt, superficial meaning of these elements has changed, a deeper underlying meaning remains, symbolizing privilege, inequality, and class interest. A culture is often elusive to those who live in it precisely because, while the past has a massive impact on the present, the meaning systems of the past, the interpretive frame through which earlier generations saw and constructed a world of objects, ideas, and institutions, is only partially understood, if at all.

Cultural change is continuous but rarely cataclysmic. Rather than rejecting the past totally, people more often filter it selectively. They change or forget past meanings, yet artifacts and stylized forms of behavior remain. For example, the Tudor-style house, the symbolism of which we shall discuss later, is seen by the groups we have studied as a prestigious architectural style, but they have only the vaguest idea why this should be so. Were they to know the 19th-century symbolism of the Tudor house, they might be less attracted to it, or at least ambivalent about it. The meaning of objects of this kind is continually being replaced by new or modified meanings. The changes are complex, leaving contradictions between artifact and use, meaning and behavior, and rendering the web of meanings called culture opaque.

The dominant image of the English landscape

Residential landscapes simultaneously contain many different meanings which are conveyed to those who can understand, at different levels of abstraction. The landscapes of élites symbolize social class, and, within class, status groups, and, more personally, memories and sentiments of youth and acquaintances of the past. Why has an English landscape type been adopted by an élite in America and Canada, and why have the country house and garden become its archetype?

The image of the English country house in contemporary North America is based upon a 19th- and 20th-century English revival of the country-house tradition (Girouard 1981). In the late 18th century, the view of the urban English upper and upper middle classes toward the country and country pursuits became increasingly romantic. At the close of this period, a network of good roads made the estates being transformed through enclosure accessible to an urban-based élite (Girouard 1981, pp. 214–18). The idealized country residence was re-created in peripheral parts of the 19th-century English cities (Lowenthal & Prince 1965, pp. 189–90). In both country and city, the effect that was sought during the Victorian era was both pastoral and picturesque, a landscape that evoked a mood of romantic nostalgia for the rural past. In the countryside, according to Lowenthal and Prince (1965, p. 192):

> The favored landscape is what Turner denoted 'elegant pastoral' as distinct from merely 'pastoral'; it calls to mind traditional upper-class tastes and pursuits. What is considered 'essentially English' is a calm and peaceful deer park, slow moving streams and wide expanses of meadowland studded with fine trees.

In a city such as London, the picturesque ideal had the qualities of 'closeness, variety, and intimacy, and the ever-recurring contrasts of tall and low, of large and small, of wide and narrow, of straight and crooked, the closes and retreats and odd leafy corners' (Pevsner 1957, p. 105). In both city and country in specific instances, the new was made to look like the old and to blend unobtrusively with 'natural' surroundings that landscape architects had designed to improve upon nature (Girouard 1981, p. 228). During the 19th century, the country house, and its garden transplanted into the city, was the architectural manifestation of this ideal.

In England during the latter half of the 19th century, nostalgia for the countryside, more specifically the life of the gentry, took the form of taste for an 'Old English' style in houses, which was to blossom into the rage for 'Tudor' that swept well-to-do suburban areas and diffused down to the middle classes during the first third of the 20th century (Wiener 1981, p. 66). Coupled with the Tudor revival was a dramatic increase of interest in the preservation of old buildings. The result of these two trends was 'a generalized historicity and rusticity – the purpose of which was to convey a feeling of Old Rural England, rather than to adhere to any particular and consistent style' (Wiener 1981, p. 650).

At one level, this development simply represented a yearning for an idealized rural past, a recurring pattern, Raymond Williams (1973) tells us, whereby successive generations of upper and middle class English people idealized a reconstructed and partially fictive past. The irony, he notes, is that in the late 19th and the 20th centuries, 'there is almost an inverse proportion ... between the relative importance of the working rural economy and the cultural importance of rural ideas' (Williams 1973, p. 248). Underlying both the 'Old English' imagery and the preservation movement is another set of symbols; according to Williams (1973), these find their roots in the class struggle associated with the Industrial Revolution.

Another interpretation is that this architectural cult of the past was intimately and explicitly bound up in a conservative, upper-class denigration of capitalism, industrialism, and the new manufacturing classes who were increasingly challenging the fading supremacy of the landed, aristocratic élite (Wiener 1981, p. 64). Building in this style, and the preservation of the old, not only symbolized but concretized a critique of industrialism, and represented an attempt to return to an older way of life. At the turn of the last century, contemporary ideas of design were excluded *because* they were modern, and represented a new industrial and social order which was thought unable to provide a satisfactory living environment (Wiener 1981, pp. 64–72).

Some members of the late 19th-century landed gentry saw the rustic, anti-bourgeois symbolism of the English Tudor and country-manor styles, but not all consciously made this link (Wiener 1981). As these styles were imitated more widely, the anti-bourgeois symbolism was submerged. They came to represent a derivation of élite landscapes, but lacking the anti-capitalist connotation.

In North America, as in England, the country house had its urban counterpart. One case we consider, Westchester County, New York, is rural, or, at least, 'exurban,' the other is in the city of Vancouver, Canada. Different elements of the country-house style are stressed in the two areas: the pastoral ideal in Westchester and the 'Old English' house in Vancouver. Both have in common the 'estate character' of the area. In 19th-century England, estates often comprised tens of thousands of acres, but, in 20th-century North America, an 'estate' is much more modest. In Westchester, despite residents' demands for a minimum lot size of 20 acres to preserve the 'estate character' of the area, municipal officials settled upon a 4-acre minimum, arguing that this was sufficient. In marked contrast, in Vancouver, lots in our study area were at least 1 acre. Therefore, the notion of a country estate is vague, and its specifics vary dramatically according to cultural context.

The landscape of anglophile élites: Westchester and Vancouver

Our first study area, an affluent suburban town (i.e. township) in Westchester County, is a 'picture-postcard' village of unspoiled beauty, cherished by its residents, some of whose forebears lived in the town in the 17th and 18th centuries. The town consists of several hamlets of white wooden and red brick shops and public buildings, some dating back to 1789. All around are gently rolling hills, open meadowlands with horses grazing, woods of oak and hemlock, rivers, ponds, and swamps. Tall maple and oaks overhang the roads, many of which are of dirt and lined with dry-stone walls and wild flowers. Although passers-by cannot see many of them, the hilltops are dotted with late 19th-century and early 20th-century mansions, now hidden by tall trees and approached by long gravel driveways. Many are complete with one or two gatehouses, gardeners' cottages, and stables. Young couples find that such gatehouses and cottages can be made into sophisticated 'apartments,' now that many are no longer occupied by servants.

As one resident put it, the people of the town see their community as a: 'sanctuary from the buffetings of a too-competitive world. To those who know its rich store of natural resources and its priceless heritage from history, it is a sanctified holy spot.'

Interviews with more than 40 residents reveal an almost universally shared preference for a decidedly English style of landscape. The terms 'pastoral,' 'bucolic,' 'rural,' and 'historical' crop up over and over again in reference to what residents value about the landscape. The open meadowlands, stone walls, great oaks and other deciduous trees are all valued, but perhaps the most highly valued symbols of the town are the country estate with its rambling main house and informal, often over-grown gardens, the opportunities for riding on dirt roads and bridle trails, and fox hunting. This taste for the pastoral and old, the respect for old families and 'old money,' for all that is well worn, is English in origin. It contrasts with some of the neighboring towns, where one finds a prefer-ence for a more Germanic landscape of conifers and rock outcroppings with well designed contemporary architecture, or a preference for the more Mediterranean formal garden, columns, and neoclassical elegance. The cult of the old allows a certain seediness of house and garden; it is studied seediness, however, such as one finds in the aristocratic English model it reflects.

This Westchester town occupies what was once some of the choicest farmland in the county. Late in the 19th century, the area became a popular location for the building of gentlemen's estates, and for riding and fox hunting. Among the prosperous commercial class, building country estates was a conscious or unconscious mimicking of the English landed gentry, and paralleled the same movement in England. In England in 1900, the new rich set up country houses, were given titles, and took the train to their offices (Girouard 1981, p. 301). For some, country houses symbolize tradition, and standing; the model was clearly outlined for the uninitiated through *Country Life* magazine: the houses were presented discretely and made to look as old as possible. As one contributor to *Country Life* put it, 'land had ceased being a major source of wealth and the country house was now valued more as a symbol of ancestry than of economic power.' Yet the rural, 'aristocratic' ancestry of the property owners, both in England and elsewhere, was often fictitious.

Today in Westchester, the model of the English country house has prestige, and its origins appeal to many, even those whose ancestry is not English. The landscape tastes of the residents and potential buyers of houses are clearly reflected in real-estate advertisements. Many are obviously designed to recall the country-estate ideal, usually emphasizing the setting more than the house. Advertisements for houses in the area appearing in the *New York Times* real-estate sections in 1982 and 1983 have such headings as 'In the grand manor' (sic) – horse country; 'English garden'; 'Rolling hunt country'; 'Country gentlemen'; 'English park setting'; 'Maples, meadows, old stone walls'; 'Pastoral views'; 'Dirt road and rolling fields'; 'Listen to the hunting horn'; 'High meadows'; 'Turn of century estate' in the heart of horse country; and 'Peaceful open rolling land'.

Symbols of the English landed gentry are today considered prestigious among many groups in North America. One finds people of different class and ethnic backgrounds favoring some of these landscape elements. For example, a recent article in *Esquire* magazine (Smith 1982, p. 14) stated:

> The art form favored in the dining rooms of most Wall Street houses is English sporting prints, pheasants, retrievers, shooting sticks, pink-coated riders taking a stirrup cup before pursuing a fox. None of the proper ancestors of true Wall Streeters wore pink coats, and there was no tradition among the urban Dutch, the urban Jews or even the counting-house English, of pursuing foxes. But that British image continues to be projected.

Builder (1982, p. 32), a magazine for home builders and architects, recently published a survey of American preferences for different types of houses. The two most highly favored were farmhouses and Tudors, which suggests both an anti-urban bias and the influence of English styles. The Vancouver neighborhood we have studied makes explicit the tie to England. More than any other neighborhood, it symbolizes the prestigious cultural (i.e. British) heritage of the city in the minds of citizens and city officials alike. This suburban district was located and designed in the first quarter of the 20th century under the control of the Canadian Pacific Railway (CPR), a major landowner in Vancouver then as now (thanks to outright grants to induce the railway company to locate its Pacific terminus in the city). It was the culmination of a series of fashionable districts developed by the CPR in the burgeoning cities of the Canadian west. Company officials (and their surveyors/designers) were undoubtedly familiar with the élite residential areas in such major centers of 'Anglo' socioeconomic power as Toronto and Montreal, and with certain parts of Ottawa (the nation's capital), where railway and national politics were commingled.

The design reflects a late 19th-century vision of residential architecture and landscaping (Hardwick 1974, pp. 105–6), expressed by such phrases as 'picturesque landscape,' 'garden city,' 'naturalism,' and 'country life.' These were key phrases defining the later phases of the romantic movement in architecture and landscape design both in England and North America. Streets were laid out to follow the contours of the hilly topography. The district was consciously designed to reflect the picturesque 'country home' approach to the residence that had been popularized by A. J. Downing and Calvert Vaux in America, and J. C. Loudon and P. Webb in England. Most of the houses which dominate the area's architecture recall half-timbered Tudor structures and the romanticism of the neo-Gothic. The area was designed to have, what the residents now like to term, a 'secluded estate-like quality' with 'grand-scale houses' partially hidden behind landscaping. Access to the typical property is marked by entrance posts and, in the case of the largest properties, by gatehouses. The climate, which is like that of southern England, contributes to the image.

The anglophile culture of the élites that we have examined helps to explain why they have copied the manor-house style. Presumably this particular style was adopted because it has been the élite cultural model in Britain from the 1850s to the present. In Vancouver at the turn of the century, members of the Canadian-born élite went so far as to bring over some of the most famous country-house architects in Britain (such as Baillie Scott) to create 'authentic Tudor-style houses' for them. Of course, as Prince suggests with respect to England, 'The Tudor we now look upon is not sixteenth-century Tudor, but what twentieth-century builders think Tudor ought to look like' (quoted in Lowenthal 1975, p. 32). The style of the gentry represents for anglophile élites, in both the USA and Canada, the image of themselves which they wish to convey. These élites are the New World counterparts of the bourgeoisie that the late 19th-century British aristocracy was trying to fend off (Wiener 1981). They are the children of trade, people whose families made their money in dry goods, timber, steel, and the like, among whom 'old money' is money that may have been made as late as the early 20th century. Yet, at a deeper level, the disparagement of 'new money' embodied in the aristocratic critique of the bourgeoisie remains. What one finds in North America is a distorted image of the struggle between the aristocracy and the new bourgeoisie in 19th-century England. In North America, the struggle, as one would expect within a social context with no aristocracy, is taking place entirely within the bourgeoisie, between the old commercial class and the new. The old commercial class, which forms the élite in the two North American areas, has followed in the footsteps of successful 19th-century English businessmen in taking on the trappings of an older aristocratic tradition. It displays an appreciation for the Old English style and tries to preserve its residential landscapes, with early 20th-century Tudor and neo-Gothic copies, and despises the *nouveau riche* who have moved into its preserves and put up either late 20th-century copies or houses of contemporary design.

What often exacerbates the division between 'old' and 'new' money are the ethnic and cultural differences between an old 'Anglo' élite and a new élite whose background is more diverse, drawn not only from non-Anglo-Saxon Western Europe but also from Eastern and Southern Europe, and, increasingly in British Columbia, from Asia. The distance separating them is not merely that between a newly affluent English bourgeoisie and an established English gentry, but the distance between a North American bourgeois copy of that gentry and a newly moneyed group, of which many know nothing of English landscape tastes and some even find them unattractive.

In our examination of the origins of the English country-house tradition and its transportation to the New World, we have focused upon a set of cultural symbols in the built environment. Throughout this discussion there has, of course, been an undercurrent of the class and status-based nature of this landscape. Although the English symbol is crucial for understanding this upper-class residential landscape type, it does not exhaust the messages that can be read in it. It also symbolizes class and status in a way that is analytically separate from its image of England.

Controlling the residential landscape

For our purpose, the residential landscape has two interrelated but analytically distinct sets of cultural meanings, one having to do with class, the other with status. These meanings will have communicative value extending across the society. The size, style, and decoration of a house, the size of the lot, the type and amount of landscaping, and the location and reputation of a neighborhood within a city or town all represent class. That is to say, they represent economic power in a society where personal success is largely marked by the possession of objects (Agnew 1981). Social-class distinctions are clearly acted out in the residential environments for all to see.

Americans, and, to a lesser degree, Canadians, are ambivalent about social class (Porter 1965, Sennett & Cobb 1973). On the one hand, and especially in America, there is the ideology of equality, the notion that all are born equal, and in some sense remain equal for the remainder of their lives. On the other hand, there is the ideology of social mobility – the ideal of the self-made man who rises in social class. Both stem from a bourgeois critique of aristocratic privilege and of a society in which position is based on ascriptive status, rather than success in economic competition. Although all segments of American society would reject the idea of aristocratic privilege as the basis for an acceptable social order, there is evidence to suggest that important segments of the upper class in North America mimic an aristocratic tradition, and adopt ascription as (in part) a basis of social life, at least in the realm of consumption. Forms of ascriptive behavior were also to be found within the realm of production, and perhaps still are. The importance to the 'eastern' business establishment of attending an 'Ivy League' university, and the exclusion of Jews from many large corporations, are examples of ascriptive behavior. In short, there appears to be a persistent tendency among those who have risen to the top of North American society to block the type of social mobility that they themselves experienced. Charlotte Curtis, a journalist who has long observed the American rich, describes this tendency nicely when she writes (Curtis 1976, p. x):

> While professing a dedication to the principle of equality, Americans have consistently worked at being unequal. They close ranks, change rules and move onward whenever threatened by whatever levelling-up the marauder appears to be gaining on them, which seems to have been constantly.

This ascriptive social organization within the upper class creates status groups, which, as Weber pointed out, have different 'styles of life' centered around consumption. The existence of status groups within a class-based society poses some interesting dilemmas, both of a theoretical nature for the social scientist, and of a practical nature for the actors themselves. The principal dilemma is this: in a society based on economic class – one in which there is no formal ascriptive basis such as an aristocracy – the upper class may be extremely permeable. In theory, those who earn great wealth enter, and those who lose a portion of their wealth drop out and become members of the middle class. But the workings of the upper strata of North American society show that they are not quite so permeable. In a class society where success is largely marked through the possession of objects, houses, cars, jewels, furs, and the like, identity, in part at least, can be bought. The link between objects and identity has been readily grasped and exploited by manufacturers who assure us that, if only we will consume their products, we will become more beautiful, wiser, and achieve a higher status among our peers. An example of this marketing of identity is to be found in one of our study areas where a developer built some expensive townhouses on the former property of one of the area's old families. The advertising campaign for these townhouses stressed the fact that they had been built on a former estate, and suggested that the future owners of the units could acquire an upper-class image by purchasing a unit. The advertisement concluded by stating that one could demonstrate one's social standing by living in such an environment.

The fact that identity in capitalist societies can, at least in part, be bought, and no formal mechanism for marking status exists, is a problem for segments of the upper class, which we call the old élite.[2] Put slightly differently, there is an 'internal' struggle within the upper class between different status groups – between an entrenched old élite and a newer segment of the upper class that is vying with the old élite for social prestige. This status struggle within a class is in part a conflict over the residential landscape. The conflict sheds light not only on the rôle played by the environment in the formation and maintenance of identity, but also on the concepts of class interest and class identity. The old élites that we have studied, both in Westchester and Vancouver, form what Weber calls status groups. They comprise the 'old' families, entrenched élites whose money goes back at least one generation, and often several. They see themselves as a kind of local aristocracy, modeled upon their version of the English upper class, residing in an environment that has been designed in the English image over several generations.

The old élites show little solidarity with other members of their economic class, at least in consumption. Quite the contrary, members of these élites single out the newer members of their class, the *nouveau riche*, as the people they must oppose. Individuals who may speak about the poor, and even the middle class, in quite generous terms are invariably hostile toward new members of their own class. One influential member of the Vancouver old élite said, in particularly evocative terms, 'We would like to encourage artists, professors, and other nice people without a great deal of money to purchase coach houses in our area. These are the sorts of people that we want, not those awful *nouveau riche* people who build monstrosities.' Implicit in all this is the assumption that middle-class professionals would not change their landscape: they would move into the coach houses and no one would notice them. New money, on the other hand, has deployed its economic power to change the landscape by constructing new mansions that reflect tastes not shared by the old élite.

If an old élite's control over residential land breaks down, and if enough money can buy property in the neighborhood, in North America such a conflict could be seen as one between status groups rather than classes. However, the old élites have skilfully manipulated the political process in order to reassert some control over the landscape. Zoning laws have been used, both in Westchester and in Vancouver, to protect their landscapes from unwanted damage. Élite values do not simply survive; they must be fought for.

Westchester There is politics in preserving landscapes, which may involve zoning and environmental protection (as in Westchester), or the institution of strict design guidelines (as in Vancouver). Lowenthal and Prince (1965, p. 193) say of England:

> From the condemnation of planning and regimentation, one might well suppose the picturesque to be a series of happy accidents, and conclude that the desired impression of roughness and irregularity was entirely fortuitous. Nothing is further from the truth; the picturesque is contrived and composed with as much care as any geometrical layout.

The picturesque landscape of suburban Westchester is carefully planned and vigorously monitored. As early as 1928, members of the local garden club, and other politically active groups in the Westchester town who were concerned about the natural environment of the area, instituted a zoning code for the town which would preserve its beauty for future generations. The present residents still care deeply about protecting the natural environment and preserving the town's historical heritage. This is done through tightly controlled zoning laws, wetlands ordinances, historical preservation districts, and the vigilance of citizens willing to devote their time to opposing new development by forming neighborhood organizations and attending town meetings.

The preservation of this picturesque, idyllic landscape, with its unspoiled country atmosphere, absence of neon signs or other symbols of the modern commercial era, and authentic historical townscapes, has not been without social cost. To understand the degree of government control and planning that has produced a landscape of such 'natural' beauty, one must place it within the context of the larger social, economic, and political realities of the New York metropolitan region of which it is a part. More people are now employed in suburbs than in central cities. Many suburbs, however, are able to regulate the numbers and types of people who can live there by establishing zoning laws, building codes, subdivision regulations, and restrictions against multifamily housing and mobile homes. Such exclusionary activities have exacerbated the fiscal problems of central cities, restricted the access of urban residents to suburban jobs, and contributed to house price escalation in suburban districts (Cox 1979). The Westchester study area has over 90 percent of its area zoned for single-family housing at a 4-acre minimum. Given that the majority of towns surrounding it also have exclusionary zoning (80 percent of the residential land *in the county* is zoned for a minimum of 1 to 4 acres), over 90 percent of the New York metropolitan area's population cannot afford to live in most of this exclusive county (Shipler 1974, p. 114).

How are we to account for the residential landscapes of Westchester? Who or what is to be credited with preserving the natural beauty and historical heritage of this Westchester town? And what explains the inequitable distribution of private and public resources within the county that necessarily goes hand in hand with the preservation of picturesque landscapes? The answer, in part, lies in the individualistic ideology found in North America which refuses to acknowledge collective responsibility (everyone, it is believed, earns his own place in society). Interviews among town residents and less affluent residents of nearby towns confirm this. The nearly universal attitude is that if one can afford to buy a 4-acre lot, one deserves it.

The zoning is taken for granted as right and natural, and the interdependence between the various types of environments throughout the county and metropolitan region is not acknowledged. Therefore, highly restrictive planning measures can be used to achieve the illusion of an unplanned, natural environment populated by gentlemen farmers. None of them, however, could privately afford the amount of land one would have to own in order to live in such a landscape, without a strong local government to control development and restrict the access to the town of people who, simply by their numbers, would spoil the environment for those who live there.

Even the more subtle landscape features that make the town appear so attractively quaint, such as dirt roads, are not simply a relic from the past, but are carefully preserved at great expense to the taxpayers of the town. Dirt roads require far more time-consuming maintenance than hard-surfaced roads. Time and again, controversy over dirt roads in the town has resulted in passionate pleas to retain them. Very proper, upper-class ladies have been successful in halting the paving of such roads by lying down in front of town trucks and bulldozers!

There has been a threat of lawsuits against the town over the issue of exclusionary zoning. However, of more than 40 residents interviewed, only 4 mentioned exclusion as one of the purposes of the zoning. These four lived near one of the hamlets behind the commercial district where housing was poor and the lots were small. Thus they did not represent the socioeconomic status of the great majority of the town's residents. However, less affluent residents of the town and surrounding areas generally agreed that the large-lot zoning was beneficial, protecting the rural atmosphere of the town, and giving hope to those who could not afford 4 acres but enjoyed the thought that, if they worked hard and were successful, they, too, might be able to live in such a beautiful setting. They felt that, in any case, those who could afford it, deserved it.

Environmental protection, a socially acceptable rationale, was often cited as the purpose for large-lot zoning, (see also Frieden 1979). Whether this is a genuine cause or a conscious manipulation to mask the underlying rationale is open to question. The town and its lawyers have been able to make environmental concerns the basis of defending the existing zoning code and the increasing restrictions on development through new wetlands ordinances and even more stringent subdivision regulations. The popularity of the ecology movement throughout the wider society has greatly aided the town in its efforts to maintain the quality of the environment for the residents.

The following is a trivial example, but one which clearly illustrates several points that have been made: the reverence for what is old; the love of nature, particularly of deciduous trees in open meadows; and the ability of members of the town to convince the wider public of the value of preserving the town's green spaces and historical resources. There is a very large oak tree, that is thought to be 500 years old, standing at one end of one of the town's most prestigious residential roads, a long winding dirt road. The tree stands on a small plot of land owned by the town and enclosed by a stone wall. Beyond is a large open field which was bought by a builder. Residents of the town, particularly those who live nearby, were distressed at the thought of any new construction so near the revered tree. They launched a campaign to raise enough money to buy the land back from the builder, and succeeded in doing so. One informant disclosed that donations to the fund to save the open space around the tree included the proceeds from a bake-sale held by children from a poor neighborhood in a city 25 miles away.

The belief, expressed by the residents, in the value to the wider society of preserving large, open areas of green space, and protecting the historical heritage of the town by halting further development, is sincere. Not only those who live in the town, but many others who are confined to poorer, more urbanized areas and therefore do not benefit directly from the town's country atmosphere, do not appear to recognize the interdependence among the towns and the negative effect that large-lot zoning has on the housing situation of the metropolitan region as a whole. Seventy percent of those who were asked if they believed that large-lot zoning in one town affected surrounding areas said no. This privatism, or the belief that individuals or towns are independent of one another and should have the right to decide use of the land without regard to others, is a characteristic of highly individualistic societies which has proved advantageous to those wishing to preserve their own neighborhoods.

Vancouver From its very creation in the early 1900s, the builders and residents of the Vancouver study area have struggled to maintain an English image. The Canadian Pacific Railroad, which owned and developed the land on the outskirts of their city, also controlled the layout of the streets and even checked the plans of the 1150 homes that they helped finance in the area, to assure that they conformed to the company's standards on price, quality, and appearance (Holdsworth 1977, Bottomley 1978). The railway had the area zoned for single-family housing, and produced the most expensive and fashionable residential area in the city, thereby greatly increasing the value of their unsold adjacent land. In the 1920s, in order to increase their control over the neighborhood, residents, with the company's blessing, successfully lobbied the provincial government to give the area a special zoning code that would limit the land-use control powers of the city. But even with such political gains, the area could not withstand the economic pressures of the Depression, which drove many owners of larger mansions to abandon them, and others to take boarders in secretly. (The latter threat to the single-family nature of the area was increased when the federal government passed a wartime edict in 1941 allowing boarders in all residential districts in Canada.) During the 1930s, a property owners' association was created whose purpose was to preserve the character of the area and to lower taxes for the residents so that they could afford to maintain their mansions. This association has continued to serve as the watchdog of the area, reporting violators of the area's codes to the province or the city, and taking violators to court when necessary. In the late 1960s, despite a massive lobbying effort by the property owners' association, the province turned the zoning control of the neighborhood back to the city. The association then persuaded the city to create a special zoning category for the area and amend the city's charter to allow special interest groups, such as the property owners' association, to prosecute violators of the zoning code. Within a few years, the association decided that these restrictions alone were not going to preserve the nature of the area completely, as some demolition of large homes and subdivision of properties continued. The property owners fought these changes, preparing briefs that were presented to the city planning department whenever a subdivision or demolition application arose. They were constantly on the lookout for violators of the area's zoning; they patrolled the neighborhood looking for unauthorized construction, and even hired private investigators to weed out illegal boarders. Although their action greatly retarded change in the area, they could not stop it completely. The association therefore decided that stronger political action had to be taken, in the form of a new and more restrictive zoning code for the area. Not only did they want subdivision and demolition to stop, but they wanted to control the appearance of all future development in the area. This degree of landscape control was to go even beyond that exerted by the railroad in the early days.

The association successfully lobbied the city, and was allowed to create a citizens' committee to draft a plan to preserve the neighborhood. The committee, which was dominated by members of the association, was to work in conjunction with the local area planner, and the resulting plan would guide all future development in the neighborhood.

The shaping of this plan, and hence of the landscape, took place within the broader arena of Vancouver politics. Political opinion in the city over the past decade has focused on two major issues, one of which was a liability and the other an asset from the committee's point of view. The liability was that the city was experiencing a housing shortage which stemmed from a lack of land, while the association planned to increase minimum lot sizes. The asset was that the other major political issue in the city for the past decade had been 'livability,' which stressed local community participation in government, the fostering of visually and socially distinct neighborhoods, and the preservation both of green space and of areas of historical significance to the city.[3] The association successfully played down the impact of the plan on the housing shortage, and argued its case on the basis of livability.

It was fortunate for this committee that the ideology of livability provided a culturally acceptable way of putting forward its own landscape tastes, not simply as being in the interests of an élite, but of the whole city. The ideology of livability was used to convert class interest into general interest.

The plan which was finally worked out with the city planning department was to institutionalize English landscape tastes in the neighborhood. The preamble to the official plan made this quite clear. The architecture in the area, it stated:

> was greatly influenced by the Romantic Movement and consists of a sophisticated manipulation and blending of various styles based on earlier historic examples. Many houses are modelled after the Tudor style. The dominant approach, however, was to create a country-estate in an urban setting.

The plan hoped not only to preserve this image, but to enhance it. As a sympathetic city councillor who attended one of the planning meetings stated: 'The problem is you want to design guidelines to make people imitate a 1920-style imitation Tudor.' The committee realized that it would not be a simple matter to make new development resemble English country houses of the early 20th century. Some imitation Tudors that had been recently built were considered unacceptable. A committee member summed up the association's feelings:

A new house has recently gone up which is a Tudor imitation. But the timbers are matchsticks and the leaded windows are tape. This is simply awful. How can we avoid it? How can we legislate against it? What we want are houses built with traditional materials.

Perhaps nowhere in the plan does the English landscape ideal emerge more clearly than in an architectural rating of existing houses that was appended. The houses were divided into categories according to how closely they conformed to the country-house ideal. Unacceptable architecture did not meet the standards of 'the English picturesque landscape tradition . . . and . . . the building could be removed entirely with little or no regrettable loss to the architectural fabric of the area.' The plan further guaranteed that no more houses that are not compatible with the 'English picturesque landscape tradition' would ever be built. Moreover, its design guidelines are simply the latest and most thorough attempt to exert a kind of cultural control over those who move into the area. They cannot keep the new élite out, but the design guidelines can maintain the old élite's taste, forcing newcomers' housing and landscaping to look like their own.

It may seem odd that the old élite should seek to force others to emulate their tastes, since one might think that they would wish to mark the differences between them and people they disdain. However, since the new élite has already entered their neighborhood and taken over a part of their identity, the old élite's goal is simply to make them disappear from view. Since they are excluded from the old élite's networks and clubs, the design guidelines that will make future development resemble the old élite housing will accomplish this. As an observer at the planning committee's meetings, one often has the impression that, in many respects, the old élite is primarily interested in creating an illusion: they make new houses resemble old ones; garages appear to be coach houses; and new houses look like the coach house or the servants' quarters of the large house on an adjacent property. But they can only create the *illusion* of an English landscape of the 19th century, of estates with servants. Even their cherished priority of maintaining the area as one of single-family detached houses was negotiable so long as the illusion remained. As one committee member said, reflecting the general committee's views: 'If the house is well designed, who cares what the use is, so long as it looks single family and the parking is concealed.' It is indeed ironic that members of the old élite insist that there should be an 'honest use of materials' in the design of buildings when the whole landscape is fakery.

This debate over neighborhood preservation reflects nostalgia (a belief that a city should have an area of historic significance), but also, and this is an element not often noted in regard to preservation, the use of a tool by which one status group within the upper class tries to fend off another. Not all members of the old élite see this connection. For some, the issue is simply historical preservation; for others, there are strong elements of status struggle symbolized by the fight to preserve a particular landscape; and, for yet others, it is simply a sentimental attachment to the landscape of childhood memory.

It is interesting, although not surprising, that while many members of the old élite see this as a struggle between themselves and what they term the *nouveau riche*, this fact is suppressed in the political arena. While drawing up the plan, the committee consistently downplayed class, and emphasized the physical nature of the area or its historical merit. In societies as ambivalent about class as those in North America, this is strategically necessary. For example, the following interchange took place at a committee strategy session regarding an early draft of the plan:

We should decrease the emphasis on the well-to-do exclusiveness of the area. Is this emphasis good public relations? Does it add to our claim of historic preservation?

We must present the neighborhood as an area of historical signifi-cance to people in the suburbs as well as the rest of the city. Perhaps any mention in the plan of rich people will turn them off.

Yes, remove any reference from the plan to helping people maintain large properties. The press will pick this up as a preoccupation of ours. Do you want to see this printed in the press?

Not only did the old élite skilfully define the debate around the popular issue of preservation, they were also able to portray it as a struggle between the interests of residents and those of developers. Opposition to developers, which is genuine among the old élite, was used to gain allies, which they could not have done had they portrayed their adversaries as the new rich moving into the houses built by developers. Opposition to developers was, in this instance, a successful political stratagem because it cut across class lines in a society that prefers not to think in terms of class. One does not have to be wealthy to dislike developers, whereas the dislike felt by the old élite for the new would have been dismissed as upper-class snobbery. As objects of nearly universal scorn in 1970s' Vancouver, developers were useful scapegoats for the purposes of the old élite because they serve to mask class sentiment.

Three years after the committee was formed, the plan passed through the city council and became law. For the old élite, it represented a great victory, for it institutionalized their taste. All new development had to conform to the design guidelines which they had created, and the acceptability of a proposed dwelling was to be decided upon by a permanent design-guidelines committee that was dominated by area residents. The preservation of landscape and, more broadly, of cultural values usually does not just happen, but must be fought over within the political arena, for our society is heterogeneous, different classes, and often status groups within classes, have differing values, tastes, and material interests that they wish to preserve.

Conclusion

We have focused our attention on a particular urban residential landscape, the English country-house complex, and argued that it has symbolic meaning within North America, particularly among certain upper-class groups. This landscape conveys multiple messages which differ according to time, group membership, and individual knowledge. We have shown (following Wiener 1981) how the symbolism of this landscape in late 19th-century Britain was 'aristocratic' and anti-bourgeois. We contend that this landscape was progressively adopted by a bourgeois élite in 20th-century Britain and North America as a symbol of privilege and high status. For North American anglophile élites, it came to represent a symbolic link to pre-industrial Britain, and a form of cultural resistance to the *nouveau riche*. Membership in the old élite is signified through a set of cultural symbols. The landscape is a tangible statement of who the group is, the past they claim as their own, and their current values. It has come under increasing pressure during the 20th century. The large lots that are integral to this landscape type would not survive if there were a free market in land, for it is more profitable to divide them. The landscape can only be maintained through political action, which has taken the form of zoning laws and design guidelines which effectively legislate taste. In both case studies, the preservation of the cultural landscape typical of a particular class is skilfully portrayed as being in the interests of the wider society. This is accomplished through the use of culturally acceptable themes such as environmental and historic preservation, and 'livability,' and the downplaying of culturally unacceptable categories such as class.

The fight to preserve this landscape in North America has gone on for over a century. Attempts to portray this landscape style as a valuable historical and environmental resource have been successful, perhaps too successful in the eyes of certain members of the old élites, for it has helped to boost its popularity, as shown by the mass production of so-called 'bypass Tudors' in Britain and 'mini-Tudors' in North America. Among the new, moneyed upper class, it has also appeared at times in large developer-built Tudors, which the old élite consider poor replicas of early 20th-century models. As it has diffused, the symbolic meaning as well as the physical form have changed, and each group has disdained its successor's model.

The irony, then, is that the propagandizing that has been necessary to preserve the landscape has resulted in a profusion of what old élites consider to be unacceptable copies of their houses. When modern copies are built, they threaten the meaning of the landscape held by these groups and thus the integrity of the groups themselves. The very effort of cultural preservation, therefore, contains within it the seeds of cultural change. Political action can retard this change, but cannot ultimately prevent it.

Notes

1   For a discussion of these antinomies in geography, see Agnew and Duncan (1981); and for a critique of the structural–deterministic view of culture in geography, see Duncan (1980). The most recent review of cultural theory is to be found in Ley (1983b).
2   The term old is used in a relative sense here. In some areas, an old élite goes back several hundred years, while in others it might not stretch back beyond the early 20th century. The term old simply distinguishes it within an area from newer members of the economic class.
3   A discussion of some of the political implications of livability is found in Ley (1980, 1983a), and Ley and Mercer (1980).

References

Agnew, J. A. 1981. Homeownership and identity in capitalist societies. In *Housing and identity: cross-cultural perspectives*, J. S. Duncan (ed.), 60–97. London: Croom Helm.

Agnew, J. A. and J. S. Duncan 1981, The transfer of ideas into Anglo-American geography. *Prog. Hum. Geog.* **5**(1), 42–57.

Bottomley, J. 1978. *The business community, urban reform and the establishment of town planning in Vancouver, B.C., 1900–1940*. Dissertation, University of British Columbia.

Builder 1982. **5**(12), 32.

Couper, M. and T. Brindley 1975. Housing classes and housing values. *Sociol. Rev.* **23**, 563–76.

Cox, K. R. 1979. *Location and public problems*. Chicago: Maaroufa Press.

Curtis, C. 1976. *The rich and other atrocities*. New York: Harper & Row.

Duncan, J. S. 1973. Landscape taste as a symbol of group identity: a Westchester County village. *Geogr. Rev.* **63**, 334–55.

Duncan, J. S. 1980. The superorganic in American cultural geography. *Ann. Assoc. Am. Geogs* **70**, 181–98.

Duncan, J. S. and N. G. Duncan 1976. Housing as presentation of self and the structure of social networks. In *Environmental knowing*, G. T. Moore and R. G. Golledge (eds.), 247–53. Stroudsberg, Pa: Dowden, Hutchinson & Ross.

Duncan, J. S. and N. G. Duncan 1980. Residential landscapes and social worlds: a case study in Hyderabad, Andra Pradesh. In *An exploration of India: geographical perspectives in society and culture*, D. E. Sopher (ed.), 271–86. Ithaca, NY: Cornell University Press.

Firey, W. 1945. Sentiment and symbolism as ecological variables. *Am. Sociol. Rev.* **10**, 140–8.

Frieden, B. J. 1979. *The environmental protection hustle*. Cambridge, Mass.: MIT Press.

Gans, H. J. 1962. *The urban villagers: group and class in the life of Italian-Americans*. New York: Free Press.

Geertz, C. 1973. *The interpretation of cultures*. New York: Harper & Row.

Girouard, M. 1981. *Life in the English country house*. Harmondsworth: Penguin.

Hardwick, W. 1974. *Vancouver*. New York: Macmillan.

Holdsworth, D. W. 1977. House and home in Vancouver: images of West Coast urbanism, 1886–1929. In *The Canadian city*, G. A. Stelter and A. F. J. Artibase (eds.), 186–211. Toronto: McClelland and Stewart.

Ley, D. F. 1980. Liberal ideology and the post-industrial city. *Ann. Assoc. Am. Geogs* **70**, 238–58.

Ley, D. F. 1983a. *A social geography of the city*. New York: Harper & Row.

Ley, D. F. 1983b. Cultural/humanistic geography. *Prog. Hum. Geog.* **7**(2), 267–75.

Ley, D. F. and J. Mercer 1980. Locational conflict and the politics of consumption. *Econ. Geog.* **56**, 89–109.

Lowenthal, D. 1975. Past time, present place: landscape and memory. *Geogr. Rev.* **65**, 1–36.

Lowenthal, D. and H. Prince 1965. English landscape tastes. *Geogr. Rev.* **55**, 186–222.

Perin, C. 1977. *Everything in its place: social order and land use in America*. Princeton, NJ: Princeton University Press.

Pevsner, N. 1957. *London, Vol. 1: The cities of London and Westminster*. Harmondsworth: Penguin.

Porter, J. 1965. *The vertical mosaic*. Toronto: University of Toronto.

Pratt, G. 1981. The house as an expression of social worlds. In *Housing and identity: cross-cultural perspectives*, J. S. Duncan (ed.), 135–80. London: Croom Helm.

Rapoport, A. 1981. Identity and environment: a cross-cultural perspective. In *Housing and identity: cross-cultural perspectives*, J. S. Duncan (ed.), 6–35. London: Croom Helm.

Seeley, J. R., R. A. Sim and E. W. Loosley 1963. *Crestwood Heights: a study of the culture of suburban life*, New York: Wiley.

Sennett, R. and J. Cobb. 1973. *The hidden injuries of class*. New York: Vintage.

Shipler, D. 1974. The attack on snob zoning. In *Suburbia in Transition*, L. Masotti and J. Haddon (eds.), 112–17. New York: New York Times Press.

Smith, A. 1982. The Wall Street spirit. *Esquire* **98**(1), 12–14.

Wiener, M. J. 1981. *English culture and the decline of the industrial spirit*. Cambridge: Cambridge University Press.

Williams, R. 1973. *The country and the city*. London: Chatto & Windus.

13 *Commentary*

JOHN A. AGNEW, JOHN MERCER, DAVID E. SOPHER

Dominant approaches in urban studies tend toward one or the other of two forms of reasoning. The first is rationalist or conceptual: actual cities and people are understood as explicable only as they can be deduced from a general or abstract theory of society. The actual is thought to be real only when it can be captured by the concepts of the theory (DiTomaso 1982). This is the essence of structural–functional theorizing in social science. In urban studies, it is exemplified by the work of Castells (1977), Harvey (1978), and Dear and Scott (1981).

The second form of reasoning is empiricist or instrumentalist: actual cities and their inhabitants are understood through models that 'simplify reality' by identifying and ordering 'critical variables.' The classic example is the model of *homo economicus*. Other examples are the ecological models of urban sociology and urban geography (see Introduction), in which the emphasis is on fitting a predicted pattern of urban land use or activity to an empirically observed one. The focus on outcomes rather than on causes or reasons has been heavily criticized (Laslett 1980, Szymanski & Agnew 1981, Sayer 1982).

An alternative form of reasoning is exemplified, we believe, by the cultural-context approach proposed in this book. In the terms used by Bourdieu (1977), the approach involves the 'dialectic of strategies' rather than the 'fallacy of the rule,' or 'the mechanics of the model.' It leads to the *explanation* of urban form, growth, and life through cultural context. A theory of cultural context guides one in a search for critical causal connections and associations. The object is neither deduction of empirical outcomes from a universal theory nor induction of a theory from the way curves fit each other. The concepts used are guiding, rather than fitted (Schrag 1975). Laslett (1980, p. 219) proposes such an approach:

> In contrast to the search for generalizations about outcomes, which allows the possibility of multiple starting points, a search for generalizations about causes allows for multiple outcomes to result from a more limited set of causes.

For our purpose, the 'causes' are those conceptualized by the term cultural context.

Unlike many contemporary urban theorists (e.g. Saunders 1981), the authors of this book do accept 'the urban' as an object of study. The reasons for doing so are presented in the Introduction. At the present stage, it is enough to say that we share the position that cities form contexts in which cultures and societies are produced and transformed, just as cities are themselves produced and transformed by those cultures and societies. Writing of English cities in the 19th century and early 20th century, Williams (1973, p. 278) touches upon this 'duality;'

> Out of the very chaos and misery of the new metropolis, and spreading from it to rejuvenate a national feeling, the civilizing force of a new vision of society had been created in struggle, had gathered up the suffering and the hopes of generations of the oppressed and exploited, and in this unexpected and challenging form was the city's human reply to the long inhumanity of city and country alike.

Some specific virtues of studying the city in cultural context can be seen from the individual essays. First, the essays do not start with fixed categories into which the substantive material is squeezed. Rather, they are interested in explaining urban phenomena by linking cultural contexts with urban 'outcomes.' Karl Marx – who might seem a most unlikely candidate for citation in this connection, given what his disciples have done to his work – was sensitive to the issue. In 1877, Marx wrote in a letter (cited in Carr 1961, p. 82):

> Events strikingly similar but occurring in a different historical milieu lead to completely different results ... By studying each of these evolutions separately and then comparing them, it is easier to find the key to the understanding of this phenomenon; but it is never possible to arrive at this understanding by using the passe-partout of some universal historical–philosophical theory whose great virtue is to stand above history.

Second, all the essays locate their explanations of urban phenomena beyond the city itself. Their focus is upon the cultures that serve as the symbolic 'glue' of the societies in which they have developed. But, as a number of authors point out (particularly Murphey, Bater, Claval, and Lewandowski), cities can often be centers of power within societies, and this power is manifested in the cities. Thus cities can be seen as representing the political and social orders signified by a hegemonic culture.

Finally, various authors demonstrate the utility of 'cultural context' rather than 'culture' as the necessary operative concept. From Abu-Lughod, with her sense of a global capitalist culture rapidly incorporating the Arab World, if not without resistance, to Claval, with his emphasis on a European cultural context, and Walton, with his proposal of distinctive 'class' cultures within the city of Guadalajara, culture is seen as more than a concept with national origins. Furthermore, in the hands of some authors (such as Claval, Walton, Lewandowski, Western, and Rapoport), cultural context involves an elaborate interweaving of hegemonic, residual, and emergent cultures operating at different geographic scales.

Some problems

However, the approach is not without some general difficulties, which have been discussed in the Introduction. In addition to these, some particular issues and dilemmas are illustrated in individual chapters. Some chapters, for example, lack specificity in their concept of 'cultural context:' it is not clear whether they imply a superorganic, mentalist, or practical explanation of culture. Not too much need be made of this point, however. Many of the authors are concerned with the continuing 'operations' of cultural signification, rather than with the question of genesis. Nevertheless, there is a danger that a static and reified image of culture may be adopted by default, rather than being consciously constructed, something that has often happened to the concept of culture at the hands of cultural anthropologists and cultural geographers (Duncan 1980).

A related problem arises when context is defined on a national scale, as it is in many of the chapters. This is understandable in those by Allinson, Bater, and Murphey, in which historical analysis suggests that the national scale does have overriding importance. But even in these, there is a danger of overemphasizing the national scale. There is little doubt, however, that in the contemporary world, the state or national context is of hegemonic significance.

In the Introduction, we made a contrast between culture as a 'way of life' and culture as 'a realized signifying system.' We prefer the second definition because it is clearer, more specific, and closer to the dominant sense of culture in contemporary social science. Culture as a way of life, being all-inclusive and not clearly distinguished from concepts of social and political order, has tremendous redundancy. Many of the chapters retain this less specific usage. This need not be a defect in the collection as a whole, since no matter how the writers mean to define culture formally, they do present its central symbolizing elements.

Traditional cultural approaches in the social sciences, then, have seldom been aware of links between culture and political and social orders. One reason is that culture has been defined in a very general way: culture is a way of life. Another is that cultural continuity and tradition, rather than change, have been emphasized. It sometimes appeared that only 'traditional' peoples had culture; we 'moderns' had lost ours. On the other hand, we had political and social orders that had evolved over time; they did not. This contrast reaches its extreme in Lévi-Strauss' designation of societies as either 'hot' ('historical') or 'cold' (cultural?). Most of the essays in this book reject the distinction as they explore one or another of the links between culture and the distribution of wealth, stratification, the institution of power, status hierarchies, and the strength of bureaucracies. Yet there is a hint in some chapters that cities are constructions of the mass, or even egalitarian constructions, since cultural context itself seems to be regarded as the social construction of the mass. The problem is especially evident in the chapters that range widely over time and space and, as it happens, in some that focus on societies in Asia and their cities.

The view of culture that has been dominant often entails another bias. This is the tendency to adopt 'the view from above.' In many societies, only the views of political and social élites are readily apparent to the outside observer. This can lead to a partial, and perhaps distorted, understanding of the cultural context in question, a danger, however, that the contributors to this book have, by and large, avoided (but see Ch. 12). The classic case is that of orientalism, the Western study of Islamic culture that has recently been criticized as élite-based antiquarianism because of its approach and subject matter (Said 1978, Turner 1978).

Another danger is the tendency to retreat into an idiographic mode of presentation that often verges on an extreme cultural relativism. The essays in this book manage, by and large, to steer clear of this danger, too, by using common terms and making casual comparisons. But some degree of cultural relativism is inevitable (Campbell 1972, p. xiii):

> Cultural relativism points to the fact that among the peoples of the world there are many different belief systems. The anthropologist or any other social scientist is a product of one of these cultures. He inherits from this culture a set of primitive unconscious assumptions about the world and its categories which affect not only his everyday life in his home culture but also his activities as a scientist when he goes to study another culture.

However, the danger of ethnocentrism – projecting 'our' categories on to 'them' – does not make it impossible for us to understand them, or them us, because of linguistic unintelligibility and cultural uniqueness (Lukes 1977, pp. 152–3). Murphey strikes the right note when he castigates Western students of Chinese cities for their ethnocentrism, but does not himself drift into an idiographic dead end. Studying the city in cultural context is hard but, we say, not impossible!

One solution to the problems we have identified is to approach the city in cross-cultural context, rather than in the context of a single cultural milieu. Even the study of a single case can be comparative if it refers to other situations and uses common terms (Grew 1980, p. 777). The advantage of a more explicitly comparative approach is that 'to look at other cases is to see other outcomes' (*ibid*, p. 769). This serves as a necessary check on the validity of the links between cultural contexts and urban outcomes that the cultural-context perspective is trying to discover.

The virtue of comparison

Let us digress for a moment to review the comparative research that has been done in urban studies, and to show the value of doing much more. The extremely fragmented nature of the work led Masotti and Walton (1976) to doubt whether it constituted a 'field,' and not much has changed since then, certainly not in the development of theory (Walton 1981).

Comparative urban research shines a light on possible interaction effects between cities and cultures, because research that is confined to a single national setting is in effect 'controlling for' important cultural processes. It is true that regional cultures may have significant effects within a country; for example, northern English cities and towns exhibit different forms and yield different urban experiences from those in the south. Nevertheless, it is always perilous to examine one context alone.

Attempts (such as those of Lojkine (1977) and Castells (1977)) to state universally applicable propositions about the development of cities under modern capitalism have been roundly criticized. Not only have these authors failed to make careful comparative analyses, they have even abstracted 'at an unjustifiable level of generality' (Harloe 1981, p. 183). Writers need to become self-conscious about the limitations imposed on their work by their immediate context. Comparison may show that what appears self-evident and expectable in one context is a problem requiring explanation in another.

Another strength of the comparative method is its ability to generate new questions. It can uncover unsuspected variation, and thus lead to a redefinition of traditional problems (Grew 1980, p. 765). Hasty generalization based on a single context may close off further examination, or confine it to the same context. Premature closure and wilful short-sightedness are less likely with the comparativist's approach. This approach in turn gives new importance to the facts yielded by local studies.

Finally, comparisons would help to demonstrate how, as we have said, cultures are continually being made and remade. They would show how different cultures may emerge from apparently similar antecedents, as in the case of urbanism in Canada and the United States. Although British colonial settlement in the New World, and English liberalism, were common to the formation of culture there, different political cultures and different kinds of cities developed subsequently in the two countries. The question, raised in the 'fragment thesis' a generation ago (Hartz 1953), has generated considerable discussion (Lipset 1963, Hartz 1964, Truman 1971, Horowitz 1978, McRae 1978), as well as some comparative urban studies recently (Goldberg 1977, Mercer 1979, Goldberg & Mercer 1980).

Drawing comparisons: a first step

How, then, can the chapters in this book contribute to comparative urban studies? We propose to show what they can yield in this respect by following two particular themes as treated in some of the essays. We hope that the discussion will serve two purposes: to be a model that will show how much more of value might be extracted, and to demonstrate the worth of comparative study in reaching a greater understanding of cities.

On the surface, American and British social thought and literature, both popular and élite, are against the city (White and White 1962, Williams 1973, Fischer 1976; for a different view, see Siegel 1981). A number of the papers point to the existence of a similar attitude in other cultural regions. Claval finds that city dwellers in northwestern Europe tend to deny their urban identity, and he wonders whether their attitude may not have Protestant roots – dissent from the city and turning to rural life as the source of health and virtue. Does this apparent distaste for the city lead to the British planning philosophy and strategy which, as described by Hall (see also Hall et al. 1973), seek to contain the city? The economy of a compact city and perhaps some celebration of urbanity are also involved, but clearly a desire is being manifested to preserve the countryside, at least in a physical sense, from what we may interpret as some form of defilement. Paradoxically, the desire to be rid of the influence of the city, while retaining it as a market-place and generator of wealth, is (in Hall's thesis) the motive underlying American suburban culture. It is a social form that has spread beyond America, but unevenly, and it is a question whether long-standing 'attitudes to the city' have played any part in moderating this spread.

Bater's chapter brings another point of view to the subject. The pre-Revolution Russian élite also viewed the city negatively, fearing that it might be unmanageable, and therefore attempted to control its growth. Moreover, the élite was never strongly committed to the city as home, being drawn from a class of country gentry, as 19th-century Russian literature makes clear. The geographical consequence of this was the marked seasonal alternation in élite residence between city and country estate. There are much weaker parallels to this behavior in Western European society, both in the past and today.

Murphey's comments on the city in imperial China shows that anti-urban attitudes are not confined to the West. Mostly founded by the state, the cities were the periodic targets of an aroused peasantry who saw them as symbols of oppression and exploitation. The urban élite enjoyed the status and material benefits of city life, yet 'longed for the countryside.' Their sentiments implied a view of the city as a place of evil-doing, in which would be included the amassing of wealth, a view not unlike that of Wordsworth and the English Romantic poets.

A legacy from the imperial era, this attitude became muted in the first flush of industrial development, and the appearance of new forms of cities in China. But it surged up again as a result of the Maoist revolution. Mao's vision was resolutely against the city, not as the symbol of a strong central authority, but rather as a symbol of all that was loathsome and pernicious in Western capitalism, with its attendant miseries for worker and peasant alike. The favored planning and development strategy, as Murphey outlines it, grew out of the positive view of the countryside and the negative view of the city.

The contrast with the shift in attitudes toward the city in the Soviet Union is instructive. The fears of state bureaucrats before the revolution were replaced by the hopes of a government that saw the city, now the Soviet socialist city, as an instrument to bring about, in Bater's words, 'a new and higher form of society.' But some Russian writing since the revolution gives, in Bater's review of it, an unflattering impression of the city that is at variance with official positions. The materialism and privatism attributed to urban residents in the Soviet Union are remarkably like the behavior observed by Murphey among the privileged, consumption-oriented urbanites of contemporary China, a condition that is not unique in socialist countries; we may recall the 'new class' exposed by Djilas (1957) in Tito's Yugoslavia.

Against these largely negative attitudes toward the city, we must place some contrasting views. Within Europe, Claval distinguishes the central and southern parts as marked by an élite preference for residence close to the foci of collective existence. An orientation to the city center was an element of the culture taken overseas by colonizers from those parts of Europe, and is thus reflected in the morphology of Guadalajara (analyzed by Walton). The center is the focus of the civic culture that he identifies, and that can be taken to transcend the particulars of that Mexican city.

Nevertheless, Guadalajara, together with other Latin American cities, is undergoing the suburbanization of upper-class groups, at least those sharing in Walton's 'modernity culture.' In other regions, too, orientation to a traditional central focus in the city appears to be undergoing transformation. In older cities in the 'oil and sand' countries described by Abu-Lughod, the suddenly affluent local population appears to be abandoning central residential districts to live, work, and shop amid the trappings of 'modernity' at the edge of the traditional city.

On the other hand, the persistence of a central orientation can be discerned from Lewandowski's observations on Madras. Colonial symbols in statue and street name, particularly numerous in the heart of the city, are being replaced and supplemented by symbols of a Tamil identity. The vitality of 'the center' as symbolic focus coexists with new geographic orientations manifested in the building of new temples and cultural centers at the edge of the city.

We have been leaning toward an interpretation of a strong preference for residential location at the center, and the maintenance of its symbolic power as indicators of a positive attitude toward the city. There is, however, no firm evidence on the point in the chapters by Claval, Walton, Lewandowski, and Abu-Lughod. Our survey suggests, then, that anti-urban attitudes, at least in élite expression, have existed over a broad spatial and temporal span, in many *different* cultural contexts (cf. Ch. 12). Such attitudes are by no means a systematic outcome of urban experience, and 'pro-urban' attitudes, although less prominently noted in these essays, have also existed under similarly diverse cultural circumstances. Attention to those circumstances is evidently called for.

A second theme for comparative interpretation is the nature of the form and related social pattern of cities. We showed in the Introduction that few studies of morphology have been made across cultures, or even across nations. If urban form is conceived more broadly to incorporate social grouping (what is called the 'internal structure' of the city), the intellectual limitations of ecological and other structural explanations that fail to attend to cultural context are disclosed.

The city, we repeat, is not only a product of culture, it has a part in the genesis of culture. City form is a signifying system. It has symbolic meaning which is conveyed to city dwellers and rural visitors, and is absorbed by them and acted upon by them. Dramatic changes in city morphology and social patterning generate new sets of meanings. Conventional reliance on the market as an allocation mechanism, on transportation technologies as determinants, and on ecological principles to explain form appears misleading. The diversity of form treated in these papers, and the directed changes in form that they record, cannot be accounted for by such explanations.

The same conventional attempts at explanation cannot accommodate the contrast between planned or directed change and 'autonomous' or 'spontaneous' change. Several contributors are aware of this contrast, or regard it as fundamental. Planned change is likely to reflect some form of state control or purpose, and is usually designed to make a particular kind of symbolic statement. Almost always, planned changes are the product of a small group, often one that has been professionally trained; spontaneous changes are more diverse in origin. Rapoport distinguishes the two kinds of changes as belonging to high-style and vernacular orders, respectively; while Claval speaks of *architecture savante* and vernacular architecture.

Bater treats the matter systematically in writing about the Soviet city. Before the Revolution, the nature of Russian culture, what was believed and what was practiced, had a great deal to do with urban form. The basis of social stratification in Russia was quite different from that in the 19th-century West. The need to use residence to mark and maintain status (Sopher 1972) was not so great in Russia. The consequence was a different urban form. Certainly, the ability to pay and the technology of transportation had some effect, but not in quite the same way as in the other capitalist monarchies of the day; there are some interesting parallels here with modern Tokyo.

In contrast to the ineffectiveness of control over urban form before the Revolution, planned forms came into vogue soon after. Miliutin's concept of the linear city and its implementation in certain urban areas nicely illustrates Rapoport's idea of a high-style order. So does the bureaucratic decision to give the city center an ideological rôle. This required it to be redesigned physically to accommodate 'massive, orchestrated public ceremony,' as was also done in central Peking under Mao. In the Soviet scheme, housing was assigned a dormitory function, and was built accordingly. Nevertheless, living in the reconstructed Soviet city conveyed a clear sense of a new stratification – of a new society, if not that of official Soviet myth. The city form encountered in daily life was integral to the making of a post-Revolution culture. Bater also skilfully portrays the clash of old and new cultures, and their associated morphological and social patterns in Samarkand, Kazan, and other places outside ethnic Russia.

The directed, self-conscious re-ordering of form to make symbolic statements of a religious kind, with the state as willing instrument or innovator, is noted in the chapters on particular metropolises in India (Madras) and Mexico (Guadalajara). In Tamil Nadu, the state government is actively fostering Tamil self-consciousness. One way of doing so is to build cultural centers which contain both *Hindu* temples and secular space. Lacking resources, the government is, however, limited in the amount of re-ordering it can achieve. It cannot abandon the buildings of colonial government, but it can make a modest, cosmetic addition to them. This provides a new element in a symbolic code comprehensible only within the cultural context of India, and specifically Tamil Nadu.

In Guadalajara in the 1920s, the city government undertook a massive project of renewal that created a public-sector complex in the center of the city. It was given the form of a huge cross, with the principal cathedral standing at its center. Yet this followed by little more than a decade the revolution that had eroded the national authority of the church, transferring it to the emerging one-party state.

More recently, the state has been arranging the provision of services and other elements of the economic infrastructure to benefit large-scale commerce and industries headquartered elsewhere in Mexico, often the subsidiaries of multinational corporations. Although inducements of this kind are common elsewhere, Walton thinks that Guadalajara's political élite provides them extravagantly because success in attracting new industry and building infrastructure is the foundation of success in national politics. That urban morphology has, therefore, a decidedly political complexion is widely understood.

The power of the state to change social patterns and to convey specific meaning by altering urban form is nowhere clearer than in South Africa. Western tells how whole new residential districts, the Black African townships, were built, and how particular social groups were displaced (as were the Cape Coloureds), or prevented from entering the city (as were the families of Black male 'temporary' workers). The location and low quality of the townships reinforces the sense of Blacks and Coloureds that they are truly marginal people in urban South Africa. They see themselves as without political power, yet needed for their labor, and even as a growing market for local, White-owned industries.

To understand the conscious manipulation of urban form requires an awareness of cultural context within the nested framework discussed in the Introduction. We can enhance the picture by briefly considering spontaneous change. In the United States, by comparison with the cases we have just noted, urban planners are notably weak in their ability to alter urban form. Form there, (of the kind described by Hall) arises out of the interplay of developers, financial institutions, often, but not always, ineffective local governments, and landowners eager to profit from speculation. What developers build and put on the market is desired by people who are strongly motivated to buy the product. They want to own property, to proclaim the status attached to a particular kind of housing in a particular location, and, mostly, to live in a single-family dwelling (Agnew 1981).

Hall claims that the life lived in both old and new suburbs is intensely private and familial, and that mobile spectators find quite as much stimulation in suburbs as they would downtown as pedestrians. The physical product of the American city and its social patterns are thus a reflection (a mirror, as Murphey calls it) of American society and its beliefs and practices. Although Hall does not develop the point as the Duncans do, suburban residential areas tell us a great deal about the hegemonic culture. The developers, after all, protest that they only build what the public wants and what the market will bear (Perin 1977). But this does not tell us the origin of the individual's private wants, their social construction, as we contend.

We can see the need for a comparative reading of what the chapters of this book contain on urban form, its construction, its changes, whether directed or spontaneous, and its interpretation by those who live there. Finally, we believe that studying the city in cultural context points toward resolution of large problems in contemporary urban studies. As we have conceded in the Introduction, many issues remain to be dealt with in achieving this goal. In the Introduction, we described the problems in the abstract, and in greater particularity in this chapter as they appeared after a reading of the essays.

A set of commitments is central to both essays and commentary. These come down to what are called, in the philosophy of science, epistemological fallibilism and ontological realism. One says that knowing is partial and culture bound, but not inevitably so, the other that cities and cultural contexts are real and exist independently of our thinking about them. In both respects, we have moved away from much current writing in urban studies, in particular, and in social science, in general. We believe that this route to understanding resolves major problems. We have yet to see whether the difficulties of adopting the perspective itself can also be resolved.

References

Agnew, J. A. 1981. Homeownership and identity in capitalist societies. In *Housing and identity*, J. S. Duncan (ed.), 60–97. London: Croom Helm.

Bourdieu, P. 1977. *Outline of a theory of practice*. Cambridge: Cambridge University Press.

Campbell, D. T. 1972. Herskovits, cultural relativism, and metascience. In *Cultural relativism: perspectives in cultural pluralism*, F. Herskovits (ed.), V–XXIII. New York: Random House.

Carr, E. H. 1961. *What is history?* New York: Knopf.

Castells, M. 1977. *The urban question*, London: Edward Arnold.

Dear, M. and A. J. Scott 1981. Towards a framework for analysis. In *Urbanization and urban planning in capitalist society*, M. Dear and A. J. Scott (eds.), 3–16. New York: Methuen.

DiTomaso, N. 1982. 'Sociological reductionism' from Parsons to Althusser: linking action and structure in social theory. *Am. Sociol. Rev.* **47**, 14–28.

Djilas, M. 1957. *The new class: an analysis of the communist system*. New York: Praeger.

Duncan, J. S. 1980. The superorganic in American cultural geography. *Ann. Assoc. Am. Geogs* **70**, 181–98.

Fischer, C. S. 1976. *The urban experience*. New York: Harcourt Brace Jovanovich.

Goldberg, M. A. 1977. Housing and land prices in Canada and the US. In *Public property? The habitat debate continued*, L. B. Smith and M. Walker (eds.), 207–54. Vancouver: Fraser Institute.

Goldberg, M. A. and J. Mercer 1980. Canadian and US cities: basic differences, possible explanations, and their meaning for public policy. *Reg. Sci. Assoc. Paps* **45**, 159–83.

Grew, R. 1980. The case for comparing histories. *Am. Hist. Rev.* **85**, 763–78.

Hall, P., H. Gracey, R. Drewett and R. Thomas 1973. *The containment of urban England*, Vols. 1 & 2. London: George Allen & Unwin.

Harloe, M. 1981. Notes on comparative urban research. In *Urbanization and urban planning in capitalist society*, M. Dear and A. J. Scott (eds.), 179–95. New York: Methuen.

Hartz, L. 1953. *The liberal tradition in America,* New York: Harcourt Brace.

Hartz, L. (ed.) 1964. *The founding of new societies.* New York: Harcourt Brace.

Harvey, D. 1978. The urban process under capitalism: a framework for analysis. *Int. J. Urb. Reg. Res.* **2**, 101–31.

Horowitz, G. 1978. Notes on 'conservatism, liberalism and socialism in Canada.' *Can. J. Polit. Sci.* **11**, 383–99.

Laslett, B. 1980. The place of theory in quantitative historical research. *Am. Sociol. Rev.* **45**, 214–28.

Lipset, S. M. 1963. *The first new nation.* New York: Basic Books.

Lojkine, J. 1977. *Le marxisme, l'état et la question urbaine.* Paris: PUF.

Lukes, S. 1977. On the social determination of truth. In *Essays in social theory*, S. Lukes (ed.), London: Macmillan.

Masotti, L. H. and J. Walton 1976. Comparative urban research: the logic of comparisons and the nature of urbanism. In *The city in comparative perspective*, J. Walton and L. H. Masotti (eds.), 1–15. New York: Sage Publications and Halsted Press, Wiley.

McRae, K. D. 1978. Louis Hartz's concept of the fragment society and its applications to Canada. *Etudes Canadiennes* **5**, 17–30.

Mercer, J. 1979. On continentalism, distinctiveness and comparative urban geography: Canadian and American cities. *Can. Geog.* **23**, 119–39.

Perin, C. 1977. *Everything in its place: social order and land use in America.* Princeton, NJ: Princeton University Press.

Said, E. 1978. *Orientalism.* New York: Random House.

Saunders, P. 1981. *Social theory and the urban question.* New York: Holmes and Meier.

Sayer, A. 1982. Explanation in economic geography: abstraction versus generalization. *Prog. Hum. Geog.* **6**, 68–88.

Schrag, C. O. 1975. Praxis and structure: conflicting models in the science of man. *J. Br. Soc. Phenomenology* **6**, 23–31.

Siegel, A. 1981. *The image of the American city in popular literature: 1820–1870.* Port Washington, NY: Kennikat Press.

Sopher, D. E. 1972. Place and location: notes on the spatial patterning of culture. *Soc. Sci. Q.* **53**, 321–37.

Szymanski, R. and J. A. Agnew 1981. *Order and skepticism: human geography and the dialectic of science.* Washington, DC: Association of American Geographers.

Truman, T. 1971. A critique of Seymour Lipset's article, 'Value differences, absolute or relative. The English-speaking democracies.' *Can. J. Polit. Sci.* **4**(4), 497–525.

Turner, B. S. 1978. *Marx and the end of orientalism.* London: Macmillan.

Walton, J. 1981. Comparative urban studies. *Int. J. Comp. Sociol.* **22**, 22–39.

White, M. and L. White 1962. *The intellectual versus the city.* New York: Mentor.

Williams, R. 1973. *The country and the city.* London: Chatto & Windus.

Contributors

Janet Abu-Lughod. Dr Abu-Lughod is currently Professor of Sociology, Urban Affairs and Policy Research at Northwestern University, Evanston, Illinois. She is the author of, *inter alia, Cairo: 1001 years of the city victorious* (1971) and *Rabat: urban apartheid in Morocco* (1980), as well as co-author or co-editor of *Housing choices and constraints* (1960), the *Cairo fact book* (1963), and *Third World urbanization* (1977, 1979). Her articles cover topics that range from contemporary urban developments in the United States, to the history of urbanism, and to demography, labor force, migration, and urban changes in the Arab World.

John A. Agnew. John A. Agnew is an Associate Professor of Geography and Director of the Social Science Program in the Maxwell School, Syracuse University. He is a graduate of Exeter and Liverpool Universities and obtained his PhD at the Ohio State University. His research interests include the social psychology of urban life, problems of explanation in urban studies, and political regionalism in multinational states. He is author or co-author of a number of books and articles.

Gary D. Allinson. Gary D. Allinson received his PhD degree in 1971 from Stanford University. He is the author of two books on Japanese urban life, *Japanese urbanism* (Berkeley 1975) and *Suburban Tokyo* (Berkeley 1979), as well as numerous articles on the social, political, and economic history of modern Japan. In 1983 he became the Ellen Bayard Weedon Professor of East Asian Studies at the University of Virginia.

James H. Bater. James H. Bater is Professor of Geography and Dean of the Faculty of Environmental Studies at the University of Waterloo. He graduated from the University of British Columbia and received his PhD from the University of London. He has written extensively on the historical geography of Russia and on cities and town planning in the Soviet Union. His books include *St Petersburg: industrialization and change* (1976) and *The Soviet city: ideal and reality* (1980); he is at work at present on a book on the Soviet Union, as well as a monograph on the historical geography of the Russian city.

Paul Claval. Paul Claval is Professor of Geography at the University of Paris-Sorbonne. He has written extensively on the philosophy of geography and the social sciences, and on the concepts and theories of several branches of geography, including urban geography. Among his many books and articles are *La logique des villes* (1981) and *Les mythes fondateurs des sciences sociales* (1980). A work on the history of the city in Europe is to appear soon.

James S. Duncan. James S. Duncan is an Associate Professor of Geography at the University of British Columbia. He is a graduate of Dartmouth College and received his PhD at Syracuse University. His major research interests are in housing and identity, and the social psychology of the urban built environment. He has conducted fieldwork in Canada, the United States, India, and Sri Lanka. He is the editor of *Housing and identity: cross-cultural perspectives* (London: Croom Helm 1981) and a number of articles in geography journals.

Nancy G. Duncan. Nancy G. Duncan is a doctoral candidate in geography at Syracuse University. She has conducted fieldwork in India and the United States on housing and identity. She is presently writing her dissertation on theories of land-use control and suburban development in the United States. Her publications have appeared in a number of edited collections.

Peter Hall.   Peter Hall is Professor of Geography, University of Reading, England, and Professor of City and Regional Planning and of Geography, University of California, Berkeley. He is the author of a number of books on urban geography and planning, including *London 2000, The world cities, The containment of urban England, Urban and regional planning,* and *Great planning disasters.* He is currently working on the relation of industrial innovation to regional and urban growth.

Susan Lewandowski.   Susan Lewandowski is Member, School of Social Sciences, Hampshire College, Amherst, Massachusetts; she has taught history at Amherst College and been involved in research on developing areas at Massachusetts Institute of Technology. Her PhD in history is from the University of Chicago, for research on urban development in South Asian cities. She is the author of *Migration and ethnicity in urban India* (1980), and of chapters in *The rise and growth of the great port cities* (1979) and *Buildings and society* (1980), in addition to articles in leading journals of urban history and Asian studies.

John Mercer.   John Mercer is Associate Professor of Geography at Syracuse University. He graduated from Glasgow University and received his post-graduate degrees at McMaster University. He taught formerly at the University of Iowa and the University of British Columbia. His research interests include comparative urban analysis (USA and Canada), urban housing and public policy, and local government reform and re-organization.

Rhoads Murphey.   Rhoads Murphey is Professor of History at the University of Michigan, where he was formerly Professor of Asian Studies and Geography. His PhD is from Harvard University, in Far Eastern History and Geography. His writing and research have been most concerned with China and South Asia, especially with the nature and meaning of the city in those regions, where the phenomenon of the great port cities has received particular attention from him. The ten books he has written range from *Shanghai: key to modern China* (1953) to *The fading of the Maoist vision* (1980). He has been Excutive Secretary of the Association for Asian Studies since 1976 and edited the Association's *Journal of Asian Studies* for several years.

Amos Rapoport.   Amos Rapoport is Distinguished Professor of Architecture at the University of Wisconsin, Milwaukee. He is the author of *House form and culture, Human aspects of urban form* and *The meaning of the built environment.* He has edited and co-edited four books, and written approximately 100 papers, articles, etc. His main interests are man–environment theory, the role of cultural variables, and cross-cultural studies. He spent the 1982-3 year as visiting fellow at Clare Hall, Cambridge and was the recipient of a Senior NEA Fellowship and a Graham Foundation Fellowship.

David E. Sopher.   David E. Sopher teaches geography at Syracuse University. He received his undergraduate training at St John's University, Shanghai, and at the University of California, where he obtained his PhD. He has had an abiding interest in cultural geography, particularly the geography of religion, and has found a special regional setting for this interest in the Indian world. He is the author of *The sea nomads* (1965) and *Geography of religions* (1967) and the editor of *An exploration of India: geographical perspectives on society and culture* (1980).

John Walton.   John Walton is Professor and Chair of the Department of Sociology at the University of California, Davis. He is author of a number of books and articles on the subjects of politics, political economy, developing nations, urbanization, social class, and the international economy, including *Elites and economic development* (University of Texas Press 1977), *Labor, class, and the international system* (with Alejandro Portes, Academic Press 1981), and *Reluctant rebels: comparative studies of revolution and underdevelopment* (Columbia University Press 1983). He is currently writing a critical introductory book on sociology, and doing research in social history.

John Western.   John Western is an Assistant Professor of Urban Studies at Temple University, Philadelphia. He graduated from Oxford University, took a Master's degree at the University of Western Ontario, and then obtained his PhD at the University of California, Los Angeles. His teaching experience includes two years in Burundi, Central Africa. In 1974–6 he held a research scholarship at the Centre for Intergroup Studies, University of Cape Town, South Africa. He has a number of publications on the Coloured population in Cape Town, most notably *Outcast Cape Town* (Minneapolis: University of Minnesota Press and London: George Allen and Unwin and Cape Town: Human & Rousseau 1982).

Index